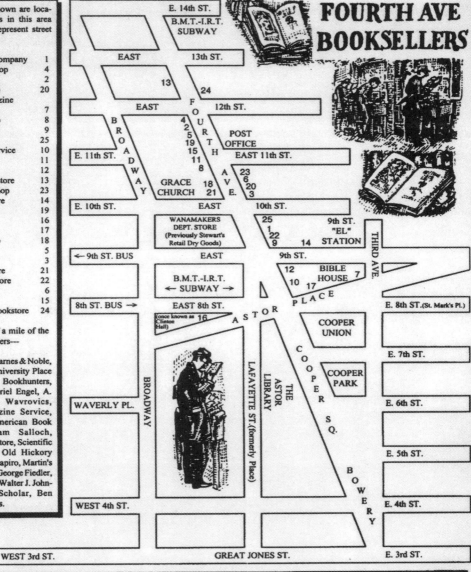

FOURTH AVE BOOKSELLERS

KEY: Numbers shown are loca-
[ti]on of Bookshops in this area
[on]ly - does not represent street
[ad]dresses.

[Ab]erdeen Book Company	1
[Am]erica's Bookshop	4
[An]chor Bookshop	2
[Ar]cadia Bookshop	20
[As]tor Place Magazine And Bookshop	7
[At]lantis Bookshop	8
[Bi]blo and Tannen	9
[Bo]oks 'N Things	25
[Co]lonial Book Service	10
[Co]rner Bookshop	11
[Eu]reka Bookshop	12
[Fourt]h Avenue Bookstore	13
[Fr]iendly Music Shop	23
[Ge]lman's Bookstore	14
[Gr]een Bookstore	19
[—] Hershbain	16
[Le]on Kramer	17
[Pa]geant Bookshop	18
[Ra]ven Bookshop	5
[Lo]uis Schucman	3
[Sc]hulte's Bookstore	21
[St]ammer's Bookstore	22
[St]rand Bookstore	6
[(Va]nity Fair)	15
[Sa]muel Weiser Bookstore	24

[W]ithin a radius of a mile of the
[4t]h Ave. Booksellers---

[Sp]echert-Hafner, Barnes & Noble,
[Da]uber & Pine, University Place
[Bo]okshop, Seven Bookhunters,
[Pe]rry-Fisher, Gabriel Engel, A.
[K]uschke, Louis Wavrovics,
[A]brahams Magazine Service,
[Jo]seph Kling, American Book
[A]uction, William Salloch,
[M]alley's Book Store, Scientific
[Li]brary Service, Old Hickory
[Bo]okshop, S.R. Shapiro, Martin's
[Bo]okshop, Henry George Fiedler,
[—]Thomas Heller, Walter J. John-
[s]on, American Scholar, Ben
[Bl]oomfield, Wex's.

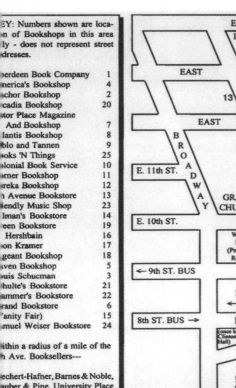

E. 14th ST.
B.M.T.-I.R.T. SUBWAY

EAST 13th ST.

13
24

FOURTH AVE.
EAST 12th ST.
4
2
5
19
15
11
8

BROADWAY

POST OFFICE

E. 11th ST.
EAST 11th ST.
23
6
20
3

GRACE CHURCH 18
21

E. 10th ST.
EAST 10th ST.

WANAMAKERS DEPT. STORE
(Previously Stewart's Retail Dry Goods)

25
1
22
9
14

9th ST. "EL" STATION

THIRD AVE.

← 9th ST. BUS
EAST 9th ST.

12
BIBLE HOUSE 7
10 17

B.M.T.-I.R.T. ← SUBWAY →

PLACE

8th ST. BUS →
EAST 8th ST.
(once known as Clinton Hall)
16

ASTOR

E. 8th ST.(St. Mark's Pl.)

COOPER UNION

COOPER SQ.

E. 7th ST.

WAVERLY PL.

BROADWAY

LAFAYETTE ST.(formerly Place)

THE ASTOR LIBRARY

COOPER PARK

E. 6th ST.

E. 5th ST.

BOWERY

WEST 4th ST.
E. 4th ST.

WEST 3rd ST.
GREAT JONES ST.
E. 3rd ST.

FOURTH AVENUE BOOKSELLERS & A FEW LANDMARKS OF NOTE East of Broadway (a few still remaining).
MAP c. 1950 Orig. drawn by Mahlon Blaine with a few historical modifications [not drawn to scale].

BOOK ROW

BOOK ROW

An

Anecdotal and

Pictorial History

of the

ANTIQUARIAN BOOK TRADE

MARVIN MONDLIN
&
ROY MEADOR

Foreword by Madeleine B. Stern

CARROLL & GRAF PUBLISHERS
NEW YORK

Book Row
An Anecdotal and Pictorial History
of the Antiquarian Book Trade

Carroll & Graf Publishers
An Imprint of Avalon Publishing Group Inc.
245 West 17th Street
New York, NY 10011

First Carroll & Graf edition 2004

Library of Congress Cataloging-in-Publication Data is available.

ISBN: 0-7867-1305-4

Printed in the United States of America
Interior design by Simon M. Sullivan
Distributed by Publishers Group West

To All Antiquarian Booksellers, Past—Present—Future, Who Find Homes for Old Books—and specifically to John Huckans, Editor of Book Source Magazine; *Robert Lescher, Agent; Herman Graf, Publisher, who contributed to make this book a reality and share our gratitude.*

CONTENTS

FOREWORD

by Madeleine B. Stern

✂ THEY OCCUPIED A comparatively small area of New York City, that collection of phenomenal booksellers who began to ply their trade from the 1890s to the 1920s and beyond, on and around Fourth Avenue south of Fourteenth Street, in sight of the aspiring Grace Church. Yet they left an indelible mark in the lives of book lovers fortunate enough to have visited them. They left their names in the diaries and journals of bibliophiles, in the letters of collectors, in the archives of libraries, in the memories of readers who journeyed to Book Row America.

Now, thanks to the labors of Marvin Mondlin and Roy Meador, Book Row America has been reconstructed, its colorful cast of characters brought to fascinating life, its substantial influence traced, even its shelves restocked. This long-awaited restoration of New York's Fourth Avenue dealers resuscitates a place and a time, an important but thus far unrecorded period in the history of books and those who treasure books.

Book Row America had its own special aroma, the incomparable and unforgettable scent of books and dust, paper and ink, type and binding, the dazzling anticipation and excitement of seekers after books. But most especially it boasted a phalanx of booksellers whose variety was extraordinary. It is that cast of characters to whom the co-authors give their closest attention. The biographies of those booksellers are here, as well as their characteristics. The facts of their lives are provided as well as the flavor. Mondlin and Meador begin their saga with that scholarly and swashbuckling individual, that "czar of the auction room," George D. Smith, who is first to walk upon this book-laden stage.

The details of Smith's fabulous and grand-scale exploits lead the way to an enticing sequence of book people. They are all here, those magicians of the bookstall, in their infinite variety. Their often incredible comments, their legendary transactions are recorded. From the aggressive, generous Isaac Mendoza, who welcomed "Anything That's a Book," to the representatives of a later age, they are gathered here, those onetime denizens of Fourth Avenue.

Their stories are told with accuracy, vigor, and enthusiasm: their adventures with books and book buyers, their aid in developing libraries from the Morgan to the Huntington. Their personal idiosyncrasies and their achievements are remembered. Anecdotes are recounted that crystallize the nature of these merchants in books, and interesting asides elaborate the experiences of proprietors of Fourth Avenue bookstalls who moved on to far larger backgrounds—Dauber & Pine, Schulte's, the Strand. In these pages the reader is introduced to their customers, from the lone anonymous browser to a presidential collector, from the hopeful scout after a "sleeper" to the scholarly searcher for special editions.

From a small field, this book reaches into large consequences and significant enterprises. Its text is graphically detailed, skillfully restoring the life of America's Book Row. And that text is generously enhanced by a multitude of illustrations that depict interiors and exteriors, catalogues and advertisements, images recalling the nature of shop and shopkeeper.

What, then, ended the existence of this enclave of booksellers? Economics encroached upon bibliophilism. The Depression, followed by the steady rise of property values in the Fourth Avenue region and the decrease of customers, was without doubt a principal cause. Yet, in a sense, with reference to such surviving firms as the Strand, the saga of Book Row is "a continuing epic that . . . moves forward in both reality and fiction." It is because these authors regard this history in such a light that they have been able to reconstruct it in such precise but elaborate detail. Certainly the personnel who carried on Book Row gave birth to a legend that has endured.

In this volume the ghosts are clothed again in flesh and blood. Book Row America returns to life and resumes its strategies, its dealings, its collecting, its dispersing. Customers still search for plums, and in the aura of Grace Church, the business of books is once again an exciting adventure.

*A successful bookseller is a man of infinite resilience, strong diges-
tion, tolerance of odd people, and ability to breathe dusty air and
crawl through cobwebs in search of the golden book."*

—LAWRENCE CLARK POWELL

FROM THE 1890s the secondhand and rare book seeker's favorite New York City for nearly eight decades—followed by two decades of slow decline—encompassed a special area on and around Fourth Avenue, mainly south of Fourteenth Street and Union Square to Astor Place. Seven concentrated blocks on Fourth Avenue, plus a few side streets stretching west to Fifth Avenue and north to Twenty-third Street, supplied crowded sites for several dozen bookstores.

Book hunters and collectors—nationwide, worldwide—knew the neighborhood during those decades as the New York Booksellers' Row, or more often just Book Row. The booksellers, by design or destiny, craft or luck, settled in one of the city's most fascinating and felicitous communities, north of the financial district and the Lower East Side, south of Herald Square, midtown, and the theaters of Broadway. For many, in memory, it is still Book Row.

Book Row was within easy reach of the city's millions. Grace Church, where General Tom Thumb got married, stood at the heart of Book Row. Near Union Square a statue of Washington was named "George the Veracious" by O. Henry. At Joe Smith's Saloon, at Fourteenth Street and Fourth Avenue, actor Hugh D'Arcy was inspired to write "The Face upon the Floor," about the demise of an artist from unrequited love and strong drink. When prohibitionists used his poem as a campaign song, D'Arcy said he would jump in the Hudson rather than help America go dry. His poem, he insisted, was "an admonition to be kind to drunks." That suggests a good slogan for book lovers: Be kind to booksellers everywhere even if they're not always nice, since what they sell is great. The fine Shakespearian words Enobarbus used for Cleopatra also fit booksellers from Fourth Avenue to wherever: "Age cannot wither them, nor custom stale their infinite variety."

Fourth Avenue bookshops came in a variety that approached the infinite, from narrow, hole-in-the-wall crannies to multistory buildings with sagging floors creaking from the weight of their volumes. Many shops were fronted by stalls and bins outside on the sidewalk with thousands of bargain books enticing pedestrians to pause, browse, and often enter. Early in World War II, when New York City officials for murky reasons sought to ban sidewalk book stands, Book Row dealers took a pioneering step and formed their historic Fourth Avenue Booksellers' Association to take arms against the city's unreasoned and unreasonable edict. It wasn't that Book Row didn't want to cooperate patriotically with the war effort. The dealers there were proud, along with their peers, when President Franklin D. Roosevelt on May 6, 1942, sent American Booksellers at their association's annual banquet this statement:

> I have been a reader and buyer and borrower and collector of books all my life. It is more important that your work should go on now than it has ever been at any other time in our history: in a very literal sense you carry upon your bookshelves the light that guides civilization . . . books never die. No man and no force can abolish memory. No man and no force can put thought in a concentration camp forever. No man and no force can take from the world the books that embody man's eternal fight against tyranny of every kind. In this war, we know, books are weapons. And it is a part of your dedication always to make them weapons for man's freedom.

On Book Row they liked the sound of that. But along with appreciation, Book Row being Book Row, there were no doubt rivulets of cynicism about the city's bureaucratic sidewalk fanatics, concern about sales to cover the rent, and the chronic aches and pains that daily beset every small business. In his January 1, 1944, "Trade Winds" column for the *Saturday Review of Literature,*

Bennett Cerf wrote about a bookstore that prosperity passed by. One partner said, "I can't understand it. Here we go busted, and only yesterday I read where President Roosevelt was saying that business was never better." The other partner said, "Maybe Roosevelt had a better location than ours!" That has an unmistakable Book Row flavor.

Movie director Robert Benton, in *Bookstore* (1999), by Lynne Tillman, called working in a bookstore one of the greatest jobs he ever had, but he admitted lacking the courage to run one: "The people who run these small bookshops, it's heroic." Again, in thought we dash back to Fourth Avenue, and memory revisits Book Row.

The booksellers who congregated on Book Row were colorful, charming, crotchety, impossible, delightful, dense, brilliant, unpredictable, standoffish, friendly characters. Take a barrel of adjectives, and all will apply to those remarkable booksellers. Writer Fran Lebowitz in a wry comment for *Bookstore* seasons criticism with affection for them as a group: "Remember Fourth Avenue when they had all the secondhand bookstores? You had to beg those guys to sell you a book. You had to scream and yell to get their attention because they were reading. You remember those old grumpy horrible guys? You would say, How much is this? They'd grumble, I don't know. Put a figure on it."

Typically in a Book Row shop, the proprietor right off the bat wouldn't or couldn't say whether a particular title was available. You'd be directed to a section where a copy might be found. Of course, if you didn't locate the title, you might find something else to take instead.

Some shops were impressive, specialized, antiquarian enterprises operated by highly knowledgeable bookmen; some were clean, orderly, general used-book stores with shelves packed full of promise; some were notoriously scruffy book caves where occasional worthwhile first editions and elusive titles awaited searching and patient eyes, along with thousands of unwanted volumes priced at a dollar, fifty cents, and even less. Or make an offer. Bargaining between proprietor and customer was never a complete stranger on Book Row. Congenial bargains for Book Row regulars were a taken-for-granted fact of life.

On Book Row there was no appetite for being fussy about "used" and "secondhand" versus "antiquarian." Such competing terms were simply alternative descriptions for books of varying quality, price, and appeal. They began their lives as new books, then moved on from earlier owners by way of Book Row to appreciative buyers—with a small profit staying behind in the cash drawer at the bookshop.

Various Book Row proprietors and employees would have been quite comfortable at a university faculty meeting. Others would have to skip the meeting to see their parole officers following release from incarceration for illegal anarchist activities. A few among Book Row personnel could have served plausibly in a pulpit; still others perhaps would have done all right joining Bonnie and Clyde and teaching lessons to bankers.

Wayne Somers, who frequented Book Row as a student, collector, librarian, and bookseller, wrote in 1990, "I find that I, at least, feel a certain kinship with even the most benighted bookseller, provided he is not actually a crook." Yet Somers remembered something of an adversarial relationship between customers and various dealers. "One learned to walk on eggs, speak to the proprietors as little as possible. The only exception I recall was Wilfred Pesky, who seemed a kind soul." Milton Reissman, a specialist in children's and illustrated books at Victoria Book Shop, reported holding his Fourth Avenue dealings to a minimum: "Too many madmen for me."

Whether mad or slightly sane, Book Row dealers for the most part could not serve convincingly as templates or models for booksellers in the sentimental Roger Mifflin mode as depicted by Christopher Morley in *Parnassus on Wheels* and *The Haunted Bookshop*. Book Row was a place of businesses, and businesses more often than not are places of constant struggle and hard work.

Valentine Mitchell in *Morocco Bound* (1929) wrote about the bookseller whose secret daydream was to load up on liquor, tell off Christmas shoppers, and when the celebrated bookstore sentimentalist Morley entered he had a special greeting in mind: "Morley pictures the life of a bookseller as one of ease in which the shopkeeper sits around smoking a pipe. I should like to have Morley pop in so that I could wring his blooming neck." If Christopher Morley's biblioenthusiasm veered somewhat from accuracy about day-to-day bookselling, especially at holidays, the shops on Book Row were glorious havens for many customers, and the proprietor could feel free to gripe as long as we could root among the books. We viewed Book Row proprietors and their scouts, whatever their personalities and moods, as informed toilers in the trenches who attended the sales, searched the attics, inspected the boxes, prowled along dusty shelves, heeded the clues, and followed the spoors to obtain the books that adorn collections, that enrich libraries, that entertain and educate readers.

In the 1930s book collector Stan Nosek attended Stuyvesant High School on East Fifteenth Street with ten cents a day for the subway and "five cents spending money" from his mother. "It was a short walk to Union Square and then to Book Row," he recalled. "I loved to walk over there and browse among the book stalls." Even with just a nickel a day to invest on Book Row he could slowly acquire books to read and treasure.

Not all Book Row encounters produced the memories that friendly nostalgia feeds on. Jack Biblo, on Book Row at Biblo and Tannen for decades, admitted, "We were all a little peculiar." He cited the Russian revolutionary who ran one of the shops. He would give a customer he liked a cup of tea and throw out those he didn't like. He would state a price, and if the customer hesitated, he would double the price. Biblo described Fourth Avenue bookshops as sixteen-hour-day jobs where "sometimes you didn't make a dollar."

David A. Randall, a rare-book dealer whose reminiscences are in *Dukedom Large Enough* (1979), discovered Book Row as a boy and began there as a book scout rummaging for cheap finds to sell for a profit at posh uptown bookstores. One of his discoveries in the twenty-five-cent bin was a nondescript work by Whittier that had a verse in Whittier's hand on the back flyleaf. The store owner, cantankerous Peter Stammer, going through hundreds of books, had understandably missed the fact it was a presentation copy. Young Randall then learned the wisdom of not impetuously bragging, at least not in the victim's presence. When he showed Stammer the inscription he had missed, the bookman seized the book, tore out the flyleaf, and handed back what was then legitimately a twenty-five-cent buy. Stammer, famous for his warm heart as well as his temper, repented by giving Randall a part-time job, thus furthering the education of an eminent American bookman.

Such stories lightly lend credence to one picture of certain Fourth Avenue bookmen as entrepreneurs who wandered ashore when the Spanish Main broke up, ending their careers as pirates, and who then opened bookshops on Fourth Avenue for themselves and their scalawag descendants. Many other stories challenge this character portrait. Book Row was host to most psychological types among its denizens. For every dealer who would just as soon kick you out as let you browse, there was another who was easygoing. For those who growled, there were the gentle souls who were polite and even kind to doubtful purchasers.

Frederick Lightfoot began buying books on Fourth Avenue in 1935, when he was fifteen. "Books on stands were priced at as little as one cent in the 1930s. A nickel or a dime would buy a wide variety of books. It is impossible to convey to someone born in the last twenty years the quality of life as well as the treasures of old Fourth Avenue," he reminisced in 1989. Among Lightfoot's favorite bookmen and bookshops were Alfred Goldsmith and his basement emporium, Sign of the Sparrow. Lightfoot recalled that one of Goldsmith's customers was a collector of books on angling. After Goldsmith learned with some astonishment that the collector had never gone fishing, he took him on a fishing trip to New Jersey. The next week the experienced and hence disillusioned collector brought in all his angling books to sell.

Sonja Mirsky, who became a librarian, began venturing to Fourth Avenue in 1939. In the 1940s when she was majoring in mathematics at college and had no funds to purchase Bertrand Russell's *Principia Mathematica,* she began taking the three volumes down from a high shelf at the Strand and using them at the store to do her homework. This repeated behavior was noticed, and she heard a clerk tell founder Ben Bass, "She's never going to buy those books." Bass said to leave the browser be: "When she has the money she'll buy them." When she graduated in 1948 from City College of New York and received $50 from an uncle, she offered the money directly to Ben Bass for the $35 set. Bass examined the books and said, "They're quite shelf worn. Why don't we make it $25?"

Ordering customers to be gone; taking a collector fishing; defacing a book in a fit of pique; amiably tolerating a student browser—these and countless more incidents became the human drama and comedy of Book Row. Bookmen, like their customers, never quite fit a clear-cut stereotype of any sort. They were human and, depending on the day, the dealer, and the book involved, were likely to assume a niche somewhere between sinner and saint.

A durable if never quite sufficient tagline for New York City is "There are 8 million stories in the Naked City," thanks to a Mark Hellinger film and the television show *Naked City.* The Green Book Shop, started by Ruth and Harry Carp, was featured as background in one episode of the gritty crime series. The following day, perhaps due to the publicity, the store was robbed.

So it went some days on Book Row in the naked city of 8 million stories and countless books.

In the preface to his *Memoirs* Ulysses S. Grant in 1885 wrote, "There must be many errors of omission in this work, because the subject is too large to be treated of in two volumes in such a way as to do justice to all the officers and men engaged." A similar apologia is apropos for a volume about Book Row. This work focuses on colorful booksellers and bookstores from the 1890s into the twenty-first century. Inevitably some individuals and establishments associated with Book Row are omitted or are incompletely covered. The recollections of others who were there may generously complement those that follow.

Across the decades many books flowed through Book Row from sellers to dealers to buyers and around again in a continuing cycle. With each came a story. This book records some of them as it commemorates a time and place where books mattered more than anything else among a special group of colorful and memorable individuals. Let's start with George D. Smith.

Hymn to Fourth Avenue

by Eli Siegel

Ah, all the books waiting for you
In the crowded bookshops of Fourth Avenue.
Experiences galore;
Experiences you'll adore.
Bibliographical thrills
New as the hills.
Mental fountains,
Emotional mountains.

II

In books, you'll find what you are looking for.
In books is that which makes existence more.
Our hopes in life are often in an old bookstore.

III

A book in Schulte's perhaps can explain
A puzzling thing. A book to lessen pain
Is now in Weiser's, rich in mental gain.

IV

Surprise is waiting on the Biblo shelves.
Green Book Store volumes tell about ourselves,
And bring us news: the word that shines and delves.

V

The same is true of all the other shops.
Our lives are there in all their skips and stops,
In all their valleys, all their mountaintops.

VI

Come, then, and see what's in Fourth Avenue.
Ah, all the wealth that's old and all that's new!—
And what a page, a book, can do and do.

BOOK ROW

CHAPTER ONE

The Smith a Mighty Bookman Was He
G.D.S. and Bookselling from Fourth Avenue to the Collecting World

*In the good old days when George D. Smith was Czar of the
auction rooms, all other dealers and collectors were under a terrific
strain the moment he appeared.*

—A. S. W. Rosenbach

EVERYONE HAS KNOWN since grade school about Longfellow's smith: "A mighty man was he." Except for bookselling and book-collecting insiders, few now know about New York's book Smith, the redoubtable George D., who was a mighty bookman indeed during the first two decades of the twentieth century. In the auction rooms, behind the scenes when great private libraries went on the market, and guiding Henry E. Huntington in shaping perhaps the finest private library of them all, George D. Smith was viewed as the czar, Napoleon, George the Great, and a host of similar, not entirely flattering, encomiums. Disparagement by disgruntled and defeated foes was also inevitable.

Antiquarian bookselling has not been free of the human appetite to apply dubious superlatives such as "greatest." Devotees and disciples of bookselling maestro A. S. W. Rosenbach of Philadelphia acclaimed him bookseller number one for his scholarship, big-money buys, and crucial additions to major collections. Yet the facts don't support the claims of Rosenbachians that their man towers over Smith. Rosenbach, who seems never to have suffered from shyness about seeking attention, knew with a touch of envy that Smith was the antiquarian book czar and said so in *Books and Bidders* (1928). Among all the booksellers who began on Book Row and graduated to uptown esteem and profits, George Smith soared highest and consumed more ink as newspapers publicized his deals.

Dig under the surface, and probably most booksellers qualify as colorful characters. From all accounts, G.D.S. was a character's character, an innate showman, workaholic, charlatan, genius, and self-starting original whose nature and exploits ensured that he would be talked about, for and against, whenever his peers got together (stop dawdling and open the bottle) in a reminiscent mood. As the leading mover and shaker of antiquarian bookselling, Smith became a competitor about whom it was probably not possible to be neutral. Most of his contemporaries in books, at least those who expressed themselves on the written record, liked him fine. Charles P. Everitt, the Americana master seller and author of *The Adventures of a Treasure Hunter*, called Smith "perhaps the greatest American book merchant of all time. . . . He never read anything but an occasional racing form; his word was said to be better than his checks, which sometimes bounced; he died at the one time in his life when he was worth a million dollars."

If a symposium were held to describe the ideal bookseller, among winning descriptions would no doubt be "learned and scholarly" (or at least "literate"), "scrupulously honest with customers," "consistently fair with peers." Such noble traits didn't stand out with horse-betting, poker-playing, chance-taking, go-getting George Smith. He did, however, have other indispensable assets, including a commitment to work eighteen-hour days, a tenacious memory that never forgot a book, the go-for-it nerve of a gambler, brilliant business instincts, the knack of being lucky, loyal friends such as Henry Huntington, and sincere, almost selfless dedication to the noble cause of getting those friends the very best books possible, wherever they might be and at whatever lengths short of murder. Charles Heartman called his friend Smith the "Gentleman Bookseller."

The gentleman title means, let's hope, that G.D.S. wouldn't have approved of Spanish monk Don Vincente, whose book-collecting extremism inspired Gustave Flaubert's first published story, "Bibliomanie." The monk robbed monastery libraries, abandoned holy orders, and opened a bookshop in Barcelona; and he *may*, after being outbid, have burned the house of a fellow collector—with the collector in it—but not before stealing the work on Castilian laws by Lamberto Palmart, the first Spanish printer, which had started the trouble. Don Vincente was executed in 1836, and Flaubert's story was published in 1837, when he was fifteen. A. S. W. Rosenbach in *The Unpublishable Memoirs* (1917) wrote, "All honour to poor Don

Vincent of Aragon. His name shall always be tenderly cherished by lovers of books!" George D. Smith would have calmed Don Vincente down and convinced him there was a neater way than theft and arson to win his prize, not to mention that killing just wasn't a practical strategy for book collecting. Let George Smith agent the deal, do a little trading, sweeten the pot, offer something the other collector wanted more, and so forth.

A. Edward Newton in *The Amenities of Book-Collecting* (1918) called G.D.S. an enigma and asked himself, "What are the qualities which have made him, as he undoubtedly is, the greatest bookseller in the world?" Answering that question would be an education in the art, challenge, and all-out battle of antiquarian bookselling. Since Smith was a book entrepreneur on Fourth Avenue in the 1890s, examining his 1890–1920 career should help explain not only the dealer but also the phenomenon—and mystery—of Book Row.

Matthew J. Bruccoli, in "George D. Smith and the Anglo-American Book Migration" (*Antiquarian Bookman*, 1994–95), stated without equivocation, "George D. Smith was the greatest American bookdealer." Bruccoli based this claim on Smith's book acquisitions and the collections he helped build. Many others, including historians and Smith's contemporaries, made equivalent assertions on his behalf. Smith's exploits often made him appear a virtuoso among amateurs in the frenzied chase for book treasures. Henry E. Huntington had no more money than several other well-heeled, well-intentioned book collectors of his day. Huntington created a greater library than they did because he had George D. Smith to complement his own intelligence, taste, and drive. When "the Old Man," as Smith affectionately referred to his chief patron, was warned about some of Smith's unscrupulous methods and unethical actions, the collector calmly replied, "He got me the books. I wouldn't have a library without him, would I?"

The accusation bearers, with dreams no doubt of replacing Smith as Huntington's rare-book provider, made the mistake of forgetting how Henry Huntington and his uncle Collis P. Huntington put together the railroad empire and built the fortune that could afford very expensive rarities, whether books, art, or trinkets. Huntington told Clarence S. Brigham, who collected books for the American Antiquarian Society, "I think that I have spent twenty million on books, and slightly more on art." Not all, but many of the top-dollar book deals were George Smith deals. Richard S. Wormser in a profile about Smith pointed out that most of the great (and wealthy) collectors beat a path to his shop because of the outstanding books he found and offered to them, and also "possibly in part because they saw, in his activities, methods similar to those by which some of them had amassed their fortunes."

G.D.S. was naturally decried as ruthless, reckless, crude, unlettered, and dangerous by stodgy traditionalists and by those who came in second once too often on deals shrewdly managed and won by Smith. His triumphs made him the bookseller most revered and reviled, depending on whom you represented and what you thought of his cunning, tactics, and nearly unlimited resources, thanks to the bottomless pockets of Huntington and other collector clients. During that run-wild era of antiquarian book collecting, big fortunes from nineteenth-century robber baron days required respectable investment outlets in high culture such as art and books. George D. Smith repeatedly proved that he was a skilled, unbeatable guide when unique books were a pecuniarily endowed hunter's goals. But G.D.S. was no book snob. His 1890s catalogues from Fourth Avenue feature excellent books at low prices. "Excellent books at low prices" isn't a bad description of Book Row at its best.

From Brooklyn to Stock Boy to the Book-Collecting Stars

George Smith's series of catalogues from his store at 830 Broadway with Alfred J. Bowden and later, on his own, from 69 Fourth Avenue pinpoint him as the first world-class antiquarian bookseller physically situated in the Book Row area.

The only information on record about his childhood is that he was born in Brooklyn in 1870. Whatever conventional schooling he received was finished by 1883, when he went to work for the firm of John Wiley & Sons at Astor Place. John Wiley was the son of Charles Wiley, who ran a downtown bookstore and published Cooper's novels early in the century. The lack of a formal education seems not to have been a handicap for Smith then or later. Like Benjamin Franklin and Mark Twain, who used print shops as their universities, George Smith would obtain the only higher education he needed in bookstores and auction rooms.

Smith's first bookstore job was short-lived, since Wiley terminated bookselling in 1884 to concentrate on publishing. Selling books may have struck the boy as a career worth pursuing, or maybe he just needed another job quickly. He went to work as a stock boy in the bookshop operated by Dodd, Mead & Company at Broadway and Eighth Street. He couldn't have found a better place to serve an apprenticeship in antiquarian bookselling. While sweeping the floors, running errands, and handling stock, he could watch and learn from Robert Dodd and his staff of experts about the acquiring and selling of rare books and manuscripts.

John Tebbel, in *A History of Book Publishing in the United States* (vol. 2, 1975), described the Dodd, Mead retail outlet in front of its publishing offices as a business that kept hours every day except Sunday, though it did take time off for the blizzard of 1888. Young Smith got a half hour for lunch and probably wasn't overworked, since a dumbwaiter transported books from floor to floor. His future actions confirm that he had ample on-the-job opportunities to watch and learn.

He was also smart enough to keep a low profile and avoid irritating the elders. One thing he learned about himself was that he possessed an unusually absorbent memory, capable of retaining specific details about books from catalogues, sales, or auctions. He didn't have to read the books to remember their titles, edition points, prices, buyers, and where they fell on the scale of importance to collectors. Even as a teenager, he was on his way to becoming a human incarnation of *Book-Prices Current,* augmented and deluxe.

Smith didn't stay long at Dodd, Mead. When William Benjamin left the company in 1886 to open a store of his own at 744 Broadway, he took the teenager with him. He had been impressed by Smith's eager energy and extraordinarily reliable memory. If Dodd, Mead was Smith's high school, the new store was his Harvard and graduate school combined. He learned much from the astute and versatile Benjamin, whom he virtually hero-worshiped, according to bookseller Charles F. Heartman in a 1945 privately printed, thirty-two-page memorial tribute to George D. Smith. Benjamin dealt in books, autographs, and prints. This wide range helped alert Smith to the fact that there was money to be made on a multitude of collectible items other than books. Throughout his career, he showed readiness to seize opportunity by the forelock, however peculiar any particular forelock might be. In 1916, thirty years after he began working for Benjamin, Smith encouraged Huntington to consider "a most important item," an antique Italian reliquary with compartments containing a lock of John Milton's hair on one side and a lock of Elizabeth Barrett's hair on the other. Huntington wasn't interested in literary hair, but at Smith's urging he did take the Shakespeare bookcase from a 1914 sale. The case held ninety-five worthwhile Shakespeare items, but the sales kicker was that it had been made out of wood from forty different structures connected with Shakespeare's life. Who could resist?

At the store, Smith began meeting—and sometimes impressing—major league collectors, permanent luminaries in the sport that A. Edward Newton called "the best and safest hobby," because it was year-round and could be played everywhere. The star roster visiting Benjamin's store included theater producer Augustin Daly; the first Grolier Club president, Robert Hoe; and the third Grolier Club president, Beverly Chew, as well as Rush Hawkins, Frederick Robert Halsey, Elihu Dwight Church, Charles Foote, and others. These early contacts would facilitate and accelerate Smith's rise from stock boy to antiquarian books impresario.

Who could have guessed that years later Smith would buy all or part of some of their magnificent collections for his clients and his stores, or that the Church and Hoe collections would almost overnight turn obscurity into fame and thrust greatness permanently upon him? Who could have guessed? Apparently the Leon brothers. Heartman in his G.D.S. booklet reports that they visited Benjamin's store before leaving America for their return to Europe. Benjamin said that when they returned, they would find him the American Quaritch. "Not you," said one of the brothers, pointing at Smith. "That boy George will be the American Quaritch." So it turned out, though limiting Smith to being another Quaritch may have been an understatement. In later years, more often than not, it would be Smith himself who would prevail over England's own premier bookseller, Bernard Alfred Quaritch.

A BUSINESS OF HIS OWN

At the summit of success, George Smith recalled, "I had not been with Dodd, Mead a month when I began to dream of having a business of my own." The dream must be fairly routine among young, low-level workers. What is not routine is seeing it happen by the age of twenty. The catalogues they issued confirm that by 1890, "A. J. Bowden and Geo. D. Smith" had an operating bookstore at 830 Broadway—next door, in fact, to the current Strand Book Store, at 828 Broadway. They called their joint venture Mitchell's Rare and Standard Books, with "Prints, Autographs, Etchings, Etc., Etc.," available as well. An attractive 3-by-5.5-inch card identified Mitchell's and its managers and quoted a line from Shakespeare as a quality come-on to the literati: "Come and make choice of all my library, and so beguile thy leisure." The bookmen improved the original line, by changing "take" to "make" and "thy sorrow" to "thy leisure." But let's face it, stage entrepreneur Shakespeare would have been flattered to be quoted, and pleased that the boys were dipping into and playing around a bit with *Titus Andronicus*.

A stylish little prospectus mentioned that Mr. Alfred J. Bowden was "many years with several of the principal houses in London" and that Mr. Geo. D. Smith was "formerly with some of the leading booksellers of this city." They called themselves the managers of the house, which could imply there were other owners or investors behind the venture at the start. The prospectus announced the plan to issue catalogues at frequent intervals for rare, standard, and new books, some imported. Mitchell's assured customers that experienced London agents would be serving them with expertise based on "thorough knowledge of the best quarters in which to look for good books on the other side." Bowden's firsthand London experience, whatever the specifics, gave some credibility to this claim.

In addition to customary guarantees of authenticity for documents and autographs, persistent efforts to maintain a large stock, and bindings done "with dispatch, neatness, and taste," the prospectus made an offer that seemed to go beyond normal bookstore activities. Noting the difficult problem of keeping books orderly and clean, Bowden and Smith wrote: "We shall be ready at all times to take this work, and not only catalogue, but DUST, CLEAN, ARRANGE, and generally look after a library at a moderate and fixed charge per annum." "EXPERIENCED WORKMEN SENT," they concluded. The library housekeeper pitch has the ring of a Smith effort to earn supplementary income during Mitchell's start-up years. Another typical G.D.S. touch for the bookman who would be the greatest book buyer of his age was this statement: "Experience has shown the best way to dispose of a large lot of books is direct to some respectable bookseller, who will pay—as ourselves—spot cash. By this means the vendor will avoid the long waits, the exorbitant charges, and the proverbial uncertainty of the auction room." Smith early on sought to increase stock, especially of important books, and to borrow if necessary for that purpose.

"The true booklover finds in catalogs his most fascinating reading," wrote Clarence S. Brigham in his introduction to *American Book Auction Catalogues,* compiled by G. L. McKay (1937). Brigham meant auction catalogues, but store catalogues have their fascinations too. The prices in the old ones make modern collectors yearn for a time machine. The books listed tell much about the tastes, attitudes, and customs of their times. Clearly, historians and archaeologists shouldn't ignore bookstore catalogues.

The first Mitchell's catalogue, for December 1890, has Smith's name listed first, a switch from the name positions on the prospectus. This became standard practice on catalogues that followed. The Mitchell's catalogues show the expected features of book sale brochures from over a century ago, fabulous prices on some names and titles still in the mainstream, and many names and items that have faded out of sight in terms of modern interest. Autographs and letters by nineteenth-century worthies and Revolutionary-era eminences are staggeringly low by modern measures. At $12.50, an autograph document signed by Franklin was a special bargain in their 1892 "A Century of Rare Books—One Hundred Choice Items" catalogue.

From a modern perspective, the best deal in that catalogue, at $15, is the 1856, 8vo, original cloth second edition of *Leaves of Grass* containing Emerson's July 1855 letter and Whitman's long reply. Whitman died at Mickle Street in Camden on March 26, the year of the Mitchell's catalogue. Whoever bought the $15 *Leaves* second edition enjoyed a rare bargain. Not all the books that Smith bought and sold still obey his dictum that "prices were bound to increase and to go on increasing because the demand was outgrowing the supply." Some authors collected in the 1890s are in no demand whatever during the 2000s. But the Whitman, certainly, and many other of the books, autographs, manuscripts, and prints found, bought, catalogued, and sold by Smith still reflect his faith in the abiding value of great items.

Smith at the age of twenty-one boldly lived by his trust in rising prices and a born gambler's willingness to take a big chance for a big win. At the 1891 sale of the books and manuscripts collected by Brayton Ives, a founder of the Grolier Club, Smith, barely old enough to vote, wagered $40,000 at the auction. Some purchases were on commission, but many were for his own stock, and he told Heartman, "I sweat blood trying to pay." Blood sweating may have been hyperbole since he always appeared calmly confident that his book wagers would work out. Typically they did. It was then perhaps that G.D.S. began proving, and himself believing, that for success in antiquarian book-selling a prime requirement along with book savvy and salesmanship is the nerve of a high roller. The fact that he nearly always found purchasers and made his audacious plunges pay off shows that Smith added marketing shrewdness to his in-depth knowledge of the books and related items specific collectors would want and could afford. Smith's career is a living textbook on entrepreneurship for small businesses determined not to stay small.

By the mid-1890s Smith was ready to brave the deep waters by launching his own business without any visible partners or investors. Under his own name, as "Geo. D. Smith, Dealer in Choice, Rare and Miscellaneous Books," he set up shop at 69 Fourth Avenue, near the Bible House. Smith's later claim was that his start-up capital was $63. Heartman points out that whatever the reality of his cash situation, Smith's capital included his "incomparable knowl-edge of the principles of what constituted a rare book and the value of such material." Added to this was his tireless energy, good sources, and the well-wishing of collectors. "That was his capital. He made the most of it. And, of course, he had nerve. Plenty of it," wrote Heartman. But there was nothing easy about the pioneering challenge of bringing rare books as a business to Fourth Avenue, even in the protective presence of the massive Bible House.

The Bible House, maintained by the American Bible Society (ABS), con-sumed nearly the whole block bounded by Eighth and Ninth Streets and Third and Fourth Avenues. It was a successor to the original Bible House, on Nassau Street, established by the ABS to use advanced stereotyping tech-niques and produce Bibles by the thousands for shipment west through the Erie Canal. Should any particular significance be seen in the fact that the first Bible House was on Nassau and the second on Fourth Avenue and that each thoroughfare developed a Booksellers' Row? Just asking.

When he began alone on Fourth Avenue, George Smith had a small but carefully selected stock; and he knew how to upgrade his book resources steadily: Buy aggressively yet intelligently, sell creatively, and shoot the income promptly back into fresh stock for the business. Smith was also a strong believer in the power of catalogues to produce orders. After he began operating as George D. Smith, he issued over 170 catalogues, as well as mis-cellaneous bulletins and special unnumbered lists.

His Catalogue No. 1 from 69 Fourth Avenue, with 453 items, reflects the working approach he followed throughout his subsequent career. Along with enticing, professionally detailed descriptions of the best books he could muster, he included a prominent notice that he would be attending the auction of David Adee's valuable collection and would "doubtless be a large buyer," and emphasized that "intending purchasers may find it advantageous to place their bids with me." The sovereign of the New York and London auction rooms was announcing the start of his reign. Long bid the king.

Catalogue No. 3, in 1896, the last issued from Fourth Avenue, repeated the Mitchell's invitation to end the trouble and expense of maintaining large collections: "I shall be ready at all times to undertake this work, and not only *catalogue*, but *clean, dust, arrange* and generally look after libraries at a moderate rate." As with his other Fourth Avenue catalogues, No. 3, with 711 items, offers splendid books at prices now painful to look upon. Never again will the first book edition of *The Pickwick Papers* be available for $22.50, or *Little Dorrit* in the nineteen monthly parts with original wrappers for $10! George Smith always insisted prices would climb. You could put that promise in the bank at high interest on some of his 1896 entries.

Item 117 may compel reaching for references on obscurities: "FIRST AMERICAN NOVEL. THE FORESTERS, an American Tale: being a sequel to the history of John Bull the Clothier. Frontispiece. 12 mo, original boards, uncut. Boston, 1792. $15.00 / *This is the first edition in book form of the First American Novel, by an American author, Jeremy Belknap. Very rare."

George Smith won a priority position in Fourth Avenue Book Row history with his shop at 69 Fourth Avenue, but he soon moved on. His later catalogues, with several different locations in midtown and downtown Manhattan, indicate considerable mobility along with emphasis on American and English literature. His 1902 "Monthly Bulletin of Scarce Books" No. 3, from 49–51 New Street, does stray to Renaissance Italy with a rare first edition by Galileo at $45. Autographs and manuscripts are featured in some catalogues, such as "Monthly Bulletin" No. 7, from 50 New Street, with a $4.50 Walt Whitman postcard, a $3.50 John Quincy Adams letter, a $3.75 John Jacob Astor 1792 check for $1,550, a $60 Benedict Arnold letter, and an $18 Thomas Jefferson letter ordering books from a catalogue. Then as later, "infamous" did better than simply "famous"; witness the price of an Arnold autograph versus that of former presidents.

Smith's other downtown addresses included 70 Wall Street and 48 Wall Street. He operated plush midtown stores simultaneously with downtown outlets. George Smith had pioneered antiquarian bookselling on Fourth Avenue with his second store, but he clearly wasn't sentimental about the area as he bounced around Manhattan. Catalogue addresses indicate he was successively in business at 4 East Forty-second Street, 547 Fifth Avenue, and 8 East Forty-fifth Street. In 1897 he was located at 4 East Forty-second Street, near where George Washington's troops were routed by the British from a cornfield during the Revolution and where the main building of the New York Public Library opened May 23, 1911.

His new addresses generally meant higher prices on progressively classier offerings. The 830 Broadway and 69 Fourth Avenue catalogues predominantly offered literary collectibles and rarities at prices seldom exceeding a few dollars. At 547 Fifth Avenue one tantalizing catalogue features lofty costs on rare books with exquisite outer garments, including, at $500, a bejeweled *Rubaiyat* with sixty pearls and ten garnets, as well as a jewel-bedecked Tennyson poem, "The Lady of Shalott," at $1,750. His Fifth Avenue customers perusing that catalogue could choose unique productions, from fine bindings to three chairs and a sofa "attested and authenticated" as original possessions of Charles Dickens. How could a Dickens lover resist sitting where the author may have planted himself to ponder and plot his next opus in nineteen parts plus one? That Fifth Avenue catalogue took Smith and

his customers not just miles but vast social strata away from the humbler realities of Fourth Avenue and, for that matter, even nearby Forty-second Street.

From his Forty-second Street store, he began distributing *Smith's Bi-Weekly Price-Current of Books*, which included a page of "Literary Gossip" along with book bargains. The June 15, 1897, issue listed eight first editions of Robert Louis Stevenson, ranging in price from $1 for *The Wrong Box* to $6 for *The Dynamiter*.

"Literary Gossip" must have seemed flippant; it became "Literary Notes" in later issues. Whether gossip or notes, the page seems to be George Smith talking to customers with revealing frankness. The August 2, 1897, issue carries this description of Bernard Quaritch: "Mr. Quaritch's personality is an interesting one, and from small beginnings he has become the foremost bookseller of Europe. This has been accomplished by a constant faith in the upward tendency of prices of rare books, and a courage to back that opinion to the extent of his resources." Smith in 1897, at the age of twenty-seven, describing Quaritch, is also accurately describing Smith, who would dominate the rare-book market—and even Quaritch—with his own faith and courage. Mitchell's "A Century of Rare Books" catalogue in 1892 succinctly stated what proved to be Smith's antiquarian bookselling and buying credo: "Rare books have risen in price, are rising, and will rise still higher." So buy now; you'll have to pay more later.

The October 15, 1897, *Smith's Bi-Weekly* contained a literary note obviously aimed at trying to make Forty-second Street a New York Book Row. Smith wrote: "Forty-second street is rapidly becoming a book-market. Within three blocks there are six bookstores, several of which are dependent upon the Passer-by for their trade. From what I hear and can see we are all doing very nicely and would welcome further neighbors in the shape of bookmen. The more the merrier." Fourth Avenue enthusiasts may smile tolerantly at this innocent heresy, for they recognize that wherever he located, Smith's lasting influence on book collecting fostered a book-receptive climate that ultimately helped make the Fourth Avenue Book Row possible.

Smith's 1900 catalogue, from Forty-second Street, announced that a monthly journal devoted to the interests of collectors, the *Literary Collector,* would appear in October, available at $1 per year. This publication carried out a long-range plan aimed at earning greater prestige for his establishments among collectors. It was edited by Bowden, with articles by Smith and others. An obvious effort was made to keep it from being merely a house organ similar to the *Bi-Weekly*. It contained extensive advertising by other dealers and held Smith house items to a respectable and soft-spoken minimum. Many twenty-first-century book lovers would still find these periodicals informative, nostalgic, even fascinating reading about the authors, sellers, and buyers of books in their not-all-that-far-away era.

The publication not surprisingly did function with some subtlety as a forum in which Smith could air views on the state and trend of current collecting. In the November 1900 issue an article by Smith concludes with this little sermon of optimistic uplift to practicing and would-be collectors: "When the rulers of kingdoms today have crumbled into the dust and their names forgotten of the people, the memory of a maker of a great collection will be a household word in the mouths of thousands. This is the real road to fame."

It seems unlikely that Smith's ambitious customers, eager to be remembered for the wisdom, taste, and exclusivity of their collections, would have been disposed to argue with that (let's face it) somewhat fantastic claim. In fact, several distinguished collectors from the 1890s to 1920 are remembered mainly not for their acquisitions but because George D. Smith dramatically bid up many of their treasures at the final auctions of their collections.

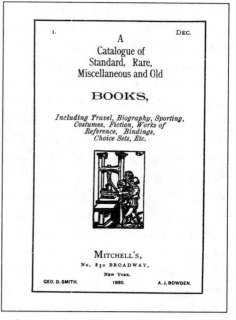

G.D.S. at the Auctions

In his *Bookdealing for Profit* (2000), English antiquarian bookseller Paul Minet writes that successful bookselling stands on three legs: shops, fairs, catalogues. George Smith skillfully used the first and third for thirty years of a highly active career. He used book auctions brilliantly and sometimes belligerently as his third and by far most powerful leg up on success.

John Huckans in *Book Source Monthly* (August 2000) noted, "The stereotyped image of the slightly detached man in herringbone tweed jacket, elbow patches to the fore, is what the uninitiated probably think of, if indeed they do think at all of, the dealer in out-of-print, antiquarian and rare books." What a far cry that romantic image of intellectual and spiritual remoteness is from the reality of spiffily dressed George D. Smith arriving in his Rolls-Royce, after checking on his stable of racehorses and on his stock holdings, to take over another million-dollar book auction, thanks to his bids, at the finest auction houses in New York and London.

Barely out of his teens, Smith was a consistently high bidder on promising books at auctions soon after he launched his own firms. "It was perfectly clear to me that the dealer who had the largest stock would do the largest business, because collectors would be obliged to go to him for their books," Smith declared. "I have never been afraid of overstocking in really rare books. . . . The best salesman in the world cannot sell books that he cannot deliver. The fundamental thing is to get the books." In March 1900, Smith, at thirty, startled his elders by risking his modest capital and buying close to a third of the books at the sale of producer and playwright Augustin Daly's theater collection. This performance challenges the arguments of those who claim it was easy for Smith to dominate auctions considering the resources behind him. Yet he began dominating such proceedings when the only resources were his own meager holdings, not access to venture capital. After the Daly sale, when New York buyers didn't rush in and bail him out of his financial predicament, Smith, undaunted, displayed his showmanship. He took the books to Chicago, publicized them vigorously, and stirred up a buzz that soon had both Midwest and New York collectors vying and buying.

The Daly exploit was typical of him. It made Smith known as a force to reckon with at sales, and it brought him a steady flow of bid commissions from major collectors. In 1908 the supreme book-purchasing connection probably of all time began, that of George D. Smith, dealer, and Henry E. Huntington, collector. Huntington, according to Rosenbach, once observed that while men come and go, books go on forever; thus "the ownership of a fine library is the surest and swiftest way to immortality." The original source of that sentiment, George Smith, is no secret; and on the scale he collected in collaboration with Smith, it was literally quite true for Huntington because of the unexcelled Henry E. Huntington Library at San Marino, California, deeded to the American people in perpetuity. With Smith guiding him, Huntington put the library together, then gave it to us.

During the first decade of the twentieth century Huntington had the money, lots of it, from railroads and other enterprises to give less time to business and more time to his book and art collecting. He had earned the right and was ready, as he remarked, to have "some fun." The fun of finding and buying rare books was already in progress for Huntington when he commissioned Smith to make purchases for him as the Henry Poor collection was sold over a period of six months, November 1908 through April 1909, by the Anderson Auction Company in New York. Acting for Huntington, Smith acquired nearly a quarter of the Poor library, which was anything but poor, with incunabula, manuscripts, and first editions—for example, Goldsmith's *The Vicar of Wakefield* and Shelley's *Queen Mab: A Philosophical Poem*. Poor had been hard hit by the financial panic of 1907 and sold his books to pay debts. Ironically, the Poor fortune came in part from railroad publications, and it was with Huntington's railroad money that Smith was bidding.

The dealer and the collector apparently hit it off while cooperating during that 1908–9 auction, and they continued to do business. Charles Heartman dismisses others who claimed to have inspired Huntington's collecting and assigns full credit to Smith for changing the railroad man from a casual investor in rare books into a full-fledged bibliophile and dedicated collector. "It was . . . when George Smith got hold of Huntington that the latter, under clever coaching, developed into a booklover," wrote Heartman.

Two big sales within weeks of each other in 1911 earned the collaboration front-page attention and alerted the book world to the arrival of a formidable, often unbeatable combination: Smith's book knowledge and shrewdness in negotiations combined with his partner's capital. The first coup was the purchase en bloc at a price reportedly exceeding $1 million of the stupendous literature collection assembled over decades by Elihu Dwight Church, a Brooklyn manufacturer of bicarbonate of soda. The Church deal added about four thousand books to the growing collection that would be housed in the library of the California mansion completed for Huntington in April 1910. Among the volumes were first editions of Spenser's *Faerie Queene*, Bacon's *Essays*, Milton's *Paradise Lost*, Defoe's *Robinson Crusoe*, Swift's *Gulliver's Travels*. The American items included the original manuscript of Franklin's *Autobiography* as well as original issues of his *Poor Richard's Almanack*. The library also featured what was then one of the world's finest Shakespeare collections.

Next came probably the most talked and written about book auction in history, the Robert Hoe sale that began April 24, 1911, and lasted until November 1912. The high-drama climax of the show came early, not at the end. Robert Hoe, another Grolier founder and the club's first president, belonged to a family wealthy from important contributions to printing technology and from the manufacture of printing presses. A notable book collector, Hoe, after seeing fine books carelessly handled when they were donated to academic libraries, had his books sold at auction so there was a better chance they would go to book lovers rather than indifferent academic book handlers. In one way, Hoe's plan backfired since the cream of the collection did go to a library, the Huntington; yet the plan succeeded too, because there the books have been lovingly cared for.

The Hoe auction resembled a book buyers' Olympics. An international group—including Quaritch and other star players from England, as well as representatives from most serious American collectors with serious money, such as J. Pierpont Morgan—assembled at the mansion rented for the occasion by Anderson Galleries. The main event occurred on Monday evening of the first day when bidding was held on item 269, a vellum Gutenberg Bible, one of the first books printed with movable type and a world-class treasure by any measure. After a facetious bid of $100 by someone in the audience, George Smith, with Henry Huntington sitting beside him, bid $10,000, and the race was on as several bidders participated and successively fell by the wayside. The race ended when Smith bid $50,000, and Huntington owned the Gutenberg Bible. A. Edward Newton was in the audience and later wrote, "No book had ever sold for so great a price, yet I feel sure that Mr. Huntington secured a bargain, and I told him so."

The sale went on, and so did George Smith's high bidding on behalf of Huntington and also for his own stock. Of the 14,588 lots, Smith reportedly bought about 5,500, including many of the standout items. Smith sent Continental and English buyers home with much less than they intended, and he speculated that the experience had taught them a lesson they would remember "about American sporting blood."

Smith's sporting blood also sent angry shivers through some of his American competitors. J. P. Morgan's librarian, Belle da Costa Greene, who came in second to Smith on too many lots at the Hoe sale, didn't conceal her dismay that the newcomers were irresponsibly attacking the Hoe books with a shovel of money. The Gutenberg Bible story made the front page of the *New York Times* on April 25, 1911. Five days later a *Times* follow-up article appeared under the head "J. P. Morgan's Librarian Says High Book Prices Are Harmful." Greene called the prices paid at the Hoe sale ridiculous and a regrettable precedent. She complained that it wasn't an auction but an en bloc surrender to Smith and Huntington: "Things have been raised to a fictitious value. It isn't even a case of paying two or three times the value of a book. Sometimes ten or twenty times the true value has been paid." George Smith must have wondered who's to say what "true value" is on a rare book.

Even while the Hoe sale was in progress, the Smith-Huntington team negotiated for and in October 1912 purchased the Beverly Chew collection en bloc to join other San Marino treasures. Chew, the third president of the Grolier Club, compiled many of the Grolier catalogues and wrote *Essays and Verses About Books* (1926). The title of one Chew poem was "Old Books Are Best." At the Grolier Club, Chew recounted how his literature collection went west. Not really wanting to sell, he responded to the request for a price with a figure he thought unacceptable. Huntington accepted. The Beverly Chew and Elihu Church acquisitions set a pattern Smith would follow with worthy collections whenever he could: Buy the whole library.

Their 1911–12 accomplishments through auctions and en bloc deals provided a working model for the future: Buy aggressively at the sales, but when possible get what you want by means of private arrangements. Thus Smith often, after learning a valuable library might go on the auction block, went to work behind the scenes, and rendered the auction unnecessary with an attractive offer.

By 1914, with his New York sovereignty secure, Smith looked to England for new book worlds to conquer. He proved equally formidable at English auctions and no less successful in arranging numerous en bloc purchases there. One 1914 purchase was the library of the duke of Devonshire which came rich with Caxtons, plays, manuscripts, and a trove of Shakespeare folios and quartos. Smith subsequently viewed the Devonshire buy as perhaps his greatest bargain.

To the chagrin of the English dealers, Smith was also unstoppable at their London auctions. Lawrence Clark Powell wrote in *Books in My Baggage* (1960), "What a show they are! as the dealers fight it out with nod of head and wink of eye, twitch of brow or flick of finger, garnering fabulous Caxtons, dazzling Books of Hours, precious manuscripts, and rare Americana." Writing about the Huntington and other libraries "formed by American capitalists, largely from European sources," Powell expressed the hope that a free flow of books would develop among all countries since "books are ambassadors that never die."

At the earl of Pembroke's sale in June 1914, Smith dominated the auction by taking 97 out of 211 lots. Later he rubbed it in by expressing regret he didn't get everything. "The squeal of the English is highly amusing, as when I acquired the Devonshire library," he was quoted in the *New York Times* on June 26, 1914. Even conspiracies to rig sales through a collaborative bidding ring failed because Smith simply kept bidding higher to get what he wanted. "My high prices caused the rest of the dealers to lose heart and they do not know yet what I am capable of," he was quoted by the *New York Sun* on July 18, 1914, under the head "American Smashes London Book Ring." An end result of Smith's shovel work in England was that several great English collections became permanent immigrants to America.

Smith's substantial purchases in England and New York from 1914 on were for himself and several other wealthy collector customers as well as Huntington. His relationship with the Californian and his public and private feats made it fashionable for collectors to deal with the number one dealer. Huntington typically had the right of first refusal, what Matthew Bruccoli labels cherry picking, on books Smith bought for his own stores. The opulent Smith catalogues after 1914 offered splendid items from the Pembroke auction and his multitude of other rare books sources.

As a front-runner, the graduate of Fourth Avenue had plenty of attackers from one side of the Atlantic to the other. He was assailed as a tyrant and accused of questionable ethics. Yet he continued to rule with relative ease until his sudden death from a heart attack on March 4, 1920. He was at his 8 East Forty-fifth Street store—working as a bookseller—when it happened. Donald C. Dickinson, writing in the *Book Collector* ("Mr. Huntington and Mr. Smith," autumn 1988), observes, "As Heartman claimed, scholars owe him an enormous debt of gratitude. His knowledge of books and his bold methods for acquiring them helped build the greatest collection of early books and manuscripts to be formed in the first quarter of this century."

Now "this century" is to us last century, and George D. Smith became a bookseller on Fourth Avenue in the century before that. He started small on Fourth Avenue; became a leviathan of antiquarian books by means of vigor, knowledge, skill, and imagination; and ultimately sent business back to Fourth Avenue by permanently stimulating the whole field of book collecting. The legend that fed the future should live on.

CHAPTER TWO

An Early Beaux Books Quartet

Isaac Mendoza · Jacob Abrahams · Peter Stammer · David Kirschenbaum

> *A bookseller must be a business man, a salesman, an advertising*
> *copywriter, a window-dresser, a bookkeeper, a janitor, a gambler, a*
> *psychologist,—but above all he must be a book man with such an*
> *intimate knowledge of his merchandise that he may recognize and*
> *satisfy a human need on the instant. . . . He is dealing in the literature*
> *of human thought and ideas, both the timeless and the timely.*
>
> —HESTER R. HOFFMAN, *Bookman's Manual* (1948)

IN MUSIC A quartet is a composition for four instruments or voices with the goal of achieving interesting effects through harmonious blending of sounds. It seems likely that any four New York booksellers could never achieve such harmony and would always, by comparison with, say, the string quartets of Haydn, Mozart, or Beethoven, be a pretty quirky quartet. Yet such a disparate group does have the inherent harmony of a shared commitment to the common theme of *books*. Each individual member of this early bookseller quartet would probably look at the others, shake his head, and call it not a string but a distinctly strange quartet.

Frederick Lightfoot, who began buying books on Fourth Avenue in the 1930s, wrote about the booksellers he knew then: "They were people of remarkably strong individuality, probably mostly self-taught to a high degree of knowledge about many subjects as well as of the books they handled, and mostly very hard-working. Some had very prickly personalities, others were kind and generous. They had few members of Dickensian uniqueness, but they were a very different breed from the merchandisers of today's new book stores."

Lightfoot's description fits our special book quartet. All four were consummate bookmen; all had strong, early connections with Book Row through Fourth Avenue bookshops or through close association between secondhand bookdealers over many years; and all four, to use an ancient cliché that still delivers more meaning than ancient clichés generally do, were booksellers of that proud, dedicated, informed "old school" Lightfoot remembered.

Isaac Mendoza and Sons—Isaac Mendoza Book Company

As about every neighborhood in Manhattan at one time or another has been the site of an interesting bookstore, the entire island qualifies historically as a collective Book City. In this account of bookselling as it developed in one particular area, until Fourth Avenue became known as Book Row, we recognize certain exceptional booksellers who were physically located elsewhere than Fourth Avenue but whose importance through long association and cooperation identifies them as vital extensions of our Book Row. They were much more than just honorary members; they were active contributors to Book Row history. Certainly one of these is Isaac Mendoza, with his Old Ann Street Book Store, incorporated in 1908 as the Isaac Mendoza Book Company.

Isaac Mendoza was born on the Lower East Side of New York in 1864, the son of immigrants from London. As a teenager, he worked for Michael J. Hynes in a bookstore on Ann Street, and he used the next dozen years at that store and others learning the ins, outs, problems, and opportunities of the business. In November 1894 he went into business for himself at 17 Ann Street, and not long thereafter expanded to 15 Ann Street. The Mendoza store operated at this location until its final closing, in February 1990. During later years it was quite accurately advertised as "New York's Oldest 'Old' Book Shop."

In *Clegg's International Directory of Booksellers for 1899* appears this entry: "Mendoza, Isaac, 17, Ann Street. *Second-hand.*" Not far away on William Street, at the corner of Ann, was the childhood home of Washington Irving. The area then was the location of New York's most active book business, with access to the executives, employees, and clients of the financial district, as well as to municipal workers from City Hall and city government offices within walking distance.

Mendoza's longevity at the same site proves the firm's skill at satisfying a diverse clientele that included, wrote Madeleine B. Stern in *Antiquarian Bookselling in the United States* (1985), "bankers and brokers, railroad titans and robber barons, politicians and passers-by." In addition to business and government customers, Christopher Morley, William Rose Benét, and other writers and collectors regularly visited the gaslit book building to browse and buy. The claim was that exceptional discipline was always needed to leave Mendoza's without buying.

The red brick building in which the shop was located had six floors and eventually contained an estimated half million books. Donald C. Dickinson in *Dictionary of American Antiquarian Dealers* (1998) observed, "With its windows set back from the sidewalk on one of the city's oldest and narrowest streets, its floor-to-ceiling shelving and tables of books everywhere, the Mendoza store was for many New Yorkers the essence of what a bookshop should be."

To maintain the large stock, Mendoza aggressively bought private libraries as well as the stocks of other booksellers and the backlist stocks of publishers. In 1904, perhaps instructing by example rare-book-selling virtuoso George D. Smith, Isaac Mendoza managed en bloc sales of the Charles A. Morrogh library, featuring first editions and illustrated classics, and the John A. Morschhauser literary collection to Henry E. Huntington. Mendoza continued to be a book source for Huntington into the 1920s.

Along with his own business, Mendoza helped other bookmen successfully enter the ranks of "generous liberal-minded men," as Samuel Johnson described booksellers. One was Charles Goodspeed of Boston, author of *Yankee Bookseller*, who in 1898 opened the shop famous for its slogan, "Anything That's a Book," and its trademarked figure of a riding and reading monk. Urged on by Mendoza, Goodspeed started with some of Mendoza's remainders and stock bought at Bangs auction house in New York, plus books from his own collection, which he had assembled by years of book hunting in "junkshops and odd-corners." Goodspeed was one among numerous individuals assisted by Mendoza and later by his sons.

When Isaac Mendoza died in 1937 he had three sons, Aaron, Mark, and David, to carry on. Aaron took over and operated the business until his death in 1960. He was succeeded by David Mendoza, who died in 1972. One of Aaron's notable deals was the sale of Christopher Morley manuscripts to the University of Texas. This produced a "huge check," noted Walter Caron, who bought the stock and the company name in 1972 and kept the store alive until 1990.

Jacob Chernofsky, in "The Mendoza Bookstore: Surviving a Century of

Change" (*Antiquarian Bookman,* April 11, 1988), wrote, "In his way, Walter is keeping alive a memory and a tradition that reflects the pride and the glory of 19th-century bookselling." The same issue of *AB* stated, "Isaac Mendoza in his time, and Aaron and David, all had a profound influence on the trade and on individuals who looked to them for guidance." Frederick Lightfoot remembered a Mendoza brother (probably Aaron) as one of the rare rare-book dealers "who took time out from marking books, etc. to talk with me and establish genuine rapport and eventually friendship." Aaron Mendoza, according to Madeleine Stern, had planned to write a history of New York City bookselling. "To that end he had crammed his roll-top desk with notes and source materials. Although he did not live to write that history, he and the Isaac Mendoza Book Company assuredly helped, and still help, to make it," Stern noted.

Walter Caron as the store's owner reflected changing market realities by concentrating on science fiction, mysteries, and regular first editions rather than the earlier antiquarian emphasis. Interviewed for this chronicle in 1990, Caron described a practice he saw during David Mendoza's management that was a hangover from the Depression era and that took place in some Book Row shops as well: methodically turning out lights to save electricity. At Mendoza's, because of the location, the bulk of the sales occurred between noon and 2 P.M., which was predominantly the lunch period for most area businesses. So out went many of the Mendoza lights after 2 P.M.

When Caron took over, he chose another way to save electricity: Make the store smaller. He closed off the top three floors, which were later rented as storage spaces. That limited the bookselling areas to the basement and the first two floors, with the third floor for storage. He substantially reduced his stock to about fifty thousand books and worked hard to maintain stock that would sell. "I religiously read the want lists, so that I got to know titles that people were actually trying to find. I educated myself by reading *AB*," he said.

RARE AND OUT OF PRINT BOOKS A SPECIALTY

BOOKS BOUGHT

LITERARY PROPERTY APPRAISED   ESTABLISHED 1894

NEW YORK'S OLDEST "OLD" BOOK SHOP

ISAAC MENDOZA BOOK CO.

2nd floor   NEW AND OLD BOOKS

15 ANN STREET   NEW YORK, NY 10038

One source of good books was the arrangement the store made to receive cartons of university press books.

When he was asked what his bookstore career had taught him about things he should have done differently, Walter Caron mentioned that one way he knew he had gone wrong was not putting out better catalogues. There was no steady policy of holding good materials for the catalogue. Thus the books offered were not the best that could have been listed. "The catalogues we issued didn't do very well, because we put the wrong titles in them," said Caron. This frank insight echoes Paul Minet's emphasis in *Bookdealing for Profit* (2000) on the importance of catalogues in antiquarian bookselling.

Caron talked about his shop's long connection with Fourth Avenue's Book Row from the early period on and about his personal experiences as a wide-ranging customer there before entering the business himself. For his own collection, he was a regular Book Row customer with strong memories of the stores and the proprietors and the book finds he made in different shops.

Concerning the historic passing of the store, fewer than five years short of its century mark, Caron commented that he would sell what he could and donate the remaining stock to various charities such as the Hudson Guild and the West Village Association. The point was made that with large quantities of old books from stores that close or from estates, it isn't always simple even to give the books away in bulk. Modern recipients of generosity expect quality gifts, or why bother? The New York Public Library, for instance, might hold back on picking up a gift of books unless a famous person was involved and there was a reasonable expectation of treasures among the volumes offered.

Whatever may have been the destiny of those remaining books at the Isaac Mendoza Book Company, the company's impressive record as part of New York's antiquarian book scene for over ninety-five years (1894–1990) will not be easy to surpass or even equal.

As the time approached for his retirement from the bookshop that Isaac Mendoza started in the previous century, Walter Caron said, "I just love dealing with books. I love books period. Even though I'm going out of business now, I'll not stop looking at or buying books."

In 1893, the year before Isaac Mendoza started his Ann Street bookstore, Jacob Abrahams opened a bookstore at 80 Fourth Avenue. In *Clegg's International Directory of Booksellers for 1894,* fourth edition, appears this entry for secondhand booksellers in New York City, with a population of 1,650,000: "Abrahams, J., 80, Fourth Avenue." Abrahams relocated to 145 Fourth Avenue in 1898 and remained there, except for one brief detour to a store on East Eighth Street, until he died in his eighties late in the 1930s.

Abrahams took in Herman Meyers as his partner, and their shop became the center of a real-life spy story during World War I. A German agent was believed to have placed secret military messages in old copies of the *Saturday Evening Post* at the rear of the store, and an explosion in New Jersey was thought to be associated with these messages. Herman Meyers was called before a government committee to tell what he knew. He testified that a well-dressed man appeared from time to time and always browsed at the back of the shop. What was he doing? Meyers couldn't say, since at Abrahams Book Store they let customers browse without interference. Somewhat similar events in Christopher Morley's *The Haunted Bookshop* (1918), the sequel to *Parnassus on Wheels* (1917) with further adventures of bookseller Roger Mifflin, strongly suggest a collaboration between fiction and reality. Subsequently, mystery writers frequented the store for ideas, and newspaper cartoonists made use of the setting as well.

In 1917, the site of the first Abrahams bookstore, 80 Fourth Avenue, became the location of Schulte's Book Store, founded by Theodore E. Schulte, who at the time of his death in 1950 was credited by *Publishers Weekly* (May 13, 1950) with first designating the proliferation of Fourth Avenue bookshops as Booksellers' Row. The linkage from Abrahams in the 1890s to Schulte's to the existence of Book Row forms a distinct record centered on a single historic site, 80 Fourth Avenue.

His 1893 opening date made Jacob Abrahams one of the earliest booksellers established on Fourth Avenue. He was preceded, of course, by George D. Smith, who had not yet moved on to greener book pastures and was still in business at 69 Fourth Avenue. Other booksellers were also active in the neighborhood during the 1890s. James Clegg's *Directory of Second-Hand Booksellers and List of Public Libraries, British and Foreign* (third edition, 1891) lists William J. Casey, 71 Fourth Avenue; George M. Dressel, 8 Cooper

Union; Funk & Wagnall's, 18 and 20 Cooper Union; William Erving, 121 Fourth Avenue; Robert Henderson, 136 Fourth Avenue; James Pott & Co., 14 and 16 Astor Place; and E. & J. B. Young & Co., 12 Cooper Union. At least three of these seven booksellers were also publishers, continuing a familiar nineteenth-century practice of combining the activities. In the vicinity of Fourth Avenue, on side streets, on nearby Broadway, and around Union Square were over twenty more dealers in antiquarian books and literary properties, along with the busy auctioneers Bangs & Co. and George A. Leavitt & Co.

If the presence of Abrahams, Smith, and the others did not at that juncture signal a trend, retrospectively it did, perhaps, in the Churchillian phrase, signal the end of the beginning that would transform the peaceful neighborhood into the city's leading place of books for several generations.

Guido Bruno, in *Adventures in American Bookshops, Antique Stores and Auction Rooms* (1922), wrote, "The location of book streets changes with the growth of a city. Seventy-five years ago the book center of New York was far downtown on Ann Street; after the Astor Library had opened its doors, Fourth Avenue became the city center and soon was lined with picturesque bookshops." During the 1890s, when Jacob Abrahams helped pioneer bookselling on Fourth Avenue, the majority of those picturesque bookshops were in the future; but a start toward the development of Book Row was clearly taking place.

In his 1922 account of bookshop adventures, Guido Bruno spelled out why it was logical and good business for secondhand bookstores to locate in the same general area: "No matter how large and complete the stock of a secondhand bookdealer may be, his neighbor's collection will be quite different. The clients of secondhand bookshops like 'to browse about' . . . they love to have a large territory in which to hunt." Consequently, they consider themselves fortunate when they conveniently find several inviting bookstores close together. In 1893 on Fourth Avenue book seekers could move from 69 to 80 and roam about freely among the other shops. And the time was coming soon when their happy book hunting grounds along the avenue would substantially expand.

Jacob Abrahams, who helped begin the beginning, immigrated to the United States from Poland, where he had been an antiquarian and scholar. His scholarly background led him to emphasize antiquarian and rare books, as his neighbor George Smith did. Abrahams was considered a finer scholar than businessman, yet he was sufficiently astute in a business sense to see early in his career that featuring magazines as well as books would bring more regular customers. Furthermore, magazines represented a genuine marketing opportunity because they were largely ignored by most other dealers. In time Abrahams offered a tremendous stock of magazines; and they eventually took over the business as the successful Abrahams Magazine Service, dealing in general and learned periodicals. The firm also developed into a large reprint publisher of scholarly books under the AMS imprint. The company became a supplier of out-of-print titles to the libraries that were the mainstays of the periodical business. AMS was also a source of congenial employment for several former bookmen who wanted to stay active, among them Noy Berenson, the nephew of Peter Stammer.

The end-of-century contributions Jacob Abrahams made in establishing the early foundations of Book Row gave him and his book and magazine business an honored position during the earliest phase of Book Row history. Amid sentimental concerns about endings, there is sometimes a regrettable if natural tendency to ignore beginnings. That should not be true concerning Book Row. It is important to remember Jacob Abrahams along with his neighbors and colleagues who represented and through their efforts extended into the future the tradition of acquiring and selling antiquarian books in New York. They were present for the start of the Book Row saga, and without them there would be no saga and no story to tell.

In the introduction to *Antiquarian Bookselling in the United States,* Madeleine B. Stern wrote, "Unlike the publisher, whose name is immortalized in his imprints, the bookseller has almost always been a ghost, whose transactions as intermediary between source and market are seldom preserved. . . . Many of these intermediary ghosts have helped to advance our civilization, but they are recalled only by a trade card or a directory listing, an auction record, a newspaper advertisement, a sales catalogue—by memorabilia as ephemeral as they themselves." We must not be content to leave the booksellers of Book Row to that unfair and wistful fate.

To be listed, of course, when no more is known than a name and a time is better than to be forgotten. A famous story by the beloved cowboy writer Eugene Manlove Rhodes, *"Pasó por Aquí,"* published in *Once in the Saddle* (1927), gives a poignant account of a famous Western landmark, Inscription

Rock, called El Morro, where early travelers carved *Pasó por aquí* and then added their names and the year, informing others they too had passed that way. To whatever extent it is possible, let there be such recognition for the booksellers who made the books available and in their special fashion helped the lights shine and the knowledge flow. Let them not be lost. Each passed this way. *Pasó por aquí.*

Manuel B. Tarshish, in a probing and admiring yet necessarily incomplete survey series of articles for *Publishers Weekly* (October 20, 27, and November 3, 1969), "The 'Fourth Avenue' Book Trade," recorded the names of Fourth Avenue booksellers from Trow's 1901 *Business Directory of Greater New York.* In addition to Jacob Abrahams and Peter Stammer, the following dealers were named: Herbert Hammond, 85 Fourth Avenue; Book Mart, 105 Fourth Avenue; Alexander Hall, 89 Fourth Avenue; Andrew McLaren, 86 Fourth Avenue; Pincus Wachester, 123 Fourth Avenue.

The following year, Phillips's 1902 *Business Directory of New York City* added secondhand book dealers as a new category. Jacob Abrahams was now at 145 Fourth Avenue and Peter Stammer occupied 123 Fourth Avenue. New names listed include M. A. Gropper at 97 Fourth Avenue and Alexander Deutschberger at 117 Fourth Avenue. Deutschberger, Tarshish noted, was described as an "old man with a long beard." Perhaps, language being flexible, he could just as accurately have been called "a senior gentleman with an impressive beard." A few years later, observed Tarshish, Fourth Avenue's hospitality for books attracted Edward Adams at 136 and Joseph Rosenbaum at 83.

Fourth Avenue bookstores in those early years were not allowed to settle down and wait peacefully for books and clients to arrive. To the itinerant impulses of some booksellers was added the unceasing dynamism and ferment of a city that was never still and never finished. Before Book Row was securely established on Fourth Avenue, during the first decade of the twentieth century, a hegira of sorts occurred as dealers left the avenue for other sites, with East Twenty-third Street the principal beneficiary. The 1906 Phillips *Business Directory* still listed many Fourth Avenue booksellers, but some former Fourth Avenuers such as Peter Stammer were now on East Twenty-third Street. By 1910 the Fourth Avenue exodus, according to the H. W. Wilson Company *Directory of Booksellers, Newsdealers and Stationers,* had left only the bearded Deutschberger, Joseph Rosenbaum, and Harry Stone.

The mass departure of bookshops from Fourth Avenue resulted mainly from the upheaval, noise, and dirt of subway construction as the city with foresight prepared for its expansionist future. A referendum approving the use of city funds to build a subway system passed in 1894, and the Book Row segment of Fourth Avenue was on one of the routes. It became difficult to sell books with a deep ditch right outside. It was even harder to persuade customers to work their way through construction sites into stores where peace and quiet were absent friends. Eventually, the city's rapid underground transit system would be a popular and speedy if not exactly comfortable transportation wonder of the world that would deliver countless customers for books by train to Astor Place or Union Square, at the hospitable downtown and uptown borders of Book Row. And so it was when the bookstores returned to Fourth Avenue—and most did after the digging was done, after East Twenty-third Street rents went up too much, and when increasing traffic forced dealers to remove sidewalk book stands. One of the first to move from Fourth Avenue to East Twenty-third Street was Peter Stammer, and among the first to move back was Peter Stammer.

Peter Stammer—"Empty Your Purse into Your Head"

Stammer was born in Russia in 1864 and died in New York in 1946. During those eighty-two years, books filled if they didn't rule most of his days. Manuel Tarshish wrote that according to Stammer's nephew and employee Noy Berenson, the bookman in the 1880s worked as a tutor for a Russian general's son until there was a falling-out and in the resulting struggle Stammer cut off the general's ear. He left Russia and became a typesetter in England.

In the early 1890s Stammer left England for the United States, where he worked in Boston as a typesetter until 1898. During his years in Boston he claimed to have set type for editions of Henry James's novels and for the first American edition of Oscar Wilde's *The Ballad of Reading Gaol*. The James claim holds up if he set type for reprints, since many of the novels were first published in the 1870s and 1880s. In the case of *The Ballad*, the facts also tend to support Stammer. He left Boston for New York around 1898. *The Ballad* was first published in England in February 1898 as the work of C.3.3 (Wilde's prisoner identification at Reading Gaol) without the author's name present.

John T. Winterich, writing about the publishing history of *The Ballad* in *23 Books & the Stories Behind Them* (1938), accepted that its first book appearance in America was "an edition published at New York in 1899 by Benjamin R. Tucker which exists in two bindings, blue linen boards and white paper wrappers." Stammer's Boston employer was publisher Benjamin R. Tucker.

Peter Stammer started a bookshop on Fourth Avenue in 1900 by using his personal library for the initial stock; thereafter, he was openly proud to have been among the first booksellers on Book Row. He began in a basement at 84 Fourth Avenue and soon relocated to 123 Fourth Avenue. The tumult of subway construction on Fourth Avenue drove him for a few years to East Twenty-third Street, but he returned to Fourth Avenue in 1910 and opened Stammer's Bookstore at 61 Fourth Avenue. Number 61 became his permanent location. The store's card emphasized that books were bought and sold, and announced: "Out-of-Print Books a Specialty." When the store reached the point where the claim was halfway tenable (with perhaps five hundred thousand books crowded into several floors), Stammer proclaimed his building, which he bought in 1919, the "House of a Million Books."

The June 1919 issue of *Pearson's Magazine* called him "the Original New York Book Hunter." The title delighted Stammer, and he used it regularly from then on. Later David Randall in *Dukedom Large Enough* (1969) called him "the king of Fourth Avenue." Stammer probably would have been pleased to receive royal recognition, though he might have growled in protest at Randall's accompanying claim that the bookman once impulsively mutilated an inscribed work by Whittier because he had missed the inscription and let a $25 item go for twenty-five cents—and justified the action on the grounds that a youngster wasn't "going to make me look like a fool." Randall added that Stammer made amends by giving him a part-time job.

Randall's account jibes with many others and reflects the probable fact that Stammer's ego, temper, and rather quixotic sense of humor often produced both impromptu and premeditated gestures of a bizarre kind, outside the bounds of conventional behavior. We might fancy Peter Stammer reading the preceding sentence and bellowing, "Get out of my store!"

Journalist Joseph J. Cohen recalled one of his memorable visits to Stammer's: "The old man himself was sitting alongside a pot-bellied stove reading. He scrutinized me as though I was a book thief and barked, 'Mister, what can I do for you?' I asked the location of the philosophy section. He gave me another sharp look and barked again, 'Mister, there is nothing in this store which would interest you.' That ended my visit." Stammer simply wasn't in the mood to let his reading be interrupted by a mere customer.

Manuel Tarshish related numerous events of this sort, although softening the indictment by stating that Stammer hid a "warm heart under a notoriously gruff exterior." He had a take-it-or-leave-it policy on prices, and woe betide those who chose to argue or question. Stammer might instantly double the price or even tear up the item while the customer watched aghast. "The book is only worth thirty-five cents—but I'm going to get six dollars for it," he would say, and then adhere stubbornly to the decision.

Ever a high-handed contrarian, Stammer sometimes deliberately picked a quarrel with a new customer who was unaware that a candid-camera type of interview was taking place. "If the customer survived, they often became good friends," wrote Tarshish, and added, "The old man would give away books to children to encourage them to read." Another example of Stammer's complicated personality involved the falling-out he had with his secretary, Bessie Gilman. They worked together for several years after that without speaking to each other, but the bookman couldn't dismiss her.

Stammer was the hero or the villain of countless stories that make him one of the most complex, interesting, and stimulating individuals the profession of bookselling ever attracted—even if various stories may have originated in Peter Stammer's imagination and are substantially apocryphal, as some have claimed. Legends tend to multiply around legendary characters. Tarshish wondered if the fact Stammer was a vegetarian explained his vitality. Vegetables somehow don't seem to explain his wrathful, indignant, and playful temperament. Maybe genes?

The terms used to describe Stammer by his contemporaries arouse a tempest of contradictions: incorrigible, destructive, impatient, ruthless, outspoken, impolite, egotistical, generous, scholarly, anticustomer, ferociously independent, reverent about books, stubborn—and many more expressions ranging from outrage to praise. He struck some customers as an alumnus of the Spanish Main who could have sailed with Captain William Kidd (before Kidd lived at 119–21 Pearl Street and later was hanged). Walter Goldwater, who became a New York book dealer in the 1930s, said, "Some people looking at him from the outside might think he was an affable old codger; actually he was a scoundrel from the very beginning."

The king of Fourth Avenue and the Book Hunter a scoundrel? Well, Goldwater *was* a competitor, which wouldn't make him wrong—or right. Others saw Stammer as a kindly and helpful bookman intent on finding what they sought either in his store or elsewhere. What seems to have been indisputable was Stammer's dedication to books and locating what his customers wanted. His talent for irascibility apparently didn't hurt business.

A scene familiar to many was Stammer in his shop reading hours on end, while for a pleasant aroma orange slices were warmed on the potbellied stove. He sold secondhand books in New York for over forty years and never pretended to be anyone but himself. His customers included writer Sherwood Anderson, actor Ralph Bellamy, and the distinguished statesman Dag Hammarskjöld, who "came in to relax." Professors from Eastern universities were regulars at the store. Stammer once said he began on Fourth Avenue because New York University and Greenwich Village were nearby, which meant book buyers. Colleges and universities were active customers as well. He supplied Harvard with an economics collection, Cincinnati's Hebrew Union College with a Judaica collection, and New York University with a journalism library.

Individuals at businesses and corporations turned to Stammer's Book Store in times of book need. When the DuPont Corporation wanted an obscure work on fixing underwater cables, a call to Stammer located the title. His price, $100: "Ninety-five dollars for my services and five dollars for the book." The sale was made.

Public libraries were among his customers; also large department stores. The Cleveland Public Library purchased several hundred books each year. The Marshall Field's Company in Chicago would send a detailed order for several thousand books, stipulating so many volumes of fiction, poetry, and the like at a specific price. Stammer typically could fill such an order from the store's enormous, constantly renewed stock.

Peter Stammer's services in finding books were effective and valuable. His book hunter title was not an honorary one. Money that entered the shop promptly left again to buy more books at auctions, thrift shops, and other bookstores. Guido Bruno in *Adventures in American Bookshops* (1922) quoted Stammer's observation that two-thirds of New York's book dealers sell most of their books to the other third. "These little book shops are our vanguards, that collect the honey for us and we come and take whatever we can use, or they bring it to us, and we are glad to have them come regularly," Stammer remarked.

Bruno reported that Stammer made the rounds of small book dealers on a daily basis, adding to his stock and looking for titles sought by his customers. Concerning the small dealers, "He is their educator and patron," wrote Bruno. "He tells them what books are worth money, and he pays a good price whenever he can use them. He is a welcome figure on rent day, and most of the treasures of these cobwebbed corners wander to the comfortable shelves of his palace on Fourth Avenue." Describing Stammer, circa 1918, as the great Fourth Avenue bookdealer, Bruno wrote that his specialty was "hunting up every book that anybody in the United States might desire, no matter when and where printed."

Stammer was by all accounts a book scout with the natural book finder's instinct and feel. In *The Adventures of a Treasure Hunter* (1951), Charles Everitt noted that except for the scout, "the books he finds in attics and libraries would mostly sleep like the dead." As a customer of other bookstores, Stammer found what Everitt called "sleepers," valuable books unknowingly priced low. Remembering his own dealings with the bookman, Everitt wrote, "Peter Stammer, the eccentric and rough-tongued Fourth Avenue bookseller, paid a dollar a barrel for thirty-one barrels of Stone & Kimball's correspondence." Stone & Kimball was a literary publishing house in the 1890s that folded after a few years because the prices of its books couldn't pay for its fine printing and binding. One of the founders, Herbert Stuart Stone, lost his life in the sinking of the *Lusitania*. Now books with his and his partner's names as the imprint are collected just because of their outstanding production values.

The thirty-one containers of Stone & Kimball correspondence, for which Stammer paid $31, included letters from the big-name authors of the period, among them Robert Louis Stevenson and George Bernard Shaw. Stammer let Everitt take what he chose from the mass for $1,200, but he refused to sell the letters of Fiona Macleod. "Stammer, who could be charming to his friends, would let me have nearly anything I wanted; but about Fiona Macleod he remained obdurate," Everitt wrote.

Remember Fiona Macleod, the Scottish romanticist, who wrote *Pharais* (1894), *The Sin-Eater* (1895), and other works? She was all the rage until it came out, partially through the Stone & Kimball letters, that *she* was actually *he*—Scottish writer and Celtic revivalist William Sharp, long concealed behind the skirted pseudonym. Since it seems unlikely Peter Stammer was a

Fiona Macleod fancier, he probably held the letters back briefly to be contrary and for fun to frustrate Charles Everitt. Eventually he sold the Macleod materials for $100 to Everitt, who in turn sold them to a Minnesota collector of 1890s authors.

Donald C. Dickinson, in *Dictionary of American Antiquarian Bookdealers* (1998), described Stammer's business as "a general, secondhand, out-of-print bookshop with bargain bins on the sidewalk." "Stammer did not deal in rare materials on a regular basis but knew how to market them when he had a chance," noted Dickinson. The evidence is that Stammer knew the book field well and paid close attention to scarce and rare items when they appeared. He might occasionally for theatrical effect attack a customer verbally and refuse a sale, but he did run a secondhand book business profitably over four decades.

Stammer kept his business going until he was eighty. In 1945 his nephew and longtime employee Noy Berenson took over the running of the bookshop. Stammer's son-in-law Lazarus Greenberg several years later succeeded Berenson as the manager. When the store finally closed in 1969, it had existed nearly seven decades through the rise-and-fall years of Book Row history and had itself contributed to that history while living up to the founder's advertising slogan, "Empty your purse into your head." Manuel Tarshish called Stammer's closing the end of a bookselling era. "Leave at once! Get out of here! Bookselling must go on!" we can imagine Peter Stammer shouting to protest end-of-an-era thinking.

David Kirschenbaum—Carnegie Book Shop

Longevity coupled with nearly nine decades of active bookselling in Manhattan established David Kirschenbaum as the unchallenged dean of the New York booksellers during several of those decades. He was born in Poland in 1896 and passed his ninety-ninth birthday before his death in 1994. He was thirty-two years younger than Peter Stammer, yet the starting points of their New York bookselling activities were only four years apart. Stammer opened his store in 1900, the year Kirschenbaum's family arrived in the United States. Kirschenbaum in 1904, at the age of eight, was selling books on the sidewalks of New York from his father's pushcart.

Kirschenbaum thus belongs to the first generation of Fourth Avenue booksellers. With Jacob Abrahams and Peter Stammer, he shared the trait of staying alive a very long time, avoiding the unpleasant word "retirement," and selling books many years past the age when most people one way or another call it quits. Kirschenbaum also displayed an attribute that was not common enough among the Fourth Avenue bookmen of the early generations—a cheerful willingness to remember the past and to talk about his bookselling years and colleagues.

"I never missed a day's work," he matter-of-factly told an interviewer for this account in 1990. That interview by coincidence took place on the same day the bookstore of Isaac Mendoza closed. Kirschenbaum's tenacious attention to business was part of the legend among booksellers and the book collectors he served so well and long. In another interview, he talked about his bookselling decades to Nicholas A. Basbanes, author of *A Gentle Madness* (1995). In that work, Basbanes reported that Kirschenbaum was present at every major book auction in the city for the eighty years from 1911 to 1991. As a teenager, he was a runner at the 1911 Robert Hoe sale, which George D. Smith dominated, and he attended all the other great auctions through the 1991 Richard Manney sale. "You know, I think I am the only person alive who remembers the Hoe sale," he remarked at the 1990 interview.

A teenager, David Kirschenbaum opened his first New York bookstore at 198 East Broadway in 1910. He remembered that one of George D. Smith's stores was not far away, on New Street. Six years later he moved to Second Avenue and First Street. The following year, in 1917, he started a bookshop at 79 Fourth Avenue. During the next ten years he successively had three shops on Fourth Avenue. One of his stores, in the vicinity of 85 Fourth Avenue, occupied a four-story building that housed his stock of a hundred thousand books. In the 1920s he also operated a store on Eighth Street, which was one of the first in the city to deal in remainders.

Another Kirschenbaum with Book Row credentials was David's brother Louis, who had a Ninth Street bookstore before he became the proprietor of American Book Auctions. He conducted sales on Thursday or Friday evenings upstairs in a building at the corner of Eleventh Street and Fourth Avenue. These auctions, which featured low-priced items, were well remembered by Book Row regulars. Milton Reissman clearly was a close-up observer at the auctions. In a 1989 statement, he said, "Louis Kirschenbaum would stand next to the auctioneer and squeeze the auctioneer's leg to transmit a bid so no one could see what he was doing."

In 1928 David Kirschenbaum moved again, to Fifty-seventh Street, next door to Carnegie Hall, which stood at the corner of Seventh Avenue. Carnegie Hall was constructed with a million dollars from Andrew Carnegie early in the 1890s, concomitantly with the opening of secondhand bookshops on Fourth Avenue. When Kirschenbaum moved there, in effect Fourth Avenue joined what was already the country's most famous concert hall. It made good business sense for the bookman to name his Fifty-seventh Street store Carnegie Hall Books.

One more name change, to Carnegie Book Shop, and one more address change, to 140 East Fifty-ninth Street ("One flight up; elevator on premises, opposite Bloomingdale's"), lay ahead in the 1930s for what became perhaps America's most distinguished antiquarian book business. Kirschenbaum guided the creation of major private and institutional collections, with the assistance, from 1940 on, of Irving Halpern. The Carnegie Book Shop offered expert appraisal services and featured rare books, manuscripts, prints, and autograph materials.

Kirschenbaum served many of the great collectors—Henry Bradley Martin, Charles E. Feinberg, DeCoursey Fales, David Borowitz, Philip Sang—and lived to see collections he had helped build become permanent treasures for future generations at the Library of Congress, the William L. Clements Library at the University of Michigan, the New-York Historical Society, the Pierpont Morgan Library, and the Fales Library at New York University.

The existence of the Haliburton Fales Library at NYU illustrates Kirschenbaum's repeated effectiveness in bringing about happy marriages between collectors and institutions. With Kirschenbaum's help, New York bank president DeCoursey Fales assembled a magnificent English literature collection with first editions, pamphlets, letters, and much more. Fales was an obsessive collector who couldn't say no to anything he liked. The result was inevitable overcrowding and a "The books go or I go" ultimatum from his wife. How long, one might wonder, did the banker agonize over the choice between his books and his spouse? David Kirschenbaum may have saved the marriage and the collector's peace of mind when he persuaded the university to accept the collection with the proviso of keeping it intact as a special collection (the first at NYU) and giving the donor lifetime access to the collection as a consultant. Fales had the library named after his father, and as an unpaid consultant, he helped the special collections at NYU multiply several times before his death in 1966. Another rare books success for NYU, with Kirschenbaum again in the Dolly Levi matchmaking role, was acquisition of Robert Berol's Lewis Carroll collection.

As a general bookseller, Kirschenbaum offered all types of books through his store and his frequent catalogues. As an antiquarian dealer, he was a notable specialist in Americana, including major books and manuscripts from such giants of American history as Washington, Jefferson, and Franklin. In the 1940s he paid William Randolph Hearst's mother, Phoebe, $5,000 for George Washington's autographed copy of *The Federalist*. This invaluable document in America's national memory went into the collection of industrialist Henry Bradley Martin, an heir of Carnegie's partner Henry Phipps. When the Martin library was sold after the collector's death at a Sotheby's auction in 1989–90, the collection brought over $35 million, which included $1.43 million for *The Federalist*.

In the preface to the Sotheby's catalogue for the Martin sale, Kirschenbaum reflected, "The Martin Library was assembled over a forty-year period, and for much of that time Bradley and I were in almost daily communication about the books he had bought and those he was considering. Other bookmen sometimes joined our discussions, most frequently Gordon Ray, who was part of a regular Thursday threesome at Gino's restaurant on Lexington Avenue."

Another famous manuscript that Kirschenbaum purchased at a 1971 Parke-Bernet Galleries auction was the logbook of the *Enola Gay*. The B-29 that dropped the first atomic bomb in 1945 went to the Air and Space Museum in Washington, D.C.; the logbook, the paper record of the event, went, as did so many historic documents, to David Kirschenbaum.

The bookman was interviewed in 1990 for this profile at the East Side restaurant Gino's, where he was a regular diner since its 1945 opening and was remembered with a gold nameplate on one of the chairs. At the interview, when he was shown a copy of George D. Smith's 1897 catalogue, memories were awakened of booksellers he knew in those former days: Henry Malkan; Frank Thoms; Max Breslow; Frank Bender, the specialist in architecture; A. S. W. Rosenbach; and Alexander Deutschberger, whose store, he recalled, was just below street level, with great awnings almost concealing the windows.

He noted that Erhard Weyhe, the art book specialist, began on Fourth Avenue about the same time as himself. He remembered Albert Boni as a "remarkable man" whom he had known since 1911 and who "had a place on Eighth Street, number forty-five." This was the same Boni who switched from selling to publishing and, in partnership with Horace Liveright as Boni & Liveright, inaugurated the Modern Library of the World's Best Books reprint series that has introduced countless readers to the masterworks of literature.

Kirschenbaum reminisced about Frank Shay, who wrote books, edited a song collection, *My Pious Friends and Drunken Companions* (1927), and operated a famous bookstore in Greenwich Village. He fondly recalled New York bookman Alfred F. Goldsmith. He spoke about bookseller and auctioneer Charles F. Heartman, located on Lexington Avenue at Twenty-third Street, who sponsored hundreds of book auctions and in association with Harry B. Weiss produced *The American Book Collector, a Monthly Magazine for Book Lovers* (1932–35). He paid tribute to book dealer George Baker as a great teacher of bookmen, including himself. David Kirschenbaum in turn was a teacher and inspiration to other bookmen for a remarkable span of time. He closed his bookstore in 1982 but went to his office regularly and remained an active bookman well into his ninety-eighth year.

For some reason, the great collectors in their memoirs and interviews tend not to identify by name the oftentimes even greater booksellers who made their collections possible by finding and supplying their special items. Maybe the simple reason is to keep the credit, and perhaps also to keep peace among the dealers by not singling out any for praise. An exception to this dubious practice was Charles E. Feinberg, indisputably a great collector of Whitman and others. He was, to use Carolyn Wells's pun, an exceptional Leaves-of-Grass-hopper. Feinberg paid honest tribute to booksellers who guided and helped him. In "A Collector's Note on His Collection" (1955), he credited the awakening of his Walt Whitmaniac enthusiasm to "an old book dealer who took an interest in what a boy was reading" and sold him for a few pennies a copy of *American Poems* (1872), edited by William M. Rossetti, with a selection of poems by Whitman.

Feinberg remained an enthusiast for booksellers as well as Whitman, and he singled out David Kirschenbaum for a collector's gratitude based on a long and productive association in building an unparalleled Whitman gathering that in time went to the Library of Congress and made that institution *the*

Whitman site of sites. Kirschenbaum often represented Feinberg at auctions. The dealer sat next to the collector at a Parke-Bernet sale in 1953 and paid $1,500 for the only known page from the original *Leaves of Grass* manuscript. The rest of the manuscript was lost in a print shop fire. Right after the auction, Kirschenbaum and Feinberg were offered $5,000 by another dealer for the item that was worth $1,500 minutes earlier. The dealer had refrained from bidding, because Feinberg's purchase would establish the document's authenticity. On another occasion, a competing dealer deliberately overbid for a Whitman postcard. Why, wondered Feinberg, who later wrote, "He answered that I could have the card at cost—he just wanted to bring to my attention that there were other dealers in the world besides the one who always represented me. I said it was a costly introduction."

The Kirschenbaum-Feinberg partnership wasn't always triumphant. At the February 1, 1944, Howard J. Sachs sale, Kirschenbaum, as instructed, stopped bidding at $1,000, and Gabriel Wells purchased for $1,050 a copy of the 1855 *Leaves of Grass* first edition signed in 1877 by John Boyle O'Reilly, with an 1881 inscription by Walt Whitman to Boyle, and under that an 1882 inscription that stated, "The spirit who living blamelessly yet dared to kiss the smitten mouth of his own century. Oscar Wilde." "To this day I am sorry I lost the book," Feinberg wrote over thirty years later. Recalling his auction room "win some, lose some" adventures with the bookseller, the collector declared, "Collecting has brought me welcomes and honors. Books have brought me a full life, but I've had the most fun chasing things at auctions." His frequent companion during those chases was David Kirschenbaum.

In the 1970s, asked about his career high spot, Kirschenbaum reflected and mentioned the purchase of an Audubon *Birds of America* double elephant folio for $40,000 half a century earlier. He was confident the value had increased fivefold. If accurate then, that estimate would be much too modest now, when Audubon double elephant folios can lure millions out of collector bank accounts.

One of many manuscripts acquired and sold by David Kirschenbaum was Stephen Crane's *The Red Badge of Courage*. Kirschenbaum's long career in books conspicuously earned him an all-time dealer's badge of special distinction.

CHAPTER THREE

DAUBER & PINE AND THE SPARROW SIGN
Samuel Dauber · Nathan S. Pine · Alfred F. Goldsmith

I have always maintained that any collector, rich or starving,
should pick a dealer he can trust, and trust him. A collector is likely
to be quite old before he knows more than a competent bookseller
about the books he collects.

—CHARLES P. EVERITT

✄ NEITHER BOOKSTORE WAS actually on Fourth Avenue proper. Let's call them the peripheral outposts—or rather book posts. One was a few short crosstown blocks west, at 66 Fifth Avenue, "near 12th Street" as its catalogues always helpfully noted—Dauber & Pine Bookshops.

The other was a short stroll uptown from Fourteenth Street on Irving Place (named for Washington Irving), past Pete's Tavern, where William Sydney Porter plotted O. Henry's stories and wrote "The Gift of the Magi." Then the book seeker hooked around Gramercy Park, with its statue of Edwin Booth as Hamlet and the home of James Harper, cofounder of Harper & Brothers, and continued up Lexington to the block between Twenty-fourth and Twenty-fifth Streets, stopping at number 42, At the Sign of the Sparrow Bookstore, Alfred F. Goldsmith the bookman in charge.

Both stores and their proprietors were certainly key members of the Booksellers' Row community. They were part of the neighborhood and important contributors to the record and the spirit of antiquarian bookselling in New York City during the twentieth century. In history and memory, they exemplify Book Row, and the profession of preserving and marketing used and rare books, at its best.

"I am a one bookshop man, and Dauber & Pine is my one bookshop," maintained Carl Clinton Van Doren, Columbia professor, editor of the

Cambridge History of American Literature, 1939 Pulitzer Prize–winning biographer (*Benjamin Franklin*), and book buyer. It was a nice thing to say even if we can't quite believe any scholarly professor could resist checking out the wares of other Book Row stores.

Frederick Lightfoot knew most of the booksellers from the 1930s on and used most of the bookstores throughout the area. "My favorite bookseller was Alfred Goldsmith," he wrote. "He evidently saw something in me he liked, and he edged me toward an appreciation of Walt Whitman." Alfred Goldsmith is generally assigned priority for the often repeated observation that "the book business is a very pleasant way of making very little money." One repeater was the San Francisco bookman David B. Magee, whose first bookstore job paid him "$75 per month cash and $10 in books" and who wrote, in *Infinite Riches* (1973), "Remember, the rare book business is a highly agreeable way of making very little money." Fortunately, material gains aren't everything. Bookman and Renaissance pope Nicholas V (Tommaso Parentucelli), who collected manuscripts and started the Vatican Library, declared, "I would rather have Chrysostom on St. Matthew than the city of Paris." All of us can give thanks, secular and otherwise, that Dauber, Pine, and Goldsmith chose agreeable and pleasant careers and that sometimes those careers graciously and generously granted them a bit more than a little money. As the antiquarian book business goes, they did all right for quite a few years.

Samuel Dauber and Nathan Pine—Dauber & Pine Bookshops
Peter Stammer's Protégés Become Partners

Los Angeles bookseller Ernest Dawson was asked how long it takes to learn the rare book business. He answered, "I really wouldn't know. I've only been in the book business fifty years." During long careers, Samuel Dauber and Nathan Pine productively labored a combined total of well over a century in that tome-centered business, and the record confirms that they either learned a lot or jointly had terrific instincts for the calling. Theirs was in the running during its heyday to be called the most famous used-book store in America. And Dauber & Pine is still remembered fondly whenever bibliophiles of a certain vintage gather to wax nostalgically about the great bookstores of yesteryear. Whether by happenstance or fate, the founders could be called members of a Peter Stammer alumni association.

Samuel Dauber came to the United States as an immigrant from Austria, where he was born in 1882. After a few other jobs led nowhere that he wanted to go, he worked for Peter Stammer a couple of years, starting around 1920. Dauber remembered the experience as one of the most harassing and difficult times of his life, but it must have been a valuable and instructive period too, since he laid a sturdy foundation for a brilliant career in rare books. Years after that apprenticeship, Charles Everitt in *The Adventures of a Treasure Hunter* praised Percy Wilkins at the Leary, Stuart & Company bookstore in Philadelphia for "a wider general knowledge of old books than anyone in the country *except Sam Dauber.*" Everitt had no doubt whose knowledge ranked first. Dauber in the 1920s gave him temporary employment, which stretched into years and afforded Everitt a firsthand post to observe the bookman on the job, close-up.

John T. Winterich considered easygoing Sam Dauber ideally suited to the job of bookman by temperament and inclination. He appeared to have fun buying and selling books. The title of a John Masefield narrative poem, would you believe it, is "Dauber," about an artist-sailor with the credo "No harm in sometimes painting just for fun. / Keep it for fun, and stick to what you're at." Substitute "bookselling" for "painting" and that's Sam Dauber.

After his demanding and rewarding stint with Stammer, Dauber was ready to open a bookshop of his own. He soon needed a competent associate, and Nathan Pine became his partner in 1922. Long familiar in the trade as D&P, theirs became one of the best known and most successful partnerships in bookselling annals.

Nathan Pine was born in Russia in 1892. He immigrated to the United States as a teenager and went to work for his uncle Peter Stammer in 1905 at $3 per day—a fair enough wage for a 1905 teenager. While earning he could also be another attentive bookstore student learning the business. Working days, Pine followed the lead of other youths trying to get ahead in the Horatio Alger tradition by attending night school.

Pine must have realized that for success in his chosen field he needed a wider perspective and more knowledge than he would acquire from his uncle Peter. After those beginning years at Stammer's, Pine headed for the country's midsection and worked in Chicago at one of Charles Tracy

Powner's antiquarian bookstores. Powner's was another general operation proclaiming itself a million-book place, but it also dealt professionally with first editions, variants, and association copies. Charles Powner, a lover of books and bookselling, was an Indiana schoolteacher who became a bookseller at fifty-five and reportedly died in bed while reading Mark Twain. Powner's served as a fine bookselling college, after Stammer's elementary and secondary school, for young Pine.

Around 1916, Pine awarded himself a diploma in practical bookstore management and opened a Fourth Avenue bookshop. Either business fell short of expectations or the young man still had a touch of wanderlust. During 1919 Pine was at San Francisco working for Paul Elder in his far-famed bookselling and publishing establishment. Elder illustrates that even disaster was a sometime parent of New York bookselling. When his first store was destroyed due to the 1906 earthquake and fire, Elder for a few years was a Manhattan bookseller. By 1910, he was back in California and stayed there. Nathan Pine followed the reverse course. After his San Francisco stint with Elder, he returned to Book Row and accepted Sam Dauber's invitation to become the *P* of D&P. It was a win-win move for both bookmen.

Dauber & Pine Bookshops, Inc., in 1923 took up residence on the west side of Fifth Avenue at number 66 and remained there for the life of the store. During much briefer periods than for Dauber & Pine, the same building housed the publishing firms of Macmillan as well as Albert and Charles Boni. The bookstore over the decades became such an established New York treasure and tradition that in the 1970s, when the inevitable New York demolition devils began threatening the building, protesting book publishers and book lovers fought them off and kept Dauber & Pine alive another decade, perhaps inspired by the example of Isaac Stern and his persistent team of music lovers who in the 1960s saved Carnegie Hall from would-be destroyers. Sometimes with the right team and a really high-proof brand of tenacity the demolition devils can be sent packing.

Upstairs and Downstairs at Dauber & Pine

During the years after 1923, the D&P bookselling combination had its ups and downs, but ups were in the majority. Complementing their Fifth Avenue flagship store, at one point they had three other stores operating simultaneously in the Book Row neighborhood. To most Dauber & Pine customers, however, the name meant only 66 Fifth. The store officially was Dauber & Pine Bookshops, Inc.—with the plural present even when the name covered only the single store. There seemed some logic to that plural because of the upstairs and downstairs activities at 66 Fifth, which made the place seem like two stores in one.

At the main facility, a famous working arrangement evolved. Upstairs, at street level, was Nathan Pine, sporting a beret and flaunting a benign Continental manner. He was in charge of marketing the general stock of remainders, routine used books, some almost new books, and whatever new books came in. Meanwhile Sam Dauber was downstairs ruling over the store's renowned stock of valuable rare and antiquarian books.

Most of the store's considerable walk-in trade was satisfied upstairs. With a stock of two hundred thousand–plus books, the upstairs area kept most browsers intently occupied, often until closing time. And usually when they went, they took along one or more reasonably priced books. Bibliophiles, collectors, and frequent visitors learned in time that the main book booty was belowdecks with Sam Dauber. Will Durant, author of *The Story of Philosophy* (1926), christened the basement "the fascinating catacombs." Plenty of other book lovers were no less fascinated by the books and manuscripts that flowed in and flowed out of the lower part of the shop, known as the American Room by D&P insiders.

Roy Meador was a frequent Dauber & Pine customer in the 1960s and 1970s and has book acquisitions along with many personal memories from those upstairs and downstairs activities. A few of the memories were recorded in a letter to the editor, from Ann Arbor, Michigan, published in the *New York Times Book Review*, March 13, 1977:

> For years, a stop at Dauber & Pine on lower Fifth has been a must each time I visited New York. . . . On a recent visit, I located a first edition of H. M. Tomlinson's *London River*. I wanted that and also a clipping about Tomlinson I found in another book. Mr. Pine wavingly agreed to let me transfer the clipping to *London River*. Noting my interest in Tomlinson, he went scampering up a perilous metal ladder

to the upper book deck. He moved with that special energy of a bookman, scrambling for a title.

I always think of Murray Dauber in the basement as "Old Ben." That started in 1975. I was writing a scientific biography of Benjamin Franklin and rooting through New York bookstores for Franklin items. In the Dauber and Pine basement, Mr. Dauber, whisperingly, with respect and affection, said slowly, "Old Ben. There were nice sets of Old Ben around the turn of the century. We don't see them often, of course." But off he went into the shadowy corners and returned with a rare Franklin item.

A few years before that book-questing interlude, a bad flood in "the fascinating catacombs" damaged several thousand books, many of them hard-to-find and valuable. So the 1975 Franklin search also gladly (and sadly) supplied a water-wounded first edition of J. Frank Dobie's *A Texan in England* (1945), price fifty cents. Rebound in the original cloth, it makes a poignant, lasting remembrance of the bookstore.

J. Frank Dobie was one among many authors who felt they had a New York home at Dauber & Pine. As related by Everitt, Dobie wrote about a convivial get-together there in March 1931: "I don't recollect so much of the conversation, but the geniality and warmth of the company, led by our host, remains with me so vividly that my spirits rise now remembering it." Another writer who cherished the D&P atmosphere was Louis Untermeyer: "There is no bookshop that I have more pleasure visiting and I speak as a book lover, not as an author."

The 1977 letter to the *Times* mentioned a Gilbert Millstein article in the *New York Times* (February 13, 1977) that referred to vanishing Book Row as once the Athens of the secondhand book business. The letter concluded: "Fortunately, New York still has Dauber & Pine and a few others. Don't let them go, New York, I warn you. Those stores are essential to your survival, like the birds at the Tower of London. I personally think of that Dauber & Pine basement as the heart of Manhattan."

The D&P heart finally stopped beating in June 1983, after the death in 1982 of Nathan Pine at the age of ninety and the reluctant decision of Murray Dauber, the son of Sam Dauber, who had succeeded his father in the basement, to call it quits. Thus ended the store's sixty years of distributing good books and goodwill to a phenomenal range of customers, from bargain hunters with nickels and dimes for used reading to wealthy collectors with fortunes for rarities. D&P courteously served them all with egalitarian panache from 1923 to 1983.

During the early decades, Dauber & Pine was a welcome employer for several distinguished American bookmen. Charles Everitt served downstairs with Sam Dauber as the store's Americana specialist and recounted many of his experiences there in *Adventures of a Treasure Hunter.* His admiration and esteem for Dauber are manifest throughout. Referring to Sam Dauber and a few others, he wrote, "If you had all, or even half, the trade secrets (by which I mean information not listed in any bibliography)" in their heads, you could "make a very handsome living out of rare books." "Sam Dauber's description of 'one price' is 'the most I can get for it,' " Everitt noted about the bookman who was his mentor as well as colleague.

A disastrous D&P purchase with a happy denouement thanks to an honest actor involved the collection of actress Julia Marlowe. The value of her books was enhanced by her fame and the fulsome inscriptions from stagestruck authors and admirers to the actress. Sam Dauber, reported Everitt, paid plenty to acquire the collection. When it was delivered to the D&P basement, they discovered the actress had methodically torn out all the pages with inscriptions before letting the books go. Her partner and husband, the equally famous actor E. H. Sothern, was as upset as the bookmen by the deception. Observing that his wife was sometimes "not amenable to reason," the actor-manager offered to refund the money, or would they prefer "a thousand of my bookplates for the drama books you have in the store?" The equivalent now, let's say, would be a similar offer from a comparable celebrity such as Steven Spielberg. Drama collectors, check your shelves for theater volumes with Edward Hugh Sothern bookplates; there may well be an amusing bookstore story behind them.

Everitt, who had run his own bookshop before joining Dauber & Pine, resumed independent bookselling in 1935 with a shop on Lexington Avenue that became the world's number one port of plenty for Americana collectors. A master book scout as well as shop proprietor, Everitt stood out for his deep knowledge based on a retentive memory, his wide contacts among collectors, and his flexibility. Knowing the field thoroughly was the only way to obey his friend Frank Dobie's precept that "Luck is being ready for the chance." When he made a find, Everitt could usually associate it immediately with a particular buyer. He called any books that stayed on the shelf his "mistakes." Everitt also emphasized keeping alert and ready to move in whatever direction was needed, maintaining that in selling rare books the rules are "an inch of rule and a yard of exception."

He wrote, "It is not much fun selling books to people who can afford to buy them. The real pleasure is in serving the true students, those who are hungry for books that cost more than they can afford." We can believe Everitt took pleasure from helping students, the way Peter Stammer encouraged reading by giving books away to young people. But "not much fun" selling books to those well-off? Accepting that as true takes a really major suspension of disbelief.

Everitt was succeeded as the D&P Americana specialist for several months during 1935 by Oscar Wegelin, who brought to the position a long and distinguished record as a bibliographer, cataloguer, bookstore owner, and collector of American poetry and drama. Among his many publications as a compiler were *Early American Plays, 1714–1830* (1900), *Early American Fiction, 1774–1830* (1902), and, in two volumes, *Early American Poetry, 1650–1820* (1903–7).

Following his D&P assignment, Wegelin became the bibliographer for the New-York Historical Society. A Wegelin gathering of American plays went to the University of Rochester. His early American poetry collection was sold to C. Waller Barrett, who donated them to the University of Virginia as the Barrett Library Wegelin Collection.

THOSE PRODUCTIVE DAUBER & PINE CATALOGUES

The Dauber & Pine success was attributed in no small measure to the astuteness shown by hiring outstanding staff members. Neither D. nor P., obviously, was fearful of experts. Charles Everitt and Oscar Wegelin contributed to the firm's productive series of catalogues, which were distributed regularly to a substantial mailing list of private collectors, libraries, universities, and other potential customers. Catalogue 100 in December 1931 was a special effort, with comments from friendly authors, including Sinclair Lewis, who brought home America's first Nobel Prize for Literature in 1930, and

Christopher Morley, who never met a bookstore he didn't like. Another employee at Dauber & Pine as a cataloguer was Sam Loveman, who was recognized by other bookmen for his ability and inclination to include a sensuous note in some of his book descriptions. Loveman too eventually left to start his own store, which he called Bodley Bookshop. One of his specialty areas comprised the books and letters of the poet Hart Crane, who had been Loveman's friend.

Whoever wrote the copy for the D&P catalogues, they sold books. Catalogue 162 in January 1935 reflects a common cash-hungry symptom of the 1930s by offering 50 percent off for cash on the store's entire stock. The large discount was explained by using the marketing ploy of a preinventory clearance sale. The catalogue included large general literature and Americana sections. Some of the entries do sound as if the cataloguers were having fun while teasingly tempting buyers. Everitt was still on the D&P staff when the catalogue was done.

346 **Napoleon's Love Life.** Masson, F. Napoleon and the Fair Sex. Tall 8vo. London, 1894. First Edition. **$5.00** *Scarce. A history of Napoleon's amorous peccadilloes—they were both unfaithful to one another, husband and wife, Napoleon and Josephine.*

390 **Prostitution.** The memoirs of HARRIET WILSON. By Herself. Plates. 2 vols., large 8vo. London, 1924. **$10.00** *The autobiography of what one would call (permitting oneself the candor) a "high-class prostitute." If the reader conjectures that the title hides modesty, let him be spared all disillusion. HARRIET WILSON had faith in only one thing—money. Love was inevitable—but subsidiary.*

HE UNDERSTOOD THE LADIES

402 **Richardson's Works.** The Complete Novels of SAMUEL RICHARDSON. Edited with an Introduction by E. M. M. McKenna. Fine Plates. 20 vols., 16mo, beautifully and sumptuously bound in three-quarter olive crushed levant morocco, exquisitely and appropriately tooled and gilt, marbled fly and end-leaves, gilt tops, by ZAEHNS-DORF. Phila., 1902. **$50.00**

". . . His influence stretches far into the letters of our own and other lands, and 'some are yet ungotten and unborn,' who all unconsciously may owe much and not a little of their insight into feminine psychology, to the initiative of SAMUEL RICHARDSON."

502 Wilcox, Ella Wheeler. Poems of Passion. Sq. 8vo. Chicago, 1883. First Edition. **$5.00** *First Issue. Scarce. Poems so red-hot that they sizzle. It contains the First Printing of Pollyana's favorite poem: "Laugh and the world laughs with you."*

Wilcox collectors reading item 502 must have been amazed to see their sentimental poet's sententious verses described as hot enough to sizzle. The $5 price for Wilcox compares interestingly with the catalogue's offer of many other first editions, such as Robinson Jeffers's *Cawdor and Other Poems* (signed), $10; Jack London's *The Scarlet Plague*, $2.50; Sara Teasdale's *Dark of the Moon*, $2.50; H. M. Tomlinson's first American editions, $2.00 each; Mark Twain's *The Stolen White Elephant*, $5; Thomas Wolfe's *Look Homeward, Angel*, $5.

The store kept going even through the hard times of the Depression by virtue of its Fifth Avenue walk-in business and its mail-order sales produced by the catalogues. The catalogues featured low prices and sometimes playfully erotic or shocking descriptions to titillate and persuade buyers. In Catalogue 162, under the head "Latin Depravity," a book about Nero is described as a "history of the insoluble viciousness of pagan Rome during the monstrous reign of NERO. He must have been—if only one-half of the enormities ascribed to him are true—a hell of a guy."

To bring passersby inside, the store used its thirty-foot-long, ceiling-to-sidewalk front window for a display of handsome, often leather-bound books, and a never-ending promise of substantial discounts, 25–50 percent, on the already low prices. A seemingly perpetual sale was always in progress at Dauber & Pine, in full awareness that the word "bargain" is a word few can avoid checking out.

THE DAUBER AND PINE "POE"

One D&P book coup, proving again that luck favors the well informed, occurred in 1926. At auctions, whenever possible, a close inspection of all the offerings took place. Sometimes, however, bundles were made of assorted pamphlets and books and auctioned on a sight-unseen basis. Such odd-lot bundles are purchased as a bookstore gamble. At Dauber & Pine, when such wagers occurred, a common practice was to examine a bundle's contents for any immediately worthwhile items and to put the rest aside temporarily. Set-aside materials tended to accumulate.

"One evening in 1926, I knocked over a pile of these pamphlets, gathering dust for years and coming from heavens knows what sources," recalled Sam Dauber. He stooped to pick up the pamphlets, and out of one fell a publication that had been concealed there for years. A quick look and Dauber knew he had struck literary gold. The pamphlet was the first separate printing of Edgar Allan Poe's story "The Murders in the Rue Morgue," which had been printed in a short run as a salesman's sample. It was an off-print from the April 1841 issue of *Graham's Magazine,* which published the story that introduced the Parisian amateur detective C. Auguste Dupin. To Poe it was the first of his "tales of ratiocination"; to those interested in mystery history, it was the initial detective story and thus grand progenitor of the mystery genre.

Attorney, corporation director, and book collector Owen D. Young saw the pamphlet, prudently consulted his wife, and paid $25,000 for what he considered a superb addition to what was modestly described as one of the most valuable private book collections in the world. In 1941 Young donated the collection, including the Poe, to the New York Public Library, which helped establish the NYPL as possessor of one of the most valuable public book collections in the world. "The Murders in the Rue Morgue" became one of the jewels in that bibliocrown.

The Dauber & Pine experience with the hidden treasure in a dusty mound of trifles reconfirms the importance in the antiquarian field of taking nothing for granted, of never assuming that apparent junk is all junk, and of taking a serious look where it appears serious looking is a terrible waste of time. Staff and staff time are, of course, finite, and not everything, obviously, can be adequately appraised before offering it for sale. When a valuable book does slip through the screening process, a happy customer results, and satisfied customers are as good for business as a $25,000 markup on a throwaway pamphlet.

Walter Caron from Isaac Mendoza Book Company never forgot his delight in finding a rare, low-priced poetry book at Dauber & Pine. "The old man, Sam, was a sweetheart," he said. "But they apparently didn't think much of poetry. Going through the shelves I found a copy of *Dionysus in Hades* (1931) by Frederick Faust. He used the pseudonym Max Brand for westerns and Dr. Kildare stories. His Max Brand titles and those under other pseudonyms are collected now; but the poetry is what I wanted, and I found it at Dauber & Pine."

The great finds at Dauber & Pine are no more, but still great are the memories.

ALFRED F. GOLDSMITH—AT THE SIGN OF THE SPARROW
THE RISE OF THE SPARROW

The sparrow, though small, modest, and barely credible as a melody maker, has won astonishing attention from the literature makers. The fall of a sparrow betokened a special providence to Shakespeare. Saint Matthew in chapter 10 of a popular old book had two sparrows selling for a farthing and fed the egos of twelve disciples who were assured that "ye are of more value than many sparrows." John Skelton's dirge "Philip Sparrow," in a digressive poem of some fourteen hundred lines, *The Boke of Phyllyp Sparowe,* lyrically laments the death of a girl's pet bird "that was late slain at Carrow . . . *Pater noster qui* / With an *Ave Mari.*" Bede the Venerable likened human life to the swift flight of a sparrow through a warm room in winter. There's something simple, basic, ephemeral, hopeful, humble, literary about a sparrow. And among book lovers, At the Sign of the Sparrow means fine books and book talk, friendship, and Alfred F. Goldsmith, bookman. The rise of his Sparrow Bookstore adds an archive of feel-good recollections to the Book Row chronicle.

David Randall in *Dukedom Large Enough* observed that as a book scout he was slightly suspect around some Book Row secondhand shops because he had worked "uptown," which was anything north of where "Alfred Goldsmith, the Walt Whitman specialist, ran his famous shop At the Sign of the Sparrow." Book Row had to draw its circle to keep Goldsmith in, because his knowledge, amiability, probity, humor, and punctilio made him such a congenial square shooter that he elevated the hospitality tone of Book Row all by himself.

Not enough tribute poems have been addressed to booksellers by admiring collectors. Christopher Morley did report in rhyme about an Anderson Galleries March 15, 1920, auction of a John Keats letter to Fanny Brawne with a verse that ends, "The soul of Adonais, like a star. . . . / Sold for eight hundred dollars—Doctor R!" But that's really more the obeisance of a Dr. Rosenbach disciple than a heartfelt tribute.

The bulk of booksellers—take this as dogma—want cash, not verse. Most see the point of being practical. Or at least trying. Alfred Goldsmith may well have been an exception to the pragmatic rule of favoring payment over poetry. He comes across as an exception to expectation in a lot of ways. He probably would have been delighted that his customer, friend, and Whitman collector Chester James Teller wrote a poem in his memory entitled "Of A. F. Goldsmith," which commences: "A dealer in books he called himself, but what he truly traded / Was loving kindness." Teller called his friend "a merchant of good will; / A broker not so much in scriptures old and faded / As in the context of a simple heart" (*Publishers Weekly*, November 22, 1947).

Teller described Goldsmith standing at his counter, more interested in having a leisurely talk about books than a chance for monetary gain. Contemporary bookseller Walter Goldwater also pictured him never sitting down: "He always stood behind his counter and made cute remarks to people who came in." Once when book scout Abe Klein entered the store, the proprietor's greeting was, "How's the Yeats of Fourth Avenue?" "What's a Yeats?" asked Klein, playing along and in the process probably selling what he had to offer for a bit more than it was legitimately worth at the time. Customers, scouts, collectors, bibliographers, writers, and librarians always played along as they made the Sparrow a friendly hangout at the outer border of Book Row.

Based on Goldwater's recollections, we can put Goldsmith down as a lovable soft touch to book people, whether in the business or not. During the Depression years of the 1930s, he could always be counted on to buy books from needy scouts, even when there was no evidence that he was selling much himself, at a time when digestive systems and rent demanded priority over food for the mind, alias books. "If we were broke during those early thirties, we would go to Goldsmith and be able to get fifty cents or a dollar, because he would buy. . . . He was a friendly soul," recalled Goldwater. Goldsmith facetiously described himself during that period as "a once happy bookseller, now toothless, poor and filled with sorrow for no one buys books during the summer of 1933."

Born in New York in 1881, Alfred Goldsmith became a Walt Whitman enthusiast and collector at the age of twelve. He studied at the University of Pennsylvania and then worked in the paper business before turning to bookselling around 1918. His authors, Whitman and others he eclectically collected—Lewis Carroll, Edgar Allan Poe, Abraham Lincoln, Mark Twain, Ambrose Bierce, Arthur Machen—inspired his establishment of a bookshop that initially featured first editions of books he had collected for himself. Now he was ready to share his books with others at the Sign of the Sparrow.

The entrance to the small, quaint (as some said) shop at 42 Lexington Avenue required walking down steps from street level. It wasn't a ground-floor establishment, and it wasn't exactly a basement. Many small businesses in Manhattan still fit the description, slightly down but not subterranean, sort of cozy. Inside, the shop presented a diverse congregation of books, rather jumbled, and a hint of age, cobwebs, benign neglect, and intimate charm. The faux Gothic ambience fit the proprietor, who typically stood waiting, book in hand, smiling in welcome.

In this atmosphere during the decades ahead, Alfred Goldsmith would serve several of the twentieth century's great collectors. But he was equally hospitable with impecunious collectors and even those who purchased books not as objects to possess but as convenient packages of information and entertainment to read. Goldsmith was a reader himself; and though it might seem strange to some booksellers, he actually approved the same practice by others. His standing in the antiquarian book community made him one of the first to be asked by the founders to join the Old Book Table, a social club formed in 1931 that served for many years as a fraternal organization allowing competitors to meet regularly and talk books as friends. The five founders of the Old Book Table were Ernest R. Gee, Geoffrey Gomme, E. Byrne Hackett, Frank R. Thoms, and Edgar H. Wells.

Frederick Lightfoot was one of the Sparrow's nonwealthy, reading customers. He remembered the owner with gratitude as his favorite Book Row bookseller and as the friend who introduced him to Walt Whitman. Lightfoot became such a regular visitor to the shop that he gained something of an insider's perspective. "Alfred Goldsmith, known primarily as a specialist in American literature and as an expert on Whitman and Poe, also featured ephemera," Lightfoot wrote. "He received large shipments of engravings, ancient theatre bills, etc. from England where the supply then far exceeded the demand among English buyers."

BIBLIOGRAPHY, THEATER, ODDITIES, MURDER, AND MORE

Alfred Goldsmith's Whitman devotion led to his acquiring a plethora of rare Whitman editions and ephemera. As a bookseller, he saw books come and go, and often come again. He reportedly owned the same *Leaves of Grass* first edition at least six times. Consulting Goldsmith on Whitman became more than a desideratum, it was a have-to for scholars and serious collectors. It drew Whitman fanciers to the shop. Their names are legion, among them the mystery and light verse writer Carolyn Wells. She became a Whitman collector at the behest of her friend A. Edward Newton, who assured her that "as a yelper of the brotherhood of man, he is destined to take an important place."

With Goldsmith's help, Wells built a strong Whitman collection, to the point where she held an auction of her duplicates. She noted in *The Rest of My Life* (1937): "The auction was pleasant if not profitable, and I set out to buy more Whitman." Whether or not Goldsmith was involved in the Wells auction, he was a regular at New York auctions for other collectors and for himself.

It was natural, perhaps inevitable, that a Whitman man and a Whitman woman would get together. Alfred Goldsmith and Carolyn Wells got together not only as collectors but also as collaborators on a useful and now scarce Whitman checklist, *A Concise Bibliography of the Works of Walt Whitman* (1922). The preface stated that the purpose was to provide "a safe and reliable guide to these various editions, that may be of helpful interest to the collector, the student, and the librarian." John T. Winterich, paraphrasing that statement, called it a fine description of Alfred Goldsmith, "a safe and reliable guide . . . to the collector, the student, and the librarian." A bibliography of Lewis Carroll was another Goldsmith project based on the pursuit not of revenue but of knowledge and pleasure.

Winterich, like most book accumulators, sometimes accumulated too much and sought to dispose of the excess. He carried a suitcase filled with books from "the great Winterich crime collection" and offered them to Goldsmith, who named a price Winterich immediately dismissed as "ridiculous—ridiculously high." The bookman insisted on paying the price quoted. "How Alfred Goldsmith contrived to convert the mutually effacing principles of buying high and selling low into anything resembling the profit motive is beyond my economic comprehension. But I am sure he had a good time in the process," wrote Winterich (*Publishers Weekly,* November 22, 1947). Winterich emphasized his conviction that the book business was the right one for Goldsmith because he was interested in people and books: "And although he lived by selling books, he was about the poorest—or possibly the best—bookseller of my acquaintance. He never talked up a book. He never priced up a book."

Walter Goldwater, recalling Goldsmith's observation that the rare book business was a pleasant way to make little money, contended that was Goldsmith's choice, not his necessity. Along with others handling Whitmans and Carrolls, maintained Goldwater, Goldsmith could have made a lot of money but just didn't bother.

His shipments of theater memorabilia from England may have alerted Goldsmith to the possibilities of the theater market. His shop became a theatrical oasis specializing in stage books and ephemera. Broadway enthusiasts and personalities browsed at the Sign of the Sparrow for books, theater programs, and pictures of actors. While satisfying the appetites of the stars' fans, Goldsmith was also a reliable source for serious historians. George C. D. Odell, author of *The History of the New York Stage* (1927), described Goldsmith as "untiring in his effort to find for these annals curious items of forgotten lore."

Whether they knew it or not, theater fans at the store might be shopping alongside one of America's great collectors who were part of Goldsmith's established clientele. And some of the items they found at the Sparrow were indeed curiosities. Goldsmith liked to purchase odd things with a literary connection or a strange provenance. He appreciated one-of-a-kind objects impossible to find elsewhere; and he found customers with similar inclinations.

Among the big-time collectors relying on Alfred Goldsmith and buying from him regularly was William Thomas Hildrup Howe, president of the American Book Company and a notable collector of American and English literature, a literary territory in which Goldsmith was masterfully at home. After W. T. H. Howe's death in 1939, his collection of sixteen thousand books and manuscripts that Goldsmith helped so much to assemble was acquired in toto by Dr. Albert A. Berg, to be part of the Henry W. and Albert A. Berg Collection of English and American Literature at the New York Public Library. The contribution was made to the library in 1940; and when the Howe collection was examined, a few rather startling nonbook items showed up, such as Charles Dickens's desk, which was placed in the Berg Collection room under Henry Berg's portrait. Other relics of a literary nature in the Berg Collection, presumably from the Howe gathering and probably from At the Sign of the Sparrow, included Elizabeth Barrett Browning's slippers, Charlotte Brontë's portable escritoire, Thackeray's pen, and Lewis Carroll's photograph of Alice Liddell. Alfred Goldsmith, it may be said, a collector of Bierce and Machen, had an affinity for the offbeat and could communicate that taste to collectors.

Many booksellers probably have an eager taste to experience a juicy murder (literary variety) on the premises as a magnet for the curious with interest in the macabre (everybody?). At the Sign of the Sparrow Bookstore was mentioned (among others) as the inspiration and milieu, transported to Brooklyn, for Christopher Morley's *The Haunted Bookshop*. Morley identified different stores as his sources, but the Sparrow certainly had the requisite atmosphere. Considering the connection between Carolyn Wells and Goldsmith, there seems a high probability that her well-known mystery, *Murder in the Bookshop* (1936), used the store as the innocent setting for the story's dark and (always with Wells) humorous events.

THE FALL BUT NOT THE END OF THE SPARROW

After Goldsmith died on Monday, July 28, 1947, his wife asked Frederick Lightfoot if he would like to take over the store and keep it going. Lightfoot decided it wouldn't be a financially feasible step for him to take. "So I missed my one chance to join the New York booksellers' group," he recalled in 1989. "Mrs. Goldsmith gave me her husband's 'Screechless Screech Owl,' a ceramic teapot that I still have. This was just one of the evidences of his charming wit, which delighted my young daughter when she met him," Lightfoot added.

In an obituary for book dealer A. F. Goldsmith, the *New York Times* on July 30, 1947, stated, "Yesterday, for the first time since it was opened, At the Sign of the Sparrow was closed to its frequenters."

Mrs. Goldsmith kept the store open a few months longer. But without Alfred Goldsmith, the spirit of the store was gone. The store closed, and his books were sold by the Swann Auction Galleries, November 6–7, 1947. An essay by John T. Winterich, "Alfred F. Goldsmith: An Appreciation," was the preface for the Swann catalogue. The essay was reprinted by *Publishers Weekly,* November 22, 1947. Among other affectionate compliments to the bookman, Winterich wrote, "Alfred Goldsmith knew books, and was happy to share his knowledge with the friends of books—the real friends, not the phoneys. . . . Many people are a lot more knowledgeable because Alfred Goldsmith lived and dealt in books." While insisting that the honest and kindly man would have succeeded in any field, Winterich observed, "It is the great good fortune of many who survive him that he chose books. Books are more durable than the men who write them, the men who sell them, and the men who buy them. For that reason, perhaps, friendships that begin in books seem to be more durable than other friendships. Among those of us who still have books acquired from Alfred Goldsmith, whether by private treaty or by outright gift (and many of us have), some part of him will endure as a goodly memory."

Although At the Sign of the Sparrow no longer waits on lower Lexington Avenue for book seekers to appear, although it no longer invites us to step down and in, this peaceful harbor of culture and its gentle proprietor won immortality in the annals of New York's Book Row.

CHAPTER FOUR

GIANT SCHULTE'S AND A "SHIP OF BOOKS"
Theodore Schulte · Philip Pesky · Wilfred Pesky · Dave Butler ·
Louis Cohen

> *For book-sellers are various, good and bad, sly and frank, straight*
> *and crooked, wise, wayward, mean, generous, greedy,*
> *open-handed, proud, humble, quiet, noisy, well read and ill read,*
> *as other tradesmen are; but there is, I find, a numerous company of*
> *the best of them.*
>
> —HOLBROOK JACKSON, *The Anatomy of Bibliomania*

LITERARY HISTORIANS SHOULD explain why farsighted George Bernard Shaw didn't abandon the chilly British Isles and settle into comfortable writing quarters somewhere around Fourth Avenue between Astor Place and Union Square. Early in the twentieth century, with one of those clearheaded Shavian insights, he noted, "What we want above all things is not more books, not more publishers, not more education, not more literary genius, but simply and prosaically more shops." That gives birth to an axiom with the clarity of Euclid: It is easier to find and buy books where there are more places that sell books.

A considerate friend should have advised, "Move to Fourth Avenue in New York City, GBS. There you'll find wonderful little secondhand bookstores offering sooner or later practically any book that ever emerged from a printing press or a scribe's quill. The shops you yearn for are starting to settle in there at a steady and remarkable rate." Apparently no such kind and wordy friend existed, so the Irish-born playwright's response, alas, isn't available. But wouldn't his reaction have been interesting?

Shaw's unfortunately nonexistent friend would have been correct about the startling proliferation of such bookstores occurring in that particular neighborhood as the twentieth century decade that would be called the Roaring Twenties approached. During those years of "flappers and philosophers" (the title F. Scott Fitzgerald used for a 1920 story collection), the Fourth Avenue bookstore birthrate steadily increased. Available space, acceptable rents, the hopeful promise of customers delivered by subway, publishing firms in the vicinity, the city's leading department store, Wanamaker's, at Tenth Street, were among factors stimulating the process.

Also involved was a tendency Bernard M. Rosenthal mentioned in the second annual Sol M. Malkin Lecture in Bibliography at Columbia University on December 15, 1986: "Besides, booksellers always tend to go where the books and other booksellers are—and New York was the obvious place." There was no reason why bookstores should be exceptions to the innate impulse of living forms to be with their own kind.

The book dealers moving in and setting up shops were, in theory, competitors, since they sold the same commodities. But they were keen enough to realize the theory applied to used Model Ts perhaps but not to books. When the wares were books, more bookshops in a neighborhood meant more customers. A single bookshop could offer only thousands from the staggering total of books pouring from the presses, starting with incunabula and never stopping. The next store, the next shelf might deliver at a bargain price a true treasure for reading or collecting. So like ants on the march, book shoppers roamed. The born browser's incurable temptation to check next door made a community of stores—a Book Row—inevitable when conditions were right, as they were on Fourth Avenue. The Fourth Avenue Book Row probably came closer over the years than any library, collector, or alternate cluster of bookshops to accomplishing Sir Thomas Phillipps's probably mad collecting goal "to have one copy of every book in the world." Sir Thomas didn't get there; our Book Row, maybe.

The existence of such a community was good for business individually and collectively. Decades after the adolescent years of Book Row, Fred Bass at the Strand said, "There's room in this business for everybody. Another store could open across the street, and my business would increase. People like to browse from shop to shop" (*New York Times,* September 30, 1969).

The result was that A. Edward Newton in 1928 could acknowledge the glamour and romance of "prowling around in the bookshops of the old country. But the best picking is now to be had at home, especially in New York City." And when Book Row later was at its zenith in the 1940s and

1950s, Lawrence Clark Powell accurately declared, "In the concentration of bookshops on lower Fourth Avenue, the browser finds himself in heaven" (*The Alchemy of Books*, 1954).

Oddly enough, or perhaps not so oddly, book heaven had great support from a Fourth Avenue neighborhood institution known as Bible House. The building, between Eighth and Ninth Streets, was the property of the American Bible Society (ABS). It was erected in 1853 as a replacement for the earlier Bible House, on Nassau Street, to produce religious publications by using advanced technology. The new Bible House, according to Edwin G. Burrows and Mike Wallace in *Gotham,* was needed by the society to "churn out bulk shipments of Holy Writ for Sunday schools, poorhouses, prisons, orphanages, and immigrant depots—and to manage what was increasingly a worldwide crusade." The structure also eventually functioned as an incubator for New York's newest Book Row.

According to Manuel Tarshish in *Publishers Weekly,* October 20, 1969, the Bible House was the city's first building erected on a framework of cast iron columns. Thus its floors were uniquely designed to accommodate heavy loads of books. Thanks to the hospitality of the owners, a wide variety of books other than Bibles began to arrive in accelerating volumes on the premises. The Fourth Avenue Bible House proved to be an understanding landlord for small bookshops. The rents charged were not exorbitant, and the ABS was compassionately patient about overdue rent. Eviction wasn't an American Bible Society thing to do or thing done.

The Bible House became the physical location of several bookstores and served as a magnet for others nearby. The history of Book Row's evolution features the ABS Bible House as a home for secondhand bookstores and as a catalyst for the presence of others in the neighborhood. Among the booksellers associated with the Bible House was a one-time Russian anarchist who served time in a Siberian prison—the studious chess enthusiast Leon Kramer, a specialist in books pertaining to radical movements and economic theory. Libraries and universities relied on his expertise. One of his contributions was preventing the archives of the Socialist Party of the United States from being destroyed by having them preserved at the Duke University Library.

Other Bible House residents included Max Breslow with Books for Bookish People; David Kalisch and Steve Seskin's Eureka Books; and the initial incarnation of Louis Cohen's Argosy Book Store. The expression "near the Bible House" describes many Book Row shops. One of them was Schulte's Book Store at 80 Fourth Avenue.

THEODORE E. SCHULTE AND OTHERS—SCHULTE'S BOOK STORE, INC.

In a 1911 address to the American Booksellers' Association at the Astor Hotel in New York City, "The Second-Hand Book Business as an Adjunct of the Bookstore," printed in *Publishers Weekly*, May 13, 1911, Theodore Schulte called himself a "mere novice as a dealer in old books." At the time he owned and ran what he described as an "unpretentious second-hand book shop" at the corner of Twenty-third Street and Lexington Avenue.

He told the convention that they should be listening to a veteran in the old book business such as "Mr. Geo. D. Smith, the valiant knight of the auction rooms." He agreed to speak to be helpful to "fellow workers in the trade," and told his audience that he had been interested in old books and old bookshops since his boyhood, when he frequented the shops around Cooper Union, near his home, and the shops on Nassau and Ann Streets. His admission of a devotion to books in his early youth fosters doubts concerning Schulte's much later claim to Jack Biblo of Biblo and Tannen that while he sold them on a massive scale, he had never read a book in his life. The confession sounds more like the tongue-in-cheek bravado of a pianist who brilliantly plays a Brahms ballade and then boasts, "I never had a lesson in my life."

Whether he read them or not, Schulte sold books in larger quantities than most of his contemporaries during a long career. He certainly did not remain a novice dealer; and "unpretentious" was definitely the wrong modifier for his store after he moved to 80 Fourth Avenue in 1917. "Largest" was the adjective preferred by one of the most successful book entrepreneurs of his time. By 1918, Schulte's Fourth Avenue store used bold capitals on two bargain tables outside the big front windows declaring itself the LARGEST SECOND-HAND BOOK STORE IN N.Y., and that was just the beginning. Nineteen years later, the "Talk of the Town" section in the *New Yorker*, on January 30, 1937, reported, "Schulte's Book Store is, we are told, the largest second-hand book store in this country; largest in the world, for all they know," with a stock of a million-odd secondhand volumes.

Larry Moskowitz from Joseph the Provider Books, when he was

interviewed for this account and was told the quixotic claim of an old seller of old books that he had never read one, said, "So what? We are not scholars; we are booksellers. Book reading is something different. Of course, it's nice at a bookstore if you find someone who knows something about your subject, but that has little to do with bookselling. You are a merchant of books. If you are a good merchant, you can provide the people with the books they want. That's bookselling."

Theodore Schulte was born in 1867. After graduation from the College of the City of New York, he worked as a clerk at the New York branch of the American Baptist Publication Society of Philadelphia and eventually was promoted to manager. His experience selling old books began while he was working for the society and had an opportunity to buy the library of a deceased Baptist clergyman, the Reverend Thomas Rambaud. Schulte was not familiar with the books offered, but he decided to take a chance and made an offer of $180 for all the books. Anxiety hit when the bid was accepted and he received several large cases of books. "I was fearful that I would not know how to dispose of them, that I would not come out whole on the transaction, that my purchase, so entirely out of the usual order of the purchases of the Society, which dealt exclusively in new books and church supplies, would call forth severe criticism at headquarters." The Rambaud books sold, and the purchase of libraries for sale by the society continued. Schulte used these activities and his work for the society as learning experiences for the future.

That future can be said to have started in 1905 when the society decided to close its New York branch and sold the stock to Schulte, who continued to operate the establishment as his own bookstore at the Twenty-third Street location. "Personally, handling old books has always appealed to me," said Schulte in 1911. "I determined gradually to alter the character of the store from a new to an old book shop and this program has now been consistently adhered to for about five years." Love for old books was a primary reason for the change. Because of the store's Baptist origins, he continued to specialize somewhat in theological books.

In 1917 came another major change, the move to Fourth Avenue and the bookstores already there in the vicinity of the Bible House. The astuteness of Schulte's decision was underscored by a statement in *Publishers Weekly*, October 6, 1917: "A vindication of the claim that more bookstores do not necessarily mean less business is found in the reports of 'good business' from

Frank Bender's and other dealers in the Row." Bender, at 84 Fourth Avenue, specialized in art books in addition to general books.

Possibly the largest, maybe even greatest, general secondhand bookstore that ever existed until the development of the modern Strand—Schulte's Book Store—settled in at 80 Fourth Avenue, the address where Jacob Abrahams had opened his first bookstore in 1893. The location remained Schulte's site for the remainder of its existence into the 1980s. The site was owned by Grace Church, an Episcopal institution designed by James Renwick Jr., located around the corner on Broadway at East Tenth Street. The church is a famous city landmark, with an exterior of marble provided by the labor of Sing Sing convicts. In the nineteenth century it was the house of worship for upper-class families and a favorite place to hold high-society weddings. That history of association with eminent citizens contrasted with the church's later Book Row connections, and its maintenance of a homeless shelter in the 1990s richly symbolizes the dynamic nature of an ever-changing city. The importance of Grace Church and the Bible House to Book Row development and success can't be denied.

The establishment of Schulte's Book Store on Fourth Avenue in 1917 has been called the beginning of the great age of Booksellers' Row. When Schulte died at his Scarsdale, New York, home at the age of eighty-three on May 3, 1950, the obituary notes in *Publishers Weekly* (May 13, 1950) gave the bookman credit for naming the Fourth Avenue bookstore aggregation Bookseller's Row early in his residence on Fourth Avenue. "His vision and optimism bore fruit, for today it is truly the center of the secondhand book trade," *PW* stated.

The name of the store was never changed, and theology remained a specialty through four successive owners: Schulte; Philip Pesky, who became his partner in 1925 and took over in 1950; Wilfred P. Pesky, who succeeded his father in 1955; and the final owner, David J. Butler. If theology was emphasized, it was far from dominant as Schulte's expanded into a general bookstore with a very large stock in nearly all areas. When Stammer's Bookstore closed in 1969, Schulte's became the oldest remaining bookstore on Fourth Avenue.

AMONG THE BOOKS AT SCHULTE'S

Before becoming Schulte's partner, Philip Pesky ran a bookshop on West

116th Street near the Morningside Heights campus of Columbia University. Together Schulte and Pesky created an atmosphere that some considered Dickensian and a vast assemblage of books at modest prices that attracted every conceivable type of buyer.

A store with such an immense range of choices predictably drew a wide range of customers. One recipient of books from Schulte's was President Franklin D. Roosevelt. The rich and famous as well as the poor and unknown were steady customers there. Among the famous who bought books at Schulte's were Fritz Kreisler, Marlene Dietrich, Joan Crawford, and Steve Allen. Marion Davies found books she needed about the Quakers for a film role among the store's more than ample theological works.

The *New Yorker*'s 1937 visit to Schulte's led to the preservation of a book story with the flavor of great wealth about it and one thin dime: "Mr. Schulte has had all sorts of dealings with the great. . . . Mr. R.'s secretary called up once and said that he wanted a certain hymnal which he had used in Sunday school long ago." John D. Rockefeller's factotum continued that no expense was too great. "Mr. Schulte," reported the magazine, "just walked over to his ten-cent shelf, picked out the hymnal, and sent it around to Mr. Rockefeller with a bill for ten cents."

Books by the thousands awaited buyers and browsers on the main floor, in a large basement, and along a three-sided balcony. The store contained numerous book-lined alcoves illuminated by uncovered lightbulbs turned on and off by book hunters. Such a labyrinthine and bookish place naturally gave rise to stories, mysteries, legends, and speculations. One Schulte's basement story, alleged but unconfirmed, involved sudden impromptu amorous activities during a search among the shadows for French books by a bookseller and his female assistant. *Cherchez la Française.* Fortunately, even theology books are innately unshockable, and apparently *Romance in Schulte's Basement* never found a publisher.

A mystery that was published in 1919 by Doubleday, Page & Company and achieved a permanent place on the bibliophile bookshelf is *The Haunted Bookshop*, which features a fictional bookshop named Parnassus at Home. Its author, Christopher Morley, in his *Saturday Review of Literature* column, "Bowling Green" (July 4, 1925), admitted that his imaginary bookshop was a composite of Schulte's and the Brooklyn store of N. Morrow Ladd. Morley wrote that he was inspired by "the sparkling and savory piled-up alcoves of Schulte's."

The Parnassus bibliophile never complained that various other bookshops such as At the Sign of the Sparrow were credited by some for the book as well. A persistent bookshop collector and roamer, Morley without naming names dedicated *The Haunted Bookshop* "To the Booksellers," whom he saluted as upholders of "the ancient and honourable traditions" of a "noble profession."

The books for those alcoves and the many crowded shelves came from the unvarying Schulte's policy of buying books on a large scale and marketing vigorously for a quick turnover. One major source of nearly new current books was review copies from the *New York Herald Tribune* and other New York–based publications. The *New Yorker* in 1937 reported, "Mr. Schulte invariably pays one-quarter the list price of a book, and buys anything—hack love stories, children's books, the latest Huxley or Maugham, expensive limited editions, detective stories, or technical expositions." Schulte then sold the review copies at half price. A busy reviewer, noted the article, could sell enough books to pay the monthly rent on a small apartment. Ah, the good old low-rent days.

A quick, large-scale source of books involved the purchase of entire collections. Schulte around 1935 bought the Maimonides Library of fifty thousand books. In another deal the store acquired sixteen thousand books put together during World War I for U.S. servicemen. The store purchased numerous libraries assembled by individuals. One was the library of the Presbyterian clergyman, author, and professor George Foot Moore, who taught the history of religion at Harvard from 1904 to 1928.

Theodore Schulte at the 1911 American Booksellers' Association convention called "right buying . . . the life of the business." In his store, with large volume as the goal, he recognized the necessity of constant replenishment. Without frequent new consignments giving customers daily access to fresh items, "stagnation and business death are sure to result," he warned. Schulte acknowledged the importance of buying at auctions while admitting he particularly relished the excitement of the as yet unknown: "Nothing in business life can compare to the delights of first going over a consignment before one knows what the lot contains. Every new item has a fascination and gives a distinct pleasure. Some times an unexpected 'plum' is found such as a rare book or a good first edition. . . . Whether the hopes are ever realized or not, the game is fascinating and the pleasure to a book lover is more than a mere monetary consideration."

Successful buying, contended Schulte, demands "the largest possible experience," and he named several desiderata: "A thorough knowledge of all classes of books, a retentive memory, and a book instinct, which is intuitive and really cannot be learned, but which seldom fails to dig out the valuable items in a collection, combined with a certain amount of commercial instinct are the necessary requirements for the buyer of old books."

Schulte as a dealer in theological works and volunteer organist for many years at the Second Avenue Baptist Church asked himself a question some dealers probably didn't: "It is a moot question whether the dealer should disclose his knowledge of rare or unusual items, which may be in a collection offered him for sale, the value of which are not known to the seller." Schulte's conclusion: "This is a matter which must be left to the sense of honor of the dealer."

He emphasized that the selling of old books requires a lot more than just a yes or no when a customer seeks a book. At Schulte's if a customer asked for a specific title, whether the store had the title or not, clerks when possible were instructed to take the customer to the appropriate section to verify availability. Even when the book requested wasn't present, often something else was found "that will answer your customer's purpose just as well."

YES, CATALOGUES SELL BOOKS

While Schulte's principally offered modestly priced books that didn't qualify as rare or antiquarian, with so many volumes coming in, rarities did inevitably appear. In a copy of *Tess of the D'Urbervilles*, Philip Pesky found as an insert a letter by Thomas Hardy expressing his dismay that the prudish American publishers wanted to expurgate his book. Walk-in customer Donald C. Gallup, the Yale bibliographer, recalled in his autobiography, *Pigeons on the Granite* (1988), finding first editions by T. S. Eliot and others at bargain prices. Gallup noted first editions at Schulte's that came from the John Quinn auction. Quinn was an attorney and bibliophile whose large library was auctioned in New York from November 1923 to March 1924.

In a newspaper column, Burton Rascoe wrote about a 1930s Schulte's catalogue that offered signed letters by famous writers at bargain prices, including Sherwood Anderson, $2.50; F. Scott Fitzgerald, $2.50; Sinclair

Lewis, $3.50; George Bernard Shaw, $5; and several Theodore Dreisers from $5 to $25.

Theodore Schulte considered catalogues valuable bookselling tools. "Probably the most successful way of selling old books is by catalogue," he said in 1911. He added, "Catalogues are expensive and should be prepared and sent out with judicious discrimination." He considered it important for catalogues to be well organized, to focus on a specific subject, and to be sent to selected classes of customers with known interest in the subject—"and thus save my ammunition," declared Schulte. These 1911 views by a thoughtful and analytical bookman who was trying to pinpoint the best ways of selling used books anticipated by decades the practical guidelines for effective direct-mail marketing that gradually evolved in the twentieth century.

In his early experiments with catalogues Schulte found it helpful to enclose a blank asking customers to inform the store concerning special books and subjects that interested them. A card file was made of these interests, and the customer was notified if a book came in he might want. "Not only do we quote the special book desired but we find it invaluable to quote other books on the same subject or of a similar character," noted Schulte about a standard practice that often produced multiple sales. This procedure has become a standard routine, ad nauseam some might say, in all areas of direct-mail marketing.

Schulte's catalogues typically focused on particular topic areas and listed several hundred books by author, title, publishing data, and the selling price, which was generally modest. The descriptions were kept to a minimum and were strictly informational, without any advertising arias about the books as books. An exception was made only with special books, as in a rare Schulte's catalogue of six hundred items, entitled "Private Presses and Finely Printed Books," which was described favorably in the *Book Collector's Packet* (May 1933).

A more representative Schulte's offering was Catalogue No. 192 in 1938, "Anthropology and Related Subjects." While "related" was stretched some to include curiosities and humor, essentially the catalogue adhered to business with 679 items at prices never seen since: item 135, Stephen Crane, *Whilomville Stories* (1900), $1.25; item 158, J. Frank Dobie, *Coronado's Children* (1931), $1.50; item 262, Lafcadio Hearn, *Glimpses of Unfamiliar Japan,* 2 volumes (1894), $4.50; item 368, Pierre Loti, *Morocco* (1920), $1.25.

In the curiosities category would be item 42, *Batchelor's Estimate of the Expences of a Married Life in a Letter to a Friend,* by "John Single" (London, 1729–31), $5, and item 602: "*Swindling Exposed. From the Diary of William B. Moreau, King of Fakirs.* Methods of the Crooks Explained. History of the Worst Gang that Ever Infested This Country, Etc. (1907), $1.50."

THE PESKY SUCCESSORS, FATHER AND SON

In November 1949 the Booksellers League of New York honored Theodore Schulte with a testimonial dinner. He had served the league as both its president and its treasurer. He was given a scroll recognizing his "great contributions and long service to the trade of bookselling." Schulte appreciated the esteem of his peers in the "ancient and honorable profession." He had declared his own commitment thirty-eight years earlier in 1911 when he said, "The old book business offers delight to the dealer who is genuinely fond of his business, who is in fact a book lover. . . . I have sometimes said as a matter of choice I would prefer the book business if it afforded me a competence rather than another pursuit with abundance." Fortunately for thousands of book buyers through the decades, he earned that competence with exceptional dedication and skill in the business of bookselling.

The continuity of Schulte's Book Store was smoothly managed without significant change as Philip Pesky took over the store after the founder's death in 1950. The *New Yorker* article about Schulte's, January 30, 1937, remarked on shaking hands "with Mr. Schulte and his silent partner, Mr. Pesky." Pesky was described by some customers as not possessing an outgoing nature, but he was considered a good bookseller who kept the store functioning efficiently much in the same way it did when Schulte and Pesky ran it as a team.

Under Philip Pesky and later under his son Wilfred P. Pesky, who began working at the store while in high school, and then David J. Butler, Schulte's continued to be a large, general bookstore with numerous books in most areas of interest. Until the nearby Strand began to rival it in size and appeal, Schulte's carried on as the store Walter Goldwater said was "the kind of place where, if you were coming to New York and just had time to go to one place, this was the place you'd go, because the prices were reasonable, and the quantity of material was very large indeed."

The availability of nearly new, recently published books from the city's busy cadre of reviewers, among them Irita Van Doren at the *Herald Tribune,* persisted as well for several years. The bookselling methods introduced by Schulte remained solidly in effect, and the store, as before, attracted book shoppers who appreciated a lot of books among which to browse in zealous quest of they often didn't know what titles—but they'd know when they found them.

Schulte's was a crowded and therefore an inviting (or nerve-racking) place to roam and look. One customer thought of it as an enormous amphitheater containing "all the books that were ever penned." A minister from Pennsylvania called it "an infinite Elysian field of mental pasture." For some it could be an intimidating Elysian field. Bookseller and collector Maggie DuPriest reminisced about Book Row shopping: "I went to Schulte's where I would search for specific titles. I recall the balcony used to scare me. There was hardly room to put down a foot because of the books on the floor!" Under Pesky and later Butler management, Schulte's persisted as a fine place for book grazing until the fatal malaise that eventually erased Book Row started to set in during the 1970s. Schulte's went into decline and then closed in the 1980s.

Intimations of the end began to show in 1969 perhaps, when David Butler, who also specialized in theological works and thus preserved Schulte's historic role in that field, offered a customer a thousand theological books at fifteen cents each and fifteen hundred children's books at thirty-five cents each. Walter Goldwater, speaking probably in the early 1980s, noted that Butler had been one of the employees who acquired the store from the Pesky estate and ran it for several years. Toward the end, however, he tried to sell the shop's 120,000 books for $50,000, about forty cents per book. Goldwater expressed the opinion that the books by then were worth no more than ten cents each. "I don't know what the future holds," said Goldwater.

The future was as bleak for Schulte's as it was for others. Most of the Book Row stores fell prey in the 1970s to high rents and other expenses that exceeded what the businesses could afford from used-book revenue. Clearly working was the Wilkins Micawber principle that if expenditures exceed income, the result is misery, or in the case of secondhand bookstores, closings or relocations. When Schulte's reached the end, it had survived longer in the same location (80 Fourth Avenue) than any other Fourth Avenue bookshop.

Let's not slam the door on Schulte's at the close of its record run. Let's look back to better times in the 1960s, when Wilfred Pesky, representing

Schulte's, was one of the twenty-three booksellers taking part in New York's April 4–9, 1960, First Antiquarian Book Fair, at the Steinway Concert Hall. One dealer, Leona Rostenberg, according to *Antiquarian Bookman* (May 2, 1960), saw an opera prima donna make an entrance into what had always been a sacred place of music and declare in shock, "What have they done to Steinway Hall? Books!"

Wilfred Pesky considered not taking part in the fair—a booth cost $250—and he was apprehensive about his general books standing up against true rarities. He concluded Schulte's should give the fair a chance and join with the others the first time. Once committed, Pesky did it right and even had a special catalogue prepared. The results for Schulte's and many other participants proved that a book fair in New York could draw plenty of book people and many would leave as book buyers. Pesky said, "The first night I more than made expenses for the week. . . . There is something about a Fair that creates an auction-room atmosphere. I saw my own collectors buy books at net prices that they had turned down at 20 percent off on my last sale. . . . Everybody enjoyed the experience. Definitely next year."

Walter Goldwater remembered Wilfred Pesky, who died in 1966 at the age of fifty-three, as a gifted salesman of books whose gentle manner could convince a customer he was making a wise choice but as an ineffective manager who became too bogged down in excessive detail and record-keeping minutiae. Pesky's detailed records of books in stock were useful to customers, but the complex maintenance tasks involved were exorbitant for the low-priced volumes. "Most of us discovered this after a while and simply wouldn't do it," said Goldwater.

While conducting Schulte's day-to-day business, Wilfred Pesky published books on women in education and served as a founder and secretary of the Antiquarian Booksellers' Association of America (ABAA). In spite of his store's general stock, Pesky earned recognition as a bookman well informed concerning first editions and rare books. Admired as a gentle and generous person, he won the esteem of his peers. Goldwater remembered him as one of the nicest people ever engaged in the book business, and Wayne Somers, reminiscing about Book Row, wrote for this report that it was smart to remain quiet and careful around many of the proprietors: "The only exception I recall was Wilfred Pesky, who seemed a kind soul." Pesky became the friend of numerous authors, publishers, and collectors who followed the habits of decades by continuing to come to the store that had sold books to other generations before many of them were born.

When David Butler's time to take over arrived, in the 1960s, the store was still among the largest in the city. Butler previously had a bookstore at 114 Fourth Avenue and was an experienced professional. McCandlish Phillips wrote in the *New York Times* (September 30, 1969): "If the Strand is the Macy's of book row, Schulte's, at 82 Fourth Avenue, is the Gimbels." The address was numerically slightly off, but the sentiment was right. As the head of Schulte's, Butler maintained a stock of about 120,000 books on all subjects, with theology as a house specialty. He was a collector himself of bibliographies on theology. Butler issued two catalogues a year and indicated that mail orders accounted for nearly 60 percent of the business. He told Manuel Tarshish that when he took over, his plan was "to preserve the old atmosphere—but clean up the place."

Considering the store's long dossier from 1917 on, keeping alive during the Depression, hanging on after the 1950s, and giving valuable service to book seekers even through rocky periods, Theodore Schulte at the end and in retrospect probably would have—and should have—been proud of his namesake bookstore.

Louis Cohen—Argosy Book Store

"Well do I remember a young Lou Cohen and his sister Regina of the Argosy Book Store located in the Bible House. . . . We took home treasures for sometimes as little as 50 cents, but lunch then was maybe 25 cents," wrote Philip Sperling, book collector and active member of the American Printing History Association and the Typophiles.

Book Row served as a vital training ground for numerous bookshop proprietors and through the years developed a large and widely scattered alumni association of book dealers who worked on Book Row, learned all they could, and moved on. Among the Row's honor graduates, Louis Cohen ranks near or at the summit. If Book Row is envisioned as a booksellers' university, Lou Cohen was surely a contender to be designated valedictorian of the graduating class. As a historical institution, Book Row can take a doting parent's natural pride in the success of offspring. When Cohen eventually left Fourth Avenue, he stayed close to the Book Row family though his famous Argosy was located uptown at 114 and later 116 East Fifty-ninth Street.

Lou Cohen was born on the Lower East Side on July 4, 1903, the son of a baker. He was a business innovator from childhood. At the age of eight, to earn a nickel on rainy days, he would take an umbrella and meet passengers at the subway station and let them rent the umbrella to keep dry going home. Attending Bronx High School of Commerce, he accepted whatever part-time jobs came along, including one in a bookstore. After high school in 1921, he took a full-time Manhattan job at Alexander Salop's Madison Bookstore, performing a full spectrum of bookshop duties—selling, typing, packing, searching, delivering. In the evenings he studied business administration at City College of New York. His days were full, but not too full to think about a bookshop of his own.

With $500 savings and $500 borrowed from an uncle, Cohen found a suitable location at the corner of Eighth Street, across from Wanamaker's. It was 45 Fourth Avenue, in the Bible House. The large space had a dry basement and a double front window. The rent was a steep $75 per month, but the site seemed well situated for walk-in traffic; and Lou Cohen was ready for his chance to take a chance. After acquiring start-up stock from auctions, sales, and newspaper advertisements, he opened the store in 1926. His bookstore neighbors in the Bible House included Henry Blackwell, Max Breslow, David Kalisch, and David Scheinbaum.

He wanted a name starting with *A*, to appear up front in directories. That led to the romantic word "argosy," depicting a large merchant ship conveying great treasures (books!) on the seven seas to the world's ports. Maybe he was struck by Shakespeare's phrase "argosies with portly saile" in *The Merchant of Venice*. More likely he recalled lines that used to be memorized in school, from Tennyson's "Locksley Hall": "Saw the heavens fill with commerce, argosies of magic sails, / Pilots of the purple twilight, dropping down with costly bales." There were few more precious "bales" than books from the Argosy in the 1920s, but they weren't costly. Along with inside shelving, outside bins for ten-, fifteen-, and twenty-five-cent bargain books were installed. An entrance sign enticingly promised "A Book for Every Mood." The windows proclaimed OLD, RARE & NEW BOOKS and BOOKS BOUGHT & SOLD at Cohen's Fourth Avenue "book ship."

The Argosy Book Store was destined to be an intensively family enterprise. His sister Regina quit her secretary job to join him in the store. His cousin Sam Zobel designed the shop's logo. His cousin Benjamin Swann worked at the Argosy, though he eventually left to start a mail-order book business nearby. Later Ben Swann would be the director of Swann Galleries, with Cohen as a major shareholder. After Lou Cohen married Ruth Shevin in 1931, his wife also became a member of the Argosy staff. Their three daughters, Judith, Naomi, and Adina, in time became valued bookselling professionals in the Argosy enterprise.

Cohen's entrepreneurship expressed itself in multiple ways. To replenish stock he began the practice of purchasing entire libraries, even when these moves in the early days imposed heavy financial pressures. To find the books, he mailed penny postcards to those who sounded prosperous enough to have libraries. Lou Cohen recalled early morning trips from Book Row to examine libraries. When deals were made, the books had to be boxed and carried back to the Bible House.

One of the pivotal events that Cohen experienced in book buying occurred during 1935. In a miscellaneous collection of novels, nonfiction, poetry, and children's books, he discovered thirty children's books from the 1880s. What made them special was that the front flyleaf of each was signed by Sara Delano, the mother of President Franklin D. Roosevelt. Cohen sent the books as a gift to President Roosevelt, who responded with an appreciative letter. The bookman and the president continued to correspond, and the Argosy became a source for President Roosevelt's naval history collecting. Decades later came another presidential mission for Lou Cohen. Jacqueline Kennedy in 1960 asked him to assist in the development of the White House Americana Collection. He didn't refuse the assignment, for which he was indisputably qualified.

A mid-1930s milestone for the Argosy, dictated by space needs and Cohen's ambitions, was the move to East Fifty-ninth Street. There the Cohens established one of New York's best-known—and best—antiquarian bookstores, still operating in the twenty-first century over seven decades after its start at the Bible House.

On Fourth Avenue, the Argosy began the practice of utilizing quality catalogues to sell rare books. Catalogue 40, "First Editions of English Authors," in 1932, offered part of a library that the inside front cover described as one "fastidiously built up during the years 1910 to 1927—years of magnificent opportunity." "This catalogue will repay careful reading," the copywriter declared under the headline "A Little Inevitable Enthusiasm *(Enforced upon a blase cataloguer by some extraordinary books).*" Who could close the catalogue unexamined after such a rapturous buildup and the assurance that "every effort has been made to give an exact description of condition and of all material points"? Whatever the response in 1932, contemporary collectors would whistle—and then burst into tears—at the prices for firsts by Joseph Conrad, Thomas Hardy, D. H. Lawrence, Oscar Wilde, and others. How about item 261, the Shakespeare and Co. 1922 *Ulysses,* by James Joyce, immaculate, $75. Or item 262, the Egoist Press 1922 *Ulysses* at $40 with this description:

> Rare. It was our impression that a large part of this edition was destroyed by the Goths and Vandals—otherwise known as the Society for the Protection of Mrs. Grundy. However it seems that there was merely a fire in the New York Postoffice during which 500 copies of "Ulysses" were destroyed. Heroic firemen, injured trying to read Ulysses amid the flames, were discharged without compensation.

SOCIETY FOR THE SUPPRESSION OF VICE VERSUS THE ARGOSY

Ironically, later in the 1930s, while still at the Bible House, Cohen had need of the attorney who defended *Ulysses* against obscenity charges when his store fell victim to "comstockery." That's George Bernard Shaw's word for "licensed bigotry" or narrow-minded, prudish attacks on art by straitlaced antivice crusaders. Shaw's run-in with the smut suppressors began when Anthony Comstock, a founder in 1872 of the New York Society for the Suppression of Vice, savagely attacked Shaw's *Mrs. Warren's Profession* as lewd and obscene. Comstock made himself notorious during a long and, to many, ludicrous war on obscenity targets.

Comstock was succeeded as New York's morality czar by John S. Sumner. It was Sumner's men from the Society for the Suppression of Vice who infiltrated Cohen's store at the Bible House, bought an under-$5 paperback with a lurid, sexually suggestive cover from the Argosy's curiosa section, and gave

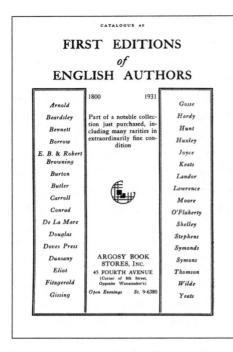

Cohen a subpoena to appear in court for dealing in prurient materials. Cohen had to take the attack very seriously, because other bookstores had been closed by Sumner's vice squads. "I was scared and angry by turns at the ridiculousness of the situation," Cohen recalled. He went to court with Argosy catalogues and testimonials demonstrating that his wasn't a store for sex addicts. He lucked out in drawing a sympathetic judge who dismissed the case in five minutes.

However, Cohen and his Fourth Avenue bookseller colleagues continued to suffer the threat of harassment from Sumner's porn patrols. Although the Argosy apparently was not among them, *Antiquarian Bookman* (April 15, 1991) noted: "During the Depression there were a number of antiquarian or used-book dealers who would regularly sell what the laws at that time considered pornography. Many of them needed the business to survive."

The regular purchase of private libraries and bookstores kept the Argosy supplied with a large stock and made it a bookstore where both collectors and institutions increasingly found books in a wide range of fields. The Argosy became a selling center for first editions and rare books of every type as well as artworks, autographs, catalogues, ephemera, maps, posters, and prints. Maggie DuPriest, recalling her regular stops at the Argosy, wrote, "I would get a lot of Floridana and other history books I needed from their third and fourth floors. But it was their basement that I loved the most because I could find more ephemera and old booksellers' catalogues, exhibition catalogues, etc., which I kept for my own collection. I also bought maps from The Argosy."

Seeking Benjamin Franklin materials and knowing the Argosy to be an Americana archive, Roy Meador called the store. "Yes, we have early Franklin sets," replied the Cohen daughter working in Americana. She described a five-volume set of William Duane's 1809–18 edition of *The Works of Dr. Benjamin Franklin in Philosophy, Politics, and Morals:* "The bindings are excellent. The paper is foxed but will last another hundred years." They came to Ann Arbor, Michigan, and are beautiful books, still splendidly preserved over 180 years after bring printed and bound. William Duane made and Argosy sold books to endure the whips and scorns of time. The Argosy price: $60 for the set.

Lou Cohen became widely known as a buyer of libraries, small and large, sometimes very large. Among individual libraries he acquired were those of department store owner Marshall Field, author John Gunther, and actor-singer Paul Robeson. The library of Dr. Henry Hart gave the Argosy close to seventy-five thousand books in medical history and associated topics. Cohen, in *AB Bookman's Yearbook* (1968), called the Hart acquisition "my most memorable book buy."

He bought entire bookstores as well. "Only Lou Cohen at Argosy had the capital. I sold him two stores of books," observed Louis Wavrovics. Certainly memorable in terms of scope were Cohen's purchases of the Aberdeen Bookshop's stock of close to a hundred thousand books and the O'Malley Bookshop's stock of close to thirty-five thousand books for the Pennsylvania State University Library. He maintained productive working connections with important university libraries throughout the United States.

Lou Cohen was among the founding members in 1949 of the Antiquarian Booksellers' Association of America and a member of the Old Book Table. When he died, at the age of eighty-seven, on January 4, 1991, the obituary article by Stephanie Strom in the *New York Times* (January 6) stated, "He donated a marine research library to Israel and several thousand Hebrew books to Bar-Ilan University in Israel."

Among the tributes to Cohen in *Antiquarian Bookman* (April 15, 1991), Justin G. Schiller's related his childhood delight from finding L. Frank Baum books in the Aunt Jane's Niece series among the open bins at ten cents each or three for a quarter. He told Cohen about the discovery. "I remember his expression of honest joy that I found something I really wanted," wrote Schiller. "He did love the business and the pleasure of bringing books and people together."

Most bibliophiles probably remember that special bookman's love in connection with the East Fifty-ninth Street location, where he migrated in the 1930s. We remember that love in connection with Book Row, where he began at 45 Fourth Avenue in the Bible House when the twentieth century was only twenty-six and Louis Cohen was twenty-three, with a book world to conquer.

CHAPTER FIVE

BOOK ROW AND THE BOOKSELLERS' ASSOCIATIONS

*I remember the money in my pocket and decide to go to Tward
Street to buy myself a storybook. . . . Each title pulls me like a
magnet. Each booklet has its own mystery, cleverness, and bizarre
intrigues. But I can't buy them all. I have to choose. I spend my
last kopeck and carry home a stack of books. The street and the boys
on it no longer concern me at all. I have only one wish: that my
joy not be interrupted, that I have the time to read everything
from beginning to end.*

—ISAAC BASHEVIS SINGER

THE FOURTH AVENUE Book Row came into existence to accumulate in
one convenient area those curious physical objects called books and to make
them easily and readily available to readers, students, bibliophiles, collectors.
To satisfy such a highly diverse customer base, Book Row had to achieve a
uniquely democratic mingling of very different products. The uptown specialist bookstores might get by with a numerically small stock of antiquarian
rarities in specific categories bearing eye-popping price tags. Book Row shops
typically needed books for every biblioappetite, purse, and billfold: nickel-
dime-quarter-dollar outdoor bin bargains, good secondhand editions, unusual
and uncommon editions, oddities available nowhere else, scarce and rare treasures to bring eager collectors, even erotica and exotica for special tastes. "What
books do you want? Let us get them for you."

Chacun à son goût—everyone to his taste—became a Book Row credo.
Individual bookstores and their proprietors varied widely. Collectively they
were socially and politically egalitarian and nonsectarian. Evangelists of tolerance, they offered something for everybody who wanted books for ideas
from masterful to mad; who sought volumes delivering amusement, beauty,
titillation, thrills, wisdom, communion with clever minds, insight into
people, support for nutty notions; who wanted books not so much to read as
possessions to admire for their fine bindings; who wanted books as smart

investments to accrue in value; who just wanted books. No need actually for the bookseller to know why. Book Row was there to answer all book wants, or at least make a persistent and experienced effort to do so.

Nor did Book Rowers rest on their bibliophilic and bibliographic oars and simply deal in books. Book lovers often evidenced an intense satisfaction from acquiring material items and ephemera associated with their favorite books, authors, fields of interest. So on Book Row there was strong incentive for the bookseller to be ready if possible when customers asked about manuscripts, autographs, letters, prints, pamphlets, pictures, pipes, dentures, you name it, anything that might have appeal to a buyer seeking greater closeness to a cherished author. The willingness to buy was motive enough to be ready when customers sought books. The identical rationale applied concerning readiness to respond when they asked for anything that might be sentimentally related.

Fourth Avenue booksellers were businesspeople selling wisdom, dreams, fantasies, and association trivia to an extremely broad group of customers who shared the conviction they could find their answers or their pleasures in books, though not the same books. And not from the same booksellers. That's why Book Row, a diverse collection of individualist booksellers, came into being on Fourth Avenue, clustered in and about the Bible House and along Fourth Avenue and adjacent streets, to serve an even more eclectic and individualistic clientele.

The booksellers of Book Row assembled near, around, about, and on both sides of Fourth Avenue. They were there to deliver knowledge and ideas, good, bad, indifferent; to deliver aesthetic satisfaction; to deliver whatever could be expressed in words or pictures, printed on paper, and tied together in a suitable manner.

And the booksellers, like the books, were all different too—different in outlook, interests, intellect, ambition. Yet Book Row at the same time was a collective entity and thus can be viewed as a unit despite the individual differences evident in the participants. "We dealers both loved and hated each other, but we stuck together," said Harold Briggs of Books 'N Things.

FORMATION OF THE FOURTH AVENUE BOOKSELLERS' ASSOCIATION

The late 1930s and the early 1940s brought an unprecedentedly dangerous era that engulfed much of the world in desperate strain, peril, and terror. When the Second World War struck like a global nightmare, the bookshops were not aloof from the conflict. Books and the freedom to read were among the great causes for which battles were to be waged. Churchill in his six-volume history-memoir of World War II called the period leading up to war "the gathering storm" and wrote, "It is my earnest hope that pondering upon the past may give guidance in days to come."

"Nobody could sleep," Norman Mailer would write at the start of *The Naked and the Dead* (1948), his novel on combat in the Pacific. The early 1940s were a time when sleep came hard for everyone everywhere, from bookstores to battlefields. "The War—we call World War II 'The War' as though there had never been another—was the ultimate experience for anyone in it," wrote Andy Rooney in *My War* (1995). It was a time in the United States of national mobilization, determination to fight, home-front resolution, and quite a few impetuous, wrongheaded acts by various governmental entities. On the West Coast government orders and troops herded thousands of good citizens with Japanese ancestors into concentration camps. On the East Coast New York City municipal authorities ordered booksellers to clear the sidewalks of their bargain stands. Whether they loved or hated one another, it was clearly a time for booksellers not only to stick together, but to join together and form a united front in the face of irrational urban tyranny that would probably worsen if not opposed with a common effort. Emerson offered the booksellers relevant counsel in his 1836 journal: "Sometimes a scream is better than a thesis."

The dealers weren't inclined to hold up the war effort in defense of the right to sidewalk stands for cheap books, but the city's edict was screwy in essence and deserved a collaborative protest. It wasn't as if a clear strategic need existed to keep Fourth Avenue free for marching marines. The dealers were not disposed to act recklessly or impetuously. Anatole France made a point about prudence in *The Revolt of the Angels* (1914) when he observed, "To die for an idea is to place a pretty high price upon conjectures." But taking bargain books off the sidewalk was no conjecture, it was city nonsense going too far. There was a genuine cause for action within reason.

Since the rapid expansion of Book Row in the 1920s, there had been occasional comment among some of the dealers about the merits of forming a Book Row league of booksellers, an organization where dealers could express views, discuss problems, exchange opinions, and, where indicated, act together for the general welfare. Many of the stores contained copies of Edmund Burke's *Thoughts on the Cause of the Present Discontents* (1770), in which he warned first his fellow Englishmen and then later the booksellers, "When bad men combine, the good must associate; else they will fall one by one, an unpitied sacrifice in a contemptible struggle." Everyone knew Benjamin Franklin at the signing of the Declaration of Independence said it shorter and more memorably: "We must all hang together, or assuredly we shall all hang separately." Whatever the variations in the size of their operations, the booksellers knew that no one of them was superfluous and that the existence of a group of antiquarian bookstores in one area had proved beneficial for all.

Before the 1940s, speculative talk had not precipitated action. In 1942, faced with the order from New York City authorities to remove bargain stands from the sidewalks and the prospect of further curtailments, Book Row dealers met and out of the discussions that followed emerged the Fourth Avenue Booksellers' Association, which would function, sometimes cooperatively and energetically, sometimes erratically, on behalf of its members for over a quarter of a century.

Concerning the establishment of the Fourth Avenue Booksellers' Association, Manuel Tarshish, in his *Publishers Weekly* series "The 'Fourth Avenue' Book Trade," wrote, "The Association was the result of necessity. Used-book dealers are notoriously individualistic.... The precipitating cause, according to Eleanor Lowenstein of the Corner Book Shop ... was an order from the New York City authorities that all dealers had to remove their bargain stands from the sidewalk in front of their stores. This was like waving a red flag before a literary bull."

While that was a publicly stated rationale for the movement toward bookstore unification, at least a strong complementary motive came from potential labor troubles and the long-term threats to all from a strike by employees at Schulte's Book Store. Although many, perhaps most, of the Book Row dealers were liberal to radical in their political and social views, impromptu and ill-advised worker strikes were no doubt as unappealing to the booksellers as they were to Fortune 500 corporations. Proprietors of the other bookstores promptly circled the wagons and rallied around Schulte's when disturbing labor challenges appeared.

The Fourth Avenue Booksellers' Association organizational meeting took place on May 25, 1942. The group initially established headquarters at 73 Fourth Avenue, which had been the location of Ben Weiser's Pickwick Bookstore. The group subsequently moved to 113 East Ninth Street, the site of Stanley Gilman's Bookstore, across from the Bible House. The association that evolved from the combined endeavors of the Book Row dealers who participated at the start was among the first of its type in the United States. Most later booksellers' groups benefited from the experiences of this early New York experiment in cooperation. At the end of the 1960s the Fourth Avenue Booksellers' Association was known as the oldest such group in continuous existence.

This is the original slate of officers for the Fourth Avenue Booksellers' Association:

President—Mac Ness, Samuel Weiser Bookstore
Vice president—Harry Gold, Aberdeen Book Company
Treasurer—Albert Saifer, publisher of the *Booktrade Wants* newsletter
Recording secretary—Stanley Gilman, Gilman's Bookstore
Corresponding secretary—Eleanor Lowenstein, Corner Book Shop
Publicity—Karl Seidenberg

An important pioneering activity by the early members of the association with long-term value for the antiquarian book trade on Fourth Avenue and elsewhere was to confront the challenge of preparing a constitution and bylaws. The discussions led to the drafting of a groundbreaking fifteen-section document, which was the first such constitution for an antiquarian organization in the United States and became a working model for the future.

FOURTH AVENUE BOOKSELLERS' ASSOCIATION CONSTITUTION AND BYLAWS

Sec. 1. The name of this organization shall be *The Fourth Avenue Booksellers.*

Sec. 2. Its object shall be the *Promotion* of Bookselling relationships and the *Publicizing* of Bookselling Activities going on in the vicinity bounded by Fourteenth Street on the North; Astor Place on the South; Third Avenue on the East; and Broadway on the West.

Sec. 3. The Executive Committee shall consist of a President, Vice

President, Secretary, Corresponding Secretary and Treasurer, who shall be elected at an Annual Election by the members personally present and voting, for a term of one Year.

Sec. 4. Any member absent, or not present by Proxy, will of necessity agree to any amendment actions or responsibility incurred by the members attending.

Sec. 5. Regular Meetings will be held Monthly and any Special Meetings at discretion of the Executive Committee. Notice of meetings shall be sent by Mail to the members.

Sec. 6. The President, acting as Chairman, shall preside at meetings, preserve order, generally exercise the customary functions of presiding officer.

Sec. 7. The Vice President shall officiate in the absence or disability of the President.

Sec. 8. The Secretary shall keep accurate records of the minutes of the proceedings, and Corresponding Secretary conduct the correspondence and keep the records of the Organization.

Sec. 9. The Treasurer shall collect and receive all moneys due the Organization and shall disburse the same under direction of the Executive Committee. He shall keep accurate records and make financial reports whenever called upon to do so.

Sec. 10. Any Bookseller conducting business within the prescribed territory may make application for membership. Membership Fee being $2.00 per year beginning May 1st to April 30th, each year.

10.1. A colored placard will be supplied all paid up members and displayed in their windows on their premises.

Sec. 11. All Elections to be conducted by Closed Ballot.

Sec. 12. A quorum to constitute at least 10 voting members present at hour set for regular meetings.

Sec. 13. Any approved extra-activities entailing financial outlay shall be prorated among the members in a form to be approved of, at a membership meeting. No extra financial obligations shall be entered into except upon a vote of a membership meeting.

Sec. 14. Amendments to these bylaws shall be first submitted to the Executive Committee in writing who shall in turn inform the membership thereof at the next membership meeting. At this meeting the

Executive Committee shall also give a report as to its approval or disapproval of such amendment. Such proposed amendments shall not be voted upon at the meeting where they are introduced but at the following meeting. Special notice by mail is to be sent to the membership of the amendment and when it is to be acted upon. The bylaws may be amended only by a two-thirds vote of the membership present.

Sec. 15. Special memberships, without voting status, may be had by other Booksellers and Laymen interested in the Fourth Avenue Booksellers and the furtherance of their activities, who wish to take advantage of any benefits that may accrue from such Special Membership. Fee for such Special Membership to be $5.00 with no other fees or duties. A printed card showing their status will be supplied when membership is paid.

CHARTER MEMBERS OF THE FOURTH AVENUE BOOKSELLERS' ASSOCIATION

Aberdeen Book Company
Altree Bookstore
Anchor Bookshop
Arcadia Bookshop
Banner Bookshop
Biblo and Tannen
Bookshop for Bookish People
Books 'N Things
Corner Book Shop
Coronet Bookstore
Eureka Bookshop
Fourth Avenue Book Store
Gilman's Bookstore
Green Book Shop
A. Hershbain
Ben Kaplan Bookstore
Moskowitz Bookstore
Pickwick Bookstore
Raven Book Shop

Schulte's Book Store
Stammer's Bookstore
Strand Book Store
Samuel Weiser Bookstore

Representing the new association, Theodore Schulte arranged to meet with the appropriate city officials concerning the booksellers' position on sidewalk book stands, and the situation was amicably resolved. Book Row shoppers in the decades that followed continued to be able to hunt for exciting book surprises outside their favorite bookshops between Astor Place and Fourteenth Street, in the fresh air. The association helped the bookstores function as a community in an atmosphere of conviviality that made competition friendly and even symbiotic. The shops would never be the Fifty Musketeers; yet "All for one, one for all" became a pragmatic guideline if not a motto under the rubric of association cooperation for mutual advancement.

The description Charles E. Goodspeed gave in *Yankee Bookseller* (1937) of the comparable Boston used-book neighborhood was no less precise for the Fourth Avenue phenomenon: "This limitation of area resulted in considerable intimacy between the various shops where, fertilized by regular visits of scouts and the daily round of bargain-hunting customers, a spice of gossip flourished which relieved any monotony in the routine of trade without diminishing the prevailing spirit of good-fellowship. In fact such competition as might be found in the trade was more in purchasing than in selling."

The association gave the bookstores a foundation and framework for salutary interaction during the war years and through the peacetime phase of relative prosperity that followed at the end of the 1940s. And the association was available when the 1950s gradually and threateningly began to usher in the problems of urban change and rising rents that would persistently plague booksellers during the remaining years of Fourth Avenue as the city's vital center for secondhand books.

CAMPAIGNS, CAUSES, CRUSADES, COMPLICATIONS, UNCERTAINTIES

Among the first collaborative projects of the association in the 1940s was the creation of a catalogue offering one thousand titles from the stocks of nine contributing members. During the rest of the decade the association helped maintain harmony between the members and acted as a benign monitor and guide. The value of the association to the members was affirmed by the smoothness of operations and the maintenance of communal calm while each bookstore vied with others for books and customers.

The association functioned as an effective peacemaker to help minimize the effects of inevitable intramural disputes as the pressures of outside forces began to threaten members' survival. That success occurred in part because the various dealers became skilled at working things out between themselves. The effectiveness of the association from its beginning was clearly due to the professional perception and wisdom of the members in voluntarily permitting that effectiveness.

The association assumed as a primary task that of gaining greater recognition for Book Row. In 1952, the association president, Steve Seskin of Eureka Bookshop, noted that relatively few citizens outside the book community knew of and appreciated the convenient presence of Book Row at the heart of Manhattan. He emphasized the importance through the individual stores and the association of making it widely known that "there is a book for every taste and for every need here." The dilemma was that such acknowledgment was probably already too late.

One expression of the campaign for recognition was a cooperative advertisement on the book page of the *New York Times* with the headline "Visit the Book Center of the World." As the association secretary, Stanley Gilman prepared lists of book requests that resulted from the *New York Times* publicity and circulated them freely among all the members as shared leads.

By the mid-1950s, however, it was increasingly apparent that problems waited ahead for the book center of the world as property values steadily rose in the Fourth Avenue area. The handwriting on history's wall was clear and inexorable: When property was too valuable for low-rent bookshops, the bookshops would again have to migrate in quest of affordable rents and easy accessibility to their customers.

Meyer Berger, in a 1955 "About New York" column in the *New York Times,* warned the dealers that high-priced apartment houses were marching toward them with eviction notices for the bookshops in their present locations. To the booksellers those vertical, high-rent, hypothetical dwellings for the well-to-do must have loomed like the Martian machines in Orson Welles's *War of the*

Worlds 1938 Halloween broadcast come to life. The Fourth Avenue Booksellers' Association tried to fight off the invaders by publicizing Book Row as a fabulous New York and American bookselling area that stood among the greatest in the world and was fully the equal of such celebrated bookstore regions as London's Charing Cross Road or Paris along the banks of the Seine. And who knows, perhaps the campaign did slow down the march of high-rent residences and win Book Row several more years.

There was evidence in the 1950s that Book Row was recognized and valued as a New York City cultural resource and visitor attraction. The city apparently wasn't accepting the prospect of simply allowing Book Row to fade away like an old soldier, due to market forces. Martin Dodge headed a committee sponsored by the New York City Department of Commerce and Public Events to investigate alternative locations and solutions for the secondhand bookstores.

In 1956 it was suggested that the Fourth Avenue shops might move underground and occupy a new Book Row arcade in the subway walkway beneath Sixth Avenue between Thirty-fourth Street, near Macy's, and Forty-second Street, behind the New York Public Library. That alternative was not welcomed as a fresh idea whose time was ever likely to come or, if it did, one to be accepted with any enthusiasm. The prospect of trying to sell used books in a subterranean, molelike tunnel had no immediate appeal among the booksellers. The community response was to display posters declaring, "The Book Row of America Will Remain As Always on Fourth Avenue."

Yet there was really nothing that the bookshops could do to prevent the sites they occupied from becoming more valuable and the rents from becoming more unmanageable. In this period the demolition of the old and hospitable Bible House, which evicted four book dealers—Astor Place Magazine & Bookshop, Colonial Bookstore, Eureka Bookshop, and Leon Kramer—dealt the area a particularly dire blow.

In 1954 a group of buildings on the east side of Fourth Avenue between Tenth and Eleventh Streets was sold, thus serving notice on five bookstores—Arcadia Bookshop, Friendly Book & Music Shop, Louis Schucman, Wex's Book Shop, and the Strand Book Store—to find new locations. Another exceedingly serious 1954 blow hit when Wanamaker's Department Store, which had been of invaluable service to the bookstores by attracting large crowds to the neighborhood, closed its doors. Before or after shopping at Wanamaker's, many in those daily throngs had paused to browse and buy at the bookstores. Without Wanamaker's, would they be back?

Nineteen Sixty-nine and an Expanded Title

The 1950s made inroads on available or affordable Fourth Avenue bookstore sites, but some booksellers carried on and found new homes for their shops. Four relocated to nearby Broadway: Arcadia Bookshop, Raven Book Shop, Strand Book Store, and Samuel Weiser Bookstore. Wex's Book Shop moved to Third Avenue.

Time did what time does best—it passed—and in 1969 the association, acknowledging current realities, rose like the phoenix under a more accurate name, the Fourth Avenue / Broadway Booksellers. Association officers were

President—Ruth W. Carp, Green Book Shop
Vice president—Milton Applebaum, Arcadia Bookshop
Treasurer—Jack Tannen, Biblo and Tannen
Secretary—Stanley Gilman, Gilman's Bookstore.

Stanley Gilman, let it be noted, diligently served as the association's secretary throughout its existence.

In 1969 Fourth Avenue realities were more threatening than they had been in the 1950s. Under the headline "Dealers on Book Row Fear Rent Rises Will End an Era," McCandlish Phillips wrote in the *New York Times:* "There is fear in the teeming stalls of book row, south of Union Square, that Manhattan's used book center may soon become just a footnote to the city's history. Rising rents have already driven some dealers out of the row and into lofts, where they take mail-order sales only. Other dealers do not expect to survive beyond the expiration of their present leases."

Ruth Carp, speaking as president of the association, expressed a wish that the city "would act to save the special character of the enclave." "With rents triple what they used to be, we die," she said. "It's depressing. Most of us love the contact with the customers, and it's deadly to be stashed away in some loft when you're used to the open door."

The association submitted a request to the city that the street signs on Fourth Avenue between Eighth and Fourteenth Streets be changed to read "Fourth Avenue—Book Row." Either the request was too complicated for the city bureaucracy to handle or there was insufficient interest to take action at City Hall. No street name changes occurred. No significant steps were taken by the city to save Book Row.

Plans were also discussed among association members to hold a Fourth Avenue book fair concomitantly with an art fair in Washington Square. Several association members had taken part in the April 1960 book fair at Steinway Concert Hall and been impressed by the ability of book fairs to draw crowds and produce sales. This idea too was allowed to wither and disappear with no action taken. A sense of resignation and submission to the inevitable erosion of the Book Row way of doing business seemed to prevail.

If there was little the Fourth Avenue / Broadway Booksellers' Association could do in the path of apparently inexorable change, the association's record was cause for pride as an innovative, pioneering example of effective cooperation between booksellers. The association added a new and instructive chapter to the long history of the venerable trade that had served readers and collectors since Johannes Gutenberg and his contemporaries perfected a better way of printing a Bible.

ANTIQUARIAN BOOKSELLERS' ASSOCIATION OF AMERICA

In 1949, seven years after the formation of the Fourth Avenue Booksellers' Association, the Antiquarian Booksellers' Association of America was created, with several Book Row dealers among the founders. The involvement of Fourth Avenue and Broadway booksellers in the establishment of the ABAA supports the impression that the ABAA is at least in part a lineal descendant, and book if not blood relative, of the earlier organization. The prior effort on Fourth Avenue taught useful lessons about the nature of association in the antiquarian book field to later organizers of similar groups.

Stanley Gilman, as secretary of the Fourth Avenue Booksellers' Association, and Louis Cohen, whose Argosy Book Store began at the Bible House, took part in the advance discussions that led to a full-scale organizational meeting at the Grolier Club on February 24, 1949. Nearly fifty book dealers, with Book Row well represented, took part. Book Row alumnus David Kirschenbaum focused the discussion on determining the purposes and goals of such an organization. Among the avenues explored was the need to put aside differences and join together to stimulate book buying and antiquarian collecting. What each had been doing on a limited scale individually could be accomplished better through an association that emphasized reaching and serving more customers.

An observer present at the meeting was Sol Malkin. The previous year he began publishing *Antiquarian Bookman,* which would become a long-running and useful vade mecum for booksellers. *AB* was issued at the start from the offices of *Publishers Weekly* and described as "The Weekly Magazine of the Antiquarian Book Trade." Malkin pointed out the free publicity that an organization of book dealers would receive and the potential value for a bookstore of identifying its membership in the organization. Another important issue addressed was the importance of setting ethical standards applicable throughout the profession.

The February 1949 meeting culminated in a unanimous vote to proceed, and a committee was selected to prepare a recommended set of bylaws for consideration at a follow-up general meeting in March. That meeting was held March 31, 1949, with eighty-one booksellers taking part in the election of interim officers and the scheduling of an initial annual meeting to be held in February 1950. No organization quite exists until it adopts a name. The March 1949 session took care of that requirement by agreeing to call the nascent group the Antiquarian Booksellers' Association of America.

One of the bookmen with strong Book Row connections who participated in the creation of the ABAA, Louis Wavrovics, reminiscing for this account, wrote, "I am proud that in one of the formative meetings of the ABAA, I proposed and it was accepted that any book person in good standing, not necessarily a member, would be entitled to help from the benevolent fund."

Walter Goldwater of the University Place Book Shop took the initiative in establishing the ABAA's membership dues, which began at $10 per year, plus an additional $5 for each additional (later called associate) member. Goldwater and his wife, Eleanor Lowenstein of the Corner Book Shop on Fourth Avenue, were active participants in the ABAA's programs. Wilfred Pesky of Schulte's Book Store, one of the Fourth Avenue booksellers who emerged as a leader in the ABAA, was among the founders and served the organization as a secretary.

On May 29, 1999, the ABAA celebrated its fiftieth anniversary and looked ahead confidently to an expanding future for antiquarian booksellers both in traditional bookstores and via burgeoning electronic media with access to a global market. Through the Internet, prospects apparently widen to a mile short of infinity.

Bernard M. Rosenthal, in his December 15, 1986, Sol M. Malkin Lecture in Bibliography at Columbia University, "The Gentle Invasion," credited Continental émigré booksellers of the 1930s and 1940s, who left (or fled) Europe and settled in New York to sell antiquarian books, with having major roles in establishing the ABAA and in winning credibility for the term "antiquarian bookseller." We can grant the Continental knowledge, scholarly insight, and important contribution of these great booksellers in finding and marketing what Richard S. Wormser (second president of ABAA, 1952–1954) labeled "uncommon rare books" and in helping establish the ABAA. The parallel and arguably equal contribution of Book Row booksellers to the same cause should also be acknowledged.

The ABAA was organized to stimulate book collecting and set high standards for the profession. By joining the ABAA, a bookseller agrees to comply with the organization's rules and regulations regarding fair practice and to obey as well the international code of fair practice that governs bookselling, dealer to dealer and dealer to customer. The ABAA stated its objective to encourage interest in rare books and manuscripts and to maintain "the highest standards in the antiquarian booktrade." The obligation to set and enforce standards led to the establishment of the ABAA Code of Ethics, whose enforcement has resulted in members being censured, suspended, and expelled for code violations such as selling forgeries, unethical business practices, and fraud.

The 1986–88 president of the ABAA, Edwin V. Glaser, commenting on "The ABAA at Fifty," stated, "For many members, the ABAA truly came of age in the 1980s when a prominent former member was expelled because of his alleged failure to abide by the Association's Code of Ethics." A courtroom confrontation resulted when the expelled dealer fought back, and the ABAA, upholding its principles in this landmark case, won. This courtroom vindication of the ABAA's position and its consistent emphasis on rigorous standards have made the membership insignia an instant confidence builder among book buyers.

Glaser as ABAA president at the thirty-eighth annual meeting in 1987 summarized reasons for booksellers to be members. He called it obvious that active participants in the profession would "want to join together with your peers for mutual examination of the issues facing all of us, to exchange ideas and information, to create cooperatively such things as book fairs and directories, and to provide a respected entity that will assure others in our universe, such as collectors and librarians, that membership is a hallmark of quality and reliability. And lastly, but just as importantly, to provide a vehicle for socializing and good fellowship with our peers." Glaser could have been echoing sentiments manifest at the start of the Fourth Avenue Booksellers' Association forty-five years earlier.

First Fair and the ABAA Bookshop

Great Britain's trade association, the Antiquarian Booksellers Association, was founded in 1906. An international body, the International League of Antiquarian Booksellers (ILAB) / Ligue Internationale de la Librairie Ancienne (LILA), was organized in 1948. The 1948 effort in Europe served to inspire and accelerate the parallel move in New York. The ABAA in 1949, the year after its formation, joined this organization. Madeleine Stern wrote in *Old Books, Rare Friends* (1997), "Antiquarian booksellers all over the world had found that, despite differences in nationality and individuality, they shared a common purpose: to make rare books understandable, desirable, a part of modern life."

Stern considered the founding of the ABAA a remarkable mid-twentieth-century achievement in view of the highly independent and individualistic natures of antiquarian bookmen. The same brand of amazement accompanied the 1942 formation of the Fourth Avenue Booksellers' Association, whose charter members clearly shared in spades the attributes of independence and individualism found throughout the profession. Collective self-interest dictated the 1942 move, and the Book Row example was well known to the founders of the ILAB and the ABAA. The ABAA started with a dominant New York City component, but it grew rapidly into a national organization with over three hundred members committed to the ideals of fairness and just treatment rigidly demanded of them.

A successful antiquarian book fair held the previous year in Great Britain led up to the ABAA's sponsorship of the Antiquarian Book Fair held in April 1960 at the Steinway Concert Hall on West Fifty-seventh Street, with admission free to all. Several Book Row firms took booths and reported what many then viewed as surprisingly excellent results. The enthusiasm of visitors and the profits of dealers made the fair a triumph, and its success led to book fairs soon becoming a nationwide enterprise that is still booming in the twenty-first century.

From New York to Everywhere, U.S.A., book fairs became a popular means of displaying wares to collectors and to new prospects eager for bargains or just curious about what's going on. Now book fairs, the same as catalogues, are a proven means of reaching the public and in the process selling books, sometimes highly valuable books. Half a century after the start of the ABAA, Lawrence and Nancy Goldstone, in *Slightly Chipped: Footnotes in Booklore* (1999), wrote about ABAA fairs as events "filled with treasures. . . . It is awe-inspiring to walk up and down the aisles seeing one museum piece after another." At a New York ABAA fair they marveled to see a "pristine first edition" of Sir Isaac Newton's *Philosophiae naturalis principia mathematica* (1687) and to see it "snapped up immediately" at $210,000, which the dealer called "a very reasonable price."

Cooperative bookselling worked well at book fairs; would it also work in a similarly cooperative bookshop? The ABAA in 1963 experimented with this untested concept by opening an association bookshop, the Antiquarian Booksellers Center, at Rockefeller Center. The center served as a popular site for exhibiting antiquarian books provided by ABAA members, and it continued in operation until 1987. Located on Fifth Avenue, the center attracted walk-in visitors with passports from many countries, and it reaffirmed what had been demonstrated on Book Row, that cooperation among booksellers was no chimera. It could happen, it could work, and it could benefit those who took part.

The ABAA, unlike the Fourth Avenue Booksellers' Association, has been an organization demonstrating the will, stamina, commitment, and health for institutional longevity. The ABAA membership credential is a convincing and reassuring one for collectors visiting an unfamiliar bookstore. It indicates that while you may pay plenty, you probably won't overpay (not much anyway) and you can trust that what you buy is what you're told you're buying. Those are not trivial benefits in connection with antiquarian items.

Speaking on the occasion of the ABAA's fiftieth anniversary, Edwin V. Glaser observed, "Despite the many and profound changes in the technology of bookselling—more to the point because of those changes—an ABAA and what it stands for is just as vital to a healthy antiquarian book trade today as it was in those formative years . . . two elements are the same as they were in 1949. A book is a book is a book, whether bought and sold in printed catalogues, at a book fair, or on the Internet. And a dealer is still rewarded for his or her expertise, experience, and reputation for fair dealing, for which the ABAA logo stands as a hallmark."

In April 1997 at the annual meeting of the Grolier Club at New York, the president of the ABAA, Bob Fleck, talked about the ABAA in the next century. The title of the address, "ABAA in 2001: Predictions and Pipe Dreams," made clear that the ABAA would still be committed to and resourceful in the cause of inspiring collectors and delivering books to make those collectors simultaneously a lot happier if a little poorer monetarily. Thanks to the antiquarian booksellers, the readers and collectors of 2001 and beyond will of course be considerably richer spiritually and culturally.

CHAPTER SIX

BOOKSELLING IN THE FAMILY WAY

Samuel Weiser · Stanley Gilman · Scheinbaum Brothers · Other Relatives

*My whole theory is that unless one is producing a real
bibliography—with a big B—a catalogue ought to be interesting.
No amount of appearances of infinite learning and scholarship and
that sort of thing can compensate for dullness.*

—GEORGE PARKER WINSHIP

New York City is world famous as the hometown of Big Business, with two capital *B*s. The great financial, industrial, entertainment, communications, and mercantile enterprises maintain corporate headquarters downtown and up in Manhattan, with Wall Street and Madison Avenue as symbolic reference points. Any Who's Who for corporate America emerges top-heavy with New York addresses.

American big businesses present themselves as staunch defenders of capitalism and free enterprise. Yet most are owned by thousands of stockholders, directed by complex management teams, and dependent on high-volume sales to millions of customers worldwide. American big business, in short, as it evolved in the twentieth century, by the twenty-first century was a fine example of old-fashioned collective ownership, sometimes called—are you ready for this?—socialism. But don't tell the New York Stock Exchange or General Motors they can be admired as socialist enclaves. Why upset them with the truth?

Heading back toward Fourth Avenue, the facts are that big business is just the tip of the money berg in New York, that the city on a much larger scale is also millions of people and block after block after block of small businesses. Small businesses from mom-and-pop shops to start-ups with big business aspirations are generally far removed from collective ownership. They typically are the creations of one or maybe a few entrepreneurial partners wagering their own savings and what they can borrow on a new business. Their anxious hope is that hard work and skill will make up for lack of funds and that they'll make a go of it. In secondhand books, some did.

Since the days of William Bradford in colonial times, an encouraging number of those New York small businesses have been bookstores. Los Angeles bookseller Jake Zeitlin wrote about himself and other small business booksellers, "We are the last of the free enterprisers." Free enterpriser, entrepreneur, gambler, dreamer, hard worker, scholar, bibliophile—all these terms and more fit the book dealers of Book Row. Most were strictly on their own, starting on a shoestring, with books from their own libraries or book scouting safaris, and enough cash for shelves and the immediately due rent. A small initial outlay, some personal shelf building, putting up a sign, and they were in business. They weren't turning, as modern high-tech businesses may, to the government's Small Business Administration for a chorus of start-up benefits and breaks. The SBA, established in the 1950s, didn't even exist when the shop builders of Book Row began, and if it had existed, most dealers would have taken for granted it wasn't for them. They could think of themselves perhaps as frontline soldier-patriots, since Franklin Roosevelt had hailed books as "weapons in the war of ideas." Yet even in wartime, patting themselves on the back as merchants in the weapons business would have appealed little to the congenial, peace-favoring eccentrics of Book Row.

Louis Wavrovics was involved in the launching of several small bookstores for himself, his brother Ernest, and others. He wrote, "Let it not be said that I was unavailable when book people needed help. I set up Peter Lader in Martin's Book Store on West Third Street. He had no capital. But he was a customer of ours, and I sensed that he would be happy only in the world of books. I turned over to him a small bookstore I bought, the shelving, the remaining books, and paid the coming month's rent. From such humble circumstances, some bookshops then came into being. Another time for $10.00 worth of used lumber and $10.00 for my labor I built, complete with shelving all around and counters, a place for Larry Sackin, then a book scout. There are many other instances from those days." He also recalled negotiating for Herbert Oxer to acquire a store with a stock of six thousand for $300. Louis Wavrovics reminisced in 1990 from his retirement home at Palm City,

Florida, and acknowledged, "I still sell a few books here and there, every now and then. Bookselling is a lifetime dedication."

Book Row can proudly claim many such dedicated alumni. The city that allowed Book Row to appear (and eventually disappear) doesn't suffer from a shortage of bookstores and never, let us hope, will. Eve Claxton wrote in *New York's 50 Best Bookstores for Book Lovers* (2000), "New York has always been a great city for book lovers, an often persnickety crowd whose every change of taste the city has unfailingly accommodated; so that it has, over the years, become emblematic of the changing currents of bookselling. And it has reflected those changes while reclaiming its core of very special, idiosyncratic bookstores."

The city no longer has but well remembers the special, idiosyncratic, once cherished bookstores of Samuel Weiser, Stanley Gilman, and the Scheinbaum brothers, Al and Sam.

Samuel Weiser—Samuel Weiser Bookstore

The *International Directory of Antiquarian Booksellers* for 1958, on ten-plus pages, lists the antiquarian booksellers for New York City. The third name from the end of the long list is "*Weiser, Samuel*, 117 Fourth Avenue . . . Occultisme/Occultism."

Samuel Weiser, described by a contemporary as a small version of Groucho Marx with a mustache and cigar, began his career in bookselling at Brentano's. By then, Brentano's had evolved from its nineteenth-century status as Agosto Brentano's newsstand in front of the New York Hotel into a literary hangout for Henry Ward Beecher, Edwin Booth, and other writers and actors near Union Square. Brentano's was a publisher and major bookseller when Weiser as a young man worked there as an employee. Brentano's gave beginning bookmen a grounding in selling both new and rare books.

The same as its competitor, the Scribner's Bookstore, Brentano's included a rare book and binding department, which was headed for a time by Laurence Gomme. In 1949 Gomme was celebrating his fiftieth year as a bookseller when he was unanimously elected the first interim president of the Antiquarian Booksellers' Association of America, at the time of its formation. (The redoubtable Walter Goldwater, who had something controversial to say about practically everybody, observed concerning Gomme, "Since he had an English accent, which he had preserved for sixty years, that having the English accent and being old, people assumed that he knew something. . . . I've never discovered whether it was true or not.")

Samuel Weiser, after an apprenticeship at Brentano's, in the 1920s began a long career running his own bookstores; and there was no question that he did know a lot about books and what it took to sell them on a large scale and earn a good living. Also in the book business at an early age was Sam Weiser's younger brother, Ben, who had first worked as a Brentano's messenger boy running errands after school.

Starting in 1926 Sam Weiser owned and ran the Samuel Weiser Bookstore at several different locations in or near the Book Row area. *The Encyclopedia of New York City* (1995), under "booksellers," lists Samuel Weiser as a specialist in the occult located at 132 East Twenty-fourth Street. His principal locations were for many years 117 Fourth Avenue and later 845 Broadway and 734 Broadway near the corner of Astor Place.

Ben Weiser worked with his brother starting early in the 1930s. In time he opened his own bookshop nearby, the Pickwick, at 73 Fourth Avenue. The war years took Ben away, but he rejoined Sam Weiser in 1949. The Weisers offered a large number of books in traditional areas. They also developed major specialty areas, including the occult, New Age, and Eastern philosophy.

The Weisers learned that a store benefited from the recognition it gained as a specialty house in book domains where most bookstores offer only a small number of titles. The literature in the occult and related fields was vast, and those interested in such subjects turned out to be plentiful. The store gained a worldwide following among magicians, students of the supernatural, and many others intrigued about topics often dismissed elsewhere as curiosa.

The Weisers became recognized as international experts, and their business correspondingly developed a customer base that reached far beyond America's borders. Among their customers were the famous magicians, spiritualists, conjurers, and others of like bent. One patron said to use the store was Ehrich Weiss, the illusionist and son of a rabbi, whose own books, including *The Right Way to Do Wrong: An Exposé of Successful Criminals* (1906), *Handcuff Secrets* (1907), *The Unmasking of Robert-Houdin* (1908), *Miracle Mongers and Their Methods* (1920), and *A Magician Among the Spirits* (1924), are now valuable to many collectors. History knows Ehrich Weiss better by the name he took as the world-famous performer and escape artist Harry Houdini. Writing in the article on conjuring for the 1926 *Encyclopaedia Britannica,* Houdini credited his success to "great physical strength" and to being "slightly bowlegged."

The success of the Samuel Weiser Bookstore can be credited to the customary nourishments of bookshop well-being—diligence, persistence, hard work, knowledge, stock maintenance, and enduring commitment, as well as commitment to endure.

THE WEISER MOVES

Following its tenure at the Fourth Avenue location, the store joined others in the move to adjoining Broadway due to the costs of urban change and the surge of appetites for greater income than bookstores could pay from properties on the avenue. Broadway turned out to be a hospitable locale for Weiser and several others, such as the Strand. The Samuel Weiser Bookstore became an important fixture on Broadway. The move from Fourth Avenue to 845 Broadway gave the Weisers a space of six thousand square feet, including a large basement where they stocked over a hundred thousand volumes, with substantial holdings in Americana, biography, history, literature, philosophy, theology.

The store's primary focus continued to be the categories that had made it a bookstore celebrity among occultists and that produced significant sales from both walk-in and mail-order customers. A not uncommon Book Row practice was to place interesting books in basements if they were dry, warm, and usable. Many of the Weiser occult titles were stocked in the capacious area downstairs. Book Row regulars remember book quests in Weiser's basement as well as several other subterranean spaces where lights were low and hopes were high.

Sam Weiser was a gentleman bookseller admired among his peers. Maggie DuPriest shared her memories of Sam Weiser for this account. She noted that she first became friends with her Book Row colleague when he visited her bookshop in Miami. "It was Sam who told me that I could not be a bookseller and a book collector," she wrote. "You see, I wanted to keep all the special things that came my way for my own collection. It did not take me too long to learn that I did not have enough capital to keep everything I wanted."

When DuPriest was next in New York, she decided it was a good day to walk from where she was on Seventy-fifth Street to the Weiser Book Row location. "It was in the middle of July and as I went downtown, I began to feel very strange. When I finally arrived at Weiser's I promptly fainted, the first and only time I did that. Sam was there, but I think it was his son Donald who revived me with a cold glass of lemonade. I don't remember what I bought then, but they always had books not in their specialty, and I used to get some wonderful buys there."

Sam and Ben Weiser built up the Broadway store and ran it jointly until Sam Weiser had a heart attack and was forced to curtail his activities. Ben Weiser subsequently ran the store, and he was joined by his nephew Donald Weiser, the son of Sam Weiser. In the 1960s, under Donald Weiser, the store, following an old New York City tradition, added the profitable reprinting of occult material and the publication of selected volumes to its operations.

Late in the 1960s, the Samuel Weiser Bookstore underwent another metamorphosis and migration. Led by Donald Weiser, the store moved farther down Broadway to number 734, close to Astor Place. The 845 Broadway site that had served the Weisers well was taken over by Robert Richman. Richman had been in the book business since 1917, with shops in Chicago, Detroit, Newark, New Haven, and Bridgeport. Richman began his first incarnation in the Book Row area with three hundred thousand books of general stock and the assistance of his wife, Ann Richman, along with Abe Katz and Jack Garbus. Richman, then in his seventies, told Manuel B. Tarshish for his *Publishers Weekly* articles, "I never made a dime—but we've had so much fun!"

At 734 Broadway, the Weiser Bookstore, chiefly under Donald Weiser, assisted by Fred Mendel, concentrated on its specialty areas with new books as well as old. The primary stock was the forty thousand occult titles taken along to 734 Broadway from the 845 basement. The books at the new address occupied two floors, and they kept Weiser's a world leader in the occult field. The store offered both imported and domestic works and also functioned as a book wholesaler. Eventually the publication division of the company was separately maintained at 625 Broadway. Donald Weiser put his father's long-lasting Book Row business through one more geographic leap, from Manhattan to Maine, where he continued to sell books and serve customers.

The Samuel Weiser Bookstore was one of the bookshops issuing regular catalogues that were fun to browse and sources of good buys. As a specialty store, it reflected the observation by Robert A. Wilson, proprietor of New York's Phoenix Book Shop, in *Modern Book Collecting* (1980), that "catalogs issued by specialist dealers are probably the most important means of acquiring the better items you need." Wilson highlighted the importance of dropping everything and checking through a catalogue immediately upon its arrival, to avoid losing out to a quicker collector. Following this dictum no doubt repaid the recipients of Weiser catalogues as they made haste to get their orders in.

No effort was invested to make the catalogues anything more than functional lists of books with adequate descriptions. The salesmanship lay in whatever appeal a particular book had and in a modest price that could make the appeal affordable. The Weiser catalogues would not win a top place in book-collecting history, praise that C. Thomas Tanselle, in "The Literature of Book Collecting," from *Book Collecting* (1977), assigned to catalogues taking more of an "imaginative approach," such as those from Scribner's in the 1930s, when John Carter and David Randall supervised rare books there.

The Weiser catalogues were as unpretentious and straightforward as the book trade was generally on Book Row. They mingled a horde of low-cost items with a few higher-priced rarities, and it was the reader's job to choose. Most catalogue prices were modest, and quite a few fell below the $2 threshold that Charles Everitt considered rock bottom for a catalogue. He wrote in *The Adventures of a Treasure Hunter,* "The catalogue dealer is one step up the social ladder. With the present-day price of printing, any book he catalogues at less than a couple of dollars must be regarded as a loss leader, even if he got it for nothing, as he very probably did, tossed in with some tidbit that he paid good money for."

The Weiser 1976–77 catalogue from 625 Broadway of their own occult and Oriental philosophy publications as well as selected titles from other publishers included a number of Aleister Crowley Equinox reprints priced as low as $1.50. The original editions of many Crowley titles now cost hundreds, sometimes thousands, as is the case of *The Diary of a Drug Fiend* (1922). This catalogue has a cover mildly decorated with occult symbols and offers books in the store's specialty area under the headings General, Alchemy, Astral

Projection, Astrology, Color & Aura, Gurdjieff, Herbs-Cooking-Health-and-Acupuncture, Magic, Oriental, Palmistry & Handwriting Analysis, Qabalah, Sufism, Tarot, Tarot Cards, and Witchcraft. These were books seldom if ever encountered in catalogues from other bookshops. It cost $4 to get a collection of rituals for pagan holidays. A book by two practicing British witches, Patricia and Arnold Crowther, *The Witches Speak* (1976), for $3.50, "dispels much of the false publicity surrounding Witchcraft."

At the 845 Broadway location, Weiser issued a number of topic-oriented catalogues. Number 65, "Biography and History," included 1,765 entries, starting with Harold Acton's *The Last Medici* (1932) at $3.50. Examining this catalogue, current collectors and libraries have to lament if they consider today's much sadder, since far from Weiser's, prices. When a price soars above $10 or even $5 in a Weiser catalogue, it commands attention. Among the highest prices noted in Catalogue No. 65 is $12.50 for an 1849 edition in three volumes of Washington Irving's *The Life and Voyages of Christopher Columbus* (1828).

Catalogue No. 68, "Archeology, Classical Studies, Anthropology, Mythology, Folklore, Witchcraft," has 1,193 entries and ends with A. E. Waite's *Devil Worship in France* (1896) at a whopping $15. The Weiser cataloguer in No. 68 may have gotten a bit lightheaded when, among all the $2 and $3 prices, he had to post "1132 Beaumont, John. *An Historical, Physiological and Theological Treatise of Spirits, Apparitions, Witchcrafts, and Other Magical Practices* (1705), $50.00," and at $60.00, item 366, "Higgins, Godfrey. *The Celtic Druids* (1829)."

Later catalogues, such as No. 81 ("Americana") and No. 82 ("Philosophy—Psychology—Theology") carried on the Weiser policy of good typography and clearly defined categories to facilitate reading. No. 81 is a modern grab bag of dreams for collectors of western Americana, with Stanley Vestal's *Sitting Bull* (1965), $5; John and Alan Lomax's *Cowboy Songs and Other Frontier Ballads* (1945), $5.25; and two J. Frank Dobie first editions, *Cow People* (1964), $4; and *The Mustangs* (1952), $5. These were bargain prices then, cause for refined shouts of triumph later.

There may be a tinge of cruelty in teasing ourselves about prices that used to be. However, the catalogues of Samuel Weiser and others also convey a strong sense of the values, interests, attitudes, and views that used to be prevalent as well. We learn about the past from perusing the book catalogues for bookshops that were—and whose books still are. History professor Ulrich B. Phillips provided an inscription for the William L. Clements Library at the University of Michigan: "In darkness dwells the people which knows its annals not." Book catalogues are part of those annals. Poet Leigh Hunt declared, "A catalogue is not a mere catalogue or list of saleable things, as the uninitiated may fancy. . . . Judge then, what the case must be with a catalogue of books, the very titles of which run the rounds of the whole world, visible and invisible, geographies, biographies, histories, loves, hates, joys, sorrows, cookeries, sciences, fashions, and eternity!"

Since the Weiser books ranged from archaeology to theology and witchcraft with large concentrations on occultism, Orientalism, philosophy, and world religions, the poet's reference to finding the "visible and invisible . . . and eternity" in book catalogues was certainly accurate about the Weiser catalogues. No. 82, with 2,205 titles, was especially strong, with a wide selection in philosophy representing practically every school of thought on the phenomenon of life. But no more of those prices right now, please, we can only stand so much.

STANLEY GILMAN—GILMAN'S BOOKSTORE

The *International Directory of Antiquarian Booksellers* (1951–52), produced by P. H. Muir and Andre Poursin in English and French, was the first such publication done on a noncommercial basis and with the cooperation of national antiquarian bookseller associations. The book was published by the

International League of Antiquarian Booksellers (ILAB), organized in 1948, a year before the Antiquarian Booksellers' Association of America (ABAA). The editors, introducing the United States of America (Etats-Unis d'Amérique) section, commented on "the comparatively recent formation of the A.B.A.A." and noted that ABAA membership would be indicated where applicable in the entries.

In the New York City portion of the U.S.A. section, the first entry is "*Aeronautica*, P.O. Box 131 Cooper Station (3). *SPECIAL. Aeronautics. Aeronautique. (A.B.A.A.)*" This was the name used by Stanley Gilman for his antiquarian book business specializing in aeronautical materials. Seven years later, in the *International Directory of Antiquarian Booksellers* edition for 1958, he still used the post office box as a mail drop but was listed as "Stanley Gilman," with American history, general literature (out of print), and periodicals (newspaper history) as his specialties. Another nineteen years later, in the 1977 issue of the *International Directory*, Stanley Gilman was still present as an antiquarian dealer in the same primary categories.

The 1977 directory contained a preface by Stanley Crowe, president of the International League of Antiquarian Booksellers. He identified the directory as the sixth edition of a series that had an established reputation and value to booksellers, librarians, collectors, and "all those interested in the realm of books, manuscripts, prints and allied materials whether nationally or internationally, and of whatever period." Crowe noted that only members of their national associations were included in the directory and that "this provides an assurance when dealing with them."

These directory references for Stanley Gilman indicate his long involvement in antiquarian bookselling. Through many years that grew to decades, Stanley as well as his brothers David and Clarence Gilman became memorable figures in the history of Booksellers' Row and bookselling in New York. Stanley Gilman was described as a quiet, studious-looking, slim six-footer. If a mad movie producer had conceived the idea of remaking *High Noon* using Book Row people as the cast (and why not?), Stanley Gilman would have received the Gary Cooper role.

Following the footsteps of so many others, Stanley Gilman began his career in books as a scout before World War II. The importance of knowledgeable and diligent book scouts to the dealers of Book Row cannot be exaggerated. Gilman, from all accounts, was among the best-informed and hardest-working scouts, and several Fourth Avenue booksellers were among his regular contacts.

Gilman learned about operating a shop working for Peter Stammer. He opened a small bookstore in 1964 at 237 East Ninth Street. The stock of about five thousand books was dominated by books in Gilman's established specialty areas of aviation, ephemeral Americana, and journalism. His continued use of a post office box reflected the fact that most Gilman sales came through mail orders. His customers were found predominantly among private collectors as well as public and institutional libraries.

Stanley Gilman issued regular book lists to alert the collectors and libraries on his mailing roster concerning his recent acquisitions. He also conscientiously responded when he could with quotations in answer to want requests received directly and to published book wants in publications such as *Book Source Monthly*.

Gilman was well respected by his Book Row contemporaries and remembered with special affection. Howard Frisch, who had a bookstore in the 1950s at 116 Christopher Street, was among the bookmen with friendly memories of Stanley Gilman both for the books and for the company. "I knew Stanley. His store was on East Ninth Street, and I used to go in regularly," Frisch recalled. The motives of the visits were twofold, to ask for specific wants and to meet his fellow bookman again for stimulating book talk.

In 1990 Louis Wavrovics, responding to inquiries about the booksellers he knew from the 1940s on, wrote, "I have fond memories of fellow booksellers, famous personalities, and interesting characters that gravitated to the shops. By the way is Secretary Stanley Gilman still around?" Wavrovics was informed that in 1990, Stanley Gilman was indeed still around. He was retired from bookselling, living with his wife, Dorothy, on Monroe Street, and enjoying a well-earned right to read more of the books he had spent decades selling to others.

THE ASSOCIATIONS' LOYALIST

As noted earlier, the two most important professional membership groups uniting the booksellers of Fourth Avenue and environs were the Fourth Avenue Booksellers' Association and the ABAA. These were the groups that gave the dealers professional status, wide contact with their peers, and a united front. Stanley Gilman was an important contributor to the founding and subsequent functioning of each.

In 1942, when the Fourth Avenue dealers held their historic organizational meeting at 73 Fourth Avenue and chose the original officers, the esteem Stanley Gilman had won among other book professionals led to his election as the recording secretary. Later, "recording" disappeared from the title, and Gilman was simply "secretary of the association," a position that in effect made him the permanent record keeper, voice, and representative of the organization.

Prior to the establishment of the ABAA, Stanley Gilman was among those who took part in the exploratory discussions, as one of "the leading figures of the time in the trade," according to Edwin V. Glaser in his 1999 paper "The ABAA at Fifty: Notes Toward a History of the Antiquarian Booksellers' Association of America."

Gilman was the only active bookseller from Book Row participating in those ABAA discussions who had been part of the 1942 Fourth Avenue efforts to unite booksellers for mutual benefit and advancement. His experience from the Fourth Avenue Booksellers' Association debates, organizing activities, and subsequent collaborative operations added a practical condiment of realistic knowledge to the ABAA proceedings. The relatively smooth launching of the ABAA owed Stanley Gilman and beyond him other Book Row booksellers a debt of gratitude plain to see but hard to measure.

Gilman's contributions to his fellow bookmen through these associations earned him recognition as an important contributor to the history of New York and American antiquarian bookselling during the twentieth century. He made these contributions while operating a mail-order book business through his post office box and keeping up a respected ABAA bookshop in a cramped twenty-by-thirty-foot space on Ninth Street.

BOOKS IN THE FAMILY

As we have seen, Book Row businesses were not uncommonly family affairs, especially among siblings. One in the family became a bookseller, and his brother or sister followed—Sam and Ben Weiser, Ernest and Louis

Wavrovics, Aaron and David Mendoza, Louis and Regina Cohen. Another surname is equally significant on the Book Row sibling list, with brothers Stanley, David, and Clarence Gilman individually and jointly achieving prominence in New York bookselling.

The Gilman brothers operated bookshops profitably; however, they were particularly noted for their success selling books utilizing lists and catalogues through the U.S. mails to reach potential customers instead of waiting for them to walk in off Ninth Street, Broadway, or Fourth Avenue. Stanley Gilman, with choice books in specialty areas, relied on carefully culled mailing lists to inform collectors and libraries about items of likely interest.

David and Clarence Gilman issued unpretentious catalogues, which were essentially book lists with few descriptions, from "Gilman's, Crompond, New York," in a wide range of categories. The catalogues were printed black-and-white with no artsy come-hither appeal about them, but they displayed a shrewd sense of skillful book advertising on the covers, with catch phrases of the type that book buyers read and often heed sufficiently to inspect the contents of a catalogue:

IF IT IS OUT OF PRINT, WE MAY HAVE IT.
YOUR GUARANTEE: RETURN ANY ITEM.
ORDER WITH CONFIDENCE; YOU CAN RETURN IT.
50 YEARS OF BOOK SELLING EXPERIENCE.
We Have About 50,000 Miscellaneous Items in Stock and About 15,000 Old Novels.

The Gilman catalogues typically concentrated on a specific area, such as "Labor and the Labor Movement" and "India, Indian Literature," but they also beguiled recipients into taking a look-see inside by adding a second, tempting, and deliberately vague category, such as "Old and Rare Books" or "Scarce and Interesting Books." (Rare? Scarce? Interesting? Let me find out what's involved here.) What was involved, catalogue readers discovered, were several hundred worthwhile, inexpensive books, all in "good, clean, sound condition" and in "original cloth binding." Considering the typical prices and the promised books, the suspicion is strong that these catalogues effectively generated sales for the Gilman brothers. The catalogue cover notice of about fifty thousand miscellaneous items and fifteen thousand novels probably produced many inquiries as readers and collectors tried to find out if the Gilmans had any specific desiderata for them somewhere within Mount Miscellaneous and all those aged works of fiction.

To round off the Gilman account and end back on Book Row, note that all three Gilman brothers, Stanley, David, and Clarence, according to Manuel Tarshish in his 1969 *Publishers Weekly* series, early in their bookselling careers were on the staff of Peter Stammer at his 61 Fourth Avenue bookshop. As other Stammer employees before them, such as Sam Dauber, they simultaneously learned the secondhand book business and suffered the cantankerous ways of their sometimes irascible boss. Youth, of course, is designed to juggle both learning and stress. If the Gilman boys occasionally had their feelings hurt, they also received practical instructions in bookselling through on-the-job experience that money can't buy.

Harry Patrick Gold in his blithely self-indulgent, impenetrable, and paradoxically beguiling verse autobiography, *The Dolphin's Path: A Bookman's Sequel to the Odyssey of Homer* (1979), included memorable descriptions of Peter Stammer, his shop, and the harassed crew. Gold depicted the Gilmans in front of the store refusing payment for a bin book because they were "in their out" and shouting, *"Pay inside!"* Another time Gold bought a batch of Stammer's bargain books because he had "spied a prize" among them, the first American printed book on sports. Stammer took the money, said, "You're too smart a lad to pay ten cents for dreck," and asked why he bought them. Gold identified the prize to the "Book Row dean" and "Peter Stammer shrieked with a deafening roar. His guts burst! The buttons snapped off his undershorts! . . . 'fools! come here! You Gilman boys let a fortune slip! You're all fired! To the river garbage scows,—jump off the pier!' The next morning, they came to man his ship. Stammer's bite seemed sharp, but lacked real teeth. His dentures bore no hate for HIS bloop. A staged fake was his blown fuse. No ire was concealed beneath his theatrical agonized whoop. The Gilman boys played their roles well; they mastered the silent undersell."

A fourth Gilman, Peter Stammer's secretary, Bessie, was also with the firm and the heroine of the well-circulated Stammer story about their falling-out that led to the silent treatment for several years because the old bookman was too much of a softie (or too smart) to let her go.

As did the Gilmans, the brothers Sam and Al Scheinbaum developed mail-order book businesses as well as successful bookstores. Sam Scheinbaum began on Fourth Avenue in a space at the Bible House in 1926. He called his store the Parnassus Book Shop. Christopher Morley's 1917 charmer of a novel about bookselling, *Parnassus on Wheels,* was well on its way to classic status in 1926; but Morley and his bookseller Roger Mifflin didn't own Parnassus. Every bookstore in a sense qualifies as another Parnassus, since the original, a mountain near Delphi in Greece, had two peaks, one consecrated to Bacchus, for readers who appreciate a small glass of wine with the next chapter, and the other to Apollo and the Muses, who give Parnassus its connection with music, poetry, and literature, and thus its distinctive literary panache.

Al Scheinbaum joined Sam at Parnassus, but left in the early 1930s for the less-confining work of being a book scout. After service in World War II, Al took over another Bible House bookshop at 45 Fourth Avenue, the former location of Mosk's (for Moskowitz), made available, as was often the case, by the death of the proprietor.

Al Scheinbaum called his bookstore the Colonial Book Service. He remained at the Bible House until it was demolished in the mid-1950s. The Colonial Book Service stayed in the neighborhood and eventually was relocated to 23 East Fourth Street, between the Bowery and Lafayette Place. A previous resident was affiliated with the large De Vinne Press business operated by Theodore L. De Vinne, printer of the nine-volume *Century Dictionary and Cyclopedia, Scribner's Monthly,* and many other periodicals and fine books sought now as superb examples of the book as a work of art.

Al Scheinbaum, assisted by Max Roe and Jack Dudzik, specialized in the humanities and belles lettres. He stored a quarter of a million books in a four-thousand-square-foot space. The Colonial Book Service issued catalogues biannually and derived over 90 percent of its sales from college libraries. The walk-in trade, however, brought the excitement and variety of human interaction, such as the time a customer selected $150 worth of first editions and tried to convert Book Row into a collector's casino by tossing double or nothing for the cost. The customers he met at the Bible House and on East Fourth Street helped Al Scheinbaum realize, "All my life has been interesting." During that interesting life, along with bookselling, Scheinbaum found time for additional service as a local theater critic.

Sam Scheinbaum after decades on Fourth Avenue at his version of Parnassus had a bookstore in the Forty-second Street area. Both Scheinbaums at their separate shops primarily offered out-of-print materials. After his New York bookselling decades, Sam Scheinbaum acted on the impulse that like a sun-seeking virus seemed to hit senior Book Row dealers who didn't stay in New York. He retired to Florida, where at one time a Book Row alumni association could have commanded a crowd. Al Scheinbaum, by the 1990s at Pleasantville, New York, had stayed closer to the familiar neighborhoods where he scouted, bought, and sold books.

Ira and Harry Friedman were another pair of bookselling brothers whose shop between Fifth and Sixth Avenues on West Twenty-third Street had a large general stock with specialties in Americana and remainders. The brothers left the area when Twenty-third Street became a no-parking zone and business suffered. Harry Friedman opened a shop in White Plains, and when he reached his late seventies sold books from his home. Ira Friedman opened a bookshop in Port Washington. Following his death, his son-in-law, with no experience in secondhand books, started the Kennikat Publishing Company, which kept Ira Friedman's name and legacy alive.

James F. Drake was a key member of the rare-book staff that Robert Dodd assembled at Dodd, Mead & Company, Eighth Street and Broadway, in the last fifth of the nineteenth century. Drake joined Dodd, Mead in the 1880s. By 1905 he had a West Fortieth Street shop of his own, initially called the Association Book Company, later James F. Drake, Inc. His objective for the business, he claimed, was "buying and selling free from the friction of bargaining." Drake became known for his great books, especially association and inscribed works, and for his great customers, including William Loring Andrews and Henry E. Huntington. Drake was the first president of the Old Book Table and "the ideal bookman," according to Sol Malkin. He was also the father of another major book duo, *James H. and Marston E. Drake*, who ran their father's business after his death in 1933. Among book people Marston was known as the Colonel, in reference to activities beyond the bookstore. Walter Goldwater remembered their determined focus on first editions and their association with Stevenson, Kipling, and Galsworthy titles and collections. After the brothers died, James in 1965 and Marston in 1966, the stock was appraised by Laurence Gomme and sold to the University of Texas at Austin. John R. Payne wrote about the acquisition in "James F.

Drake Inc., New York and Texas," *Library Chronicle of the University of Texas* (February 1972). "The tradition of the Drakes lives on at Texas," observed Payne. Such book migrations from New York to the American Southwest make Book Row America a geographic bibliofact.

The three sisters in books, Louis Cohen's daughters *Judith, Naomi, and Adina,* at the Argosy Book Store, formed in all likelihood the greatest sister combination for bookselling that ever existed or is likely to come along. In the April 15, 1991 issue of *AB,* Jacob Chernofsky reported that Judith Lowry specialized in modern first editions, that Naomi Hample took charge of manuscripts and autographs, and that Adina Cohen worked with rare books and was active in all departments. "All three of the sisters consider themselves interchangeable with one another," Chernofsky noted.

I. R. (Ike) and Jack, the brothers Brussel, would have to receive votes as the outstanding brother combination in bookselling and they are certainly strong contenders as the best-remembered book brothers. Ike, as he was known almost everywhere antiquarian books were marketed worldwide, compiled important bibliographies on American and English first editions, called himself "the Last of the Great Scouts," and used the acronym LOGS after his signature. Jack Brussel approached equity in fame with his brother as a book scout, owner of Book Row shops, and publisher of unexpurgated erotica classics in moderately priced reprints. The Brussels merit and will have a more detailed segment of their own in these Book Row chronicles.

Let these relative references end with *Adolph and Samuel Stager,* father and son, of the Cadmus Book Shop on West Forty-sixth Street and other Manhattan addresses. They were pretty far uptown from Fourth Avenue, but they seemed to have the Book Row spirit by adding the spice of eccentricity and the wine of novelty to their bookselling activities. Cadmus was particularly recognized for its Americana, due to the strengths in that area of Stager and his colleague over an eighteen-year period, Charles P. Everitt. At its midtown location, Cadmus did well from both walk-in and catalogue sales. The catalogues include fascinating tidbits about the books offered and make entertaining, informative reading nearly half a century after the books and their prices are just friendly ghosts of the past. Here is an item from Catalogue No. 193 in 1956, "Personalized American History":

340 WEEMS, Mason Locke, HIS WORKS AND WAYS. Vol. 1, a bibliography of his writings, by Paul Leicester Ford. Vols. 2 and 3, his letters, 1784–1825. Edited by Emily E. F. Skeel. Facsimiles and illustrations, 3 vols., Royal 8vo. boards, gilt tops, untrimmed, New York, 1929. $110.00

Only 200 copies printed. Weems was pastor of George Washington's parish in Virginia, but forsaking the cloth, he made connections with Matthew Carey, the Philadelphia bookseller and publisher, and for 31 years was an itinerant salesman for him. This period was not just plain sailing for him, as he and Carey had many a breezy tilt and hurricane quarrel, as the letters show. The bibliography, which the brilliant Ford undertook, was not finished by him, but completed after his demise by his sister. It is one of the most thorough of any bibliographies, giving an account of 254 issued of Weems' various works, of which 84 are the famous "Life of Washington". In our opinion, one of the tour de forces of American biography.

The scope and contents of the Cadmus catalogues suggest that the store itself must have been a browser's delight for those drawn to American history and Americana. Walter Goldwater, reminiscing in his colorful fashion about the New York booksellers of his day, clearly felt a certain wry fascination with the Stagers at their West Forty-sixth Street store. Both Adolph and his son (who was called "Son") were usually at the store. In all weathers and seasons, the elder Stager kept his hat and usually his coat on as if just dropping in. Outdoor garments indoors was a disguise, according to Goldwater, because for years he collected on a disability insurance policy in effect if he didn't work. "Actually, he was the one who was in charge of the shop," said Goldwater, but he was always in a position to claim he was just visiting his son. Goldwater's yarn is a good one; let's hope it's true. Samuel Stager took over the store from his father in 1943, and it continued as a Stager family business into the 1950s.

Bookselling on Book Row and across New York City was often and sometimes fascinatingly a family affair.

CHAPTER SEVEN

A Book Row Odysseus and Other Bookmen True
Harry Gold · Milton Applebaum · Henry Chafetz · Sidney Solomon

*I want a poor student to have the same means of indulging his
learned curiosity, of following his rational pursuits, of consulting
the same authorities, of fathoming the most intricate enquiry, as
the richest man in the kingdom.*

—Antonio Genesio Maria Panizzi

Notwithstanding librarian Randolph G. Adams's famous warning
to collectors, "Librarians as Enemies of Books" (*Library Quarterly*, July 1937),
historically the libraries of great collectors have often gone to institutions
such as university and public libraries. At such book service centers, fine collections have sometimes been stored and handled with conserving love and
preserving respect. In other places, as Adams noted, inherited collections
were treated as just more books, often old and thus "useless." It depends obviously on whether the librarians involved can be book lovers as well as efficiency and administration lovers.

Some collectors with pelf, persistence, and commitment, and perhaps
devoted offspring, have their collections maintained in perpetuity at special
libraries designed both to serve an appreciative public and to protect irreplaceable and invaluable rarities. In this farsighted group were John Carter
Brown (thanks to his son John Nicholas Brown) at Brown University,
William L. Clements at the University of Michigan, Henry C. Folger, Henry
E. Huntington, and J. P. Morgan.

Book people know about them and insist on time in Ann Arbor for the
Clements, in California for the Huntington, in Providence for the Brown, in
Washington, D.C., for the Folger, and in New York for the Morgan. Such
stops honor not only magnificent books but also the resourceful finders and

buyers of outstanding books. Superb collections occasionally do land at existing libraries and receive devoted care, for example, the Harry Elkins Widener Collection at Harvard.

Italian revolutionary Antonio Panizzi, later Sir Anthony Panizzi, fled Italy under sentence of death, became a librarian, and in spite of that, is a shoo-in, first-ballot inductee for the book lover's hall of fame, which should, of course, be on Fourth Avenue—let the committee be formed. He made the British Museum Library a center of the book by purchasing more books; by building that oasis of scholarship the reading room; and, through friendship with collector Thomas Grenville, by acquiring the Grenville Library of over twenty thousand volumes for the British Museum. Yet even book lover Panizzi, who advocated putting books within reach of all, couldn't adequately protect the Grenville collection at first. "For years the books lay on the floor in piles and parcels, a scandal which must have almost broken the heart of Holden, Grenville's devoted personal servant, who came with his master's library and was in attendance on it for many years thereafter," wrote Arundell Esdaile.

Panizzi goes into the hall of fame because he made the British Museum more of a people's library. For instance, immigrant Karl Marx had a reader's ticket to work in the reading room on *Das Kapital, Kritik der politischen Oekonomie,* and other works. Panizzi wanted books made available freely to the poor and not preserved as an exclusive perk of the well-to-do. He believed the probably dangerous idea put forward anonymously in the seventeenth century that "man without learning and the remembrance of things past, falls into a beastlye sottishness."

Book Row booksellers reflected Panizzi's wish to put books in every hand and home. They did business by the librarian's then revolutionary notion to offer good books in every field of learning not exactly free but pretty close, especially in the 1930s and later, when the paperback uprising made even new books available for a quarter, and for a lot less when secondhand. The book dealers through the Book Row years fought for and held on to their right to offer nickel, dime, and quarter sidewalk books, junk perhaps to picky collectors but sometimes great finds for grateful readers.

When paperbacks exploded on the book scene, most dealers made room for them. Then the world's best books from Homer to Hammett became available on an even larger scale for pennies. As readers have testified since the birth of printing, the right book at the right time can brighten and even transform a life. Book Row enriched, uplifted, or changed many a life for a dime as an affordable book appeared at a bright moment. Author Roy Meador found such a ten-cent book at the Strand in the 1950s, Apsley Cherry-Garrard's *The Worst Journey in the World*, and wrote in the May 29, 1978, *AB* about finding a lifetime companion.

In 2000, Fred Bass at the Strand still put paperbacks in sidewalk carts and sold them at forty-eight cents each, five for $2. "I don't make any money on them; I just don't want to throw them out," he was quoted in *Book, the Magazine for the Reading Life.* Selling books that made little if anything was never uncommon along Book Row. And thus books entered countless hands and homes—and minds! Profits were nice, and of course essential once in a while, but making low-cost literature widely available was a genuine incentive. It was a key reason perhaps why Harry Gold, remembering his youth, wrote, "He loved the World of Books as most love life; / A Bard-Bookman, oh! he yearned to become." He also acknowledged, "One cannot self-crown oneself 'BOOKMAN.' Such humble renown only can be earned." He too enjoyed significant antiquarian discoveries, yet one of the ways Gold won such renown was through large-scale marketing of low-priced books for the benefit of the many.

HARRY PATRICK GOLD—ABERDEEN BOOK COMPANY

Harry Gold indicated in his bookman's memoir, written in epic-poem style, that he was by "inept shoplifters harassed" during his years dealing in secondhand and antiquarian books on Fourth Avenue. Author Marvin Mondlin remembers him as a five-foot-six bookseller usually found sitting on an elevated platform at his Aberdeen Book Company shop, near the entrance, where he kept a watchful eye on the customers he didn't know. Swiveling his head on the lookout for thieves, he applied the maxim that eternal vigilance is the price of keeping books to sell.

Harry Gold opened his first Book Row store in 1925 on the top floor at 95 Fourth Avenue and remained there until 1940. Aberdeen had several locations, and the first two by coincidence followed fifteen-year cycles. From 1940 to 1955, Gold ran his shop at 65 Fourth Avenue. The third move was to a large space at 140 Fourth Avenue, where he had an immense basement as well as a large main floor. Aberdeen prospered at that location, but Gold left it in 1961 when an opportunity came to sell his lease to a film company, Berkey Films, for an amount sufficient to purchase the building at 308 Fifth Avenue, where Aberdeen stayed until he retired to Chapel Hill, North Carolina, in the mid-1970s. In retirement, he worked on his remarkable memoirs and died at the age of eighty-six in 1990.

During his Book Row years, Harry Gold did more than sell books; he also was an advocate for bookseller rights and accepted leadership responsibilities among his peers. In 1942, he was elected the first vice president of the Fourth Avenue Booksellers' Association, and he continued as an active member until the late 1950s.

THE MERCHANT PRINCE OF PAPERBACKS

Are paperbacks really books, or just cheap pretenders? Harry Gold would not allow himself to fret about such issues. He never sniffishly dismissed paperbacks as unimportant in the manner of some disdainful booksellers, past, present, and no doubt future. To Gold, paperbacks resembled books, they read like books, so what if they had soft covers and fit in the purse or pocket? They were enough like books for Aberdeen. Plus customers wanted them more and more.

Aberdeen's stock through the years was distinguished from that of neighboring bookstores by the depth of its up-to-date technical holdings, including books in science, medicine, and technology. "He had sections with just about everything in mathematics and the sciences," recalled Walter Caron of the Isaac Mendoza Book Company. "Also some erotica, occasionally," Caron added as he reflected on the books he observed at Harry Gold's places.

Gold also departed from his Book Row colleagues by assembling a large concentration of paperbacks decades before these lower-priced volumes, in the 1940s and 1950s, began a surge to prominence and before their resulting presence in most new and secondhand bookstores, as well as newsstands, bus stations, airports, highway stops, supermarkets, and drugstores. Gold featured the earliest paperback lines in the 1920s and 1930s, successors to the dime novels of an earlier age. He kept adding new titles as the practicality, economics, and customer appeal of the paperback format stimulated the development of fresh lines by publishers with foresight and maybe a dash of gambler's nerve.

The Aberdeen was the store to visit for copies of tiny volumes from the three-by-four-inch Little Leather Library, such as Plato's *The Trial of Socrates* (1921), or the slightly larger (three-and-a-half-by-five-inch) and considerably more ubiquitous Little Blue Books, published like pamphlets at Girard, Kansas, by socialist Emanuel Haldeman-Julius. Starting in 1919 with Little Blue Book number one, *Rubaiyat of Omar Khayyam*, Haldeman-Julius published hundreds of five-cent and ten-cent books taken from the classics, by established authors, and on controversial topics such as sex and socialism. Will Durant's best-selling *Story of Philosophy* began as a Little Blue Book series. By mid–twentieth century over 300 million Little Blue Books had been sold. Haldeman-Julius died in 1951 and his company soon did the same. But stubbornly tough copies of those Little Blue Books still turn up. And with over 300 million copies out there circulating, they're generally still cheap, though typically not as cheap as they were when new.

In 1929 Charles Boni introduced his handsome line of paperbound books with Rockwell Kent designs and illustrations, the Boni Paper Books. From Europe came the Tauchnitz reprints of English and American modern classics. In 1932 came the Albatross Modern Continental Library using the sailor's good-luck sign as a symbol. The first Albatross was *Dubliners* by James Joyce; number 20 was *The Maltese Falcon* by Dashiell Hammett. In 1935, Allen Lane at the Bodley Head launched Penguin Books with *Ariel* by André Maurois and *A Farewell to Arms* by Ernest Hemingway.

Harry Gold at Aberdeen on Book Row managed to acquire copies of all the paperback lines, including those marked for copyright reasons as not to be sold in the United States. The paperback idea and market promise highlighted by the quick success of Penguins made an American variation inevitable. Robert de Graff was certain that Penguin-type paperbacks would do well on the western side of the Atlantic. In 1938 he conducted a market survey using Pearl S. Buck's *The Good Earth* as a sample with his questionnaires to assess what readers wanted. De Graff learned from the surveys and was ready to recruit financial partners. Richard Simon and M. Lincoln Schuster signed on for a 49 percent share in the resulting corporation. The result was Pocket Books, Inc.; the creation of Gertrude, the reading kangaroo, as a company symbol; and a remarkable experiment

THE
TRIAL OF SOCRATES
—
PLATO

Translated by F. J. CHURCH, M. A.

LITTLE LEATHER LIBRARY
CORPORATION   NEW YORK

in mass-marketing twenty-five-cent paperbacks.

De Graff's plan to make Pocket Books profitable involved the basic economic approach of exponentially raising quantities while slashing production costs. It worked for Model Ts, why not for books? Pocket Book sales began in 1939 with the first title, *Lost Horizon* by James Hilton, "complete and unabridged," of course. What started as an experiment rapidly revealed itself as the opening move of a paperback boom that continued for the rest of the twentieth century and shows no inclination to stop—ever—notwithstanding implausible electronic challenges to the book. In 2000, paperbacks were no longer twenty-five cents (laughter allowed), but they were still proportionally about the same as in 1939 when compared with hardcover costs.

As a cost control measure, the Pocket Books founder at the beginning gave his enterprise a Book Row connection. The staff worked in quarters on Fourth Avenue. Not far away, Harry Gold was already selling imported and domestic paperbacks. The Pocket Books market-making strides in time gave a dramatic boost to that phase of Aberdeen's business. At his 140 Fourth Avenue location in the 1950s, Gold used the vast basement for the unrivaled display of over fifty thousand volumes. There table after table of neatly stacked paperbacks stretched into the distance. The immense number of Harry Gold's basement books made his among the world's largest selections of paperbacks. When he moved to Fifth Avenue, he continued to feature general and scholarly paperbacks along with science and technology bound volumes. Among America's earliest paperback dealers on a large scale, Harry Gold was a bookman ahead of his time who was in position to benefit when the paperback flood arrived and never receded.

Paperbacks from the earliest lists of Penguin, Pocket Books, and others are now themselves sought by collectors. History gives them a certain cachet in the annals of modern publishing; rarity gives them value. Although the print orders for many paperbacks were large, they weren't constructed or priced to be saved after reading. A few were saved by possessive or astute readers, but most went from the initial owners to dealers such as Harry Gold. He could make them available at modest prices and thus carry on the tradition of delivering good books to readers who couldn't afford a First Folio or even a hardcover *Nineteen Eighty-Four* yet appreciated having Shakespeare and Orwell volumes of their own, as Book Row paperbacks.

Harry Gold prospered with paperbacks, but he warned that this was not the route to travel to become a bookman. "Some fools fondly think / That when in paperbacks they sink / Daddy's hard-earned cash, / Into the magic circle they'll crash, / . . . The title 'Bookman' cannot be bought," he wrote.

Bookselling Travels in the Realms of Gold

Walter Goldwater with a tinge of cynicism observed, "Not too many people are completely pure in the book business, actually." He remembered Harry Gold as one of the dealers who bought stolen books, including Edgar Allan Poe titles taken from the New York Public Library, and who as a result was incarcerated for a time. This didn't interfere much with his career, Goldwater admitted, since he "came back to Fourth Avenue and later on became quite big again."

Gold mentioned his occasional run-ins with the authorities, though he alluded mainly to a police sergeant's insistence he keep his Fourth Avenue sidewalk cleared of snow and ice. It is difficult to know for certain, but Harry Gold may have told all, or almost all, at least some of all, in his 320-page autobiographical epic, *The Dolphin's Path: A Bookman's Sequel to the Odyssey of Homer* (1979), which he published himself at Chapel Hill, North Carolina.

This preposterous, funny, audacious, rambling, sometimes charming work may qualify as the strangest memoir ever written by a Book Row alumnus. It is stylistically an off-the-wall escapade; but the bookstore insights and stories—here's hoping they're true—make Gold's recollections informative and worthy of attention.

The author adds warnings: "Can a bookman ever / Fact from fable sever?"

and, "Every Book about Books reeks with bold lies / Of the vain author's mind-busting fabulous buys / Of a rarity, stupidly underpriced . . . sandwiched twixt two duds." He admits great discoveries do happen and notes finding a thousand-dollar book priced at $1 "on the fourth floor low shelf of my own building. / Slight knee-bending would have revealed its spine's gilding."

A patient and careful reader learns that Gold's youth was endured "beneath the quivering shadow / Of the Elevated in / railroad flats of an East Side slum" where "pushcart life did hum." Books were his means of escape, which he read "in his secret nook, / Under the sink." He began in the book business when he got "a carload, sight unseen, for one buck" and "dug out nuggets,—first editions, five, oh!"

The reader slowly learns the narrator entered the book business and perhaps had Albert Einstein and Niels Bohr as customers. Or did he read their books and imagine them as customers? "Let those who wish, grumble; / But by our great men, we have measured time."

We're told about buys that paid off. At an auction he got "a bundle of dusty tomes" and was told, "Bookman, you're nuts!" Nuts by no means—he saw what others missed. The dilapidated batch held nuggets: "Eugene Field's rare leaflets of verse were the secret lure" from which he "harvested a rich crop."

The convoluted verse twists and turns like a maze with enough literary references for the careers of several avant-garde poets. However, a Book Row narrative emerges with convincing stories of bookmen Gold admired, shoplifters, encounters with vice hunters, the daily grind and joy of selling antiquarian books on Fourth Avenue. He portrayed himself thus: "Bookseller 'Odysseus,' brash, gamin sparrow, / Was Gotham born and bred, / Incredibly alert, overspry with go, / Deceptively well-read. / Small, he exuded perpetual surprise; / His ever-turning head / Hid a beak-sharp judgment within elfish guise." Message: You with books hidden in your pants, beware. Bookman is watching you.

Gold remembered the part-time clerk who wondered if Whitman's *Leaves of Grass* belonged with books on gardening or pharmaceuticals and the clerk who shelved Faulkner's *Mosquitoes* with books on insects. Were they putting him on, or just representatives of the postbook generations? He remembered a perfidious manager mailing expensive books from the store to confederates who sold them back for cash. Customers, male and female, concealed books in their bags and clothes. Small wonder Harry Gold grew suspicious, wary, vigilant of both customers and crew.

This latter-day Odysseus was a dedicated though disillusioned observer who accepted his calling even though "bookstores are phasing out" with "bookmen cast adrift on phantom ships, / And daily beaten by hunger's whips" while "money grubbers deem them insane." Still, rewards were there and even a trillion-to-one chance might come through.

He related the improbable true tale of the petite woman who entered from a Rolls-Royce, read a title off a card, Jared Smith's *Arithmetic*, and asked, "Is there a trillion-to-one chance—at any charge—that you have this book in stock? My father's book." Fate sent her to the Aberdeen. He had the book, leather-bound, 1860. And it was actually her original book with her name in it, "To sweet Penny, from Father." "The trillion-to-one-chance came through!" Incredible elsewhere, the event was almost second nature at a secondhand bookstore on Fourth Avenue. "Yes! Trained bookmen retire filling the Ace / In a straight flush in true life's poker game. / Life is a gamble, but whom dares one blame? / Or should one? There's no need to moralize, / For all straights are filled in a bookman's eyes," concluded Gold.

There are bitterness and disappointment present; but there are also friendly, even affectionate memories of others on Book Row when he was there: Regina Cohen, Milton Applebaum, Peter Stammer, the Gilman brothers, Dave Randall. There were the customers he remembered. There was Thomas Wolfe, who cashed checks at the store, his $100 New York University paycheck for teaching freshman English and checks from Asheville relatives. In the 1940s there were Eleanor Roosevelt and Albert Einstein. Gold wrote about Einstein, "This eon's Archimedes. . . . We would speak of many things, but rarely of the war. I was particularly impressed by his love for the beggar, Francis. I recall he said, 'If we could take all the known and unknown laws of science and put them all in a cosmic blender, all we would get would be a single droplet of the essence of God! Francis, in his way, had the same thought.' "

There are bookmen stories. Take that winter night of sleet and snow during the Depression when his shop was host to Christopher Morley, John Winterich, Sol Malkin, Sam Weiser, Ben Bass, Ike and Jack Brussel: "As nearby Grace Church tolled its vesper bell, / Talkative Kit, and Book Row's Paladin, / John, pummelled others, argued and prattled, / Bibliophiles all, roughly they battled / In a merry, friendly, bookish tussle." The tension mounted as they fought over the points in a Henry James first edition, "disputing only as true bookmen can." We the readers enter that winter's fray and thank Harry Gold for inviting us to that nighttime bookish brawl.

Walt Whitman, who wrote, "The dirtiest book in all the world is an expurgated book," would have loved Gold's account of a visit from John Sumner and three antivice cohorts who posed as tourists. Sumner wanted something spicy, sizzling, hot. How about a copy of John Cleland's notorious 1748 brothel classic, *Fanny Hill, or Memoirs of a Woman of Pleasure*, the book that earned twenty guineas for Cleland, millions for generations of publishers, and kept morality watchdogs on guard and happily snooping ever after? Gold found a levant-bound copy, price $100. The deal was made, the book was handed over for Sumner's marked money, and then out came handcuffs to take down another "smut dealer." But this time the book dealer had outfoxed the vice fox. The book said "Fanny Hill" on its spine and title page, but it was a bound dummy volume with nothing but blank pages inside. Case reluctantly dismissed. Perhaps the vice hunters indulged themselves in a blankety-blank. Gold used *Fanny Hill* dummies as a window display.

Harry Gold's book yarns, book facts, and bookman memories with their echoes of the past make readers tolerant of the author's excesses in *The Dolphin's Path*. We believe what Kit Morley declared that winter night on Book Row: "Bless the soul of every bibliopole. And starved browsers who keep bookmen alive . . . it's book glue on which we bastards thrive!" And we believe Harry Gold spoke for himself and many another bookseller when he poignantly wrote, "Farewell to his shop is a torture rack / To any bookman in his final years."

Milton Applebaum—Arcadia Bookshop

Sharing his memories for this account, collector and Book Row frequenter from his early teens Frederick Lightfoot wrote, "It is unfortunate that no one took moving pictures of Fourth Avenue and its proprietors in its heyday. However, what we can record in photographs and words may keep alive a germ of individuality to flower again, sometime, somewhere."

The wish for Fred Lightfoot's nonexistent Book Row film grows strong as we strive to revisit the Arcadia Bookshop at 79 Fourth Avenue and to see again its proprietor, Milton Applebaum. He was one of the bookmen who conscientiously tended to business, selling books, and made no special effort to leave a record of himself and his Book Row years.

And he may have been Appelbaum, not Applebaum; there is no certainty either way. Most printed accounts use *le,* so that's the choice here. The European preference probably is *el.* Yet Milton Applebaum and his wife, Dorothy, apparently were content to have their surname written *el* or *le,* take your pick. Their attitude was: "What's in a name? One gets tired of correcting others. Don't make a big deal about it. Can we help you find a book?"

Applebaum was described by a customer as a dealer with an encyclopedic memory who could direct a buyer seeking a specific title straight to the right location for one book among fifty thousand. He was also noted for the constant presence of a cigar in his mouth and his skill at billiards. The ability to win at pool was an unusual talent along Book Row, where chess was more often the game of choice among the booksellers.

In his youth Milton Applebaum, together with Sy Silverman, worked at Abraham Geffen's large bookstore, which compared in size with Peter Stammer's and Schulte's stores. To Walter Goldwater and Book Row regulars, Applebaum and Silverman were thus always the Geffen boys. "Nobody ever called them anything else except the Geffen boys," said Goldwater.

Abraham Geffen began on Book Row in the 1920s. In *Clegg's* (1936–37), his listing is "Geffen, A. Books. 79, 4th Avenue." Harry Gold in *The Dolphin's Path* called Abraham Geffen a quiet neighbor except when he quarreled with Peter Stammer. "He was a credit to the booktrade. A scholarly gentleman, he left his private collection of scarce Folklore, Antiquities, and Anthropology to the Hebrew University of Jerusalem," wrote Gold. Walter Goldwater called Geffen "a little man who was also quite unpleasant." What is truth? Depends whom you ask.

Harry Gold admired Abe Geffen and considered Applebaum and Silverman fortunate to have him as their bookstore mentor. He also came to respect Milton Applebaum during his training by Geffen and later when he was on his own. In Geffen's voice, Gold addressed Applebaum in his epic poem: " 'Milton Applebaum, before I am through / With life, I'll make a Bookman out of you.' / The old sorcerer did, and that is true!"

To be a bookman, the apprentice had to learn how to use a broom, to bargain, to arrange a show window display, to wear gloves for clean hands, and to talk from both sides of his mouth. " 'I'll teach you the joy of humility; / But more important the rare quality / Of listening with patient dignity.' / Smiling, his Master's teachings Milt did maim, / He bought Abe's bookshop and retained its name. / Milton, in his way, true 'Bookman' became." Thus spoke Harry Gold about Milton Applebaum. There's something friendly and satisfying in the approval of bookman for bookman.

Sy Silverman after World War II army service went into publishing. Milton Applebaum took over the Geffen shop and kept it going with the help of his wife, Dorothy. Always known as the Arcadia Bookshop, the store concentrated on the social sciences, technology, and literature. Like many others among the bookshops, Arcadia could boast a distinguished clientele through the years, including a governor of New York State (Franklin D. Roosevelt before the world knew him as FDR); a president of the United States, Herbert Hoover; and two American poets whose fame certainly rivals that of presidents, Carl Sandburg and Robert Frost.

The Applebaums kept their bookstore operating on Fourth Avenue as long as they could. But theirs was one of the five bookshops forced to move in the 1950s when buildings on the east side of Fourth Avenue between Tenth and Eleventh Streets were taken over by developers. As Walter Goldwater recalled, "He continued the shop on Fourth Avenue as long as he could legally keep it open when the building was supposed to be torn down. He fought them tooth and nail for several years after it was supposed to go, but eventually had to leave and took a shop on Broadway." The Arcadia Bookshop did not have to move very far when the forced departure from Fourth Avenue finally took place. The old name soon appeared at the new site, 856 Broadway, and it was book business as usual for Milton and Dorothy Applebaum.

In the Broadway store, Applebaum had space for about seventy-five thousand books on two floors. He continued the identical specialties as before, standard and out-of-print material in the social sciences, technology, and literature. A major dilemma, however, was how to accommodate and display books effectively in less than half the space Arcadia had had on Fourth Avenue. The Applebaums managed, and the store on Broadway continued to have about the same amount of business as it did on Fourth Avenue. Their regular customers had no problem finding them at the new location since the Arcadia was still conveniently accessible in the Book Row neighborhood.

Since Milton Applebaum did not issue catalogues, the bulk of sales came from established clients and general walk-in traffic. Relying on sales from the street worked well during the peak years on Book Row, since the existence of numerous bookstores in one small area attracted large numbers of book hunters and buyers. During later years, with Wanamaker's gone and the number of bookstores slowly declining, that attraction diminished, and attracting purchasers off the street became more difficult and less predictable. Thus, it was a tribute to the Applebaums and the Arcadia Bookshop that their gross sales on Broadway held up and remained about the same as before.

STAYING WITH BOOKS FROM BROADWAY TO ALBUQUERQUE

Maintaining sales was not enough, though, at a time when the cost of staying in business was steadily climbing. Raising book prices wasn't a workable solution for secondhand stores such as Arcadia. Customers came to the store seeking hard-to-find items at hard-to-beat prices. If Book Row proprietors hiked prices substantially, many customers would obviously take a hike elsewhere and some would simply not show up. The cost of keeping an open-door bookshop running, coupled with rising rents, by the late 1960s was proving lethal for many bookshops in the Fourth Avenue and Broadway neighborhood. The Arcadia was not fated to be an exception.

The Arcadia Bookshop was still open in late 1969, but Milton Applebaum by then was reconciled to the inevitable. He couldn't raise prices sufficiently to meet high rent and operational expenses. The problem of finding competent help further complicated the challenge of keeping the Arcadia going in its fifth decade. The wages a secondhand book dealer could pay were insufficient to recruit and hold reliable full- and part-time assistants. No Sy Silvermans or young Milt Applebaums eager to learn the used-book trade at low pay from an old hand were showing up. The truth of his friend Harry Gold's line "Farewell to his shop is a torture rack" became heartfelt and personal for Milton Applebaum.

At the end of the 1960s, the Applebaums decided to give up bookshop retailing and to sell books henceforth by mail order, as others among their Book Row contemporaries were slowly and often reluctantly doing. There was less satisfaction in the mail order process than in meeting the customer directly and helping him find not only the books he wanted but often other books as well. When bookselling via mail order, the much lower costs of doing business had to offset the loss of one-to-one human contacts with the physical books at hand to show, to hold, to sell, to buy.

There was, of course, a major obstacle for some booksellers with the mail-order method of marketing books. They just couldn't learn to like the chilly and impersonal nature of the process: getting an order by letter or telephone, wrapping up the book, standing in line at the post office, buying insurance, sending it off. These activities didn't fit their long-established methods and customs of bookselling the Fourth Avenue way. Where was the interaction, the communication, the discussion, the searching, the bargaining? Where was the fun?

Milton Applebaum left Book Row, but it turned out that he couldn't abandon the traditional way of bookshop bookselling absorbed decades earlier from Abe Geffen on Fourth Avenue. As had other aging New York bookmen before him, Milton Applebaum followed the sun. But ever the maverick who played bookman pool instead of chess, he settled in New Mexico instead of Florida. There eventually the "Geffen boy" opened another street-front bookshop in Albuquerque. Harry Gold was right: a "true Bookman" Milton Applebaum became, and he never changed.

Henry (Chip) Chafetz and Sidney B. Solomon—Pageant Book Company

"Fame is the spur," warned Milton in "Lycidas" (1637), "to scorn delights, and live laborious days." The poet probably didn't have booksellers in mind, though their days were laborious, since most were spurred to little fame, and many found delights in the noble work of spreading books around.

Curiously, on Book Row, a good chance at becoming well known especially came to those in partnerships who named their stores after themselves, for example, Dauber & Pine, Biblo and Tannen. Considering the long life and success of the Pageant Book Company, the names of its founders might also be more widely recognized if in the 1940s they had called their bookstore Solomon & Chafetz or Chafetz & Solomon. By any names, their Book Row achievements deserve to be known.

If only we had a record of the original discussion that took place to select a shop name before the Pageant opened on Fourth Avenue in 1945, when World War II ended. "Chafetz & Solomon?" "No, I like Solomon & Chafetz." "Can we compromise and call it Pageant?" "Agreed." Thus reasonable booksellers might reason together. Or did they?

Whatever the process, "Pageant" was selected; and the two young World War II veterans combined their resources, brief experience, and large hopes to become bookstore proprietors on Fourth Avenue in peacetime New York City. Chafetz and Solomon acquired the experience that gave them the start-up knowledge, nerve, and ambition to open their own store the same way the Gilmans learned (by working for Peter Stammer) and Milton Applebaum learned (with Abe Geffen): They took jobs on Book Row.

The apprentice technique was an old one in practically every craft and profession before schools took over. Until complications set in and they started lawyer factories at Harvard and elsewhere, even a would-be lawyer used the Abe Lincoln method and "read" law with a working attorney until he knew enough to call himself an attorney. The same with bookselling as with lawyering.

Secondhand bookselling held on to the apprentice custom throughout the Book Row years. Then the surest and quickest way for beginners to start was as employees in Book Row shops under established bookmen who could teach them a thing or two. Thus old bookmen trained young bookmen by handing them the broom and then slowly saturating them with book knowledge. Fourth Avenue bookshops utilized the apprenticeship system to perfection, as the accomplishments of the graduates repeatedly testified. Going stores had the benefit of young, eager, aspiring bookmen laboring long hours and accomplishing the multitude of tasks required; the aspirants served in an environment that helped them grasp the fundamentals of the ancient calling. From there on it was a learn-while-doing business.

Henry Chafetz and Sidney Solomon, prior to their joint ownership of the Pageant, similarly attended Fourth Avenue's bookseller "college," where the tuition was to work hard for modest recompense in one of the shops. According to Manuel Tarshish in the 1969 *Publishers Weekly* series on the Fourth Avenue Book Trade, their 1940s classroom was the bookstore at 138 Fourth Avenue specializing in art and philosophy, with its owner, George Rubinowitz, as their faculty adviser. Astute bookman Rubinowitz, interviewed over four decades later, remembered "Chip and Sidney" well. "Sidney Solomon was here awhile during the war. Then he went into the army, and when he came back he opened a store together with Chip," Rubinowitz recalled. Henry Chafetz became familiar with Book Row while attending New York University. He served in the army air force, 1942–45, rose to the rank of first lieutenant, and was awarded an Air Medal with oak leaf clusters. When both were released from military obligations, they invested themselves jointly in making the Pageant Book Company a success on Fourth Avenue. Louis Wavrovics remembered their start. "To help them fill empty spaces, I sold them a thousand books very cheaply," he recalled. Dealers helping dealers was a perennial facet of Book Row life and business.

Like various other Book Row businesses, the Pageant was mobile, with different addresses. The location of the store, starting in 1952 and for several decades, was 59 Fourth Avenue. This is the address that appeared in the 1958 and 1977 editions of the *International Directory of Antiquarian Booksellers*. The directories identified the Pageant's areas of specialization as Americana, fine arts, general literature, geography (old maps), illustrated books, old prints.

In the 1994–95 edition of the *International Directory*, the Chafetz and Solomon bookshop, nearly half a century after its start, was listed as the Pageant Book & Print Shop with Shirley Solomon, a daughter of the founder, as the proprietor. The store's specialties then were still Americana, art, literature, and old prints and maps. Such continuity on Book Row was not uncommon earlier in the century, but it was rare during the century's second half. Thus the stamina and durability of the store created by the army and air force buddies in 1945 impressively stand out in the historical record of Book Row.

THE PAGEANT PARTNERSHIP REVISITED

Different folks see different blokes. It is interesting when probing memories of Fourth Avenue booksellers to hear the contrasts and contradictions. Chip Chafetz was described as a slight, wiry, sharp-eyed, witty man. Milton Reissman thought he kept a youthful quality even as he aged. Chafetz's partner, Sid Solomon, was seen as heavyset and gruff. Larry Moskowitz, who knew them both, considered Chafetz "quiet, until you got to know him." He thought

Solomon put on an aggressive manner as a defense to hide a certain vulnerability and reluctance to admit when he didn't know something he thought he should.

The Pageant had a narrow front window and aluminum frame door that opened into a large area of three thousand square feet. It maintained a varied stock of over a hundred thousand books. Many of the books were on wall shelves rising fifteen feet to a high ceiling. In the open space, tables and bins contained large quantities of old, unusual, rare, and valuable prints and nineteenth-century illustrated magazines, representing Pageant specialty areas. The Pageant became a store favored by print collectors and their representatives seeking exceptional items.

Book collectors don't always understand the collecting passion for prints, but it is intense and genuine. Book Row was methodically searched at intervals over many years prior to the Pageant for one ardent collector of naval prints from America's wars and seagoing history. The collector who sought prints to complement and give greater meaning to books, manuscripts, and maps was Franklin D. Roosevelt. His naval collection was displayed at his Hyde Park library. Chafetz and Solomon had been fighting the war that Roosevelt led when the collecting president died. Yet perhaps FDR's well-known collecting enthusiasm helped make prints a strong area of concentration at the Pageant.

Another area of strength, according to Maggie DuPriest, was the vast pamphlet collection. She wrote that on buying trips to Book Row, she went through other stores first so she could have all the rest of her time at the Pageant. "Over the years the Pageant became a haven for me, and Chip and Sid were very good friends," she wrote. "One time Sid showed me a small box of pamphlets and told me they had tons up on the third floor. Indeed, there literally were tons, boxes piled almost to the ceiling." She spent four days "sorting through the most fascinating collection of ephemera I had ever seen." DuPriest returned again and again to the Pageant pamphlet horde and found many "treasures." She noted that there were thousands on every conceivable subject, from murder trials to the bombardment of Fort Sumter. Most, she indicated, were from the nineteenth century, with many eighteenth-century American imprints as well. "I always had free run of their establishment," she recalled gratefully.

The partners were active buyers at New York auctions and issued catalogues in fiction and Americana at irregular intervals. Their business predominantly came from walk-in trade. They also benefited from buying visits by other booksellers, print dealers, and collectors in the Pageant's areas of specialization.

When the second Antiquarian Book Fair was held, April 3–8, 1961, at the Park Sheraton Hotel in New York, the Pageant Book Company, which missed the first fair, took part. Henry Chafetz expressed satisfaction with results. He said Pageant would come back for more fairs. He was particularly pleased with the sale of two Gutenberg facsimiles his firm's publishing arm had produced.

The partners founded Cooper Square Publishers, Inc., to issue scholarly reprints. They made a success of this venture with reissues of distinction such as Margaret Stillwell's *Americana and Incunabula*, I. N. Phelps Stokes's *The Iconography of Manhattan Island, 1498–1909*, and much-admired Gutenberg Bible facsimiles.

How Henry Chafetz Viewed Book Row

Henry Chafetz not only sold books, he wrote them, and he had a biographical entry in *Contemporary Authors*. It is unusual for book dealers to find the time—and talent—to produce books of their own, but it happened encouragingly often on Book Row. Chafetz's published writings included *The Lost Dream* (Knopf, 1955) and a history of American gambling, *Play the Devil* (C. N. Potter, 1961). He also wrote two charming books for young people based on folklore. One was *The Legend of Befana* (Houghton Mifflin, 1958), a Christmas story about gifts given to the children of Italy. The other was *Thunderbird and Other Stories* (Pantheon, 1964), a beautifully printed and illustrated book of American Indian legends, including the story of "The Peace Pipe." Chafetz dedicated this book "To the children, not born yet, of my sons, Michael and Eric. They also shall know these stories."

Chafetz used his writing skills for an article about Book Row published in *Hobbies* and reprinted in *Want List—The Book Trade Weekly* (January 26, 1953). He described the Book Row of that day as an area with over twenty-five bookstores containing "two and a half million old and out-of-print books, all cluttered together within four streets." He noted that New York's Book Row had the charm of the bookstalls along the Seine in Paris and

Charing Cross Road in London. "Book Row has the same simplicity, equal treasure prospects, and the similar quaintness of old bookshops all over the world," he wrote, and warned that "intellectual stimulus and bibliophile interest" would erode if bookshops vanished from Fourth Avenue. Look around today; he had a point.

"Bookbuying is a passion, and bookselling is an adventure, and the seller of old books combines these two qualities in his daily business. . . . He trades in the everlasting dreams and emotions of men," observed Chafetz. He admitted that while Book Row dealers derived satisfaction from sharing in America's scholarship and weren't focused on buying and selling expensive books, most of them did secretly think about finding a very rare and valuable item in a load of cheap books. "It is the only clean wholesome illusion they quietly possess. And on rare occasions book treasures have turned up in obscure little buys," admitted Chafetz. "Book Row is an unconventional world of books and business where all kinds of people come seeking all kinds of books," wrote Chafetz about the business he entered at the end of a war as his chosen occupation of peace.

CHAPTER EIGHT

THEIR MEMORIES OUTLIVED THE BOOKSHOPS
Ben and Jack Rosenzweig · George and Jenny Rubinowitz

*To earlier generations, books were as natural a source of information
and entertainment as broadcasts are to the young today. . . . William
Dean Howells tells us in his autobiography how people felt about books
in his native town on the Ohio around 1840. The river steamer would
come up to the pier every so often—nobody knew exactly when—and
amid goods of all kinds would unload a barrel of books. Within a few
minutes of landing, these books would have been sold.*
—JACQUES BARZUN

A NEW YORK bookseller who bought and sold books in large quantities,
by the box if not the barrel, was Frank R. Thoms, whose bookstore with
Charles Eron, Thoms & Eron, was located at 89 Chambers Street, not far
from the New York Municipal Building, the courthouses, City Hall, and the
Manhattan side of the Brooklyn Bridge. City municipal workers who agreed
with Montesquieu that any distress could be relieved by an hour's reading
might, during the lunch hour, leave metropolitan bureaucracy behind, get a
bargain classic at Thoms & Eron, and read it on the bridge's pedestrian
walkway with sea breezes and the Statue of Liberty for company. In the 1950s,
Roy Meador joined the bridge readers with *David Copperfield* while doing
Manhattan jury duty.

Thoms & Eron was a familiar fixture in downtown Manhattan for more
than fifty years from around the turn of the century. The store was about twenty
feet wide, running from Chambers through to Reade Street, with high ceilings
and oak-paneled walls. The 1951–52 *International Directory of Antiquarian
Booksellers* listed the Thoms & Eron specialties as standard sets, standard
works, reference books, and fine bindings. The 1936–37 *Clegg's International
Directory* included rare and secondhand books among the store's basic stock.

Quick, large-scale sales of books on the grand scale seemed the store's
principal modus operandi. During its peak years in the 1920s and 1930s, the

store was said to sell more books than any other. Considering the mass deals for which Frank Thoms was well known, that is a less than startling fact. Rapid turnover was considered sacred dogma at T&E. When books were still there after a week, Thoms often slashed the price 50 percent. This kept books flowing, gave great buys to other dealers, delighted customers, and kept Thoms happy observing the volumes moving in and out.

The Chambers Street site near City Hall made the store a healthy hike through Chinatown to Book Row, but the links between Frank Thoms and his friends among the booksellers "up north" gave Thoms & Eron a strong Book Row connection over the years. Walter Goldwater obtained books for his first store from Thoms & Eron bargain stock after the book scout Abe Sugarman, the uncle of Goldwater's first wife, advised going to T&E because "they have very good volumes on their tables." Goldwater described the store as enormous, with tables of books priced from ten to thirty-five cents and with frequent special deals allowing even more books for a dollar. "Mr. Thoms was always ready to make a deal on any large quantity," said Goldwater. "I would go down there and listen to him and take his advice. I remember him judiciously saying, 'If you don't buy, Walter, you can't sell.' " Thoms subscribed to a generally accepted opinion among bookmen that smart buying is the main ingredient of success and that, by comparison, selling is the easy follow-through.

Sol Malkin of *AB* in the May 9, 1966, issue wrote about working his way through school as a book scout in the 1920s. He would buy books at ten to fifteen cents each from Frank Thoms and sell them to Book Row stores for a profit. The Book Row dealers knew what went on; so did Thoms. They shruggingly allowed the hard-working youth his profit. "Let him make his buck," was Sam Dauber's casual reaction. Malkin recalled about T&E, "What a fabulous shop that was! Frank Thoms had every possible connection, and would get in loads and lots of books, new and old, closeouts and remainders, and would delight in turning them over the same week, indeed the same day if possible."

Frank Thoms was a founding member of the Old Book Table. During the 1940s he became a generous donor of rare ephemera to the Brooklyn Public Library. After Frank Thoms died in 1950, the stock and the store were bought by Fourth Avenue bookman Benjamin Rosenzweig for his growing business.

Benjamin Rosenzweig—City Book Auction
Jack Rosenzweig—Banner Bookshop

Ben Rosenzweig purchased the Thoms & Eron stock and business with a twofold purpose. He could dispose of the stock through his weekly auctions, and he could use the store as an outlet for material that didn't sell at the auctions. As Walter Goldwater remembered, "He bought the place for a price which we would now consider extremely low, made an auction gallery out of it, sold week after week at auction, and then had a bookshop besides." Goldwater's impression as he observed the T&E transaction and Rosenzweig's purchase of other bookstores was that his goal was "to buy up every shop that was available." Rosenzweig was described as a tall, heavyset man who was intensely active and hardworking. He was fired by ambition, like George D. Smith, and like George D. Smith he died suddenly of a heart attack at the early age of fifty-seven.

Ben Rosenzweig's younger brother Jack, also a Fourth Avenue bookman, was less driven. Still active in the 1990s when he was in his eighties, Jack Rosenzweig talked in 1994 with Marvin Mondlin about his brother Ben and their Book Row activities together and apart. "Books interested me since I was a child," he said. "On that historic street, when I first saw so many booksellers together, I felt that in a certain way they were supporting literature and influencing writers. I met writers down there. Fourth Avenue brought lots of people, it brought strange contacts as well as wonderful ones; it attracted writers, clergymen, doctors. I once shook hands with Carl Sandburg. One customer was an Italian who traveled as a Bible salesman and became an atheist. Another good customer was a Catholic librarian from Georgetown University. One day the Italian and the librarian had a great discussion. It was fun to listen and hear both sides."

The Rosenzweigs began with books in Brooklyn before their Book Row and City Book Auction years. There were three brothers. Two became booksellers—Ben, the oldest, born in 1905, and Jack, the youngest, born in 1911. "My middle brother was never merchant material," said Jack Rosenzweig. "He got his doctorate and became dean in the School of Education at Brooklyn College."

While they were boys, their father, formerly a tailor, bought a Brooklyn candy store that, in addition to sweets, sold treats for the imagination in the form of romances; children's and young people's books like the Bobbsey

Twins, Tom Swift, Horatio Alger titles; and Rafael Sabatini novels. This was early in the twentieth century, and other popular sellers included dime novels in the Nick Carter series created by John R. Coryell and turned out almost like candy bars by Frederick Van Rensselaer Dey. The business gradually expanded to include newer books and a neighborhood lending library. Young Ben eventually ran the store's book business for his father and thus began mastering the trade. In 1929 Ben left to open his own bookstore on the boardwalk at Coney Island in the Half Moon Hotel. Jack took his place at the candy store.

Eventually Ben Rosenzweig had three bookstores in the Coney Island area. Besides helping his father, Jack assisted his brother in the Coney Island bookstores. "At Coney Island, we had many well-known authors in to sign autographs. Heywood Broun spent the whole day with us. He was good fun," Jack recalled.

As the Depression deepened and new book sales declined, Ben gradually switched to secondhand books in his Brooklyn stores. He began attending auctions in New York and making large purchases at book warehouses. These activities brought him to the attention of the Fourth Avenue book dealers. The New York book sorties also brought Fourth Avenue to Ben Rosenzweig's attention as the next terrain of opportunity where he could spread his wings and ambitions. He soon disposed of his Brooklyn operations and, after trying several temporary Book Row locations, established himself at 122 Fourth Avenue.

After suffering a heart attack, their father sold the Brooklyn candy-book-library business, and Jack Rosenzweig was sent to Book Row to assist his brother, then at 97 Fourth Avenue. "To my eyes, when I first saw Fourth Avenue it was a new world," wrote Jack Rosenzweig. "I saw more bookstores than I had ever seen in my life, and I thought, can all these stores survive on the sale of used books?" He learned they had been accomplishing that feat for a long time and were still briskly buying and selling books on a large scale.

In effect, Ben and Jack seem to have become partners during the 1930s, with Jack always very much the junior partner. The Rosenzweigs took over the space at the northwest corner of Twelfth Street and Fourth Avenue and stocked it with fifty thousand books purchased from a private dealer in Brooklyn.

Gentle George and jousting Jenny Rubinowitz, booksellers and champion ballroom dancers, made their Fourth Avenue Book Store an oasis of plenty where even celebrities were welcome if they were readers. That's George in the doorway.

Asked how Book Row stores stayed open during hard times, a bookseller replied, "Our wives worked." Mony Grunberg, here at the Altree Bookshop in 1935, married a teacher. The Altree was the first on Book Row to sell original works of art.

After *Book,* the bibliophile's favorite four-letter word is no doubt *Sale.* The Exceptional Library of Philosophy on Sale eloquently reminds us where we are. An overhead sign confirms the Street of Books, Fourth Avenue.

Three-for-a-quarter books clearly appealed to pedestrians in the fall of 1954 at Samuel Weiser's Occult and All Subjects Bookstore. Observe that the "Browsers Welcome" sign is partially covered by a browser.

"Step down to Books" invited Alexander Deutschberger's walk-in bookstore. He had a Fourth Avenue bookshop early in the twentieth century. The Al Jolson show bill for *Robinson Crusoe, Jr.* dates this picture around 1916.

It's late spring, 1926 at East 12th and ahead toward Union Square is the bold announcement: BOOKS. A generation later the Star Delicatessen site will become the Samuel Weiser Bookstore, a richer delicatessen for inquisitive minds.

VIEW IN FOURTH AVENUE, N.Y.

In 1861 only an awesome knack for prognostication could have seen beyond this scene to the next century when nearby Grace Church hosted bookshops and the tranquil city block was home to Schulte's, Schucman's, Arcadia, Pageant, Strand.

On the East side of Fourth Avenue in August 1900, sidewalk book seekers could choose among ten cent treasures at the "Cheapest Book Store in the World." What were that day's bargains? Maybe the cigar store Indian noticed.

Seymour Hacker collected rare books in foreign ports as a wartime mariner and launched Hacker Art Books in 1946. Founded by a book-savvy sailor, the unique shop with international standing lives on in 2004 as a Strand acquisition. *Reproduced with the permission of Hank O'Neal.*

Graduate students learned to count on Bernard Kraus's Raven Book Shop as a last-hope place to find elusive scholarly works. Strong in literature, criticism, scholarship, the Raven was among the first on Book Row to specialize in ephemera.

Smiling among the books is Gertrude Briggs who kept Books 'N Things alive for artists, Beat poets, writers, and collectors after her husband Harold died in 1968. Although the shop moved a lot, devoted customers found it.

Louis Wavrovics, pictured here, and his twin brother Ernest, were known as the River Bargemen because they bought and sold books from an East River barge. Louis, recalling countless, colorful book deals, said, "I have had a very interesting life."

Samuel Weiser is on the job at the store he made internationally known for occultism and related arcane areas. New Age works and eastern philosophy were further strengths. Great magicians, including Houdini, made books disappear from shelves—by paying for them.

Ben Weiser, Sam's younger brother, had his own Pickwick Bookstore, then joined Sam. After ill health made Sam slow down, Ben and Sam's son Donald ran this book oasis for conjurers, spiritualists, and patrons of the supernatural. Even the strange was ordinary on Fourth Avenue.

In 1953 between 10th and 11th Streets, the Strand, Arcadia, and Louis Schucman's offered a bookish vista. Readers could admire their finds or decide about good buys left behind over "tea" at the Colonial Bar and Grill. *(Photograph by Louis Dienes, 1953)*

Only a thick atlas could comprehensively map Book Row from the 19th to the 21st centuries. This impressionistic schematic by Mahlon Blaine served the area for a bookplenty, still bookshop booming time in the 1950s.

The Call of the Auctioneer

While dealing in books with his brother on Fourth Avenue, Ben Rosenzweig soon decided he would become an auctioneer to sell more books and increase revenue in the process. The auctioneering venture started with selections from their own books, consignments from other dealers, issuance of a catalogue, and an advertisement in the *New York Times Book Review* regarding time and place. "The first sale was so successful, we began putting out a weekly catalogue for regular Saturday auctions," noted Jack. Ben wrote the catalogues; his wife, Sydelle, typed them; and Jack did the mimeographing and collating.

The development of an auction business served Ben Rosenzweig as a logical solution to the perennial challenge facing used-book dealers of quickly getting rid of stock that didn't sell readily over the counter at the store. With more books continually arriving if the bookman was doing his job of perpetually building stock, unsold books in a bookstore could be the equivalent of a skin rash. They had a tendency to accumulate and spread and take up shelf space that was needed for better candidates. Rosenzweig's solution was clearly more profitable than dumping them for garbage trucks to haul away. Through his weekly auctions, he sold large quantities of books in bundles for which the highest bid was sometimes a quarter or even less. There was seldom a bottom limit; the high bidder, no matter how low, normally took the books.

The auctions were held at the Fourth Avenue bookstore, and as the activity caught on, Rosenzweig formalized it with the name City Book Auction. To speed up the auctions and work through a maximum number of items, the auction catalogue dispensed with thorough descriptions in favor of stark brevity. Then the auctioneer would simply give the number of an item and ask for bids. This way, according to Walter Goldwater, the City Book Auction could process up to a thousand items a day, compared with the few hundred managed elsewhere. "Since he was being paid by the piece by the people who put the things up, he always knew he was ahead. This idea was later taken on by Swann, who became the only remaining medium-priced auction in the city," observed Goldwater. Using this approach, Rosenzweig sold his own books individually and in bundles and auctioned books on consignment for others, taking a percentage for the service.

Rosenzweig's auctions were not designed or conducted as glamour events. The whole purpose was to move as many books as possible as quickly as possible. Philip Sperling in 1990 reminisced about the auctions as colorful, businesslike occasions where dealers, collectors, scouts, and ordinary customers—bibliophiles all—sat on wooden benches. "They took home treasures for sometimes as little as 50 cents," wrote Sperling. Walter Goldwater recalled purchasing worthwhile seventeenth-century items for fifty cents each.

The war years of the 1940s proved to be a stimulus for the Rosenzweig businesses, and Ben soon joined the unofficial yet prestigious Book Row alumni association by relocating uptown to the Fifties near Fifth Avenue. The 1951–52 *International Directory of Antiquarian Booksellers* gave the address of City Book Auction as 119 East Fifty-seventh Street and listed its specialties as "All Subjects."

During this period as well, Ben Rosenzweig stepped up his acquisition efforts. The old Thoms & Eron store gave him an established facility where books could be sold and auctions held. Rosenzweig had been familiar with the store much earlier, when he was a student at the nearby New York Law School on William Street. Another important acquisition was G. A. Baker and Company, the bookstore led by Max Harzof, whom David A. Randall in *Dukedom Large Enough* called the finest all-around bookman he had known. Harzof's first bookshop was at 730 Lexington Avenue, and auctioneers from then on affirmed his successful bids with the word "Lex." Harzof died in 1942 and his associates after several years sold out to Rosenzweig, who disposed of the valuable sets, first editions, and other stock through his auctions and store outlets.

Marvin Mondlin was employed by Ben Rosenzweig in the 1950s to manage the Thoms & Eron retail outlet. At his employer's request, he qualified for an auctioneer's license and assisted Rosenzweig in the weekly auctions. The auctions became major enterprises, and a staff evolved to conduct them: Nat Kaplan, who fought in Israel as a member of the Irgun; Max Breslow, then in his sixties, who had owned the Bookshop for Bookish People at the Bible House; and Victor Bristow, an experienced bookseller from Bristol, England, whose primary job was preparing the sales catalogues for City Book Auction.

Rosenzweig took Edward Zelniker, a bookman from Spring Hill, Alabama, and Sam Wolf from Westchester, New York, as associates in City Book Auction. Wolf owned an enterprise called Superbooks, a connection that somehow led to a falling-out between Wolf and Rosenzweig, Wolf's discharge, and subsequent litigation. This may have seemed routine daily business for the litigious and tirelessly on-the-run Rosenzweig.

As successful businessmen sometimes do, Ben Rosenzweig made enemies. But he also worked exceptionally hard, created jobs for others, made friends, and from the record does not qualify as a foreclose-the-mortgage villain. Through his stores and auctions, he made a lot of people happy with a lot of books. Until he could open his Anchor Bookshop at 114 Fourth Avenue, Irving Warshaw maintained stands of books outside the Rosenzweig facility at Twelfth Street and Fourth Avenue. The auctions held inside that large enterprise became admired features of the area's book business during decades that book lovers looking back might call a golden age for affordable and plentiful secondhand books in New York City.

GOING INDEPENDENT

In the 1930s, Jack Rosenzweig started working as a subordinate partner with his brother in the Fourth Avenue bookshop and in the launching of City Book Auction. In time the younger brother felt the pressure of working both as a retailer with long hours in the store and as a multifaceted auctioneer's assistant as well. The fact Ben didn't raise his pay even as his duties expanded became a sticking point between the brothers. Then came another frustration for the younger brother from what he considered further unfair treatment. Various bidders who couldn't attend the weekly auctions asked Jack to bid for them on specific lots they were interested in, and they agreed to pay him the standard 10 percent commission for the service. This did not interfere with his duties at the auction, and he accepted the assignments. When brother Ben got wind of this arrangement, he appropriated the commissions himself, presumably on the grounds that Jack was his employee. Disagreements like this eventually led to the breakup of the brothers' partnership.

Jack Rosenzweig took advantage of his independence to obtain his own Fourth Avenue bookshop. The owner of the Benday Bookshop at 84 Fourth Avenue was moving to California. Jack helped the owner pack the books being shipped to California and then bought the remaining stock and the fixtures. Under Jack Rosenzweig, the shop became the Banner Bookshop. Originally it had been Frank Bender's store. When Bender sold out, the new owner called the shop Benday to retain something of the original name. By coincidence or intention, the word "benday," after the American printer Benjamin Day, refers to a printing method of using dots to produce shaded areas on a printed page.

Bender had been a leading Fourth Avenue dealer during the 1920s and into the 1930s. He specialized in architecture books and before opening a store sold books on the road. When he began, he had money for the first month's rent and lumber for shelves, which he made himself. There were no funds left to fill the shelves with respectable stock.

Then Father Fate or Lady Luck or both stepped in to help. A customer offered him $250 for a copy of a seldom seen book on ancient Rome if he could find one. Within hours, Bender saw it listed in a catalogue for an auction. At the auction, Bender nervously waited for the item to be called. It was his day. No serious competition presented itself. He bid and got the book for $6. The pleased customer fulfilled his promise. "That was the first real money I made," said Bender, who was able to stock Bender's Bookstore and to keep it going through a typically lean start-up period until it was well established on Fourth Avenue.

After starting Banner Bookshop at Bender's former location, Jack Rosenzweig often had Frank Bender as a visitor. "He was a wonderful person. He sat and talked with me often. He missed meeting and conversing freely with the customers about the books they were interested in and thus adding to his own knowledge," recalled Rosenzweig. Bender once said, "I love to talk to them even if some of them are cranks."

Rosenzweig ran the Banner Bookshop during the period when antivice squads and pornography prowlers were snooping around Book Row in search of "dirty books" soggy with forbidden eroticism. "All the book dealers knew all the undercover investigators," he said, "and the zealous characters trying to trap us were too naive to realize it. No dealer was going to get caught offering them erotica." He remembered one investigator who came in and slyly asked, "Have you got anything that's really 'hot'?" Rosenzweig answered, "Yes, I have a beauty." He rewarded that pursuer of the "real hot" with a copy of *The Lay of the Last Minstrel,* whose title gave the smut and lust chaser a quick if temporary thrill.

Jack Rosenzweig at the Banner Bookshop specialized in prints, which he carefully catalogued and filed to facilitate access and efficient control. He also built up his general stock by purchasing entire libraries when he could afford them and could reach the sources and make deals before competing bookmen found the castles and crossed the moats. A friendly relationship with Ben Rosenzweig was restored and maintained in spite of Jack going on his own. Jack consigned some things to his brother, but he did most of his business with established customers and walk-in traffic.

While operating the store, Jack began taking night courses in engineering at City College of New York. City College started in the 1840s at 17 Lexington Avenue, not far from the area where Book Row later would take root and flower. City College steadily evolved into a vital New York City natural resource offering a cherished means of higher education for poor students from the Lower East Side and other sections of the spreading city. In 1907 City College settled into its own campus at 138th Street and Convent Avenue. No less valuable reservoirs of portable knowledge are Brooklyn College and Queens College, later spin-offs from City College.

A special amenity of City College for the general public—on a par with the amenity called Book Row—was the May 29, 1915, donation by Adolph Lewisohn to City College of Lewisohn Stadium, located north of 136th Street between Convent and Amsterdam Avenues. There, from 1918 until the mid-1960s, occurred one of those cultural gifts to the people that made New York City special: the long series of low-priced (sometimes free) concerts held each summer for all of us. We sat in the summer twilight on one of the six thousand concrete seats, or stood if we came too late to sit, and waited until dark for Oscar Levant to play *Rhapsody in Blue* or for some equally inviting musical event. Lewisohn Stadium summer concerts brought out the stars under the stars.

While waiting, we read stimulating (what else?) yet inexpensive books from Book Row. If a summer shower hit, we shielded ourselves after a fashion with the *Times, Forward, Daily News, Herald Tribune, Journal American, Post, World-Telegram and Sun, Newsday, Morning Telegraph, Racing Form,* or *Variety* (those were the days!) and kept reading until it was too dark and the music began. Perhaps not by coincidence, virtually paralleling the decline and fall of Book Row, the summer concerts ended in 1966 and the stadium was torn down in 1973. *Requiescat in pace* to another memorable, lost city marvel comparable to the bookstores of Fourth Avenue.

After the December 7, 1941, attack on Pearl Harbor, with the strong likelihood of being called into service, Jack Rosenzweig sold his bookshop at a loss in 1942 and focused on completing as much of his engineering education as he could before going into the army, which he entered in 1943. His training resulted in an assignment to army engineering duties. When he was released in 1946, he never returned to bookselling. Because of his expanding interest in Judaica, he attended Hebrew Union College.

Although he stopped running a Fourth Avenue bookshop and didn't resume selling books, Jack Rosenzweig's love of books never flagged. He became a collector, mainly of history and literary materials. "My book interests now are all Judaica. I have a twelve foot wall in my Florida room crammed with books. Just looking at them still makes me happy," he wrote in 1994.

George and Jenny Rubinowitz—Fourth Avenue Book Store

Several husband-and-wife bookselling teams became well known as they worked together in the various shops on Fourth Avenue and throughout the Book Row neighborhood. Among these book-dealing duos were Harold and Gertrude Briggs of Books 'N Things, Harry and Ruth Carp of the Green Book Shop, and Walter Goldwater and Eleanor Lowenstein, who sold books together and in their own separate stores. Add to this trio a famous fourth team to complete a Book Row quartet of couples, George and Jenny Rubinowitz. In that quartet, we'll give the Rubinowitzes the first-violin chair in terms of the lasting impression they made on their bookselling peers and countless customers.

When the Book Row memories of customers and sellers are visited, George and Jenny Rubinowitz seem to have been given more than an equal share of amused, respectful, and somewhat frightened recollections. Rubinowitz stories tend to portray George and Jenny in good-bookseller / bad-bookseller terms— George gentle and understanding, Jenny tough and sharp as tenpenny nails. "I liked George Rubinowitz, but then he had that wife," said Milton Reissman. "I heard she died taking a bath. I wouldn't have blamed George had he drowned her." This comment from a Book Row regular commands attention since other book dealers, male and female, never earned responses at a comparable level of ferocity.

Reissman remembered George Rubinowitz as a dancer of professional ability who was "bossed around" by his wife, Jenny. He did admire Mrs.

Rubinowitz's knowledge and acumen as a bookseller: "She was shrewder than most of the other Fourth Avenue dealers when it came to foreign books. She knew what she was buying." What bothered Jenny Rubinowitz, according to Reissman, was what she was selling—at prices she immediately assumed were too low. He recalled in the early 1970s finding what he considered reasonably priced books in the Rubinowitz warehouse. "Jenny died a little when I brought the books down and always claimed she had planned to sell them at a different price. That is just the way Jenny was," observed Reissman reflectively.

The Fourth Avenue Book Store was located at 138 Fourth Avenue and had a long record, from 1940 to 1982, of selling books to New Yorkers and visitors from all over. The store in 1942 was among the charter members of the Fourth Avenue Booksellers' Association. The shop was described as a small establishment, twenty-eight feet deep with a twenty-four-foot front, offering approximately twenty thousand well-selected titles, with art, literature, and reference books as specialties. Early customers remembered seeing a small balcony inside. Lucy Kolk served the shop for years as a diligent assistant. Among eminent customers who used the Fourth Avenue Book Shop was Franklin P. Adams, known for the "Conning Tower" column in which young writers yearned to be recognized and for his reign as a know-a-lot pundit on the *Information Please* radio program. Other name customers among the regulars included writer Thornton Wilder and actors Zero Mostel and Joseph Schildkraut Jr. The store was used as the background for a story in *Seventeen* magazine. Catalogues were occasionally issued, but most customers walked in and dealt directly with genial George or formidable Jenny.

Every bookman seemed to have a Jenny Rubinowitz story. Walter Caron noted that when he went to the Fourth Avenue Book Store, he nearly always dealt with Jenny. It was an experience not to be forgotten. "She would sit down, look at me and say, 'Have an eye,' meaning to keep an eye on the store for her," he commented. Jenny's sometimes aggressive manner didn't discourage Caron from going back to the store for the excellent book buys he sometimes made there.

"Sure, I bought books at the Fourth Avenue Book Store. An interesting shop. He was fine, she was impossible in an intriguing way," recalled Larry Moskowitz, echoing the general opinion that George Rubinowitz was a gentleman bookseller while his wife, Jenny, was somebody special, unique, atypical, out of the ordinary, impossible. The applicable adjective depended on varying personal experiences at the unforgettable Rubinowitz bookshop on Fourth Avenue. He was sometimes described among his peers as soft-spoken George while she was loud Jenny, reminiscent of Jenny the Pirate in Weill and Brecht's *Die Dreigroschenoper (The Threepenny Opera)*. The respect and bemused appreciation she received from her Book Row colleagues was also shown by the fact that she was sometimes affectionately called Mrs. Fourth Avenue.

Another frequenter of their shop considered both George and Jenny friendly and helpful booksellers but viewed the shop as too cramped for comfortable browsing. This made it a bookstore to enter for a specific title in their specialty areas but not a place to linger.

Jenny Rubinowitz was often seen at auctions, and observers remembered her for giving them an exuberant show of zeal and enthusiasm in action. At American Book Auctions, run by Louis Kirschenbaum on Fourth Avenue, her custom was to sit up front near the auctioneer and to make her bids conspicuously, even frantically. This may have been—probably was—a strategic ploy on shrewd Jenny's part. Others may have dropped out early, considering it pointless to bid against a nut.

George and Jenny were recalled for this account by Bill Weinstein in 1990. "Whenever I bought three or four books and George agreed to knock off a dollar or two, she would get madder'n hell." Weinstein was collecting books on gems and jewelry, and he carried index cards of the items he wanted. George would go through the cards to see if anything listed had come in since the previous visit. One incident around 1950–51 convinced Weinstein that George too had his share of Book Row eccentricities. George examined the index cards, gave a big smile, and had an employee take Weinstein down to the dirt-floor, low-ceiling cellar. "We stooped and almost crawled along. Two bare bulbs hung from the ceiling. We stopped at a big wooden box. The clerk reached in and pulled out Kunz's *The Book of the Pearl*. I was so excited I hit my head on the floor above. I asked what else was in the box. It turned out to be filled with George Frederick Kunz books I had been hunting for years! The box and the books looked as if they had been there a considerable period. The volumes were priced between $10 and $18 apiece."

As he paid for these finds upstairs, the collector remarked, "Mr. Rubinowitz, I like you, you seem to be a nice man. I'm curious, how long have you had these books that you knew from my cards I've been trying to find a long time?" The bookman replied, "Oh, maybe ten years." Asked the next obvious question, why he hadn't been shown the books before, George Rubinowitz said, "There was no one here to take you. I don't go downstairs anymore." "Why didn't you just let me go downstairs?" Weinstein wanted to know. "Oh . . . well . . . I knew you would come back."

Such confidence in the likelihood of a regular customer's return was characteristic of Book Row. George Rubinowitz could afford to postpone a collector's possessive raptures with the reasonable expectation of making the sale when circumstances were right, astrological signs were suitable, the store needed the sale, or he finally got around to it. Plus a stash of valuable books with a reliable customer lined up for them was a kind of annuity, so why hurry? Add the facts that there was no clerk available to show the customer to the cellar, that George didn't go downstairs, and that no one had the nerve to ask Jenny. If this didn't exactly reflect the highest level of customer service, it showed a *laisser aller* attitude that was also fairly common along Fourth Avenue. Then too there's the undeniable fact the collector did return and the rare Kunz gem books were sold to him.

"The real booklover cannot resist entering a secondhand bookstore. If he finds a carefully chosen, well displayed and reasonably priced stock he will come again and again," Morris H. Briggs wrote in *Buying & Selling Rare Books* (1927). Customers coming again and again was a given that book dealers relied on. Those customers by virtue of their loyalty and frequency of appearance often seemed to be like unpaid, exceptionally eager members of the staff. Once George mistakenly left the front door open overnight. When he went to work the following morning, he found a familiar early-bird customer cheerfully running the business for him until he arrived.

George Rubinowitz could count on volunteer assistance from devoted customers just as others on Book Row could count on him. His shop was the place where Sidney Solomon and Henry Chafetz acquired the experience they needed in bookselling to start their Pageant Book Company after World War II. Irving Warshaw was another dealer who had reason for being grateful, as Rubinowitz made it possible for him to open his own bookshop in 1940.

Prior to the establishment of his first shop on Astor Place, Warshaw kept book stands in front of Benjamin Rosenzweig's City Book Auction facility. In

1941 one of his customers was the revolutionary Cubist sculptor Jacques Lip-chitz, who had recently arrived in the United States and was happy to find someone on Book Row who could hold a conversation with him in Yiddish. Warshaw's small store, with a general stock of about eight thousand books, was later located at 114 Fourth Avenue. At his Fourth Avenue store, War-shaw enjoyed pointing out that from 1847 to 1850 Herman Melville lived with his wife, Elizabeth, across the street at 103 Fourth Avenue, where he wrote *Mardi* (1849), *Redburn* (1849), and *White Jacket* (1850). Warshaw could gen-erally offer customers inexpensive copies of those and other Melville titles that provided not only great reading experiences but also a historical con-nection to the neighborhood where the author lived and worked. In *White Jacket*, the creator of *Moby-Dick* wrote what the Fourth Avenue Booksellers' Association might well have quoted as a come-hither advertising slogan to one and all: "Somehow, the books that prove most agreeable, grateful, and companionable, are those we pick up by chance here and there; those which seem put into our hands by Providence; those which pretend to little, but abound in much."

GEORGE RUBINOWITZ REMEMBERING BOOK ROW

George Rubinowitz died in the spring of 1997 at the age of ninety-eight. A few years earlier he shared with Marvin Mondlin his memories of Book Row during what he called "the golden age of Fourth Avenue." Before opening his bookstore in 1940, Rubinowitz was a dissatisfied housewares salesman. He knew books in some way should be his vocation since he had loved them and read them from childhood. Benjamin Rosenzweig was his friend, and he spent all the time he could during the 1930s at Rosenzweig's Coney Island bookstore in the Half Moon Hotel. "It turned out that Ben and I shared more than books and friendship. His family and mine came from the same small town near the German border. His father and grandfather were friends of my father and grandfather. My father was a tailor and designer, but I still don't know where to put a needle."

Rubinowitz was born in that town close to the border. At the age of five or six he was impressed by the village blacksmith and thought he wanted to become one and make sparks fly. Then a Cossack client of his father's asked the children what they wanted to do, and he was embarrassed when he was called "a born blacksmith." "I decided right then that I was going to be a man of learning. I stopped going to the blacksmith shop and began reading books, all the books I could get," he said. The commitment to reading stayed with him into his nineties as he read books on a broad range of topics in English, German, Hebrew, and Yiddish. "When I was younger, I wrote poetry in different languages. Now the hobby that keeps me going is, you wouldn't guess it, ballroom dancing," he said.

He was a good student in school and attended a seminary to be a rabbi. "I never really wanted to be a rabbi. My motive for the rabbinical studies was to acquire the learning." The blacksmith ambition of the six-year-old didn't entirely disappear. As an adult he collected books and prints on the legends and lore of blacksmiths. "I found one print of a boy in a blacksmith shop who looked exactly like me. I said, 'That's me!' and kept the print."

After the family immigrated to America, there was some consideration about continuing to prepare for a career as a rabbi. But his career inclinations were in other directions. Rubinowitz eventually informed Ben Rosenzweig about his growing interest in owning a bookstore. Rosenzweig didn't forget and notified Rubinowitz when a suitable opportunity presented itself. "He was instrumental in helping me get started in the book business on Fourth Avenue." When he was well situated as a book dealer, his former housewares employer visited the shop and confirmed the wisdom of his decision to switch careers. He said, "George, you are where you belong. This is for you."

He must have been where he belonged, and the profession must have been the one for him. He sold books on Fourth Avenue for forty-two years, from 1940 until 1982. "I know the finer ends of antiquarian bookselling and seeking expensive rarities for the rich collectors. But my view is that beautiful books should be available to everybody. The readers, the heart of the matter, were the people we mainly served on Fourth Avenue," he observed.

Initially Rubinowitz ran the bookstore by himself with the help of employees such as Sidney Solomon. His wife, Jenny—they were married in 1939—was then a teacher in a parochial school. She came to share Rubinowitz's love of books, and eventually she stopped teaching and joined him around 1946 as a coworker and partner in the bookstore. He remembered the occasion when he foresaw the approaching change in their lives. At a bookstore on 125th Street, he showed Jenny a beautifully bound copy of *A Midsummer Night's Dream,* and she kissed it. "I thought at the time, she's hooked on books," said Rubinowitz. The arrangement in their Fourth Avenue store became a permanent one.

"When I started the bookstore, I was sort of like the proverbial elephant in a china shop. I was a reader, but I didn't know the mechanics of buying and selling in a retail establishment. My customers helped teach me what I needed to know. I think every successful bookseller owes a great debt to his customers," said George Rubinowitz. "I listened to my customers, and I read books on the subject to avoid mistakes and to make the right choices."

He did much of his study to prepare for Manhattan book dealership in the Brooklyn Public Library's main branch at Grand Army Plaza and Eastern Parkway, near Prospect Park. The symbiotic relationship between libraries and bookstores was well served for George Rubinowitz at the Brooklyn Library, which was in the final stages of construction when he opened his bookstore in 1940. The library had a decent collection of worthwhile works about bookstores and dealers. "One of the books I especially remember was a diary kept by a bookseller," Rubinowitz noted. "He eventually went broke as I recall. I learned useful lessons from his experience. I came to terms with the fact that bookselling is a business, and I had been involved in business. I reasoned that I could apply what I knew from the business world in relation to books and thus avoid pitfalls."

A division of labor came into effect at the Fourth Avenue Book Store when Jenny Rubinowitz joined the staff. George made the longer journeys by car in pursuit of books, while Jenny attended the New York auctions. "Jenny liked auctions, and she became skilled at the art of making good acquisitions through her bids. I went to the auctions myself mainly when Jenny wasn't available," said Rubinowitz. She developed the ability to recognize distinguished bindings, to know important books from Europe, and to see things that less attentive dealers missed. She cultivated her aptitude to identify special qualities, to bid boldly when necessary, and to buy a bundle of largely unimportant items if it held something promising.

Auction purchases added to their general stock at the store and the nearby warehouse where some of the better things were stored. Through the years purchases on the road and at auctions gave them a number of "sleepers" and some valuable books. One purchase that was not a sleeper, for which they paid $800 at auction, was a book of Louis Philippe's letters. He was the

French king from 1830 to 1848, but had lived several years in the United States during the 1790s, when the French Revolution made France unhealthy for aristocrats. The book was an investment based on knowledge of its value. "We sold it to the Morgan Library and made a good profit," said Rubinowitz.

George Rubinowitz remembered that the Fourth Avenue Book Store had its share of celebrity customers. "I became friendly with Zero Mostel in a personal way," he said. "He laughed when I told him if he dropped the Mostel he'd be just a Zero. Sam Jaffe the actor was here and Thornton Wilder. But all our customers were great, famous or not famous. Jenny and I liked to sell books to people who were buying them to read."

On September 30, 1969, the *New York Times* published an article by McCandlish Phillips, "Dealers on Book Row Fear Rent Rises Will End an Era." The tone of the article largely reflected gloom on the part of active dealers about the future of Book Row. The proprietor of the Fourth Avenue Book Store, however, was quoted as one of the optimists. The *Times* reporter wrote, "He does not fear the encroachments of the newer visual media or the reduction of print by microfilm. He reasons that books are part of education and 'education will never stop.'" A lead picture for the article showed the bookman placing a volume in a handsome window display behind large letters and figures for the Fourth Avenue Book Store's name and number.

That wasn't how Rubinowitz wanted the picture taken. "I had a very nice display," he said. "I was pretty good at displaying books. I asked the paper's photographer to wait while I put another book in an open space where I had removed a book that sold. He didn't wait. He took the picture while I was stretched out and leaning over with the book. I stood up and said you can take the picture. He said it was done already. When the article ran, my sister-in-law saw it and cried, 'It's George!' Guess what my brother said: 'What happened? Did he get arrested?'"

George and Jenny Rubinowitz became familiar competitors at ballroom dancing contests. "We sometimes won in fox-trot, tango, cha-cha, paso doble. I knew the music and could create my own choreography," the ballroom-dancing bookman stated as he remembered with pride those occasions of victory away from Book Row. Dance contest dates, when possible, were profitably aligned with searches for more books to replenish stock.

After Jenny Rubinowitz died from a heart attack in 1980, George kept the store open another two years. One quirky thing he began doing after Jenny was gone was taking books home. "In this business you buy a hundred books, sell ten or fifteen, and have to store the rest. I started filling up shelves where I lived, including the kitchen cabinet, where I replaced dishes with books. Someone visited and had food to put away, but the kitchen was full of books," he remarked with a chuckle. He decided to retire when his lease approached its expiration date. He gave some of the books to a Florida library and sold the store to a purchaser found for him by his friend Jack Tannen at Biblo and Tannen.

"I'm still in the mainstream of life," insisted the retired bookman. "I traveled twice to Israel, to Turkey, to the Bahamas." He made it clear that books remained very much a vital part of his existence. "I gave books away and sold many of them," he said. "But I still have a lot of books, some valuable, some not. I love to look at them, and I love to read them."

CHAPTER NINE

THE WINNING PAIR OF JACKS
Jack Biblo · Jack Tannen

*The qualifications for conducting the ideal secondhand bookstore
are so high that it is extremely probable that the possessor of them
could do a good job at running the United States Steel Corporation and have plenty of time left over to assist Henry Ford. . . .
Many of the largest rare and new booksellers of today started in
with a few hundred secondhand books, a hundred feet of pine
shelving and a store on a side street.*
—MORRIS H. BRIGGS

IN THE INTERNATIONAL sport known as draw poker, a pair of jacks often qualifies as an opener. On Book Row, a very special pair of Jacks, Jack Biblo and Jack Tannen, were great closers—of book sales, thousands of sales, at their famous shop known throughout the wide world of books as Biblo and Tannen.

Morris H. Briggs, rhapsodizing about the skills and knowledge demanded of a secondhand bookseller, speculated in his 1927 manual, *Buying & Selling Rare Books*, that the best among them would have no trouble in the less demanding job of managing a big corporation. However accurate that might be, there's little likelihood either of the Jacks would have given up bookselling to be CEO at Dupont, General Electric, or any other blue chip powerhouse and moneymaker.

The actions and the words of the two Jacks speak loudly that they were born bookmen. Jack Biblo even had a majestically apropos surname that made any bibliophile instantly think "book." Starting the year after Briggs made his audacious and, let's face it, reckless claim regarding booksellers, the two Jacks lived with and sold books together for half a century, 1929–79, under the rubric that gave birth to legends, Biblo and Tannen. Their store became a center of book quests and hopes fulfilled for several generations of loyal customers. Bookseller Maggie DuPriest was one of those customers. "In New York on buying trips, I bought a lot of local history books and marine science books from Biblo and Tannen. I used to go there first," she wrote for this account.

"I have been a dealer in old and rare books for almost fifty years and hope to continue for another twenty-five. Booksellers seem to live to a ripe old age, possibly due to the literary dust we are constantly breathing. . . . There is a fascination about the antiquarian bookstore that cannot be described. I have tried to express this quality for almost fifty years," wrote Jack Tannen in his 1976 guidebook, *How to Identify and Collect American First Editions*. "It's a business that's more than a business," he said reflectively in the 1970s, "but if you want to make money, forget it."

Jack Biblo never had any doubts about his future: "I always knew I was going to be a bookseller." Late in his long bibliopolic career, during the 1980s, he was still operating a "retirement bookstore," Biblo Books, at Brooklyn Heights. His wife, Frances, observed that outside of youthful ambitions to read every book in the public library and to look for Tarzan in Africa, "running a used-book store was the only ambition he ever had." About bookselling on Fourth Avenue, Jack Biblo acknowledged the work required sixteen-hour days "and sometimes you didn't make a dollar," but still, "it was a joy."

THE JOURNEYS TO BOOKS OF THE TWO JACKS

If not for strategic name changes when the founders were young, their bookstore joint venture could have been called Biblowitz and Tannenbaum. Shortening and changing names was fairly common among immigrants and their progeny for many reasons—simplification, Americanization, show business, anti-Semitism, business. Jack Biblowitz, born October 18, 1906, in the East New York section of Brooklyn, jettisoned his "witz" in the 1920s because of the anti-Semitism prevalent then and because Biblo looked better on a small storefront. Book Row storefronts typically were cramped for space.

Jack Biblo's formal schooling ended before he was fourteen so he could go to work. He attended the same New York school, P.S. 149, as David Kaminsky, who would change his name to Danny Kaye. Jack was out of school, but never out of learning. As he worked at a variety of menial jobs, Jack Biblo's life was taken over by reading at the libraries of Brooklyn and later at the library with the lions on Forty-second Street in Manhattan. In his teens during the 1920s, he sold newspapers at a midtown kiosk while the voracious reading regimen continued.

While working in the Catskills as a waiter during the summer of 1928, he thought about his future and came to the conclusion that as a bookseller he could keep reading and also earn a living. He borrowed $300 from his mother and used that as slender capital in the fall of 1928 to build shelves and obtain stock at an auction for his first bookstore at 229 East Fourteenth Street, where the rent was $50 per month. Decades later Walter Goldwater would reminisce about the inauspicious beginnings of Biblo and Tannen, "who started business just before I did on East Fourteenth Street as poor little creatures and who have since then become quite large, substantial, and have bought their building on Fourth Avenue."

Jack Tannen was born January 1, 1907, at Warsaw, Poland. The Tannens came to the United States when he was nine and settled at St. Mark's Place in the Lower East Side. Young Tannen learned English quickly and made rapid progress at P.S. 25. He attended Dewitt Clinton High School, the first public high school for boys in Manhattan, whose students have also included James Baldwin, Burt Lancaster, Neil Simon, and Lionel Trilling. At eighteen, Tannen quit before graduating to hitchhike across the country and accumulate experiences, as he said, to write a novel. On his quixotic quest, he worked his way west by visiting synagogues and reading the Torah as a kind of wandering rabbi. "They would feed me, give me a couple of dollars, and I would go on my way," he explained.

The desire to write began for Jack Tannen when he was in high school and read the works of Ben Hecht, especially *Erik Dorn* (1921), the rebellious story of an unconventional and cynical (aren't they all?) journalist who wonders at the end "how many yesterdays make a tomorrow." Specific books would continue to influence him. "I was introduced to the book field by Christopher Morley's *The Haunted Bookshop*," Tannen told Manuel Tarshish. "I had a first edition and Morley was kind enough to tell me where to sell it."

Back home in New York, while working in a clothing shop, Tannen met Biblo and frequently visited his Fourteenth Street bookshop. In 1929 the two Jacks came together in what would be a fifty-year partnership. At first their rewards for hard work were meager at best. When they could put aside a dollar a day each, they felt themselves in the chips. "We used to buy our food from the peddlers on Orchard Street," Jack Tannen recalled about the lean years. "On Orchard Street they would close before dark and sell everything that was perishable. We would buy a large loaf of pumpernickel for a dime and a can of sardines for a nickel and two bottles of buttermilk for a quarter. That's what we lived on." He once commented, not in jest, that customers at the start showed up so infrequently both of them had ample opportunity on the job to read the entire *Encyclopaedia Britannica*.

To prepare themselves for better times, the partners studied bookselling at the New York Public Library and became careful observers if infrequent buyers at auctions. Sometimes they slept at the store and rose at dawn to visit the Salvation Army warehouse at 7 A.M., when the trucks were unloaded. They could grab whatever books were in the early morning delivery. Their hustle gained them nearly exclusive access to Salvation Army donations and substantially built up their general collection. They also arranged to acquire duplicates from Stechert-Hafner, the library supplier.

Like several other Book Row stores, Biblo and Tannen for over twenty years was migratory in restless pursuit of the optimum site. The store relocated successively to East Ninth Street near Fourth Avenue, 99 Fourth Avenue, 57 Fourth Avenue, and finally, in the mid-1950s, to 63 Fourth Avenue between Ninth and Tenth Streets. There it remained without any further moves and steadily evolved into one of New York's finest bookstores in the 1960s and 1970s.

Real Estate, Auctions, Erotica, Book Deals

The two Jacks managed to elude one of the major pitfalls—soaring rents—that threatened the survival of other Book Row stores by becoming the owners of their brownstone building at 63 Fourth Avenue. This real estate coup helped them stay in business longer than many of their contemporaries. At number 63, their twenty-foot-by-seventy-five-foot shop occupied the entire five-story building and at its peak held nearly two hundred thousand volumes on all subjects.

To augment individual book sales, they adopted the practice that Ben Rosenzweig at City Book Auction and others on Book Row successfully followed. They began holding in-house auction sales at Biblo and Tannen as a regular feature of their business. The auctions brought groups of people from beyond the precincts of Book Row and functioned as a practical way to move substantial quantities of books swiftly. The auctions also brought wider notice to their excellent general stock.

In the 1970s Biblo and Tannen established a rare-book room on the second floor, as Book Row dealers sought to compete more effectively with the posh uptown stores for the antiquarian trade. The Biblo and Tannen room contained about ten thousand carefully selected books. Interested customers were not permitted to wander freely in the rare-book room, as efforts were made to keep the experience special. Customers were escorted there, as though to a sanctuary, by a staff member and were encouraged to study the store's collection of first editions, fine bindings, and other rarities. When duly impressed, they were allowed the privilege of making purchases from Biblo and Tannen's trove of treasures. Concerning this development in the book trade, Tannen once remarked that it had become "easier to sell a fifty-dollar book than it is a seven-dollar book."

Speaking of $50, Jack Tannen remembered a $50 profit the store earned unexpectedly in its early "pumpernickel and sardine, dollar-a-day, tight-belt" phase, thanks to Harry Gold, *Fanny Hill,* and a couple with money to spend on pornography—luckily, they didn't turn out to be stealthy stalwarts from the antivice vigilantes. To fill their request, Tannen acquired *Fanny Hill* and four other pornographic books from Harry Gold at nearby Aberdeen Book Company for $100. The customers made no objection to paying $150 for the five books. "So we sold erotica for the first time and made a $50 profit! That's when we were able to visit Dick the Oysterman's wonderful restaurant at Eighth Street, west of Broadway, and Ratner's great dairy restaurant," Tannen wrote. Could selling pornography to eager adults be wrong if it provided oysters, blintzes, kugel, and pastries fit for a book-loving gourmet after the monotonous austerity of day-old pumpernickel and aging buttermilk?

At Biblo and Tannen, that first sale of legally forbidden material made it easy to sell more; and the two Jacks concurred with most booksellers who viewed censorship and the prudish laws then in existence as malicious interference with individual rights by self-anointed morals militia. Many Book Row dealers helped themselves stay in business by giving customers what they wanted, even if it was illegal, under-the-counter erotica. Considerable caution and careful assessment of customers were essential, since the laws, no matter how unreasonable, were sometimes ruthlessly enforced, and when caught, bookmen might be jailed for the offense. Abe Sugarman, for one, was arrested when he sold a copy of *Fanny Hill,* and his time in jail seriously affected his health.

After paying for the five volumes, the Biblo and Tannen customer asked about getting more such items in the future. No problem, assured Jack Tannen. The couple returned weekly for several months in 1931 to acquire a fresh batch of titillating reading, and Biblo and Tannen kept them well supplied. The finer neighborhood oyster bars and dairy restaurants steadily benefited as well as the bookmen due to this steady bonanza from banned books that the store had no trouble acquiring.

Nothing is permanent, of course, except death, taxes, and the rising value of the first editions one wants but can't afford. A week arrived and then another without the appearance of the couple. They never returned, and the racy items held for them became part of every retailer's number one concern, unsold stock that stays stuck to the shelf.

But that wasn't the end of the affair for Biblo and Tannen. In a few days, the woman called and asked the store to take the books that cluttered up her apartment. True love had run its erratic course in spite of erotic aids, and the man had gone away with another woman. He took the erotica collection and left behind about five thousand books the angry owner of the apartment wanted gone as well. Tannen assumed she intended to sell the books. He found the collection included many first editions and fine bindings. He told her the books were worth a lot more than Biblo and Tannen could pay. The woman assured him she didn't want payment, she just wanted the books out. The store accommodated her, took the books with the proviso that she could have them back if she changed her mind, and held them aside on the assumption that eventually, when she had cooled off, she would want either the books or money. She entered the store about two months later, and Tannen thought she had come for all her books. Seeing his anxious look, she quickly told him she wanted only the ten-volume, morocco-bound set of Oscar Wilde. "I found the Wildes for her. She kissed me good-bye, and I never saw her again," Tannen recalled. The books she gave the store in 1931 proved to be just the financial boost needed to keep going and to facilitate the store's first move, from Fourteenth Street to East Ninth Street.

A memorable transaction at the Ninth Street store was the sale of five thousand first editions en masse for $5,000 to the collector Joseph McCann.

The check was a more than welcome cushion for the hard days that lay ahead during that Depression decade. The bulk sale convinced Tannen he should spend time at the public library learning all about first editions in order to avoid cheating either customers or the store. When his research persuaded him McCann paid more than the books were worth, he contacted the customer and offered to take them back. McCann appreciated the gesture and was a Biblo and Tannen customer the rest of his life.

The research Tannen began with the study of reference books and bibliographies in the 1930s to make himself knowledgeable about first editions led some four decades later to the writing and publication of his *How to Identify and Collect American First Editions*. The book new cost $10. The handsome dust jacket has a picture of Biblo and Tannen on the front cover, a misspelled word ("Identity" instead of "Identify") on the inside flap, and a picture of a smiling Jack Tannen on the back cover. Many of us in the final years of the 1970s made it a point to drop by Biblo and Tannen and buy a copy of the book directly from its author, even if we had a doubt or two about how much it might help us identify and collect American firsts. For most of us, the amiability of the writing and our grateful memories of Biblo and Tannen make the book a keeper.

Jack Tannen enjoyed relating a book-buying episode in 1930 that taught the two Jacks a vital lesson about the dangers of dawdling. A call came from the Hotel Imperial about books they wanted to sell a book dealer. The two Jacks headed for the hotel and were shown to a room with hundreds of books wrapped in newspapers. They unwrapped a few volumes, a folio, a 12mo, and soon realized with amazement that they were in the presence of a fabulous collection. Trying to hide his excitement, Tannen turned to the hotel's representative and asked the price. "Seventy-five dollars," the staff man said, but he was suspicious since they had examined so few copies. Tannen explained that the collection seemed to be the sort of books, atlases and the like, they could use. He scribbled a check and the hotel man accepted it.

"Jack and I were alone with books that seemed to us to belong in the Morgan Library. We were so delighted with the books that we lost all sense of time as we stayed there examining what we had bought for several hours. That was a mistake," wrote Tannen. He noted that the first book he unwrapped was a letter from Columbus to his nephew and that two small books had jeweled bindings. These weren't just diamonds in the rough. Every book they examined was a diamond. They had wandered into a library worthy of Huntington, Clements, or Kubla Khan.

At 4 P.M., they decided it was time to stop admiring and to get going, but they had waited too long. The employee who accepted their check met them and said the hotel's attorney had intervened and made a few changes in the arrangement. Before the sale could go through, the lawyer thought the owner or his heirs should first be notified that the hotel intended to sell the books unless they received other instructions. So the hotel would hold the check, and if no one responded, Biblo and Tannen would own the books. It turned out the actual owner was suffering from senility, but members of his family of course promptly claimed the books. "About three months later, forty of the books came up at the Anderson Gallery and brought $60,000," Tannen noted. "The experience taught me a very good lesson. When you buy a library, get the hell out! Before the lawyers move in, take the books and run!"

BIBLO AND TANNEN CATALOGUES AND REPRINTS

At its Fourth Avenue locations, Biblo and Tannen, once well established and well known, benefited from a brisk walk-in trade during the years when Book Row was in effect America's unofficial capital for secondhand books. Although substantial sales resulted from the many catalogues distributed by Biblo and Tannen, a significant percentage of the store's sales also came from New Yorkers and out-of-town visitors, including collectors and other book dealers. They considered number 63 a forever friendly New York home—a place where, when you went there, the two Jacks had to take you in.

At Biblo and Tannen a modest sign at the entrance might well have read, "Abandon Hopelessness All Ye That Enter Here." The typical drop-ins entered with hopes high and brought along serendipity as their guide while they optimistically browsed for specific titles or whatever marvels might be found during any particular visit at one of America's outstanding book meccas. Biblo and Tannen attracted scholars along with the general public because it maintained rigorous standards in selecting books and in evaluating the libraries purchased for addition to the general stock. Visitors also knew that after a few days had elapsed since their last visit, the shelves, aisles, and counters would offer fresh titles newly available and carefully priced by Jack

Biblo. Like any other efficient and successful retail business, Biblo and Tannen required and received persistent attention to avoid dead stock and diligent work to keep the shelves replenished with inviting new materials.

The store earned a global reputation for a broad selection of high-quality books over a wide range of subjects, books that summoned customers to drop by regularly and avoid the painful suspense of not knowing what they were missing. If you didn't miss a book that interested you, you might miss seeing Edna St. Vincent Millay or some other literary luminary who just happened to drop in. Or take that professorial, Nobel-laureate-looking chap reading in the corner: a major league brain from NYU, Hunter, City College, Columbia, Barnard, Oxford, Cambridge, the Sorbonne, the University of Tennessee? Let him be, the two Jacks would decide, maybe he'll actually buy something one of these days, a paperback *Walden* perhaps. As Stephen Leacock put it to the American Booksellers' Association in *The Methods of Mr. Sellyer* (1914): "It is a maxim of the book business that a professor standing up in a corner buried in a book looks well in a store. The real customers like it."

Biblo and Tannen's real customers were frequently repeat people because the atmosphere, the amiable feel, the orderly look of the place were bookishly right. Their core reliables were the walk-ins, those who liked to hold a book, examine the binding, turn it over, sniff the glue, caress the cloth, check the dust jacket for tears and spots, examine the signatures, see if pages were highlighted or in some other way defaced by previous owners. They were the book buyers who investigated a book as carefully as they chose a pet, to make certain it would qualify as a durable friend before handing it to the clerk and saying, "I'll take it."

The two Jacks were brilliantly contrasted to give Biblo and Tannen its special ambience. The slim, tall, quiet philosopher in residence, Jack Biblo, was the skilled organizer and administrator, the inside Jack. He priced books, supervised the small staff, and kept the store humming at a peak of efficiency. That staff changed little through the years as loyal employees stayed on. Alice Ryter by title was the secretary and bookkeeper, but in fact she became an indispensable Jacqueline of all skills. Gilbert Wortman served the store as a general factotum, and Harold Wehlau was a skillful cataloguer. All employees, including the two Jacks, doubled as bookstore everything-elsers. Staffers had specialties, but in a secondhand bookstore, everyone naturally and by necessity masters every task and does it all.

The other half of the leadership team was the tall, bulkier, garrulous extrovert, Jack Tannen. He was the outside Jack, who ventured forth to investigate and buy libraries, negotiate with bankers and investors, meet the public, win new friends and influence collectors, make deals and sales. He had the flair of an actor and as a young man had been a performer in little theater groups. The contrasting qualities of the partners meshed smoothly for an ideal, long-lasting combination. They were touch and go, yang and yin, red and green. Predictably when Jacob Chernofsky for *AB* ("Biblo and Tannen: A Fourth Avenue Landmark," April 14, 1986) asked how they remembered their first meeting, Biblo said they immediately got along, and Tannen piped in with, "We took an instant dislike to each other." Their remarkable and outwardly smooth half-century partnership provides relevant evidence to consider when deciding which Jack to believe.

Jack Biblo acknowledged frankly that occasional differences are inevitable when two people work together five decades, but no significant consequences resulted from these differences between him and Jack Tannen. "Tannen very much wanted to be in the limelight and the public eye, and I was just the opposite. . . . We never had any serious differences," Biblo was quoted in *AB*. To outsiders that comes across as an amazing fact and a tremendous tribute to the patience and wisdom of the two Jacks.

While getting along swimmingly as partners, Biblo and Tannen also got along well with their bookmen neighbors. When George Rubinowitz was ready to retire, it was Jack Tannen who found a buyer for his Fourth Avenue Book Store property. During the Depression years if they had made a few sales and a neighboring shop hadn't, lunch money or more when needed was available at Biblo and Tannen, no questions asked. The two Jacks, of course, had no monopoly on generosity and helping a Book Row colleague. Such comradeship was a standard many Book Row regulars lived by for the common good.

Biblo and Tannen were charter members of the Fourth Avenue Booksellers' Association and active throughout its existence. When new officers were elected at the 1969 meeting, Jack Tannen was selected as the association treasurer.

The ambitious partners were never content just to wait for clients to walk in. Starting in the 1930s they began issuing frequent catalogues. Biblo and Tannen Catalogue No. 1 was dated 1936 and went in the mail during the spring of that year. Numerous catalogues were issued on first editions, Americana, and special book categories including literature, social sciences, economics, geographic areas, genealogy, biography, history, medicine, natural history, science, and philosophy. The first catalogue was a general list offering selected books in eighteen fields. The catalogues were unadorned, well-organized work lists designed for convenient use by library purchasing agents and collectors. The catalogues nearly always listed well over a thousand items each. They often warned customers: "List Alternate Selections. These are single copies only." The catalogues did not shy away from controversial items if they had scholarly merit or historical significance. Most catalogues offered a wide variety of books at prices sometimes strikingly and of course enviably modest (though not always).

CATALOGUE 77-2

646 PICASSO, PABLO. Lithographs, 1945–1948. Intro. by Bernhard Geiser. 12mo. 67 plates. NY (1948). 1st ed. dw. bkplate 10.00

1290 INGE, WILLIAM. Come Back, Little Sheba. Frontis. NY (1949). 1st ed. 6.00

1507 SHAW, B. Back to Methuselah. A Metabiological Pentateuch. Lond. (1921). 1st ed. VG in faded, slightly frayed dust wrapper. Scarce! 57.50

1573 TRAVEN, B. The Death Ship. NY (1934). 1st Amer. Ed. Author's first book 18.50

CATALOGUE 170

363 YORK, SGT. A. C. His Own Life Story and War Diary. Ed. T. Skeyhill. NY (1928). 1st ed. Sgd. by Alvin York. Scarce 10.00

663 ALGREN, N. A Walk on the Wild Side. NY (1956). 1st ed. fine, dw 4.00

849 WHITE, E. B. Charlotte's Web. NY (1952). 1st ed. vg 4.00

877 LONDON, J. White Fang. NY (1906). 1st ed. fine copy 10.00

CATALOGUE 172

444 HEMINGWAY, E. A Farewell to Arms. NY (1929). 1st ed., 1st Issue 15.00

461 KENT, R. N. by E. Illus. NY (1930). 1st ed. Signed 6.00

588 **WRIGHT, R.** Native Son. NY (1940). 1st ed. vg 6.50

589 **WRIGHT, R.** The Outsider. NY (1953). 1st ed. fine, dw 7.50

CATALOGUE 234

643 **HITLER, ADOLF.** Mein Kampf. Complete and Unabridged. Fully Annotated. Special Ed., with Dorothy Thompson's review. NY (Reynal) '39 15.00

800 **STALIN, JOSEPH.** Stalin's Kampf. Written by Himself. Ed. by M. R. Werner. NY (1940) 14.50

CATALOGUE 240

496 **HIMES, C.** Cotton Comes to Harlem. NY (1965). 1st Amer. Ed. 12.50

613 **WRIGHT, R.** Native Son. NY (1940). 1st ed., 1st issue, Fine, dw 27.50

CATALOGUE 250

244 **RIVERA, DIEGO.** My Art, my Life. An Autobiography. Illus. NY (1960) 15.00

325 (SMOKING). Tobacco Talk and Smoker's Gossip. A Miscellany of Fact and Anecdote . . . including a Selection from Nicotian Literature. 12mo. Lond. (1886). 1st ed. 17.50

796 **HAYES, HELEN.** On Reflection. An Autobiography. Illus. NY (1968). 1st ed. Fine, dw. Signed 15.00

Biblo and Tannen carefully built a mailing list, and in time up to ten thousand catalogues were periodically mailed nationwide. The catalogues became major sales producers credited with a high percentage of the store's annual sales. Catalogue sales eventually surpassed the walk-in business.

Another Biblo and Tannen endeavor involved creating a publishing division in 1961 that they called Canaveral Press. The purpose was to give new life to out-of-print works that were still popular and appealed to significant markets. Through Canaveral Press, they reprinted two dozen titles including a number by Edgar Rice Burroughs, whose Tarzan series has made Burroughs's first editions costly even when they are often somewhat the worse for wear.

There seems a certain irony in reprinting Edgar Rice Burroughs, who wrote in the presentation copy to his wife, Emma, about his first book, *Tarzan of the Apes* (1914): "My dear wife: Do you recall how we waited in fear and trembling the coming of the postman for many days after we sent the Tarzan ms. to Metcalf? And will you ever forget THE morning that he finally came? Not even this, our first book, can quite equal that unparalleled moment. That we may never have cause for another such is the wish of your devoted husband, Ed. R. Burroughs." A first edition of that first Burroughs Tarzan with a fine original dust wrapper has been valued at $50,000.

The Biblo and Tannen reprint business focused mainly on important works that appealed predominantly to libraries and scholars. Their efforts in this connection to meet an intellectual need for landmark works not easily found were praised by the *Classical Journal* and other learned publications. By means of production efficiency, the firm kept the costs of its imprints lower than was generally the case with such publications.

Particular emphasis came to be placed on the fields of anthropology and archaeology. A representative reprint title was *The Palace of Minos* (4 volumes, 1921–35) by Sir Arthur John Evans, who was curator of the Ashmolean Museum at Oxford and extraordinary professor of prehistoric archaeology. From 1914 to 1919 he was president of the Society of Antiquarians. Evans's discovery early in the twentieth century of the Minoan civilization at Crete and his excavations at Knossos are considered his leading contributions to archaeology and to knowledge of European prehistory.

A long-term intention that was never actually carried out completely at Biblo and Tannen was gradually to phase out the handling of general secondhand books and to concentrate the company exclusively on quality reprint publishing and serving the antiquarian and rare-book interests of its walk-in and catalogue customers. Before those ambitions were fully accomplished, the two Jacks in 1979 ended their half-century partnership on Book Row so Jack Tannen could take his allergies to a different climate, in Florida, and Jack Biblo could open his "retirement bookstore" in Brooklyn. The ability of Biblo and Tannen to continue as long as it did was due to the purchase of the five-story building in the 1950s, which protected them from prohibitive rents longer than many of their Book Row competitors.

Reporter McCandlish Phillips in the *New York Times* (September 30, 1969) described the two Jacks in their early sixties on the job at their store. He depicted them as lean, brisk fast-talkers with mustaches, neckties, well-pressed trousers, and horn-rimmed glasses. The reporter in tribute to their energy and joie de vivre likened them to nimble old-time vaudeville hoofers. Think maybe of Gene Kelly and Donald O'Connor at the start of *Singin' in the Rain.* "Sometimes one would start a thought and the other would finish it, or modify it, or elaborate, or contradict," he wrote.

Most Biblo and Tannen customers enjoyed the service, the conversation, and the repartee at the store. Many remembered their visits to the store fondly and appreciatively. Walter Caron reminisced gratefully, "They were considerate about saving things for me. I remember Gilbert Wortman, who was often in the basement. He became a friend of mine as did the Jacks." He recalled with a chuckle that Gilbert once had conscientiously erased pencil notations from a book of poetry that should have been left untouched until the prior ownership was known.

"I generally dealt with Jack Tannen, while Jack Biblo sat quietly nearby," said Larry Moskowitz. "Jack Tannen was something of a showman. He seemed to like dealing with people." Complimentary about the store and Tannen as an outgoing bookseller, he was critical of Tannen's book on first editions, as the Bibliographical Society of America had been, and felt that Tannen's grasp of the subject wasn't as broad and deep as the author might have wanted. No matter, added Moskowitz, "They had genuine rapport with secondhand books at Biblo and Tannen. I used to get some wonderful buys from them."

Bibliophile, librarian, and bookseller Howard Frisch remembered discovering Book Row when he was a student in the 1920s at Townsend Harris High School, the alma mater of Herman Wouk and Jonas Salk. "I was a kid and I was dumbfounded, seeing those bookstores," he said. He became a Book Row customer in the 1930s due to curiosity about the English literary eccentric and innovator Ronald Firbank, who largely subsidized the publication of his own works and once remarked to poet Siegfried Sassoon, "I adore italics, don't you?"

Frisch said in an interview for this account, "I can give you details about my first Book Row purchase. It was at Biblo and Tannen. I read a 1929 essay about Ronald Firbank by E. M. Forster. It was reprinted in his *Abinger Harvest* (1936). Forster pictured Firbank as a rare spirit, not to the taste of everyone. This intrigued me, and when I couldn't find Firbank's books at the library, I went to Fourth Avenue. I found two copies of Firbank's play *The Princess Zoubaroff* (1920) downstairs at Biblo and Tannen. I bought both copies for a dollar or two, I couldn't have afforded more. That was my initial purchase there, the first of many."

Another Biblo and Tannen story he related involved a customer who selected a book and handed Jack Tannen $2.50. The customer was told the book cost $15. The customer pointed to the dust jacket price, which said $2.50. "It was two-fifty new. Why didn't you buy it then? Now it's not new, it's used, it's tough to find, and it's fifteen dollars," the customer was told. Frisch didn't report whether the deal was consummated or not.

"When I became a secondhand book dealer in the nineteen fifties, to me Biblo and Tannen was the best store to rummage through. They had a fantastic fiction collection, and everything was alphabetized. That was good. Also their detective fiction was reasonably priced, and they gave me the usual discount so I could resell it. I knew all the bookstores then, but Biblo and Tannen was best," Frisch declared.

Not all memories of Biblo and Tannen were so positive. Milton Reissman thought that Jack Biblo may have had an alcohol problem and that Jack Tannen was less informed about books than he professed. No bookman can know for certain what another bookman knows. And it's a moot point whether drinking sometimes collided with book dealing at one store or another. Wayne Somers, a Schenectady bookseller and frequenter of the Book Row shops, recalled the time when one of the two Jacks had a glass of what appeared to be whiskey sitting on the counter while he berated a yuppie who had asked a foolish question about a book. The indignant bookman employed verbal weapons to drive the man and his wife from the store. Was he belligerent because of booze, or because of literary integrity assailed by yuppie silliness? Does it matter?

"A sale shouldn't just be to the advantage of the seller; it should also benefit the customer if you want him to come back," said Milton Reissman. He recalled an important purchase of his own from Biblo and Tannen that he believed served the store and himself well. The deal involved a large number of theater books, signed photographs and letters, and complete runs of movie magazines. It was a marvelous collection filling over forty cabinets. Negotiations began at $25,000 and concluded with a sale to Reissman for $6,000–$7,000. He was happy about the arrangement and assumed Biblo and Tannen didn't suffer.

Like several other Fourth Avenue bookstores, Biblo and Tannen had a steady trickle of famous customers, and some of them became regulars. Celebrity watchers, if endowed with patience, would have seen novelists, celebrated poets, film stars, and even a nationally admired politician who was sometimes compared with Helen Keller for his impressive triumph over a physical handicap.

The walk-in politician—an attorney seeking justice for Native Americans—was Thomas Pryor Gore, the blind U.S. senator from Oklahoma who helped organize the state and in 1907 became Oklahoma's first senator. He was Gore Vidal's grandfather, whom Vidal called Dah and whom he recalled fascinatingly in his memoir *Palimpsest* (1995). One of Vidal's memory pictures: "Stacks of books around the blind Senator's chair, piles and piles of them, all colors, all kinds." Starting as a child, Vidal read to his grandfather hour after hour for years.

Jack Tannen became Senator Gore's reader when he entered Biblo and Tannen in 1933 seeking books on economics. The books may have been needed to assist his struggle as a lawyer during his final years, in Gore Vidal's words, "to get the government to pay the Indian tribes for those lands that it had stolen from them." Tannen read the senator a long list of available titles and was duly impressed when Gore with his blindness-trained memory repeated them back without a mistake.

Theodore Dreiser was a regular customer during the store's early years. The novelist was a dedicated street stroller in his adopted city, and Biblo and Tannen was a favorite place to pause. "I was never weary of walking and contemplating the great streets," he wrote in *The Color of a Great City* (1923). He called New York "the City of My Dreams" and strolled the old avenues as a wide-awake somnambulist. The public libraries and the bookstores were favorite places that brought him in off the street during those mind-expanding walks. Dreiser shared with the book dealers a bitter encounter with the New York Society for the Prevention of Vice. The society tried to stop publication of his novel *The "Genius"* (1915) until Willa Cather, Robert Frost, and other distinguished writers rallied to his defense against frivolous and dictatorial prudery.

During a period when Ethel Barrymore was recuperating from illness, the actress's nurse came to Biblo and Tannen every week to stock up on detective stories. The nurse bought a dozen mysteries at a time. We take for granted the reader of those whodunits was Lionel's little sister Ethel. What better physician is there than a book of cleverly crafted fiction that seizes the imagination and holds on tight?

Edna St. Vincent Millay and Carl Sandburg were among Biblo and Tannen's regulars. A much-told Book Row story involved the author of *Chicago Poems* (1916) and biographer of Abraham Lincoln. Each time Sandburg visited the bookshop Jack Tannen asked him to sign his name and write his address "for the records." Eventually getting suspicious, Sandburg asked, "Are you selling my autograph?" The bookman answered promptly: "Of course." Sandburg nodded approval, made no objections, and signed again. The two Jacks profited, and it never hurt a poet to keep his name in circulation.

FAREWELL TO FOURTH AVENUE

"I never intended to give up bookselling on Fourth Avenue," admitted Jack Biblo early in the 1980s at his small weekend bookstore, 48 Hicks Street in Brooklyn, which he started as a retirement diversion "to keep his hand in bookselling." With no concern about the detailed contents of the books he handled, he continued to assess book values based on more than half a century of taking in a book's title, author, pictures, publisher, and subject at a glance and quickly pricing it for the secondhand market.

Departures from Book Row could take place without fanfares or swan songs. The owner moved the books he meant to keep, sold the others en masse or at discount, and handed the keys to the landlord with no hard feelings and perhaps the last month's rent. But sentimental memories didn't pack their valise and depart so easily.

Jack Biblo reminisced about the changes that had taken place in bookselling. "We used to buy 20 books to sell one. Today the specialist buys only one book and prices it accordingly," he was quoted in *AB* (April 14, 1986).

He recalled how certain books were treasured and with some difficulty acquired in the Brooklyn of his childhood. To rent a Tarzan book on Pitkin Avenue cost ten cents for three days. He and four of his friends chipped in two cents each and took turns flying with Tarzan on vines through the tropical wilderness. Speed reading went with the challenge and was simply a requirement to make those three-day romps in an African forest work. Decades later the sharing sessions of Brooklyn reading no doubt influenced the decision to feature Edgar Rice Burroughs titles among Canaveral Press reprints, including memorable works from the series about that jungle gentleman of few words, the well-undressed Tarzan.

Biblo noted that in the 1920s and 1930s earning a dollar a day pay for the privilege of working in a bookstore qualified as "nirvana" to him and some of his friends. Changing times, cultural upheavals, and higher prices, among other influences, made such low-pay bookstore learning experiences unappealing to later generations, Biblo lamented.

The two Jacks expressed regret that most young people were no longer interested in secondhand bookselling, and many showed complete disinterest in secondhand book buying. Those students seeking books wanted books on movies, entertainment, and business rather than the classics and literary criticism favored by earlier reading generations. The Jacks speculated that when their generation left the scene, secondhand bookstores for the most part might depart with them. Jack Tannen is quoted on the dust jacket of his 1976 book: "My life has been an interesting and joyful one," but "I am most saddened by the fact that Fourth Avenue as I once knew it is gone and of the thirty-two shops that once were there only a handful remain." In 1976, Biblo and Tannen was among the handful; at the end of the decade, it wasn't. As Tannen remarked, "It's always been a struggle, but it's always been fun."

Over two decades have gone by since those wistful speculations by the two Jacks, and there are still fine secondhand bookstores in New York City and elsewhere. So perhaps, let's hope, gloom about the bookselling future, shared by Jack Biblo and Jack Tannen as Biblo and Tannen completed its half-century journey, was not an entirely accurate prophecy.

CHAPTER TEN

Books 'n Booksellers 'n Book Lovers
Harold and Gertrude Briggs · Bernard Kraus · Harry and Ruth Carp

*Collecting first editions may simply be an irrational form of human
behavior in the same way that golf is. If asked, when I already possessed a cheap edition of Blunt's My Diaries, why I should buy, at a
considerably higher price, a first edition of this book, I should find it
difficult to say, and yet to me there is all the difference in the world,
and I am willing to pay for that difference. Illogical it is, but so is
running a lawn mower, or growing a hedge.*

—Herbert Faulkner West

✄ The booksellers of Book Row typically occupied cramped, weakly
lighted, inadequately heated, seldom air-conditioned spaces. They
cheerfully—oh, maybe with a little occasional kvetching—put up with
working conditions their mothers would have called, when they tried to be
nice, nothing short of scandalous.

They calmly endured the whips and scorns of time, the casual arrogance
of the gainfully employed, the friendly hauteur of recently published authors,
the smug tolerance of slumming celebrities, the blithe ignorance of the uninformed, the greediness of sellers, the stinginess of buyers, and uncertain gross
revenue even in the best of times.

Landlords or banks hovered close by, watchful, skeptical about this
month's rent, the next payment on the mortgage. Generally the accumulation
of capital was just a will-o'-the-wisp dream, a strategic illusion, as whatever
funds were put aside promptly went to buy yet another private library with a
half dozen possible sleepers and some basic replenishment items for the
bulging and creaking shelves that had perhaps been salvaged from another
store or made on the premises. Why stick it? Why?

The intriguing question is why various booksellers of Book Row calmly and
for years on years put up with privations, recurrent difficulties, erratic income,
financial problems, and galloping uncertainties just to keep books available,

every kind of book, for one and all. Most of the Fourth Avenue proprietors of secondhand bookstores were sufficiently talented, intelligent, informed, and capable to do much better for themselves, moneywise at least, in a variety of other fields. Many would have qualified readily to take part at better pay in the various New York office, corporation, civic, and merchandising rat races. Instead, they stuck tenaciously with the used-book race. Why?

The booksellers for the most part probably couldn't tell us exactly why. Most people, when their deepest reasons are explored, can't fully explain the course of things even to themselves. *It happened. Old habits die hard. Does it matter? The years went by. It was a living; well, practically a living. "Que sera sera." So ask Doris Day. Why? Why not?*

The reason why in most cases was probably the simple fact that the booksellers were genuine, committed, lifelong book lovers. They derived pleasure from living and working in the presence of books. They magnified that pleasure when they provided other book lovers with the special books they had anxiously and persistently sought. Booksellers relished the prospecting and thrilled when they struck gold for others in the form of elusive titles.

"I've tried to find this book for years!" when eagerly blurted by a delighted customer was the bookseller's extra dividend and annual bonus for being there and having the book, whether it was on the shelf gathering dust for years or came in yesterday. Booksellers, believe it or not, reaped a gratifying sense of service from the ability to make books conveniently and economically available to the venturesome individuals who found their way to Book Row. Since effort was needed to get there, the walk-in customers were clearly serious about books too. They deserved to be helped. They were helped.

The book dealers and the book scouts who assisted in finding the books knew they did more than most others involved with books to save precious Americana, irreplaceable ephemera, historical volumes, presentation items, inscribed treasures, and rare works of all kinds. Without them the splendid private and public libraries with rare-book collections would be pointless palaces containing empty or anemic shelves. The Brown in Providence, Clements in Ann Arbor, Folger in Washington, Huntington in San Marino, Morgan in Manhattan, Widener in Cambridge, and others were the direct results of smart and hardworking booksellers, some on or from Book Row, who sought, found, recognized, and sold the books that keep the libraries worthy of scholarly celebration.

The great collections wouldn't exist if booksellers hadn't located, identified, and then rescued vulnerable rarities from the ravages of time, the indifference of the multitude, and quite often the impetuosity of hasty heirs eager to make way for a quick deal so they could divvy up the take. The essential first step was getting rid of those beat-up old books collected by crazy Uncle Charlie, may he rest in peace, who made all those sly booksellers rich.

Book love—let's face it—that's why most of the booksellers gladly gave their lives to the noble enterprise, even those who might have jeered at the word "noble" and shouted, "Get out of here with your cockamamy grand illusions about my motives!"

"Collect, then, the books you enjoy reading," Herbert Faulkner West strongly advised in *Modern Book Collecting for the Impecunious Amateur* (1936). The sometimes impecunious booksellers frequently adopted a parallel policy by specializing in the books that meant most to them, from anthropology to zoology—whether art or first editions or Americana or poetry or economics or philosophy or history or other things.

HAROLD AND GERTRUDE BRIGGS—BOOKS 'N THINGS

If a particularly smart computer—the one they haven't built yet—could be loaded with all the applicable data (which they haven't determined yet) and asked to provide a template of the ideal book-loving, bookselling couple, it might grind its electronic gears and depict Harold and Gertrude Briggs. Harold, informed of such a result, would have deplored it as nonsense and perhaps quoted relevant lines from one of his own poems in *Selected Poems of Harold Briggs*: "Knowledge is a fraction of the mystery / perfection is a malady of youth."

Harold Briggs was described by his wife, Gertrude, as "a poet and a great reader." He was a published author, with poems in many of the journals and little magazines of his day and in a collection of poems, *Though Man Flies Angel High* (1959). He also made contributions on behalf of ex-servicemen and various liberal causes to left-wing publications such as *New Masses,* a magazine that published proletarian writers while championing unions, civil liberties, and minority rights, and the *Daily Worker,* published by the American Communist Party.

A genial bookman in appearance and manner, he was a crusader with words when the cause was right—or rather left. His pamphlet *The Veterans Fight for Unity* (1935) reprinted portions of earlier articles and scathingly reported on "the struggle of the attached and unattached rank-and-file vets against the old-line reactionary, officer-controlled organizations." He denounced the cruel, stingy treatment accorded ex-servicemen during the 1930s by the government they had served in combat for $1.25 per day: "One hundred and eighty-one millionaires were made while the vets were being blown to bits defending their profits." His poems and polemics suggest that Harold Briggs had the talent and indignation to be a major journalist and radical poet fighting in print for veterans and the underprivileged during the Depression, when the rich were still getting richer. "Twenty-six new millionaires were made last year," he wrote. "Twenty-six people wallow in luxury. Sixteen million haven't enough food, clothing, and shelter to maintain a decent standard of living."

As his wife pointed out, Harold was a great reader as well as a poet. Writing takes time away from reading, and vice versa. So choices had to be made. Harold chose bookselling, which let him work in the world of books and allowed him interludes for writing and reading.

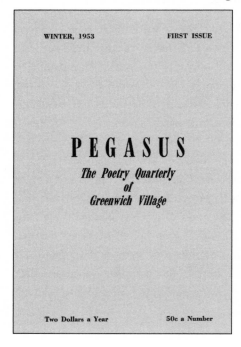

Before venturing forth with a store of his own, Briggs worked at the Samuel Weiser Bookstore, where books constituted his main pay. In the 1930s he financed his writing and reading as a book scout. A reader's knowledge and sharp eyes made him good at it. Among his book-scouting highlights were two first editions: a mint copy of *The Red Badge of Courage* for ten cents and a copy of *The Scarlet Letter* for twenty-five cents. He sold them for $125 and $100, respectively.

The call of romance and Gertrude's practicality were dual

catalysts for the first Briggs bookstore. When they talked about getting married, she questioned the hit-and-miss nature of book scouting as a realistic occupation for a family man. A typical deal at the time for Harold Briggs was to find a rare book on Book Row or elsewhere for around $2, sell it for $5 to a rare-book dealer or a store with a rare books department such as Barnes & Noble or Scribner's, and thus at the terminus of convoluted transactions earn around $3.

Gertrude remembered asking Harold what he knew that he could use to achieve more stability and earn a steady living. "I know books," he answered. Gertrude promptly suggested they start their own bookstore. Acting on a lead from Stanley Gilman, she located a place on East Tenth Street that was renting for $18 per month; and Books 'N Things was born.

"We found the space, and our friends helped build the shelves," Gertrude Briggs reminisced for this account. "So we had the store and shelves but no books. Each time Harold had a date with me, he sold more of his rare books so he could pay. When we opened the store in 1940, he was out of books. Our friends pitched in to collect more books and stock the empty shelves. There were lots of wonderful, loving people in the book trade at that time. It was a very charming store, I think, like a little European store."

In 1942 Books 'N Things became a charter member of the Fourth Avenue Booksellers' Association. The Briggses that year also relocated to 73 Fourth Avenue, at the corner of East Tenth Street, where their store remained nearly two decades and gradually evolved into a Book Row landmark. The books left behind by the previous owner were put outside and priced at a penny apiece. The penny-each disposal sale taught the Briggses a valuable lesson about never assuming everything was worthless when a considerable number of miscellaneous and apparently unimportant books were involved. Among the penny bargains, a friend of the Briggses found and considerately turned over to them a limited edition pamphlet, *Christmas Tree* (1928) by E. E. Cummings, listed at $400 in Ahearn (1998).

Their stock at the height of operations included over twenty-five thousand books and periodicals. Books 'N Things specialties focused on the literary interests of the proprietors, particularly poetry, criticism, vintage literary magazines, first editions, art, and the little magazines. The stock was also strong in press books, scholarly items, esoterica, photography, film, theater, dance, early paper Americana, and good general literature. Nostalgia items and mementos of the past authenticated the " 'N Things" part of the shop's familiar name.

In the 1950s the store was dramatically involved in a street accident, and Briggs might have been killed if he had been at his desk near the window when it happened. A three-way collision took place in the street, and one of the vehicles like a guided missile hurtled through the store window. Briggs lived to tell the tale and to continue selling, talking, and reading books on Book Row. Books 'N Things thus became living proof anything might happen in or to a Fourth Avenue bookstore!

Reminiscing about her husband, who died in 1968, Gertrude Briggs mentioned his great feeling for and knowledge about first editions and bibliography, which complemented his devotion to poetry and poets. She acknowledged that she never really shared his love of books as books, that her interest in books was that of the reader who didn't care which edition it was as long as it was accurate and complete. "Harold appreciated Kerouac and the other contemporaries. He paid attention to the writers in all the little magazines. I preferred the older classics, and the Europeans, Dostoyevsky, Proust, the German writers," she said. "So we made a good combination, modern and classical."

Harold and Gertrude Briggs also made an effective combination as the parents of two daughters, Susan and Aprille, and in the operation of the store. Aprille remembered her parents' bookstore as "kind of mysterious . . . but fun, like rummaging through an attic."

Harold and Gertrude Briggs were mutually rich in book knowledge, and both called on this knowledge when they waited on customers. Harold was the chief purchaser of new stock for the store, while Gertrude watched the counter, kept the account books, and wrote the checks. Briggs soon began issuing catalogues at the rate of about three a year, and in time they became the most productive part of the business. One of these catalogues, the last he compiled, in May 1968, just before he died, in July, became a lifelong bookseller's poignant legacy. "That catalogue kept producing sales after Harold was gone. It worked very well. All I had to do was open the orders, wrap the books, and send them," recalled Mrs. Briggs.

In 1968, Books 'N Things was no longer on Fourth Avenue. It had moved around the corner once more, to 82 East Tenth Street, next door to the location of their first shop in 1941. After her husband died, Gertrude Briggs didn't know whether she could manage the bookstore and wasn't certain whether or not she wanted to continue selling books. She remembered *AB*'s Sol Malkin telling her, "You have been around books and booksellers all your life. You don't have to know anything more."

She decided in favor of carrying on and continued to live the life of a bookseller after moving Books 'N Things to 34 East Seventh Street, across from another Manhattan landmark. The new neighbor was McSorley's Old Ale House, at 15 East Seventh, where one of the ancient slogans was "Be Good or Begone!" Joseph Mitchell in *McSorley's Wonderful Saloon* (1943) wrote that among the store's regulars were "clerks from the row of secondhand bookshops just north of Astor Place."

Books 'N Things ceased being McSorley's near neighbor when a threat to triple the rent forced Mrs. Briggs's last move, to 64 East Seventh Street in the East Village between First and Second Avenues. The plague of rising rents that afflicted secondhand bookstores was the primary reason for the migrations of Books 'N Things as it was for many other Book Row firms. Mrs. Briggs remembered that one of their landlords urged them to buy his building, and he generously offered to help them with the mortgage. They didn't accept. "Harold and I came from poor backgrounds, and we were radicals then. We didn't want to own anything," she explained from an amused and rueful perspective many years later.

Gertrude Briggs died at the age of eighty-four on February 27, 1997. She is remembered as the wife and partner of Harold Briggs, as the doyenne of Books 'N Things, and as one of the few fifty-plus-year bookselling veterans of New York's Book Row.

At the final edition of Books 'N Things, on East Seventh, Gertrude Briggs in the late 1980s calmly took note of the many changes, mostly negative from a bookseller's perspective, that she had witnessed across the Book Row area during her decades in residence. She lamented the increase in violence and tension on the streets and the area's loss of creative people, whose disappearance brought a sharp decline in the sale of art and literary works.

There were some lingering positives to acknowledge. According to reporter Kirk Johnson, writing in the *New York Times* (August 13, 1988), as she sold a book to a customer from the Bronx, she observed that "it's still a place where you can be free. For a lot of kids, coming here is a way to get away from the choking atmosphere of suburbia."

"The area has become more dangerous," she said. "Somebody held me up recently, right in the store. He asked for a book and then demanded money. I told him I had none. He took the typewriter. There's lots of stealing. Any book marked very high is certain to get lifted."

High rents drove away the bookstores that numbered nearly fifty when she arrived in the 1940s. After the bookstores were gone, the writers and artists who frequented them were gone as well. Books 'N Things on Fourth Avenue and at its other sites always attracted creative people occupied in literary and fine arts. Mrs. Briggs admitted that for years she believed Barnett Newman, the abstract expressionist, was a writer because he bought so many literary books at the store. Willem de Kooning lived nearby and was a perennial customer, as was Jackson Pollock.

"When we began, this area provided a soil for artists to grow in. It was never cutthroat. What counted was the spirit of art," said Mrs. Briggs, remembering when the avant-garde art movement used the store as a place to meet because of Harold Briggs's enthusiastic support for artistic innovation and modern movements. The store had the Artists' Club as a neighbor and was close to the Cedar Tavern, which was also a popular haunt of the abstract expressionists who frequented the Briggses' bookstore.

Book collectors and dealers were other regulars. Walter Caron was often in the store because of its fine poetry collection as well as modern and avant-garde materials. "I found several early books of poetry there for three dollars each," he stated. Harold Briggs was one of the Fourth Avenue booksellers whose knowledge and book acquisitions made him a valued expert and source for collectors. "People who started early to collect modern literature depended on Harold," said Mrs. Briggs.

Writers too were drawn to Books 'N Things by Briggs's support for contemporary poetry and writing, the ambience of the establishment, the quality of the books, and the commensurate quality of the proprietors. "On Fourth Avenue, everybody who was anybody passed by or through the bookstore," observed Gertrude Briggs. The *Partisan Review*, which spread the gospel of radical intellectualism, was headquartered nearby under the leadership of its founders, Philip Rahv and William Phillips, who were frequent Books 'N Things customers.

André Breton, the founder of Surrealism, was a customer. Others among the writers who dropped in were John Berryman, Robert Frost, Allen Ginsberg, Randall Jarrell, LeRoi Jones (Imamu Amiri Baraka), Jack Kerouac, Robert Lowell, Dwight MacDonald, Kenneth Patchen, Delmore Schwartz, and Oscar Williams. Mrs. Briggs, with the casual frankness of her late seventies, recalled Willem de Kooning as sweet and gentle and Robert Lowell as a bit of a snob. As for Kerouac: "The few times I saw Jack Kerouac, he was drunk."

A BOOK LOVER REMEMBERED A BOOK LOVER

Near the end of his life, Harold Briggs told Manuel B. Tarshish, "Fourth Avenue as a way of life is gone." He added that while the dealers engaged in strong competition, they were loyal to one another and "stuck together." Gertrude Briggs agreed the dealers were "quite competitive. But I always found them, socially, very entertaining. They were the people I most liked to be with. They had interesting stories to tell."

At the end of her interview for this account, Mrs. Briggs said, "I have nothing but wonderful things to say about the book business as I experienced it in those Book Row years and about the customers who came in. But the times have changed. I heard recently that college students were asked to name four nineteenth-century American writers, and they couldn't. They couldn't name twentieth-century writers either."

Earlier, on a happier note, she mentioned hearing from an early Book Row customer named Joe Secondi, who wrote from his home in Spartanburg,

South Carolina, after seeing the picture of her on the job at her East Seventh Street bookshop in the August 13, 1988, issue of the *New York Times*. The photograph, Joe Secondi wrote, took him back twenty-five to thirty years to his youth and a "time past that was brighter certainly because Harold and Gertrude Briggs were part of it." He thought the store looked just the same, even though it had moved from the Fourth Avenue location he knew to East Seventh Street. "Harold Briggs was—and is—one of my all-time heroes, a great man with a wonderful, sunny soul. . . . Whenever I came to New York, which was fairly often, Books 'N Things was an absolutely compulsory stop," he wrote. "I can still hear Harold's laugh even now, full of love, and goodness, and good will to man, with those wonderful smiling eyes. And for a moment or two, the reason for living is suddenly clear as the sunniness that brightened the heart." He concluded, "With wonderful undimmed memories . . . "

Such a generous, unexpected tribute from a customer who was still enormously grateful after more than a quarter of a century may in fact help answer our question "why?" Perhaps the dedicated booksellers of Fourth Avenue were often less interested in accumulating wealth, being comfortable in plush surroundings, and getting into *Who's Who* than they were in finding and selling books to appreciative customers.

Perhaps they came to believe that earning such gracious tributes from fellow friends of bookstores and lovers of books was a bookseller's medal of honor, a success mere money couldn't buy.

BERNARD KRAUS—RAVEN BOOK SHOP

In 1934 hard times were far from over, and the Great Depression seemed to have settled in for a long run. But President Franklin D. Roosevelt's New Deal policies were slowly taking hold and people were coping. Roosevelt signed the Securities Exchange Act to regulate stock markets in the future, and progress was made toward passage of the Social Security Act, which he signed into law the following year. Among national morale lifters in 1934 was a peppy little actress named Shirley Temple, who helped people forget the Depression with her movie *Stand Up and Cheer*. Crime and melodrama took over front pages and distracted everyone in July when John Dillinger was conclusively peppered in a gunfight with G-men outside the Biograph Theatre in Chicago, where he had just seen *Manhattan Melodrama,* starring Clark Gable, William Powell, and Myrna Loy.

Writers and publishers were busy too in 1934. Thomas Wolfe in Brooklyn put finishing flourishes to a 912-page novel that chronicled his years living, teaching, writing, and of course suffering in Manhattan on and around Book Row. He cashed his checks there, and the book places knew him: "From those high storied shelves of dense rich bindings the great voices of eternity, the tongues of mighty poets dead and gone, now seemed to speak to him out of the living and animate silence of the room" (*Of Time and the River,* 1935).

Also that year, Scribner's helped F. Scott Fitzgerald emerge from a long silent period by publishing *Tender Is the Night.* It was the year as well of Dashiell Hammett's *The Thin Man* and James Hilton's *Goodbye, Mr. Chips.* Booksellers in the years ahead would see these first editions grow in value. Maybe some followed an old strategy by stashing away a few copies of these promising titles when they showed up, thus forgoing present pennies for future dollars.

Speaking of Manhattan, at 112 Fourth Avenue another used bookstore opened in 1934. The founder was Bernard (known universally as Bernie) Kraus. He launched the shop in a manner fairly commonplace among start-up bookmen—he initially stocked the store with his own lovingly assembled personal library. Kraus decided that since he couldn't resist books, running a bookshop was attractive and appropriate work for him. Also to consider was the encouraging and not surprising fact that in spite of the Depression, or perhaps because of it, used-book shops in 1934 seemed to be faring better than many other businesses. Books from Book Row were a less costly and much more rewarding means of escape from trouble than most other outlets within reach of the indigent, including alcohol and debauchery. During jobless, worried, destitute times, good books available cheap could be a poor person's inviting door to joy and life-restoring companions. Bernard Kraus would offer good books.

Abraham Simon Wolf Rosenbach, bookselling monarch of the big deal whom Christopher Morley lionized as Dr. R. and who was never handicapped by humility, was asked once what he thought of impecunious collectors. Rosenbach is said to have replied cheerfully and blithely, "Don't know any." The out-of-pocket book lovers Dr. R. didn't know were welcome at Bernard Kraus's shop just as they were elsewhere along Book Row.

Bernard Kraus's specialty areas were American and English literature, with strengths in criticism and scholarly works. His store became a graduate student's oasis of last resort. It seems apropos that he entered the antiquarian book business about the same time as the appearance of milestone works by Fitzgerald and Hammett and with Wolfe's massive work a few months ahead in 1935, along with *Tortilla Flat* by John Steinbeck, the second Studs Lonigan book, *Judgment Day* by James T. Farrell, and *The Last Puritan* by George Santayana.

Santayana scared us with his cryptic warning in *The Life of Reason* (1905–6), "Those who cannot remember the past are condemned to repeat it." Yet we can fantasize tempting exceptions to that anxious maxim. The Raven Book Shop is now part of the past, and it would be wonderful to see it repeated along with the shops of his Fourth Avenue neighbors.

The name chosen for a bookstore can be an important factor in making it distinctive and memorable. Some Fourth Avenue proprietors chose their own names as the easiest exit from the dilemma of choice, and the successes of their stores made their names well remembered—Dauber & Pine, Biblo and Tannen, Gilman's, Schulte's, Stammer's, Samuel Weiser. The shops that shunned surnames ranged from the pastoral serenity of Milton Applebaum's Arcadia Bookshop to the nautical jauntiness of Irving and Irma Warshaw's Anchor Bookshop and the inviting amiability of Thomas J. Gerald's Friendly Bookshop.

Alfred F. Goldsmith and Bernard Kraus believed in the power of the birds. Goldsmith selected At the Sign of the Sparrow. Bernard Kraus named his nest of books, located upstairs, the Raven Book Shop. The raven hits readers with a high school knowledge of American literature as an ideal bird to represent a literary bookstore. The word instantly says Poe, poetry, literature, and announces the warm splendor of a cozy place with "many a quaint and curious volume of forgotten lore." The raven bespeaks a safe house where anyone can peacefully ponder, maybe stopping short of becoming weak and weary. The Nevermore bird proclaims a quiet harbor in a turbulent world where one can "borrow from books surcease of sorrow" over some lost Lenore or whatever anguish needs the healing reflection of literature.

The one-word bird splendidly symbolizes poetry and literature because of an eighteen-stanza poem featuring the feathered and winged vertebrate's name that first appeared on the front page of the January 29, 1845, *New York*

Evening Mirror. The poem struck a popular chord and made its author famous (a bibulous genius named Poe who lived for a while in the Book Row area and whose first name the Mystery Writers of America adopted for their annual Edgar award for best mystery novel). Edgar Allan Poe allegedly had to wait a year and a half for the $10 payment he was promised. The poem's first book appearance was in *The Raven and Other Poems* (1845), which contained thirty other poems in addition to the title poem, at an 1845 bookstall cost of about a penny a poem. A Jean Hersholt copy sold at auction for $500 in the 1950s. Now the price of a fine copy might easily pay for a new luxury car or a house in a good suburb, with enough left over for a modern first edition. Quoth the Raven, "Evermore."

Goldsmith's At the Sign of the Sparrow and Bernard Kraus's Raven Book Shop are affectionately remembered, but not so much for avian reasons as for the knowledge, generosity, and kindness of the bookmen who ran them. "In New York a valued friend is Mr. Alfred Goldsmith," wrote Herbert Faulkner West. "In his bookshop on Lexington Avenue I have had most charming chats with him about books and authors. His judgment is impeccable, and was long before Mr. Woollcott advertised the fact over the radio."

In any profession, there is perhaps no greater tribute than that of one's peers. "Among those in the trade, I particularly liked Bernie Kraus and his father," said Gertrude Briggs. Frederick Lightfoot, who became an important dealer in paper ephemera, archival materials, and antiquarian books with the Lightfoot Collection, began on Book Row as a young reader and collector. He particularly remembered Bernard Kraus and his father being willing to take time out from other chores to talk books with an eager teenager, answer his questions, and respect his book needs and interests. The result was lasting rapport and friendship.

"At that time, the Raven Book Shop was the only store I knew on Fourth Avenue where they made a serious attempt to stock photographs and postcards," Lightfoot wrote for this account. "When they acquired a trunk filled with stereoscopic views they realized there were collectors waiting for them. Later other dealers who had previously skipped over such materials when evaluating libraries and making purchases learned to appreciate photographs as well as related items and to make them available to collectors." Frederick Lightfoot was grateful that the Raven had been an "early bird" in that challenging area of collecting.

Associated with Bernard Kraus in the operation of the Raven Book Shop was his father, Fred, known affectionately by Book Row contemporaries as Pop Kraus. The Raven Book Shop was a charter member of the Fourth Avenue Booksellers' Association in 1942. Bernard Kraus also became an early member of the Antiquarian Booksellers' Association of America (ABAA). The Raven Book Shop was listed in the first *International Directory of Antiquarian Booksellers* (1951–52). The entry gives the shop's address as 142 Fourth Avenue and its specialties as "General Literature and History, Scholarly Books, Americana, Biography, American Civil War."

The 1950s brought the Raven Book Shop the same difficulties of rising rent and dimming prospects that beset other Fourth Avenue stores. In 1955, Bernard Kraus moved his business to a 650-square-foot space in the building at 752 Broadway, near Eighth Street. There he maintained a stock of approximately twenty-five thousand books in the specialty areas he had offered since the 1930s. The move, however, resulted in the Raven Book Shop ceasing to function as a walk-in store where browsers were welcomed. The Raven Book Shop continued as a mail-order operation with orders generated by catalogues issued twice a year. Bernard Kraus's son Jeffrey recalled in 2001 that his father often "would give illustrator Mahlon Blaine a few dollars to prepare catalogue covers for him."

The 1958 *International Directory of Antiquarian Booksellers* listed the store with the 752 Broadway address and the specialties as follows: "American and English Literature, Biography, General Literature (Criticism and Out of Print Books), History (American and Foreign)."

When he was interviewed by Manuel Tarshish for the 1969 *Publishers Weekly* series about the Fourth Avenue Book Trade, Bernard Kraus indicated that by means of his catalogues and a strong client mailing list, he expected to continue selling books with libraries throughout the world as his leading customers. That intention was effectively carried out for several years.

But time moves on, and in 1979 the Raven closed at 752 Broadway and took a short flight from Book Row to the Kraus home in Brooklyn. There Bernard Kraus continued to sell books based on *AB* quote lists, other lists, and the valuable contacts his many Book Row years generated. In 1990 Bernard Kraus, his wife, Rose, and his favorite books left the metropolitan area for a quieter reading life beyond the city. Bernard Kraus died in 1994 at the age of eighty-seven.

Considering the lasting friendships they forged with fellow booksellers and many grateful customers on Book Row, Bernard and Pop Kraus left fine memories behind and took an equal share of fine memories away. Bernard's daughter, Edith, and his sons, Alan and Jeffrey, had reason to be proud of the Kraus legacy preserved in those memories and in the annals of Book Row, where Bernard and Pop Kraus registered decades of useful service and human kindness to readers, collectors, and colleagues. Jeffrey Kraus told us that he continued the Kraus legacy as a dealer and collector of stereo views and other antique photographic images. He traced his love of photographica to the years of the Raven at 752 Broadway, where he discovered and became fascinated with such material.

Unlike the highfalutin Dr. Rosenbach, the Krauses could never say that they knew no impecunious collectors. Among the customers who walked into 112 Fourth Avenue during the 1930s and later were certainly some who debated between a book or lunch and made the wiser choice by leaving with a book. Book meals last longer and are more permanently filling than any others. You could have asked Bernard Kraus.

HARRY AND RUTH CARP—GREEN BOOK SHOP

A bookshop is known by the customers it keeps and by the quality of the books it doesn't keep as happy customers carry them away—and come back soon for more. Among the most popular Book Row stores was the Green Book Shop, operated by the husband-and-wife team of Harry H. and Ruth W. Carp. Their shop was noted for the loyalty of its many regulars, who included a number of literary celebrities plus a strong base of readers and collectors. Green Book Shop customers appreciated a reliable book place that consistently offered good literature at fair to bargain prices.

The Green Book Shop earned a reputation for the excellence of its fiction collection. It also developed a specialty in translated works, especially the novel in translation. Larry Moskowitz remembered frequently visiting the shop's fiction sections to learn what exciting new finds had invaded the shelves since his previous visit.

Another regular was Walter Caron, book collector and later proprietor of the Isaac Mendoza Book Company. An inveterate Book Row stroller with sharp eyes alert for unexpected opportunities, Caron remembered the visual feast for a bibliophile that his startled eyes devoured from the Harry and Ruth Carp window display one holiday season. Giving the holidays special attention was a Green Book Shop tradition. The entry for the shop in *Clegg's International Directory of The World's Book Trade Booksellers, Publishers, Book Collectors, etc. 1936–7* is as follows:

> **Green Book Shop.** P.: Harry H. Carp. 11, Astor Place. Fd.: 1925. 'Phone: Spring 7-1590. Bankers: Corn Exchange. Hours: 9–10. Antiquarian, new, out of print. A.S. 30,000. Window Space. Book weeks. Christmas shows.

It was a Christmas season window display that captured Walter Caron's surprised attention. His memory placed the event around the start of the 1950s. He described the moment: "One year at Christmastime I went by their store. And there in the window were two signed Faulkners! I couldn't believe it. They had just gotten them in and the price even in those years was very cheap, about $20 each. My immediate thought wasn't whether I could afford them. My thought was, I'll take them!"

Concerning the Green Book Shop and the holiday spirit, we can let ourselves speculate that the Christmas atmosphere at the shop may have been an inspirational catalyst for one of their frequent customers, writer Philip Van Doren Stern, to develop a story idea early in 1938 and to write a Christmas story he called "The Greatest Gift." When Stern's agent was unable to place the story with a magazine, the author printed it in a twenty-four-page pamphlet that he used as a 1943 Christmas card. Stern printed two hundred of the pamphlets. On the ephemera market those pamphlets would be snapped up today because of the association values that developed when his agent in 1944 sold the movie rights to the Christmas card story.

While World War II was in progress, nothing happened with the story. Its author worked for Armed Services Editions to make convenient paperbacks available free to servicemen. After the war, returning servicemen Frank Capra and Jimmy Stewart were given Stern's story. They translated it into the perennial Christmas classic *It's a Wonderful Life*. The theme of Stern's story, familiar to practically everyone because of the ceaseless rerunning of the film when the Yuletide rolls in, is that every life is immensely significant and essential to other lives, that not having been born causes enormous hardship for others, that no one is poor who has friends, and that each individual, whether aware or not, affects the lives of many different people. The importance of one individual's life in the lives of many others aptly epitomizes the careers of booksellers who put books into the hands and minds of countless readers.

Every bookseller in a sense is a George Bailey sharing "the greatest gift" through the books he obtains and delivers to others. Philip Van Doren Stern was often at the Green Book Shop. There he knew a real-life George Bailey, Harry Carp. He thought he dreamed up the whole story idea while shaving on a February Saturday in 1938, but who knows for certain about the genesis of a great idea?

The Green Book Shop was not a store specializing in mysteries. Yet among the regular customers were two of the twentieth century's leading American mystery writers. One was John Dickson Carr, master of traditional detective stories and official biographer of Sir Arthur Conan Doyle. He grew up with books in a home filled with a large library collected by his father, a lawyer and congressman during the Woodrow Wilson administration. One of his stories could have taken shape while he cruised the fiction shelves at the Carp bookshop. Called "The Gentleman from Paris," and the source for the spooky 1951 film *The Man with a Cloak*, its man of mystery is Edgar Allan Poe, played by Joseph Cotten wearing a cloak, with Barbara Stanwyck alongside as another bad, bad lady.

A loyal frequenter of the shop was writer Daniel Nathan, who teamed with his cousin Manford Lepofsky to write mysteries. They conceived the character Ellery Queen during lunch one day in 1929, changed their names to Frederic Dannay and Manfred B. Lee, and published the first of many books with "mystery" in the title, *The Roman Hat Mystery* (1929). Grab it! Their *Ellery Queen's Mystery Magazine* started in 1941, and through the years, in the magazine and anthologies, they published many stories by non–mystery writers that the collaborators blithely labeled crime stories. "The Murder in the Fishing Cat" by Edna St. Vincent Millay accompanies "mysteries" by Pearl Buck, W. Somerset Maugham, John Steinbeck, and Fannie Hurst in Ellery Queen's *The Literature of Crime* (1950). "Nearly every world-famous author has contributed to the literature of crime," wrote Ellery Queen. How many of the stories, we may wonder, resulted from Dannay's visits to the Green Book Shop on Book Row?

The Green Book Shop was started in the 1920s by Harry Carp at 11 Astor Place. Originally from Belfast, Ireland, Harry Carp served his apprenticeship in bookselling by working for a Third Avenue book dealer. In his own store, he concentrated on general literature and art books. He worked hard through the years to make the Green Book Shop synonymous with quality books in both content and format. During the 1930s the shop made a short migration to Fourth Avenue and became a valued Book Row resident at 110 Fourth Avenue, on the west side between Eleventh and Twelfth Streets.

During the 1930s and 1940s Harry Carp ran the shop while his wife, Ruth, was employed elsewhere. She was a teacher of Latin and Greek. One book dealer, when asked how he and his contemporaries survived hard times, replied cynically, "Our wives worked." Times past, times present; there's nothing new under the sun. In the case of Harry and Ruth Carp, each had important work to accomplish in his or her separate field.

At the start of the 1950s, Ruth Carp joined her husband at the store, where she became one of the great women booksellers during the last decades of Book Row. Harry Carp died in 1962, and Ruth Carp continued to operate the store on her own until the momentum of changing times forced her, in 1971, to end the shop's long service to book seekers on Fourth Avenue.

The confidence and trust her Book Row colleagues had in her was shown in 1969 when they elected her president of the Fourth Avenue Booksellers' Association. Speaking for the association, Ruth Carp told McCandlish Phillips for the *New York Times* (September 30, 1969) that the city of New York should act before it was too late to prevent the disappearance of Book Row. The city, of course, took no action, and soon it was too late.

Well past its heyday, the Green Book Shop became virtually overnight a star of show business, the beneficiary of publicity, and the victim of crime in an unfortunate chain of events. In the early years of television, a frequent nominee and winner of Emmy Awards for realistic urban drama was *Naked City*, a police show starkly filmed in New York and each week relating one of the city's "8 million stories"—the series told 138 of the 8 million. New York and its fascinating places became gritty characters in the show. Horace MacMahon as the Sixty-fifth Precinct's Lieutenant Mike Parker started each story by claiming it was filmed "in the streets and buildings of New York itself." The background for one probing episode was the Green Book Shop. The day after the screening of that *Naked City* story, conceivably as an early demonstration of the scary power of the ubiquitous tube, the store was robbed. Fame had its drawbacks.

The Green Book Shop at its peak of operations carried fifty thousand titles and displayed half of them in seventeen hundred square feet of space, with the rest in storage. Catalogues featuring literature, art, and the novel in translation were issued twice each year. A gradual reversal was noted by the Carps from the early period, when walk-in customers accounted for 65 percent of sales while orders received by mail produced 35 percent. Later the mail-order business became dominant, with 65 percent of sales.

Another transitional change, commented on by Ruth Carp, was a marked upsurge of neighborhood danger. In addition to the robbery after the showing of the *Naked City* episode featuring the store, a second robbery of the vulnerable Green Book Shop occurred. Mrs. Carp speculated that such incidents forced her to consider closing the Fourth Avenue shop and in the future to concentrate on mail-order operations from a more secure location.

She admitted such a move would be depressing for her since she loved direct contact with customers and would find working out of a loft no substitute for the rewards brought by interaction with customers in an open-door bookshop. Even the kooks would be missed. She recalled with amusement the young woman who came in all excited and exclaiming, "I heard you can pick up a book on the ten-cent stand that's worth a thousand dollars! Could you please come outside and show it to me?"

The Green Book Shop was once the subject of an article by columnist Jimmy Breslin in the *New York Herald Tribune*. Breslin was well known in his *Herald Tribune* essays for serving his city as a spokesman and sounding board of the people. Jimmy Breslin and some of his peers spoke up, but to no avail, during the period when the great and naked city stood by shrugging hopelessly as it lost the Green Book Shop and its Book Row.

CHAPTER ELEVEN

THE BOOKSELLER WITH STRONG OPINIONS
Remembering, Honoring, Fearing, and Enjoying Walter Goldwater

*All of us, I think, like to believe that we are doing something useful besides
making a large fortune; I have even met dealers who handle mainly first
and limited editions who feel, or pretend to feel, that they serve a useful
purpose in society. The dealer in special subjects knows that the chances are
that the books he supplies are being bought for use, not for display or for
appreciation in value, or even as gifts to be taken off income tax, and I find
the African field to be particularly satisfying in that respect.*
—WALTER GOLDWATER

IN THE IDIOM of a later day, Walter Goldwater would be called a man
with an attitude and a wry talent for speaking frankly. He possessed a pen-
chant for deliberately saying the outrageous. That could be amusing if you
weren't his target, irritating if you were. "Crook" was a noun he didn't hesi-
tate to use about some of his fellow booksellers, who were in most cases good
friends of his. During his own time, he was respected as a bookseller who had
strong opinions and who was fearless in expressing them, let the chips fall
where they fall. "He knew the saints and sinners, and, true to his nature,
called them by name," wrote Donald C. Dickinson in *Dictionary of American
Antiquarian Bookdealers* (1998).

Prior to his death in 1985, Walter Goldwater in an extensive tape-
recorded interview-monologue shared his encyclopedic recollections about
the bookshops and book dealers throughout the Book Row area and elsewhere in New York City since 1932, when he opened his first shop there.
The edited transcript, with name and location data provided by Marvin
Mondlin, was published in the *Dictionary of Literary Biography Yearbook*
(1993). Goldwater spoke freely about his bookselling contemporaries and
his personal views of the business. He was prompted by an unidentified
interrogator; but for the most part the interview was Walter Goldwater
winging it with insight, sarcasm, affection, panache, and a modicum of

exaggeration, concerning the Book Row he remembered, loved, missed, and casually stripped bare without mincing words.

About a bookselling couple his Olympian conclusion was, "He never knew anything about books, and she doesn't either." A venerable colleague was "a scoundrel from the very beginning." One prominent dealer "never did anything honest in his life." Goldwater's verdict on Christopher Morley's sentimental classic *The Haunted Bookshop* was, "A terrible book." Another bookman, an uptowner and thus by definition suspect, was "generally a scoundrel, I believe, and certainly dishonest." Being fair, though, to book-dealing tricksters, bunco artists, book bluffers, erotica peddlers, and first edition brigands, Goldwater cynically acknowledged, "I imagine that not too many people are completely pure in the book business, actually."

He never spared himself when dishing out the criticism. One recollection involved Harry F. Marks, a bookseller who in partnership with Harry Stone specialized in "erotica and fine bindings." Marks was an agent for Black Sun Press, and Goldwater bought a large number of Black Sun Press imprints when Marks's shop closed, including multiple copies of works by James Joyce and Ezra Pound. He remembered the purchase as decidedly clever, yet his follow-up was anything but. He hurried to the West Forties and for a dollar or two profit on each book sold them to the Gotham Book Mart and the Seven Gables Bookshop among others, thus harvesting a swift profit. Later many of the books really took off in value, and he knew if he had held them a few years he could have made a fortune. "These things have simply skyrocketed. My usual shrewd maneuver," he concluded.

In his rambling, revealing, and informative recollections, Walter Goldwater was also generous with praise for the booksellers who impressed him with their knowledge (Charles Everitt, Lathrop Harper, Michael Papantonio, Frank Thoms), their character (Alfred Goldsmith, George Preston, Peter Lader), and their business acumen (Benjamin Bass, Biblo and Tannen, Louis Cohen). One bookseller, George Van Nosdall, earned begrudging respect on a single point: He shared with Goldwater rare specific knowledge about the first issue of Anthony Hope's *The Prisoner of Zenda* (1894), which had seventeen, not eighteen, titles on the first page of the advertisements. "He was the only person besides me who knew that, and the only person besides me who cared," said Goldwater, explaining his grounds for friendship.

Van Nosdall was a member of the pro-Nazi bund headed by Fritz Kuhn, and one of New York's few right-wing book dealers. Goldwater noted that Van Nosdall regularly claimed to be swindled by others, "which was probably true, although if anybody could swindle him, we always felt good luck to him." But Goldwater credited Von Nosdall in spite of a contemptible ideological stance with the estimable virtue of at least liking books: "He really cared about books and really cared about first editions." This was an exercise in tolerance and no trivial concession for the lifelong liberal Walter Goldwater.

A Propensity for Independent Thinking

Walter Goldwater was born in Harlem on July 29, 1907. His father, Dr. Abraham Goldwater, was a political radical, a viewpoint vigorously and permanently shared by his son. Walter passed the stiff selection process for admittance to Townsend Harris High School. Then his maverick impulse to go his own way revealed itself when he was expelled for spending all his time playing chess and ignoring school. Back in high school, he graduated at fifteen, briefly attended City College of New York, and graduated from the University of Michigan at the age of twenty in 1927. Back home in New York, he worked fitfully at clerical jobs during the late 1920s while he decided what he wanted to do in life.

In 1930, he accepted employment at International Publishers, then the most prominent communist publishing organization in the United States. Inspired by the communist idealism of the era, he studied Russian in Paris and went to Russia with his wife, Ethel, in 1931. In Moscow, Goldwater helped set up the Cooperative Publishing Society of Foreign Workers in the U.S.S.R. and worked for the organization as a translator and editor. He soon became a critic of Stalinism due to the rigged trials he witnessed in Moscow and as a result was accused of anticommunist tendencies. He defended himself successfully, but he was clearly guilty of being disillusioned about the Stalin variety of communism. Walter Goldwater was never conventional or orthodox in outlook for long. Turned off by the brutality of the existing system in Russia, Goldwater and his wife came back to New York early in 1932. Russia's loss was Book Row's gain.

In 1932, with the help of his wife's uncle, book dealer and scout Abe Sugarman, he established the University Place Book Shop on University Place, a block west of Broadway. The bookish rebel at the age of twenty-five was finally on a career path that would keep him productively busy for more than half a century. Goldwater made this entrepreneurial leap by investing his own $100 savings and borrowing $500 from relatives. He began in partnership with the experienced Sugarman, whose opening advice was to obtain stock from the ten- to thirty-five-cent cheap-book tables at the Thoms & Eron bookstore on Chambers Street.

The great attraction for a start-up bookseller at T&E was the wide range of stock available and frequent books in bulk special sales, as Frank Thoms unloaded books in massive quantities and "was always ready to make a deal." It was Thoms who convinced Goldwater he must take a chance and vigorously buy books, loads of books, if he wanted to sell books.

Communication with Frank Thoms led Goldwater to his "swimming upstream" notion that consulting *American Book Prices Current (ABPC)* was not always the best way to proceed for a bookman. Thoms found a book listed at $25 and concluded that was its worth. But Goldwater's partner, Heinz Maienthau, who succeeded Sugarman, had just sold the item for about $175. "The question of looking up books and *Book Prices Current* from that moment to this has always seemed to me a matter which does not teach anybody much, unless he knows something about books in general. . . . I have always found it a very unimportant part of my business, and I believe it should be an unimportant part of anybody's business," declared Goldwater.

He added that in some instances he remembered such price-checking as a definitive guide to the buying price, and the selling price of a book "made a negative difference" and actually cost him money. He stressed the importance of learning the price range for a period of years to recognize trends. In this he was supported by Jack Tannen, who recommended consulting *ABPC* over several years to determine if a book is rising or falling in value.

In addition to acquiring books at T&E, Goldwater obtained valuable stock at the Isaac Mendoza bookstore on Ann Street. He considered it a very good shop and was on friendly terms with the sons of Isaac Mendoza. With a flair for contradiction, he whimsically called each son "stupider than the one before" while praising their store, their knowledge of first editions, and their specialization in Americana, with particular emphasis on New York. "They were always very friendly, and I was always able to buy," observed Goldwater, flaunting his own possibly tongue-in-cheek representation of the Mendoza brothers.

At the University Place Book Shop, Heinz Maienthau succeeded Abe Sugarman as Goldwater's partner until 1937. Maienthau was among Germany's countless thousands of refugees during the 1930s when tyrannical madness was replacing sanity with the rise of Hitler. He was one of the German Jews who managed to flee the country and settle in the United States. Bookselling had been his profession before leaving Germany, and this experience served the University Place Book Shop well for several years. Working with Maienthau assisted Walter Goldwater in building up his own knowledge and experience for successful antiquarian bookselling. Later Maienthau was associated with the bookselling operations of Sears, Roebuck and Company.

During the 1930s the store was nomadic in the fashion of several other Book Row shops. The 1936–37 *Clegg's International Directory* had it located at 105 University Place. More migrations lay ahead. The store relocated to 69 University Place in 1939, where it stayed put through the 1960s. The 1951–52 *International Directory of Antiquarian Booksellers* listed 69 University Place and named as specialties "Negro, Chess, Early Printed, Political Science, West Indies." The 1958 *International Directory* updated the specialties to read: "Americana (West Indies), Incunabula, Periodicals (Little Magazines), Topography (Africana), Sports & Pastimes (Chess)." Through the 1970s to its lamented final closing in 1995, the University Place Book Shop was a block east of University Place in a ninth-floor loft at 821 Broadway.

Staying alive into the mid-1990s, Walter Goldwater's bookstore was one of Book Row's longest-enduring shops. By then it and the Strand, across the street on Broadway, were among Book Row's final survivors, the last of the group from the 1930s and earlier. The store, still true to its founder under the proprietorship of Goldwater's chosen successor, William French, was still listed in the 1994–95 *International Directory* with most of its old specialties: "Africa, African-American Studies, Communism & Socialism, Early Books, West Indies."

When the shop was ensconced at 69 University Place it was described by Manuel Tarshish, in 1969, as a twenty-foot-by-sixty-foot space filled to overflowing with sixty thousand books in Goldwater's various specialties. At that time most sales were the result of orders received through the mail. Many orders were produced by the store's catalogues. Others were due to quotations on available items submitted by the owner and his staff to potential buyers. Some important orders involved purchases by libraries and private collectors whom the University Place Book Shop regularly and steadily supplied. By the late 1960s, the store no longer relied on sales directly to walk-in customers who came to browse and sometimes to buy, and in 1969 Walter Goldwater curtailed close to four decades of walk-in bookselling services. He moved his business to a Broadway loft, where he intended future sales to be generated predominantly by mail orders based on catalogues and quotations.

In its ninth-floor incarnation at 821 Broadway, the bookshop was described by Olivier Stephenson, in "The University Place Bookshop: A Labor of Love," *Village Voice*, June 18, 1985, as a store where the "seemingly stifling clutter is as charming as its affable, unpretentious owner." With poignant irony the article was published just six days before the death of Walter Goldwater, on June 24, thus denying us his reaction to the graceful epithet "affable." Concerning the loft arrangement, Stephenson wrote, "Despite what appears to be chaos, all the books are perfectly alphabetized. In fact, the inherent, albeit organized, funkiness of the bookshop is its heart and soul. And Goldwater wouldn't have it any other way." The *Voice* journalist noted that in 1985 the shop contained seventy to eighty thousand items, including "the largest collection of black studies in America, if not the entire world."

The Walter Goldwater Specialties

Walter Goldwater considered most of the Book Row businesses in the early years general secondhand and out-of-print bookstores that could not accurately be called shops with specialized strengths in specific areas. "The dealers made their living by people coming in from the street and buying books at a price which was generally low, but which represented a very, very substantial profit," he said.

Selling rare books accumulated by a bookseller in specialized areas such as fiction or Americana, he acknowledged, came later to Book Row. Goldwater believed he was partially responsible for the transition through his growing emphasis on books in several special categories that intrigued him. "When I first started in this business, there was no such thing. Everybody's was a general bookshop," he stated. He admitted that his particular interests, which grew in number through the years, were the primary reasons that he originally entered the used-book field, intending to distribute books and widen understanding about those areas of knowledge.

The bookstore's initial topics of concentration were chess, Russia, and radicalism, which were Goldwater's main fields of expertise in 1932. But those specialties were rapidly joined by others as his reading and curiosity led him to new territories for mental adventures—and books to sell. A posthumous tribute by Milton Finkelstein in *Chess Life,* December 1985, with its title appropriately recognized the scope and diversity of his intellectual explorations: "Walter Goldwater: He Was a Renaissance Figure."

The left-wing causes that he inherited from his influential father and his father's friends—among them John Reed, Emma Goldman, James Weldon Johnson, W. E. B. Du Bois, and Arthur Spingarn—remained strong and well served at the shop. Later Goldwater declared that his store specialized in *political* literature, not political *literature.*

In addition to radicalism, communism, socialism, and the political left, chess was always an important part of Goldwater's life. For chess aficionados his bookstore was the place to go for the latest, best, and rarest items on the royal game. Goldwater mastered the sedentary sport of chess strategy as a boy and never lost his love of the game. He competed in many New York City chess tournaments and was quick to boast that he had been beaten by the world's best players, including precocious teenager Bobby Fischer. At the time of his death, Goldwater was the president of the Marshall Chess Club at 23 West Tenth Street. The club was founded in 1915 by chess champion Frank J. Marshall and became famous as the site of national championships, memorable tournaments, and such historic competitions as Bobby Fischer versus Donald Byrne in 1956, playing "the game of the century." (Roy Meador, familiar with Book Row's Goldwater, was also a frequenter of Manhattan's chess clubs, with an impressive record of defeat by Fischer and other grand masters who were often available for games at a price.)

Goldwater's chess specialty merged with his best-known field of concentration, books by black authors, when he discovered an 1873 chess book by Theophilos Thompson, which he considered at that time the only book about chess by a black writer. The University Place Book Shop's tremendous holdings in black authors and black studies began to take shape soon after the store opened. The inventory reflected the owner's background. As a boy Goldwater had known several prominent black activists who were friends of his father. At the University of Michigan he was greatly impressed when he heard a lecture given by one of those friends, the black writer and civil rights leader W. E. B. Du Bois, who directed publicity and research and edited the monthly journal *Crisis* during the early decades of the National Association for the Advancement of Colored People (NAACP). In the 1950s, Du Bois's *Black Reconstruction* was issued in a new edition by Walter Goldwater.

Goldwater became more deeply involved with black studies in 1933 when Arthur Spingarn—a friend of his father, the brother of an NAACP founder, Joel Spingarn, and himself an NAACP leader—entered the store and placed a standing request for any books Goldwater could find by black authors. From then on, chess and radicalism shared the limelight with black studies and were in time overshadowed by the proprietor's commitment to make the University Place Book Shop a leading source of materials on black authors, black studies, Africana, and related areas.

If a bookstore succeeds in finding large quantities of specialized books, it must also find customers. Arthur Spingarn assisted by acquainting others with the store and by giving Goldwater leads to interested public libraries and to black universities, including Atlanta, Fisk, Howard, and Tuskegee. The Schomburg Collection at the New York Public Library was another customer identified by Spingarn. Bibliophile and historian of Africa Arthur Schomburg helped found the Negro Book Exchange and assembled a major collection of books and other materials in black history that he sold to the New York Public Library in 1926. From 1932 until his death in 1938, Schomburg was curator of the collection at the 135th Street branch; and he continued to make additions to it through purchases, some from the University Place Book Shop. The collection eventually evolved into an important research arm of the New York Public Library as the Schomburg Center for Research in Black Culture.

Goldwater methodically expanded his black authors' collection to include African books and pamphlets on the slave trade, Africana materials generally, and Caribbean studies. He wrote in "World of Africana" (1965 *AB*) that his Africana specialty started in 1951 at an Oxford, England, bookshop when he bought about 250 books on Africa, thus more than doubling the two hundred

African books he already owned. From that modest beginning, he moved steadily on, until in 1965 he could write, "I have handled somewhat more than one hundred thousand African items, and keep a stock of more than ten thousand pieces on hand." Among Goldwater's friends in the radical movement were the black authors Langston Hughes and Claude McKay. Their books, now frequently into four figures for the first editions, were always popular and often available at the University Place Book Shop.

Radicalism and mutual condemnation of Stalinist communism drew Goldwater and Richard Wright into a close and lasting friendship. "I found him to be the kind of person whom I would like to talk to all the time," he said about Wright. He visited the expatriate American writer in Paris after World War II. When Richard Wright died November 20, 1960, he was cremated with a copy of *Black Boy* for burial at Père Lachaise cemetery in his adopted city of Paris. Goldwater obtained several of the author's manuscripts, which later went to the Schomberg Center for Research in Black Culture.

Goldwater's focus on African-American subjects, Africana, the West Indies, and the wide spectrum of radical politics led the store to an associated specialty in pamphlets, antislavery publications, and black journals such as *Negro Digest* and *Ebony*.

While dealing in these specialization markets, the store kept its focus as a general bookshop with substantial holdings in literature and poetry, including large numbers of little magazines. Gertrude Briggs recalled for this account that Walter Goldwater "knew many, many things" and mentioned that when Harold Briggs at Books 'N Things was oversupplied with little magazines, Walter Goldwater either bought them for the University Place Book Shop or advised Briggs where he would find a buyer for them. With Walter Goldwater no longer available, she exclaimed, "I must have twenty boxes of little magazines that I don't know what to do with!" The University Place Book Store became widely known for its vast supply of little magazines.

In one transaction, Goldwater purchased for a penny or two each an estimated ten thousand such publications from the Pratt bookshop a few blocks away at 475 Sixth Avenue, near Twelfth Street, after the deaths of the proprietors Charles S. Pratt and his wife. Among the little magazines were large runs of *Bibelot, Black Cat, Dome, Yellow Book,* and the *Philistine*. Goldwater remembered that the acquisition included about a thousand copies of *Black Cat,* which he offered unsuccessfully to Princeton University for twenty-five cents each. He admitted he had "a great deal of difficulty" selling the publications from Pratt's. Yet, eventually he "did all right with them" through sales to the University of Connecticut, Yale University, and others. About the Pratt bookstore, he reminisced that it was taken over first by Edward Weiss, who then sold it to an English bookman who liked to discuss bicycles. "If you'd go there and talk to him about bicycles, then you could buy books at a low price sometimes," he recalled.

Goldwater underscored his credentials as a Renaissance man by developing a scholarly interest in incunabula. These are the books, pamphlets, and other printed matter produced prior to 1501 during the vast outpouring that followed the introduction of printing from movable type in the fifteenth century by Johann Gutenberg of Germany, Laurens Koster of Holland, Pamfilo Castaldi of Italy, and their contemporaries.

Goldwater's study, collecting, and marketing of incunabula resulted in his writing and speaking on the subject. He recorded his incunabula views in 1978 for an Antiquarian Booksellers' Association of America rare-book tape. Writing in *Octavo* (fall 1972) for the Society of Bibliophiles at Brandeis University, Goldwater in his essay "On Collecting Incunabula" emphasized both the pleasures and the surprisingly broad availability of incunabula items, whose age alone would probably keep their values climbing.

He argued that the 1501 cutoff date was arbitrary and that astute collectors should consider the 1501–35 period of postincunabula items as well. "Even in my comparatively short term of thirty-nine years as a bookseller, books of the 1501–1535 period have become that much older and that much more desirable," he pointed out. He noted that while tens of thousands of incunabula items exist, few appear on the market each year; and he warned that "the chances are small of finding what we in the book-business call a 'sleeper' among incunabula."

His own collection was fairly large but "not by any means a great one." Many of his incunables were fair to poor copies and sold for very little. He concluded his essay: "I believe that many people—if they decided on incunabula collecting (rather than some other mania!)—would find that not only could they afford it but that the satisfaction of obtaining something of lasting and even increasing value, and often of great beauty, would, indeed, make the price seem inconsequential. I hope that one or two of the readers of this article will be persuaded."

The future pleasures of those readers may have been on his mind when he reached the decision to put his personal library of incunabula back into circulation for collectors. He had part of his collection auctioned at the Swann Galleries during his lifetime. The remainder was auctioned by his heirs. His, as he claimed, good-but-not-great collection included among a large number of ordinary publications several items that cost from $500 to over $5,000, including a leaf of the Gutenberg Bible, the Aldine edition of *Politian* from the Venetian press of Aldus Manutius, a Spanish Seneca, an incunabulum from Constantinople, a 1493 Hebrew work, and two English incunabula.

Other published writings by Walter Goldwater related to his bookstore specialties included an essay, "Radical Literature," that appeared in *Bibliognost* (1975). His work and studies made him an authority on radical periodicals. His most important contribution to bibliography was the 1964 publication for the Yale University Library of *Radical Periodicals in America 1890–1950*. This carefully compiled annotated bibliography based on his own research and holdings of ephemeral radical publications skillfully covers an important subject and is considered a permanent, influential contribution to the field.

Following his disillusionment with Stalinism, Goldwater became a Trotskyite and was proud of the fact that he was a guide for Leon Trotsky's grandson at the New York World's Fair of 1939. In the 1950s he joined with another Trotskyite and champion of democratic socialism, Irving Howe, along with others of like mind to start the magazine *Dissent, a Journal of Socialist Thinking*, with Howe as the editor.

The sincerity and intensity of Walter Goldwater's commitment to what he believed in politically convinced Samuel Lipman, Goldwater's tennis partner and author of "Walter Goldwater: A Memoir," in the *New Criterion* (January 1991), that his friend "thought not being smart about politics was the worst indictment that could be brought against a supposedly serious person" and that "Walter was indeed a secular moralist, whose god was reason."

Book Row customer Wayne Somers, reflecting on the range and fervor of Goldwater's interests, concluded that while he had doubts about some Book Row dealers, he thought Walter Goldwater deserved Manuel Tarshish's description of the bookmen there as people with "devotion to the eternal values of the printed word." It would have been interesting to hear the subject react, with amused and probably sardonic appreciation, to such ardent praise.

Early in his bookselling career, Walter Goldwater began utilizing catalogues to produce business. He issued over two hundred catalogues, and in the course of years he came to rely on catalogues for the bulk of his sales. A 1934 catalogue from the University Place Book Shop was entitled "The Negro" and was the first of many on black and African books. Books by and about black people were listed, and those written by black authors were identified with an asterisk as in the following item from Catalogue 117, 1961–62:

538 *Wright, Richard. Escucha, Hombre Blanco! (White Man, Listen). 177 pp. Wr. Buenos Aires (1959). $3.50

The asterisk next to the name of a black writer was appreciated by some, opposed by others. "If they wanted the asterisk removed, it was removed," said Goldwater. One of his father's friends, the author and lecturer Jean Toomer, who wrote *Cane* (1923)—listed in Ahearn (1998) at $10,000—objected to an asterisk next to his name. Off came the asterisk for Jean Toomer in later catalogues. But Goldwater continued the practice because it was a convenient and simple typographic means of distinguishing black authors in the widely distributed and effective catalogues.

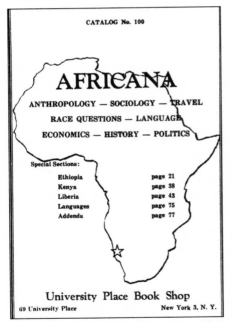

CATALOG No. 100

AFRICANA

ANTHROPOLOGY — SOCIOLOGY — TRAVEL
RACE QUESTIONS — LANGUAGE
ECONOMICS — HISTORY — POLITICS

Special Sections:
Ethiopia	page 21
Kenya	page 38
Liberia	page 43
Languages	page 75
Addenda	page 77

University Place Book Shop
69 University Place   New York 3, N. Y.

University Place Book Shop catalogues were compiled for other specialty areas including the fascinating field of incunabula. Catalogue 69, "Early Printed Books," listed nearly all of the store's incunabula and a small portion of the sixteenth- and seventeenth-century materials. The catalogue advised customers that incunabula are never really cheap but that "aside from the most expensive fifty pieces . . . the average price is no more than $10.00." A scholarly impression was made with a short description of the chief references utilized in the catalogue:

S.T.C. A Short-Title Catalogue of Books Printed in England, Scotland, & Ireland, And of English Books Printed Abroad 1475–1640, Compiled by A. W. Pollard & G. R. Redgrave, London, 1946.

BISHOP. A Checklist of American Copies of "Short-Title Catalogue" Books, Compiled by William Warner Bishop, Ann Arbor, 1944.

WING. Short-Title Catalogue of Books Printed in England, Scotland, Ireland, Wales, and British America . . . 1641–1700, Compiled by Donald Wing. New York, 1945.

STILLWELL. Incunabula in American Libraries. A Second Census . . . Edited by Margaret Bingham Stillwell. New York, 1940.

The following entries illustrate the meticulous descriptions and interesting details that are prevalent throughout a catalogue that still instructs and entertains browsers decades after the books and their prices have gone:

1. **Antoninus Florentinus.** Summa Theologica. Part III (of four parts). Venice, L. Wild, 1480. Folio. 210 leaves (first blank). Nicely rubricated, with many small initials in red and blue. Calf over contemporary oak boards, calf much worn and defective, but with nice design still clear on back cover. Margins badly worm-eaten, but text not affected. Fine large margins. $75.00 Hain 1244. Stillwell A. 778

Readers of Walter Goldwater's *Octavo* essay "On Collecting Incunabula" learn that Hain's bibliography of incunabula, published in the nineteenth century, "remains the indispensable work."

19. **Aldine Printing.** Juvenalis; Perseus. Aldine device on title. Small 8vo, 78 leaves, 18th century mottled calf, back gilt; carmine edges. Venetiis, Aedibus Aldi et Andreae Soceri, Augusto, 1501 $27.50 *Handsome, large copy of this early Aldine edition of Juvenal and Persius.*

The famous device associated with Aldine books is the depiction of a dolphin—for speed—and an anchor, for holding fast, which Aldus Manutius adapted from a coin of the emperor Vespasian.

119. **Wither, George.** Britain's Remembrancer, containing a Narrative of the Plague lately past; a Declaration of the Mischiefs present; and a Prediction of Judgments to come; (if Repentance prevent not). Extra engraved title showing map of England, etc. Thick small 12mo, full brown calf, double gilt fillet borders, leather label, by C. SMITH ; gilt edges. John Grismond in Ivie-Lane, 1628. FINE. $35.00 *First Edition, with the rare leaf of explanation facing the engraved title. Wither was unable to procure a license for this work, which explains his statement— "I was faine to imprint every sheet thereof with my owne hand, because I could not get allowance to doe it publickly." A very few blank margins neatly repaired.*

A curious and beguiling English poet was George Wither. He spent time in prison for writing a book of satires. He viewed himself as divinely inspired. And captured by the Royalists while fighting for the Puritans in the Civil War, he was allegedly saved from hanging by Royalist poet Sir John Denham on the grounds that "whilst Wither lived he [Denham] should not be the worst Poet in England."

HYMN TO TOBACCO
315. **Thorius, Raphael.** Hymnus Tabaci. (64 pages), small 8vo, contemporary morocco. Londini, T.N. pro H. Moseley, 1651. SCARCE. $20.00 *New edition, corrected. Excellent copy of this little work, by a London physician who had studied at Oxford and Leyden.*

326. **Walker, Wm.** A Treatise of English Particles. Extra engraved title. Thick 8vo, old calf. London, J. H. for G. Pawlett, 1691. $7.50 *Tenth Edition. Some marginal worming; occasional inked marginalia. Valuable especially for the flavor of its English idioms.*

The flavor of this University Place Book Shop catalogue on incunabula and the printed books of the following two centuries has a narcotic quality.

As with other intriguing catalogues from the past, one starts reading, expecting to dip in quickly, glance with mild curiosity at a few items, and promptly return to the real world. But the catalogue with its vanished books and prices just doesn't like to let go.

The no-longer-available books from another age and their descriptions hold a reader with any interest in early printed books hypnotically captive, as did Coleridge's ancient mariner with that waylaid wedding guest. Who is sufficiently weak in curiosity to pass up details on one of Shakespeare's source books, or item 79, *Aristotles Politiques*, or item 88, a 1602 edition of Chaucer with a list of "old and obscure words prooved," or item 196, Joseph Glanvil's *Saducismus Triumphastus, or Full and Plain Evidence Concerning Witches and Apparitions*, 1682, a "classic of witchcraft." Forgetting the frustration that every item is unavailable, one financially frugal benefit of perusing old book catalogues is that there's no chance whatever of overspending.

Building Associations

One of Walter Goldwater's protégés in the antiquarian book business was Eleanor Lowenstein, who worked at the University Place Book Shop before she opened her own Corner Book Shop at 102 Fourth Avenue in 1940. Walter and Eleanor started a more personal association than bookselling when they married in 1954 and took up residence in an apartment above the Corner Book Shop.

While their bookstores were kept separate, the Goldwaters often worked together on behalf of the Antiquarian Booksellers' Association of America (ABAA). Goldwater took part in the 1949 meetings at New York that led to the establishment of the ABAA, and he became a founding member of the association. At the March 31, 1949, meeting in New York of eighty-one book dealers to complete organizational arrangements and to elect interim officers, Goldwater initiated the discussion that led to the decision about ABAA membership dues.

The Goldwaters were active members of the ABAA, yet their results at ABAA events didn't always fulfill expectations. The University Place Book Shop and the Corner Book Shop shared a booth at the ABAA's second Antiquarian Book Fair, held in the Colonial Room of the Park Sheraton

Hotel, April 3–8, 1961. The April 24, 1961, issue of *AB* reported that the Goldwaters were pleased by the location chosen, the setting, and the cooperation among the participating dealers; but they were discouraged by the poor results they achieved during the event. Walter Goldwater with his trademark frankness said, "Either our fields are too specialized, or maybe we're bum salesmen—or both."

Goldwater's associations in the world of writers were numerous. One close friend was novelist James T. Farrell, creator of the Studs Lonigan trilogy (1932–35), with whom he played softball in Riverside Drive Park on Manhattan's West Side. He was the model for a character in Mary McCarthy's *The Oasis* (1949), her novel about Trotskyites launching a utopian community. The Goldwater character is described as a radical printer, "a tall, thin young man with an ovoid head who resembled a nail-file." McCarthy portrayed him rather meanly, but Goldwater was pleased anyway. Another literary friend with whom Goldwater shared political rapport was Dwight MacDonald. He lived nearby in the Book Row area on Tenth Street. About MacDonald, according to Olivier Stephenson in the *Village Voice*, Goldwater remarked with admiration, "He didn't stick to something if he didn't think it was *right*." Goldwater was impressed that his friend readily admitted being wrong as he evolved from socialism to anarchism to claiming he wasn't anything at all. "I think that was more like it," observed Goldwater, who may have been describing himself as well as Dwight MacDonald.

Another curious association that qualifies as a historical footnote to the 1930s was between Goldwater and the author of *Witness* (1952), Whittaker Chambers. Before switching over to militant anticommunism and becoming a poster boy for American conservatives, Chambers, an active communist, tried to recruit Goldwater, whose bookstore background and his Soviet experience would enable him, Chambers thought, to set up a front for communist agents. The plan was for Goldwater to run a bookstore near Columbia University that agents could meet in and use as a mail drop. Interested in the cause and possibly the intrigue, Goldwater went to Communist Party headquarters near Union Square for final approval, but, he recalled, he was denied the assignment because his knowledge of Russian made him inexplicably and unacceptably suspicious in the paranoid atmosphere of the times.

In 1981 Goldwater told John Nielsen of the *New York Times* ("Old Book-stores: A Chapter Ends," May 31, 1981) that it was time to assign the Book Row he had occupied nearly half a century an epitaph: "As a book center, the street is gone. Somebody dies, somebody becomes moribund, somebody moves to Florida. Most of us never made a substantial living anyway. . . . There aren't many young people entering this field. There isn't anybody to take over." However, through luck and foresight the University Place Book Shop was an exception.

During 1960 a young person, nineteen-year-old William French, entered the antiquarian book field by moving from earnest browser to the many-sided job of Walter Goldwater's assistant at the University Place Book Shop. In that complicated role, his initial task was to alphabetize radical pamphlets, which helped him begin developing expertise concerning the radical movement's people and publications. What began as a routine employee-employer relationship evolved into an enduring friendship and partnership. Goldwater in 1985 told Olivier Stephenson, "Somehow or other we just fitted. I didn't need somebody who did things exactly perfectly. I needed somebody who cared about the things that he was working with. We have a wonderful relationship."

When he joined Goldwater, Bill French's literary preferences were for writers such as Sherwood Anderson and William Faulkner. He soon expanded his knowledge and interest to embrace the store's specialties, including black and radical literature. In addition to his knowledge of the literature, French developed an exceptional ability to know precisely where thousands of books were located in the crowded store. He often impressed visitors by putting requested volumes quickly in their hands after a swift excursion into the towering stacks. Goldwater willed the bookshop to Bill French, who managed to keep it operating despite strangling rent hikes for another ten years after the founder's death in 1985. In 1981, French noted that the rent on the store's loft space at 821 Broadway had increased in eight years from $300 to $1,005 a month.

During the final years after the death of his wife, Walter Goldwater continued living in the apartment above the Corner Book Shop on Fourth Avenue. The owner of the building, Grace Church, had other ambitions for the site; but Goldwater stubbornly stayed put because the apartment was his Book Row home and because he still had close friends living nearby who could drop by for a meal and another session of musing about the past. The Book Row he knew might be gone; but the memories lived on, and so did a few of the people who shared the memories. During those years Walter Goldwater made philanthropic contributions from his personal collection to the New York Public Library and its Schomberg Center.

Through the 1985–95 decade under Bill French's management, the growing rent burden imposed a constant struggle to stay in business. The store was finally compelled to close at the end of 1995 due to a staggering debt of $64,000 in unpaid rent. Somini Sengupta, writing in the *New York Times* (November 26, 1995) about the approaching eviction, commented: "For 63 years . . . University Place Books has been an oasis for writers and academics interested in black literature and history." Felicia Lee reported for the same newspaper (December 31, 1995) that writers and artists devoted to the store had campaigned to help French keep it open until he found a suitable recipient for the ninety thousand books and pamphlets. The right customer turned out to be New York University. The university paid $47,500 to obtain the collection, which greatly expanded its materials for Africana studies.

"It's an agony but it's a relief because it had to be done. I was reconciled to the fact that I had to be out by the end of the year," Bill French was quoted in the *New York Times* on the last day of 1995. He was both relieved and gloomy. Writer Sharon Howard lamented, "They've been so helpful to me. It's frightening to me that they won't be there." She and the other writers and scholars who still used and loved the bookshop were sad to lose this rare New York place of books started sixty-three years earlier by Walter Goldwater, before many of them were born.

CHAPTER TWELVE
COOKBOOKS, A SCHOLAR, AND THE BRUSSEL SCOUTS
Eleanor Lowenstein · Louis Schucman · The Brussel Brothers

I never travel without books, either in peace or in wartime. . . . For it
cannot be imagined what a restful and comforting thought it is to me,
that they are at my side to give me pleasure at my own time, and to feel
how much they help me in life. It is the best provision I have found for
this human journey; and I greatly pity any intelligent man who is
deprived of it. . . . In my youth I studied for ostentation; after that a
little to gain wisdom; now for diversion; never for gain. . . . Books have
many charming qualities for those who know how to choose them.

—MICHEL EYQUEM DE MONTAIGNE

IN THE WRITINGS of the ancients there is probably no wearier statement, which is also an encouraging boast, than "Of making many books there is no end." Check chapter 12 of *Ecclesiastes* for the full citation. Fourth Avenue booksellers more than most could testify to the profusion of books and to their boundless variety. In and through and out of the Book Row shops flowed books on every subject human writers could conceive. There too were the various books that not necessarily demented authors insisted were supernaturally conceived and dictated to them as amanuenses obedient to celestial sources located above, below, or way out yonder somewhere.

The Book Row rule of demand and supply was simple: Ask and you'll probably receive, now or later, for anything resembling cash or the equivalent. "So what's the title and who was the author again? Let's start there."

Variety certainly was always a dominant Book Row characteristic. Any more or less mainstream book of a general nature with broad appeal—literature, classic, best seller, scholarly, preachy, self-help, how-to, inspirational, technical, scientific, instructional—was usually available eventually for those with time and patience enough to roam from store to store.

Countless books from the sweet and saintly to the weird and wicked outside the mainstream's normal channel were available as well. Any subject no matter how arcane, strange, precious, limited, narrow, or downright crazy that has interested human beings has been covered or at least considered in books. Sooner or later those books nearly always found their way to Book Row. So aiming for Book Row was the smart move if you needed a specific book on witchcraft, brotherly love, Serbo-Croatian history, palmistry, piety in Samoa, the butterfly stroke, vegetarianism, collecting thimbles, sneezing, business trends north of the border, or whatever.

"Filthy pictures, dirty books?" Just ask and prove you're not a smut hunter with a badge. Even when thin-skinned moralists forced the law to say no, no, many dealers on Book Row said yes, yes, and with varying degrees of readiness answered the public appetite for published realism seasoned with eroticism. F. Scott Fitzgerald in 1920, responding to the harassment of Theodore Dreiser and David Graham Phillips by censors, complained angrily in a letter to Max Perkins at Scribner's, "What in hell is the use of trying to write decent fiction if a bunch of old women refuse to let anyone hear the truth!"

If customers wanted it, they could have it as far as Book Row was concerned. Censorship was never the Book Row bookseller's cup of tea, even during Prohibition, when a cup of tea was often sweetened with a bootlegger's two-hour-old product.

Delivering maximum variety was a Book Row collective goal, mandate, and way of life. For customers, the maxim was that if shops on the east side of Fourth Avenue didn't have what they wanted, cross to the west side and, as necessary, keep bearing west to Broadway, University Place, Fifth Avenue. Or vice versa. The danger for customers as the search for specific titles went on was loading up with irresistible books they weren't actually trying to find.

What T. S. Eliot declared once about writers applies to the booksellers: "We write to keep something alive, and not because we believe in success or expect a triumph." On Book Row the common cause was strong to keep all kinds of books alive, available, and in steady circulation. Successes and triumphs weren't the main objective, but they were in fact almost daily Book Row events from shop to shop along the avenues and on side streets where books were sold. It was a moment of true success with a jolt of satisfaction every time a customer found the particular book he wanted. That was a shared triumph for the book receiver and the book provider.

Was Michel Montaigne prophetically sending posterity to Book Row when he counseled, "Let him who is in search of knowledge fish for it where it lurks"? Knowledge certainly was available in all its forms, solemn, ridiculous, useful, trivial, mortal, and divine, on the shelves of these good book providers.

Eleanor Lowenstein—Corner Book Shop

Collectors of irony's finer points may enjoy the fact that an international expert on cookbooks and the owner of a world-famous bookstore specializing in cookbooks, gastronomy, and all matters culinary readily admitted that she was never really interested in actually cooking herself. Books about cooking, not food preparation, consumed Eleanor Lowenstein's interest. She was not a kitchen person but a book person, who served her lunch guests soup from a can along with brilliant conversation about books. Sam Lipman was an occasional guest. "We ate warmed canned soup and a lunch-meat sandwich. . . . This always struck me as odd fare, coming as it did from a renowned cookbook specialist," he recalled in the *New Criterion* (January 1991).

The bookselling wife of bookseller Walter Goldwater (they married in 1954), she was the proprietor for forty years of the Corner Book Shop at 102 Fourth Avenue. Lowenstein lived with her husband and several thousand books in an apartment above the store, which typically held about eighteen thousand books on cookery, psychoanalysis, and several other specialties that intrigued the owner. Other than the books, the showpiece of the apartment was a Steinway grand piano for Walter, who studied piano as a boy. Her reply to the suggestion that she should move the books so the place could be painted was, "I'd rather live in squalor. Books and paint don't mix. Only book lovers would appreciate this shop. Housekeepers would be horrified."

The 1958 *International Directory of Antiquarian Booksellers* listed the Corner Book Shop's specialties as "Botany (Herbals), Fashions (Textiles), Gastronomy (Food & Drink, old), Theater (Cinema, Drama)." Walter Goldwater described the bookstore as a shop that always reflected its owner: "Eleanor would buy Edgar Rice Burroughs and cookery and whatever she was interested in at the moment." In addition to the listed specialties, the store featured aviation, criminology and crime, dance, juvenilia, music, perfume, photography, puppetry, radio, sea, television, and wine. Lowenstein's interests clearly ignored boundaries and limits.

Eleanor Lowenstein was born in New York City in 1909 and attended Cornell University, where she received a degree in psychology in 1929 and a master's degree in 1931. For a number of years, she was a social worker, with positions at a New York State hospital, a reform school for boys, and the Hudson School for Girls. She found herself dissatisfied with professional tasks, including an assignment as a probation officer, that didn't involve books. Later in the 1930s, she gave up social work for secondhand book-selling. She accepted a job at Walter Goldwater's University Place Book Shop and realized that buying and selling books on Book Row were activities she enjoyed and wanted to continue doing.

Lowenstein learned the ins and outs of antiquarian bookselling by working with Goldwater at the University Place Book Shop, and she was ready for her own bookshop in 1940 when the utilitarian building at 102 Fourth Avenue became available. She could live in an apartment upstairs and use the street-level space for books.

She opened the Corner Book Shop in June 1940 and became a dedicated bookseller in the heart of Book Row. Her capital when she began was about $600. The shop, despite its name, stood not on a corner, but on the west side of the avenue between East Eleventh and Twelfth Streets. "Center Book Shop" would have been more appropriate for the site. But Corner Book Shop it was, and Corner Book Shop it remained from the 1940s to the 1980s. Lowenstein may have figured that along the avenue, she would have a corner on quality.

When she started the Corner Book Shop, Lowenstein planned to specialize in psychology as she had in her academic career. However, she found her preference for rare and antiquarian books at conflict with the demand for new books in the growing science of psychology. She maintained a stock of old and, to the extent possible, recent works in psychology and related fields, but the leading specialties of the store took off in dramatically different directions.

Some areas of concentration such as textiles and theater simply reflected the owner's curiosity. Cookbooks, however, became the dominant focus of the shop, when a customer's informed talk about old cookbooks aroused Lowenstein's interest in the history of the subject, and she was offered an enticing deal by a midtown secondhand book dealer at 22 West Forty-eighth Street, Richard S. Wormser.

One of New York's least conventional booksellers, Wormser used the cable designator "Bookworm" and like some of his Book Row peers had a preference for offbeat books, which he categorized as "Cockeyediana" and "uncommon rare books." Wormser sought and sold books and publications in the fields of Americana, bibliography, cryptography, fireworks, horology, imprints, jewelry, precious stones, early science, and trades and industries. In the 1940s he obtained a large collection of cookbooks, which seemed too tame and orthodox for his bookstore. Wormser held on to a few of the earliest works and offered the rest to Eleanor Lowenstein at the Corner Book Shop.

So fate took an active hand through Richard Wormser to give Eleanor Lowenstein and her store a raison d'être and identity as America's leading bookstore in the culinary arts and the gastronomic sciences, or, as the case may be, the gastronomic arts and the culinary sciences. In the mid-1940s, acting on the Frank Thoms's rule, which she learned from Walter Goldwater, that you must buy books to sell books, Lowenstein bought the collection of cookbooks from Richard Wormser. She was an intrigued novice in the cookery field then, but she didn't remain a beginner for long. Little did Wormser and Lowenstein know when they transacted their modest deal that they had started a chain reaction that would make the bookshop a mecca in the food world and its proprietor a distinguished, noncooking authority on cookbooks. The acquisition began a remarkable specialization for Lowenstein and her bookshop, with "a clientele that ranges around the world and a stock of books that stretches back centuries," as Suzanne Hamlin wrote in the *New York Daily News* (October 21, 1979).

Who Knew What's Cooking? Eleanor Lowenstein Knew

Cookery, food, and wine became the shop's primary subject areas and accounted for nearly half of the books. Eleanor Lowenstein became a widely recognized expert on cookbooks and cooking history. She was often consulted by universities and private collectors and was utilized by food writers and compilers of cookbooks as a reliable source of information and research as well as hard-to-find, out-of-print books.

Craig Claiborne in the *New York Times*, "Shop's Clutter a Gastronomic Delight" (October 7, 1960), wrote, "One of the greatest gastronomic delights in Manhattan is the collection of culinary volumes at the Corner Book Shop. . . . It is a sort of Fibber McGee's closet of the food world. It is also the kind of bewildering jumble that could make for days of fascinating browsing for the professional or amateur food and drink enthusiast."

Lowenstein added to her stock through estate purchases and the catalogues of other dealers. She sometimes combed through bookstores in the New York area as well. Walter Caron at the Isaac Mendoza Book Company commented for this account, "We knew each other and always said hello. She was a cookbook specialist, and she came down here to buy cookbooks. She had other books on many subjects at the Corner Book Shop, and I would find interesting things I wanted there."

Stock replenishment was also accomplished through book safaris to Europe with her husband. In 1960 the Goldwaters visited 350 bookshops in ninety European cities. They shipped books to their stores in numerous packages weighing no more than eleven pounds each, which gave them the most economical shipping rate.

For Lowenstein that European buying spree produced two first editions of *Mrs. Beeton's Book of Household Management* (London, 1861), a classic on cooking, dining, and running a Victorian household, in which the author confessed, "I must frankly own, that if I had known, beforehand, that this book would have cost me the labour which it has, I should never have been courageous enough to commence it." Mrs. Beeton, let us join your club! Another Lowenstein find was Dr. Thomas Muffet's *The Nature, Method and Manner of Preparing All Sorts of Food Used in This Nation* (1655). The Little Miss Muffet who dined on curds and whey was allegedly his daughter.

Lowenstein's interest in cookbooks remained that of a bibliophile and scholar. She wrote introductions to many cookbooks and made bibliographical contributions of scholarly importance. For publication in 1954 by the American Antiquarian Society, she revised *American Cookery Books 1742–1860*, originally published by Waldo Lincoln in 1929. The Waldo Lincoln–Eleanor Lowenstein revision was among the influences stimulating intensified studies from the 1950s on within the field of American cookbooks. To include the vast amount of new data these studies revealed and to record formerly unknown titles, Lowenstein, once more expanding on her previous work, compiled the comprehensive *Bibliography of American Cookery Books 1742–1860*. This essentially new and definitive book was published in 1972 by the American Antiquarian Society and was considered a milestone accomplishment in the field.

COUNSELOR, CATALOGUER, COMMUNITY ACTIVIST

Eleanor Lowenstein left the field of social work, but the impulse to help others, in the social work tradition, never left her. She was a fountain of information for individuals worldwide with questions on cookbooks and cooking. Established customers benefited from her never-flagging commitment to find and deliver the books they needed. "Letters come in from all over the world and I answer them all, and sometimes we develop a real friendship. Right now I'm corresponding with a Japanese man who wrote asking for books on setting up a restaurant. I'm worried about him because I don't think he knows enough to open a business yet," she informed *Daily News* writer Suzanne Hamlin in 1979.

To keep customers informed concerning some of the many books available at the Corner Book Shop, she prepared and distributed numerous catalogues. The catalogues, which were as wide-ranging as the proprietor's ubiquitous interests, generally contained a few hundred titles that concentrated on a specific topic, and a few related, sometimes bizarre items.

Catalogue W-80 (1978), which focused on wine and other beverages *(les boissons)*, opened with a genial explanation for the fact that it contained several different alphabetically arranged lists: "We apologize for the haphazard use of six alphabets in this catalog, and hope for your indulgence. We had the choice of adding little groups of books as we uncovered them, or of omitting them entirely, thus impoverishing the content." The 210 books offered are mainly standard books on wine, including titles by Andre Simon, that oenophiles and collectors might appreciate, such as

31. **FISHER, M. F. K.** *The Story of Wine in California.* Photos M. Yavno, many in color. Berkeley 1962. Quarto. 35.00

Several items scattered through the six alphabets give a different, eccentric, out-of-the-ordinary impression, however. These titles and descriptions of the unusual books that follow suggest they would be fun to examine then or now:

48. **JUNIPER, WILLIAM.** *The True Drunkard's Delight.* Lon. Unicorn Press (1933) 375 pp. Section on drinking slang. 37.50

74. (Temperance) **BLAIR, HENRY W.** (U.S. Senator from N.H.) *The Temperance Movement: or, the conflict between man and alcohol.* Bos. 1888. 583 pp. Sm. quarto. Ill. inc. 4 col. plates. Folding map of Manhattan, showing locations of over 9,000 licensed places. 60.00

LES BOISSONS

CORNER BOOK SHOP
102 FOURTH AVENUE   NEW YORK, N.Y. 10003
W-80   (212) 254-7714   W-80

96. **SHAY, FRANK** (ed.) *My Pious Friends and Drunken Companions.* N.Y. (1930) Songs with music & ballads. 192 pp. Ill. by John Held, Jr. 20.00

178. **BEVERIDGE, N. E.** *Cups of Valor* (America's fighting men and their bracing concoctions; from the American Revolution to WW II) Some recipes with military associations. 106 pp. Ill. 17.50

198. **NORTH, STERLING &** C. **KROCH** (eds.) *So Red the Nose, Or Breath in the Afternoon.* Cartoon ills by R. C. Nelson. N.Y. (1935) Slim 8vo. Contributions by Hemingway, Morley, K. Roberts, R. Kent, etc. Fine copy, imperfect d.j. 25.00

The catalogues, Eleanor Lowenstein admitted, merely suggested the range and nature of the bookstore's abundance. She hoped that by naming specific titles, the catalogues encouraged customers to submit specific requests. Her search service might take a decade or more, but she wouldn't stop looking until she could match a patient client with the volume desired. Astonishment that the search had gone on so long as well as gratitude that it did were reactions she often received when she wrote or called to ask, "Do you still want . . . ?"

While building her shop into a landmark institution for gastronomes and oenophiles, Lowenstein didn't neglect or ignore the community of books and booksellers that she lived and worked in. In 1942, she became a charter member of the Fourth Avenue Booksellers' Association and accepted the office of corresponding secretary for the historic group. It was she who explained to Manuel Tarshish for his 1969 *Publishers Weekly* series that the incentive to organize the association and unite to fight came initially from New York City's infuriating no-bargain-stands-on-sidewalks order to book dealers.

When the national Antiquarian Booksellers' Association of America was established in 1949, Lowenstein became a member and was a regular participant in ABAA activities along with her husband, Walter Goldwater.

INSPIRATION TO COLLECT AND SELL COOKBOOKS

Janice Longone, the food writer, editor, and student and teacher of culinary history, with her husband, Dan Longone, as the resident wine expert, founded the internationally acclaimed Wine and Food Library at Ann Arbor, Michigan. In an interview for these pages Jan Longone stated that Eleanor Lowenstein and the Corner Book Shop were her original inspiration to start the Wine and Food Library, take the plunge, and become a bookseller also specializing in cookbooks and related materials.

She recalled going to Fourth Avenue many times in the 1960s and 1970s and being fascinated during each visit to Lowenstein's congested kingdom of books, especially cookbooks. "You would go there and see her at her desk through the locked door. You tapped on the door, and she let you in if you passed inspection; if not, she ignored you and continued working at her desk," said Longone.

Jan Longone was one of the favored individuals who was allowed inside. "Behind Eleanor's desk I always saw splendid books piled high that I was dying to look at. Staring at those books, I'd ask if she had anything special tucked away. Eleanor would follow my glance and remark that those books were held for customers. After I entered the business myself, I approved. You have to save special things for special clients," noted Longone.

On one visit Jan Longone was introduced to Walter Goldwater. Hearing she was from Ann Arbor, he mentioned graduating from the University of Michigan fifty years earlier and asked her to join them for lunch. She felt enormously honored and excited to be invited upstairs for lunch with the world's greatest cookbook and culinary authority. "We entered a dinky, unimpressive kitchen," she declared. "Eleanor opened a can of Campbell's tomato soup, warmed it up, and served it in three jelly jars. The lunch was canned soup, but the conversation was unforgettable. We talked books. That was one of the highlights of my life.

"After I began the Wine and Food Library, I still visited Eleanor regularly, sent her our catalogues, and called her often to ask questions and keep in touch," Longone continued. "After she became quite ill, I remember telephoning once when she particularly needed to talk. Our conversation went on a long time. She was especially worried then about what would happen with her books."

Eleanor Lowenstein had used her life building a remarkable private collection in addition to assembling the thousands of books in her store. Along with her own fate, she was understandably concerned about the fate of her books.

The Simon-Lowenstein Collection

In England, right after World War II, Eleanor Lowenstein visited and became friends with Andre Simon, the renowned writer on gastronomy, president of the Wine and Food Society, and noted book collector in his field. They kept in touch, and in his nineties Simon reluctantly agreed to sell her over five hundred choice books from his collection. In a January 10, 1967, letter Simon noted that he couldn't "take them with me to heaven when I go there (I hope!) so you had better enjoy them." The incredible collection included the earliest known housekeeping book; a Bernardus (1470), among three incunabula; and many other unique volumes on cookery and the kitchen that caused Craig Claiborne to call it "one of the most interesting—and valuable—cookbook collections in America" (*New York Times,* September 15, 1969).

Eleanor Lowenstein kept the Simon volumes in her private collection and added more rarities during her final years. They were the most important books at the Corner Book Shop when she died, December 1, 1980. Walter Goldwater offered the Simon-Lowenstein collection and the contents of the

Corner Book Shop to Jan and Dan Longone. The Longones were unable to undertake an acquisition of such magnitude, but they welcomed the chance to make selections from the stock. They shared the contents of the bookshop with a dealer from England and with Marilyn Einhorn, a friend of Eleanor Lowenstein. Einhorn as a sideline ran a New York book business called At the Sign of the Dancing Bear, according to Jan Longone.

Walter Goldwater told the Longones to take what they wanted, "then come upstairs and we'll negotiate a price." "Dan and I went to the basement, where apparently no one else had gone. The basement floor was covered with several inches of water. The lighting was terrible. It was wet underfoot. And there we found box after box of books, wonderful, extraordinary books. I was thrilled with what we got when I saw them in Ann Arbor. Those books were the foundation of the Wine and Food Library," stated Jan Longone about her bookshop, which many considered the natural successor to the Corner Book Shop.

The Simon-Lowenstein collection by circuitous paths, according to Longone, reached its ultimate destination when it was divided between the Mandeville Library of the University of California–San Diego and the Arthur and Elizabeth Schlesinger Library on the History of Women in America, at Radcliffe College, Cambridge. The American Institute of Wine and Food (AIWF) purchased the collection in the 1980s. In April 1990 the AIWF voted to make the collection available to these academic repositories so the books could be used for research. Jan and Dan Longone were assigned to conduct an appraisal of the books, and Jan Longone was in charge of the group that worked out the division of the books between the two recipients. "It was a Solomonic situation if there ever was one," she recalled.

In addition to books from the Simon-Lowenstein collection, the Schlesinger Library also received the Eleanor Lowenstein and Andre Simon correspondence that chronicled decades of friendship and business involving books in their shared realm of cookbooks, cuisine, and wine. Walter Goldwater in March 1981 gave the Schlesinger Library the business records of the Corner Book Shop, including catalogues, correspondence, orders, publicity items, daybooks of sales, tax papers, shop assistant records, papers related to Eleanor's bibliographic work, and other items of like nature.

Taken together, the seven cartons of papers forming the Corner Book Shop collection at the Schlesinger Library provided an unusually complete archive on a major bookshop over several decades. Such detailed records have been rare among secondhand and antiquarian bookstores, rarer perhaps than most of the books they sold. The Eleanor Lowenstein business archive at the Schlesinger Library was listed along with other bookseller archives in the *ABAA Newsletter* (spring 1997). Donald C. Dickinson, in an article for that newsletter, "Bookdealers' Archives: A Search for Buried Treasure," lamented that few such archives have been preserved, with the result that "students of book selling in the United States, particularly students of the antiquarian book trade, have a limited range of primary sources with which to work." Thanks to Eleanor Lowenstein's foresight, attention to detail, and instinct to keep records, that will not be true in the case of Fourth Avenue's Corner Book Shop.

Eleanor Lowenstein voiced concern to her friend Jan Longone not about business documents but about what would happen with her books. Many of them went back into circulation through other stores, but the best of them have been kept together in two academic sanctuaries, where they can be preserved and used for more centuries. Eleanor Lowenstein, we might speculate, would be content with the provisions made for her special books.

Louis Schucman—Louis Schucman Bookstore

Louis Schucman, like Eleanor Lowenstein, brought more advanced education than was the usual case to his long New York City and Fourth Avenue bookselling career. Born in 1908, he managed to continue his education during the Depression years and to graduate from New York University. In the manner of many other booksellers, he was drawn to the profession by his devotion to reading and his love of books.

He was also endowed (or afflicted) with an appetite for intellectual activities and attainments. The drive to learn would absorb him and dictate the nature of his shop throughout his decades as a particularly knowledgeable dealer in excellent, antiquarian, and prestigious books that were sometimes, in Hamlet's phrase, caviar to the general. "Louis Schucman was a very good, scholarly bookman," observed Stanley Lewis. These qualities attracted many customers for many years.

Earning a college degree as Louis Schucman did was not the Book Row norm. The typical Fourth Avenue bookman started in the profession very young, often as a book scout, worked as a bookstore employee, acquired some know-how, and finally found a modest amount of capital to launch a store of his own. Schucman broke with the pattern by first obtaining a liberal education.

In his twenties during the 1930s, Louis Schucman entered the book trade at an upstairs location on West Forty-sixth Street, the same Manhattan midtown book enclave that was home to Richard Wormser on West Forty-eighth Street, the Gotham Book Mart on West Forty-seventh Street, and close to the Brentano's and Scribner's carriage-trade stores around the corner on Fifth Avenue.

Because of his location, Schucman's early bookselling efforts were concentrated on generating and filling mail orders. At the beginning, he followed a common practice, which echoed the start-ups of many other secondhand bookstores in New York—offering books from his own library for sale.

That was frequently how a bookman finally realized he was a bookseller, when he could conquer sentiment, remove valued books from his home shelves, and put them up for sale. Thus the nucleus of Louis Schucman's original stock came from the books he had accumulated for himself based on his studies as well as interests in literature, history, and philosophy. In 1936 when he opened his first bookstore, he discovered that there was satisfaction in finding books for others as he gave up his own books—temporarily of course, since more books, different books, constantly poured into a working bookstore. Anyway he was and would remain a bookseller.

To augment stock Schucman resorted to the familiar paths of sales, libraries, auctions, and other book dealers. One major source he found for good books at a low price was the large-scale book business run by the Wavrovics brothers, Ernest and Louis, at 530 East Fourteenth Street, on the outer periphery of Book Row. Louis Wavrovics, reminiscing for this account, wrote, "I took to the road in those days. Good books were plentiful and cheap, especially at warehouse auctions. The operation of our shop was simple in concept. We bought books in large lots and sorted them into saleable classifications. At a small profit and with quick turnover, we sold to every Book Row dealer and got to know them closely. Times were economically bad, but we hustled and prospered. Someone from Louis Schucman's regularly came to our store."

After his start on West Forty-sixth Street, Schucman, utilizing a mail-order arangement, began a series of moves in search of the best location for his "bookstore with a scholarly bias." After midtown, the shop was relocated on Twenty-third Street, and from there continued to West Seventeenth Street. In its penultimate migration, the Schucman Bookstore finally joined the other Book Row secondhand shops. It was established as a familiar fixture at 77 Fourth Avenue, near East Tenth Street. On Fourth Avenue, the Louis Schucman Bookstore at last functioned as a full-service mail-order and walk-in business.

Louis Schucman became an early member of the Antiquarian Booksellers' Association of America. Consequently his bookstore was listed at 77 Fourth Avenue in the 1951–52 *International Directory of Antiquarian Booksellers,* the directory that made history as the first such directory based on the cooperation of national associations.

In 1954, the Schucman store engaged in a final move, and that one not far—a matter of feet—to 69 Fourth Avenue, beween East Ninth and East Tenth Streets. This site took on the attributes of permanence. The Louis Schucman Bookstore was still at number 69 when the proprietor was interviewed for the 1969 *Publishers Weekly* series by Manuel Tarshish. Tarshish described the facility as one with fifteen hundred square feet of space to accommodate a fine general selection of approximately fifty thousand books snugly ensconced behind a fourteen-foot storefront.

The 1958 *International Directory of Antiquarian Booksellers,* still based on input from the national associations, contained this entry: "*Schucman, Louis,* 69 Fourth Avenue . . . Erudition (scholarly Books & Books for Libraries), General Literature (Out of Print), History."

Louis Schucman continued to specialize in books with scholarly and intellectual appeal along with the standard lines that characterized the Fourth Avenue book trade. He too maintained well-stocked outdoor bookstands, those perennial friends of and temptations for the hurried browser. Frederick Lightfoot treasured a memory picture from the heyday of Book Row in which, starting at Louis Schucman's outdoor stands, he could see people simultaneously searching for books at three different Fourth Avenue stores—probably the Strand, Arcadia, and Schucman's, which stood side by side between Tenth and Eleventh Streets. That vision of several active stores in one small area, with people quietly examining books, chasing titles, and hoping to find specific volumes, delivered a defining moment for the entire Book Row era in New York.

During the years at 69 Fourth Avenue, Louis Schucman built up his business by frequently issuing catalogues to a proven mailing list of customers. The catalogue process included a persistent updating by weeding out names that were repeatedly unproductive and by adding names that held realistic promise of orders. Schucman knew, as did most of his Book Row neighbors, that the sine qua non for producing orders through catalogues was a mailing list of potential customers with a known interest in the kinds of books offered.

By 1969 approximately 65 percent of Schucman's sales came through the catalogues that were distributed with the indispensable help of his longtime assistant Nat Himelfarb. Nat Himelfarb, a mainstay at the Louis Schucman Bookstore, typified the widespread reliance up and down Fourth Avenue on loyal support staff. Such employees functioned in a multitude of ways and often brought to their work an astonishing repertoire of skills. These staff reliables became as well known to regular customers as the owners.

Louis Schucman from the 1950s to the 1970s held a front-row seat to observe the changes that steadily affected the secondhand book business that he had witnessed in New York City since the 1930s. He was present as attrition, due to a complicated mix of influences from rising rents to declining traffic, took one store after another. He observed that stores like his required ample space for a large number of books at low and stable rent. He also stressed the necessity of attracting large numbers of people to the neighborhood.

"When Wanamaker's was across the street, it drew many customers for us," he stated, acknowledging that the loss of that magnet for substantial crowds had a critical impact on Book Row since no comparable people puller had replaced the department store. Schucman admitted that most of his bookshop's original walk-in regular customers had moved to the suburbs and thus were infrequent buyers except through the catalogues. Another negative force in play that further wounded the bookstores was the fact that the growth of reprints reduced the demand for out-of-print volumes.

At the end of the 1960s, Schucman observed that he was guardedly optimistic about the future of the secondhand book business, though he recognized that the heart of it might not continue to be on Fourth Avenue, due to the transitional influences affecting business and population. One encouraging trend, he thought, was the growing traffic of English book dealers coming to America for books to replenish their stock. Most of them found their way to Book Row as a consequence of the drain from England before and after World

War II, the accessibility and familiarity of New York City to Europeans generally, and the international recognition that Book Row had attained by the 1960s. This was a turnaround from the prevailing practices of the previous century, when book hunting was overwhelmingly in the opposite direction. Twentieth-century historic events from world wars to intensified American industrialization and reaction to Sputnik combined to make America a dominant world power center and concomitantly a world book center, with Book Row a point of entry to an oasis of plenty.

Another important factor affecting the book business was the drive by academic institutions to maintain libraries with sufficient scope and depth to be adequate for modern research demands. Schucman was also reassured to see a substantial increase in customers representing ethnic minorities. One example he cited was his store's expanded number of African-American customers for self-help titles as well as other books. His conclusion from long observation in a bookshop focused on scholarly works for serious readers was that the zealous pursuit of knowledge through reading and the parallel demand for worthwhile books would never, should never, and could never end.

Louis Schucman died December 15, 1999, at the age of ninety-one. Born early in the twentieth century, he lived much of his life with books as a student, scholar, and bookseller. With a new century coming into view, like Moses the lawgiver at Mount Pisgah, he managed to get close but not to enter the next century. Based on the experience of decades, Louis Schucman kept the faith that thousands of the books he had circulated during his lifetime would continue their journeys in the centuries following his own.

I. R. Brussel, LOGS
Jack Brussel—Atlantis Bookshop

The Brussel brothers, I. R. and Jack, began their bookselling careers—to be crowned with successes legends are built on—as young used-book dealers in Brooklyn. They made the globe their book beat and transformed the ancient practice of book scouting from a shop-to-shop and street-to-street affair into a continent-to-continent activity, with Book Row as an intermittent home base. Each acquired an advanced education, I. R. in engineering, Jack in mathematics. Yet each turned away early from these callings in favor of bookselling and scouting to make more interesting use of their capacious memories, book love and knowledge, and Tennysonian appetite to seek, to find, and not to yield.

In his seventies the older brother, I. R. (Ike or IRB) Brussel, born in 1897 at Minsk, Russia, insisted, "I was cut out to be a big-game hunter, but had to satisfy myself with hunting books!" With IRB that was bragging, not complaining. He clearly loved the quixotic life of an itinerant bookman. In *Antiquarian Bookman*, April 3, 1948, he wrote about the importance of the book scout in bibliographical research and the immense value of the scout's knowledge in locating extremely rare books.

IRB declared, "The Trade should remember that but for the Scout many a book would remain standing on the shelves until Judgement Day." For Ike Brussel no explorer, warrior, or big-game hunter came close to matching such a life of undiluted intellectual adventuring. IRB became a book scout from Fourth Avenue to the wide, wide world and used the acronym "LOGS"—for "Last of the Great Scouts"—on letterheads and bills. His discoveries included such sleepers as a Mark Twain rarity, *What Is Man?* and an extremely scarce Robert Louis Stevenson, *South Seas*. The Twain he bought for seventy-five cents and the Stevenson for a shilling; each sold for $1,000. Another find was a copy of Henry James's first novel, *Roderick Hudson* (1875), with the author's holograph corrections.

Yet IRB warned beginners that it was knowledge and experience, not sleepers, that kept scouts solvent. "If a Scout had to depend on 'sleepers' he might just as well invite the wolf to enter by the front door," he wrote. "The Scout in the Bookselling World has to depend on his knowledge, intuition, hard work and luck." Ike Brussel was ever on the lookout for the great discovery, and he discovered an impressive array of greats. Still, it was industry plus intelligence and book knowledge that he relied on. IRB wasn't driven, as fellow scout Abe Sugarman put it, like "a donkey with the carrot of *Tamerlane* held out before him." The impression we get from IRB stories is that his carrot wasn't hitting the jackpot with a big-dollar item but the sheer excitement and perpetual fun of the search and the satisfaction of finding whatever he found.

Frequently, of course, his exceptional knowledge turned up a sleeper. According to Stanley Edgar Hyman in his article "Book Scout" (*New Yorker*, November 8, 1952), outside a Fourth Avenue shop on a ten-cent stand, Ike Brussel picked up a copy of *The James Whitcomb Riley Reader* (1915), which contained a childishly scrawled "Yours Sincerely, JWR." Brussel remembered that the partially paralyzed Riley wrote in that manner and established that the book was a legitimate Riley signed copy, making it a sleeper when the Hoosier poet was popular and much collected. Hyman gave another instance of IRB's uncanny memory. The scout found an Elizabeth Gaskell paperback mistakenly attributed to Charles Dickens on the title page and sold it to a Princeton, New Jersey, collector. Years later, IRB contacted the same collector with a second incorrect copy he thought was about half an inch taller than the first copy. It was, and the impressed customer purchased the follow-up oddity as well.

IRB ran bookshops at various times, but his nomadic heart was clearly in the hunt. His idea of bibliosport was international roaming to locate valuable rare books for those he probably considered the last of the great collectors and to strengthen the holdings of his many library customers with the key out-of-print titles they needed for scholarly respectability. John Carter, in a posthumous tribute for London's *Book Collector* and *AB* (December 25, 1972), alluded to the discriminating collectors, bibliophiles, and dealers in New York and London who "learned that if anybody could dig up a copy of some obscure rarissimum, it was Ike."

Ike Brussel entered the book business as a fill-in for his ailing father-in-law, who ran a Brooklyn bookshop. Like others before him who became booksellers by fluke or family need, once in, he stayed. As the proprietor of the GBS Bookshop on Pitkin Avenue in Brownsville, Brooklyn, IRB certainly won the admiration and devotion of one customer, young Sol Malkin, who at ten bought Liberty Boys thrillers and with IRB's encouragement moved on from dime novels to the books of Upton Sinclair and James Branch Cabell. Malkin remembered spending his bar mitzvah cash to buy a first edition, second issue *Jurgen* (1919) from IRB. He also remembered the glory and excitement in his teens of accompanying IRB on book scout sorties through Brooklyn. Malkin affectionately called Ike Brussel "our first—and in many ways still our best—dealer and mentor" (*AB*, June 15, 1970). He recounted the "ebullience—sometimes resonance" that IRB, the "LOGS, bookseller and bibliophile, bibliographer and bookman," displayed upon finding a long-sought-after title.

Deciding the role of bookman was to be his life's work, Ike Brussel in the mid-1920s ran a bookshop featuring general stock at 57 Fourth Avenue. The lure of the open road enticed him later in the 1920s to leave the shop and embrace his destiny as a professional book scout. Unlike most book scouts, he made a living at it while winning friends and building collections throughout the antiquarian book community.

Since many of the books he located as a scout were underpriced items at bookstores, often the bookstores of his friends on Fourth Avenue or elsewhere, IRB thought it both good manners and smart psychology to keep still and not brag about discovering a valuable book at a bookshop. His rationale was to avoid insulting and perhaps antagonizing people who, even if inadvertently, helped him earn a livelihood. The book scout, wrote IRB, "carries the book useless to one dealer to another dealer who needs it . . . the Scout may keep a bit of the nectar, but at the same time he has accomplished the feat of having produced two or more transactions in place of one. He has put profit into three pockets." Including, naturally, his own.

As he was esteemed on Fourth Avenue, so too he was accorded respect and welcomed by his peers in England, notwithstanding his Brooklyn version of the king's English and eccentric (for the tight little isles) attire. Even English poet A. E. Housman, who didn't suffer fools gladly or otherwise, appreciated the friendship and visits of Ike Brussel.

In addition to locating books that without him might have permanently gathered dust on unexamined shelves, IRB prepared two estimable bibliographic works of enduring value. The initial study analyzed books by English authors first printed in America, *Anglo-American First Editions 1826–1900, East to West* (1935). A year later he delivered the geographically reverse study, *Anglo-American First Editions 1786–1930, West to East* (1936), dedicated "To the Memory of A. E. Housman."

Compiled by an acknowledged expert on English and American fiction in the nineteenth and early twentieth centuries, the works were recognized as bibliographic contributions of pioneering importance and scholarly influence. "These two volumes have stood the test of time remarkably well," wrote John Carter (*AB*, December 25, 1972). The original editions of the volumes are now about as scarce and dear as many of IRB's fabulous finds.

What About Jack Brussel?

Brothers, it's true, are sometimes far from being analogues of one another, and the brothers Brussel offered living proof. Ike Brussel was consistently a creature of wanderlust with no zest for permanent locations, offices, and staffs. Jack Brussel, with several scouting interludes as productive exceptions, was more inclined than IRB to remain at home on Book Row or at his Greenwich Village apartment, surrounded by his books.

Physically, Ike Brussel was short, heavyset, and garrulous. Walter Goldwater, while admiring IRB's knowledge of first editions, stressed, "He is very noisy!" Other adjectives assigned to IRB included overbearing, arrogant, and egotistical. Milton Reissman called him a great storyteller who knew everybody and who should have recorded his stories of the eminent people he knew and sometimes supplied with books.

Jack Brussel was slimmer, taller, and quieter than his brother; he may also have been more likable. Many of his Book Row colleagues expressed affection for him as a person as well as a bookman. Reissman for this account noted that he was very friendly with the younger Brussel and always looked forward to his return from a European trip with new books. "When he came back from a trip, everybody would haunt him, eager for the sale he would soon hold of his older materials to make room for the new things found in Europe," said Reissman.

Jack Brussel at first followed closely in Ike's footsteps. He started out as a Brooklyn book dealer, running a shop for about a year near the Academy of Music. In 1922 he had a Book Row shop off Fourth Avenue, on Ninth Street. A couple of years later he moved to 110 Fourth Avenue. His next move was to Eighth Street and Broadway. At the end of the 1920s he worked as a book scout for a time and then in 1930 returned to Book Row at 100 Fourth Avenue. He left again in the 1930s to scout full-time but settled once more on Fourth Avenue in the 1940s, at 108 and then at 100, near East Eleventh Street. Thus for briefer periods and without the global commitment of his brother, Jack acted on the Brussel family trait and trade of book scouting; yet he regularly came back to the steadier and more stable uncertainty of a conventional business on Book Row.

Jack eventually settled down as the proprietor of the Atlantis Bookshop at 100 Fourth Avenue, next door to Eleanor Lowenstein's Corner Book Shop. As a shop proprietor, he could keep his scouting skills well honed right there in the neighborhood. Jack Brussel, like IRB, was no slouch as a big book hunter. One of his major finds was just around the corner from Fourth Avenue. Stanley

Edgar Hyman related in "Book Scout" that once at the Dauber & Pine annex on Thirteenth Street, Jack found for seventy-five cents an autographed presentation copy of a book by Oliver Wendell Holmes. Jack, however, didn't apply Ike's psychological strategy of concealing his find from the victim. When Ike asked him how an irate Sam Dauber learned about the Holmes, Jack Brussel answered, "I couldn't resist it, Ike. I sold it right back to him."

Among his close friends, Jack Brussel could count Harold and Gertrude Briggs at Books 'N Things. "I liked him very much," said Mrs. Briggs. "He was a mathematician. He completed his courses at Columbia. They were going to give him a job, but he didn't take it. He decided, 'They don't want a Jew,' and walked out." Mrs. Briggs was impressed by his intelligence and thought he knew more about books than his brother. "He could always buy right and make money on his books and other finds such as the wonderful Japanese prints, some of them erotic, that he brought back from England after World War Two," she said and added, "Harold and Jack loved the book business, and they loved hunting books together."

Walter Caron was another bookseller—and buyer—with fond memories. "One dealer I loved was Jack Brussel. I remember when he was next door to Eleanor Lowenstein. I was crazy about Willa Cather then and eager to read everything she wrote. Jack had a stack of old magazines containing one I was dying to buy. It was the August 1912 issue of *McClure's* containing *The Bohemian Girl*, a novella by Willa Cather, available at that time only in the magazine. It wasn't available in a book until later. I wanted just that magazine from Jack's run, and he let me take it. I never let it go. I still have that copy with the first publication of Willa Cather's story."

Frederick Lightfoot was grateful to Jack Brussel for handling nineteenth-century American photographs of historic interest before other book dealers recognized their value. He noted that Brussel acquired an impressive four-volume set of photographs from a family that circled the globe in the 1870s and collected fabulous pictures wherever they went. "Jack broke out the U.S. pictures from one volume and sold them for a high price. He gave me the remaining three and a half volumes for $50. They included multi-panel panoramas of Chinese waterfronts, etc., which individually would bring hundreds of dollars today. I passed the set on to the George Eastman House at cost," Lightfoot wrote.

In his shop at 100 Fourth Avenue, Jack Brussel's specialties included mathematics, philosophy, science, and sexology. The store was known as a source of early and unusual books, including printed books of science with copperplate engravings. At one time known as the Atlantis Bookshop, it was later called the United Book Guild.

In the 1930s Jack Brussel and his Canadian-born wife, Minna, developed a sideline business producing color prints and publishing several hundred facsimile editions and offset reprints of artistic, literary, and historic classics. One outstanding publication was a facsimile reprint of Hartmann Schedel's *Liber Chronicarum* (1493), popularly known as the *Nuremberg Chronicle*.

In the art field the Brussels reprinted George Grosz's *Ecce Homo,* a collection of the artist's early work that exposed the German military class and helped bring about a Nazi denunciation of his work as degenerate. Grosz came to the United States, where he was naturalized as a citizen in 1938. The Belgian master printmaker and artist Felicien Rops was represented among the Brussel publications with *The Graphic Work of Felicien Rops.* His prints are known for their fertile imagination, independent thinking, and sometimes licentious subject matter.

Their unexpurgated erotica publications included famous works such as *The Kama Sutra,* the long-banned Hindu manual on the techniques and philosophy of lovemaking. Another reprint was Henry Miller's *Tropic of Cancer,* when it was still officially suppressed and unlawful to sell in the U.S. "Whenever there was anything illegal, he seemed to get into it," mused Walter Goldwater about his next-door neighbor on Fourth Avenue. Whether Walter Goldwater spoke with admiration or indignation or both is anybody's guess. Clearly admiration was the verdict when he recalled Jack Brussel's fine collection of *Aesop's Fables.*

Jack and Minna Brussel's blithely casual attitude toward the law's contemporary prudery regarding some publications led to run-ins with the police and the courts. Jack Brussel generally beat the rap as cases against him were dismissed; and he continued to find, buy, print, and sell books of all kinds.

Considering the range of their involvement with antiquarian books from brilliant scouting to bookshop ownership to reprinting classics, the Brussel brothers, I. R. and Jack, should be and are well remembered for their skills, coups, flair, deeds, generosity, and colorful participation as principals in several of the twentieth century's great book stories.

In one of those stories, related by Walter Goldwater, Ike Brussel was at Foyle's in London's Charing Cross Road area. He received directions to the quite substantial medical books section, where he asked if they had any books on immunization. The British bookman replied, haughtily perhaps, with a question: "Immunization against what?" IRB might well have answered, but probably didn't as a prudent book scout in the midst of a serious hunt, "Boredom."

"Immunization against boredom" was definitely something the exploits, adventures, and accomplishments of the Brussel brothers provided for their contemporaries and their fascinated successors.

CHAPTER THIRTEEN

WHERE HAVE ALL THE READERS GONE?
Haskell Gruberger · Leon Kramer · Seymour Hacker

> *Why are not my works matters for competitive bidding in the open market?. . . . I have been told by hospital authorities that more copies of my works are left behind by departing patients than those of any other author. It does seem as if people might at least take my books home with them. If it is rarity which counts in the value of a book, I have dozens of very rare Benchley items in my room which I know cannot be duplicated. For the benefit of collectors, I will list them, leaving the price more or less up to the would-be purchaser. All that I ask is that I don't actually lose money on the sale.*
>
> —ROBERT CHARLES BENCHLEY

MANUEL TARSHISH IN his 1969 *Publishers Weekly* series on the Fourth Avenue book trade, near the end of the concluding article, speculated about the decline that began in the 1950s, accelerated in the 1960s, and brought New York's historic Book Row, with a few happy exceptions, essentially to its end in the 1970s: "Why is Booksellers' Row in a bad way now? Some argue that it is affected by a growth of anti-intellectualism in America. Some cite, on the other hand, the proliferation of paperbacks. Some point to the popularity of television, high mobility, and much money available for forms of entertainment other than books. All the dealers are affected by rising rents or the demolition of their premises."

On Booksellers' Row, as the dealers saw their rents steadily rise like a tide that never ebbed, they also saw a reduction in the number of customers venturing to the Fourth Avenue neighborhood for the books they offered. Again, a variety of reasons were advanced to explain the reduction. Often mentioned, in these pages and among bookmen, was the closing of Wanamaker's in the mid-1950s, climaxed by a Bastille Day 1956 fire that destroyed the building, which was already scheduled for demolition. Book Row never fully recovered from the loss of access to those Wanamaker shoppers.

In addition to soaring rents and fewer customers, according to some booksellers' perceptions, the secondhand book business was beset by a pervasive cultural change that saw the reading population itself steadily reduced as other media became more ubiquitous, seductive, and demanding. The book dealers along with social critics noted that couch-potatoism—countless hours in front of screens with pictures—gradually eroded the activity of reading and thus the demand for secondhand and out-of-print books that had been the basis of Book Row's existence.

Booksellers needed another verse in Pete Seeger's interrogatory song, a verse that asked, "Where have all the readers gone, long time passing?" Most bookmen recognized the necessity to face facts realistically and come to terms with whatever changes were necessary, even if they didn't welcome them. "The guy who is ignoring the market is begging for trouble. We are businesspeople," observed Larry Moskowitz for this account.

He added as a corollary, "Everything changes so fast. Some express fear there will eventually be no books at all, considering what goes on with electronics. And young people are said not to read anymore. I guess some do, but many don't. That doesn't bode well for books and the world of print. I and others with my background dread to think of a time without books because reading has been so much a part of our lives. That's what got me through childhood, the fact that I could read."

Writer Samuel Johnson pontificated, "It is always a writer's duty to make the world better." That Olympian viewpoint was shared by a high percentage of the Book Row dealers about their chosen profession. They too performed the self-imposed duty of disseminating the works of writers who had done their duty. Together writers and booksellers formed a distinct partnership to make the world better, or at least a partnership that *could* make the world better. Serious readers were always needed for the writer-bookseller collaboration to succeed.

When rents were too high and readers too few, yet another wistful verse might have been added to the Seeger song: "Where have all the bookmen gone, long time passing?" Some went to mail-order operations, some to the suburbs, some to other states, and some went to their final rewards—as retirees in sunny places with too many card games, beaches, and funny things to do with little balls to need an old-fashioned Book Row.

Among the later arrivals to Book Row was the Social Science Book Store, opened in 1967 by Haskell Gruberger at 85 Fourth Avenue. The store contained over seventy thousand books in a five-thousand-square-foot space and reflected the philosophical and scholarly interests of its proprietor. Featuring literary and social criticism, the Social Science Book Store was the last in a series dating back to the 1930s of New York City book businesses founded and operated by Gruberger.

Interviewed by Manuel Tarshish at his shop, Gruberger voiced the apprehensions of the late 1960s about what was happening to America and to Book Row from his perspective behind the counter of an antiquarian bookstore. Selling books was the business he had loved and pursued in a variety of ways since childhood. Haskell Gruberger was concerned about the changing attitudes toward books that he witnessed from his front seat on Book Row. "In the old days people really had an interest in scholarly works. Now good books are in the doldrums," he said. "Since I've been on the Avenue, there has been one call for Dante, none for Chaucer. There is too much money available for frivolities. So most people won't struggle with a serious book. Collectors have virtually disappeared. It was said that used-book dealers fared better during the Depression than any other business. I believe it. Affluence is bad for us."

His answer was for the book dealers as a group to sponsor an orientation course aimed at informing the public about "where to go to find good used books." Yet that solution—or variations such as book fairs and publicity campaigns, all of which had been suggested many times and in some instances even halfheartedly tried—was already too late and too little for the weakening patient in the late 1960s. Haskell Gruberger soon moved on to sell books outside New York City, and his Social Science Book Store joined all the others that couldn't make it through the final quarter of the twentieth century.

Haskell Gruberger was born October 3, 1911, on Allen Street, on the Lower East Side. His family lived in West Harlem at 143rd Street when as a young boy he discovered the magnetism of books at a branch library. Curiosity drove him up the stairs from the children's books to the upper level, where adults were reading, and he yearned to know what waited for him in all the inviting volumes. He wasn't much older when with pure delight he cruised the 125th Street bookstores clutching his Saturday allowance and seeking the best buys for a quarter from the outside stalls, which in those days offered as many as five or even seven books for a quarter.

William Wordsworth in "My Heart Leaps Up" had it right for Haskell Gruberger: The child was certainly father of the man. Interviewed for this account, he was asked what he enjoyed most about bookselling, whether cataloguing, buying, or selling. He replied without hesitation, "Buying books, the quest, the search, learning the answer to the big question, where are you going to find the next book?"

Gruberger's first big business deal, involving the purchase of a bookstore, took place when he was seven. His father owned a stationery and candy store with a lot of empty glass cases just right for books. The precocious entrepreneur heard about a neighborhood bookshop going out of business with about five thousand books that could be bought for around $75. He urged his father to buy the bookstore and use the books for a lending library. That initial book enterprise turned out well. It became the first of many for a born bookman. Over seven decades later he said with feeling, "I am so enamored of the book business!" Lucky indeed the person who persistently loves his work from the age of seven.

As a teenager Gruburger attended the City College of New York along with many of his friends, who aimed, with eager families urging them ever onward, to enter the conventional professions of law, medicine, or in a pinch, teaching. "The cream of the crop came to City College. Nobody had enough money to go out of town to Yale or Harvard or the University of Wherever. All they had was subway fare to City College. I was there, but I never entertained the idea of entering one of the standard professions. I think I already realized I was a bookseller," said Gruberger.

In the late 1920s, while still a student, he engaged in a special form of bookselling known as "curbing the books." This was a variant on the New York stock market practice by which dealers too poor to join the stock exchange worked on the street as "curbstone brokers." (The American Stock Exchange was once known as the Curb.) Gruberger as a curb book dealer worked for the owner of textbook stores, one in Brooklyn near St. John's College and another at 137th Street and Amsterdam Avenue. Gruberger and a partner stood on the curb in front of the colleges and made deals to buy textbooks at the end of sessions.

"We would hail the students and buy their textbooks," he recalled. When they accumulated a supply of chemistry, literature, or other textbooks needed by advancing students, they took them to the corridors and classrooms of the schools and sold them directly. As an extra profit maker, they went to the teeming Orchard Street shopping district on the Lower East Side—a block down from the street where Gruberger was born—and bought supplies of laboratory coats to sell the science students along with textbooks. By the age of seventeen, "doing some kind of business was engrained in me," admitted Gruberger.

In the summers during those years he worked at the resort hotels of the Catskill Mountains, New York State's renowned Borscht Circuit, so called because of the popularity of beet-and-potato soup by vacationing New Yorkers. Working in the hotels as a busboy and waiter, while future famous entertainers up on the stage learned how to please audiences, Haskell Gruberger saved his pay and tips to buy a bookstore.

In the 1930s an opportunity came his way to acquire a bookstore specializing in textbooks at 18 Waverly Place, near New York University. The alumnus of "curbing the books" evaluated the proposition. He decided the fixtures and the goodwill were worth more than the $2,100 asking price. With $700 from his Borscht Belt earnings and close to as much borrowed from his mother, Gruberger closed the deal and paid off the remaining debt within a year.

THE MAKING OF AN ANTIQUARIAN BOOKMAN

Haskell Gruberger began to visit the Fourth Avenue bookstores on a regular basis in his search for textbooks, and he soon made contact with other bookmen there. One friendship that grew into a partnership—and an education—was with Sy Silverman, who worked at Abraham Geffen's 79 Fourth Avenue bookshop. Silverman and his coworker at the store, Milton Applebaum, according to Walter Goldwater, were always known as the Geffen boys. Gruberger had known Silverman previously at City College. Gruberger remembered that Silverman left the college because of problems that arose over his radical 1930s politics. Milton Applebaum got him the job that gave him permanent Book Row standing as one of the Geffen boys.

A transforming and pivotal moment came for Gruberger in the 1930s when he and Silverman took a vacation trip to St. Johnsbury, Vermont. St.

Johnsbury was a New England manufacturing area that at one time or another had produced everything from hoop skirts to bowling pins. It also evolved into the maple capital of the world after grocery salesman George Cary convinced a customer to use maple sugar instead of cane sugar as a binder and flavoring for plug tobacco.

For Haskell Gruberger, St. Johnsbury was the place where he experienced a sort of epiphany and gave birth to the idea of becoming an antiquarian bookseller. While walking about the town, he and Silverman happened on a surprisingly well stocked used-book store. Gruberger browsed among the low-priced books for a few titles he could add to his home library, but he saw Silverman was clearing off shelves and taking literally hundreds of books, for which he paid a paltry amount. Later Silverman put selling prices in the books before he stowed them in the trunk of their car. Gruberger realized his friend wanted the books as stock for a bookstore and that he theoretically could make a good profit on a meager investment.

"That started me thinking right then as we drove back to where we were staying," he reminisced. "What a romantic business—buying books you can sell to others. You ride around the countryside, enjoy the beauty of nature, see the world, take an aesthetic approach to life, have the company of books, and make money. What an irresistible combination!"

The young bookman was disillusioned about the textbook business and considered it a "cemetery" for ambitions because of long delays waiting for new semesters to begin. Between semesters a big day could involve selling a bottle of ink or a pencil. Gruberger acted by selling the textbook business to a law school student and began training himself for antiquarian bookselling. He studied secondhand bookstores on Fourth Avenue and elsewhere in New York, and he began attending auctions. He started applying the guidelines he received from Sy Silverman about analyzing a book for potential value based on such key features as the author, the publisher, the binding, and in the case of a nonfiction title, scholarly characteristics like a bibliography and index.

In addition to knowledge, he also recognized the importance of a gambler's nerve. "The cliché is true that you gain experience by taking a chance and jumping in. You have to have a certain amount of courage and ego drive to get involved, to tell yourself, if Abraham Geffen or Benjamin Bass or the others along Fourth Avenue can do it, I can do it," he said.

One asset for the book business that Gruberger was born with was a photographic memory, which he discovered in the course of book-buying trips with his friend Peter Lader and Louis Scher, founder of the Seven Bookhunters, located in a loft at 45 West Seventeenth Street. Gruberger offered to work for Scher on commission, anticipating as additional benefits getting "a shipload of information, experience, and how to price a book." Under this arrangement, he represented the Seven Bookhunters both in New York and on the road. The road trips acquainted him with an interesting and useful talent that he put to good use in his different mail-order and open-shop book businesses.

"If a customer came into my shop and asked for a certain book which I didn't have, I often remembered seeing it in another bookstore on my scouting trips, say, in the philosophy department on a specific shelf at a store near the University of Chicago, for example. I could call a bookstore out west that I had visited, give the title and the location of a particular book. They would usually confirm still having it where I said," he noted. This unusual ability was attributed to Louis Scher by Stanley Edgar Hyman in his "Book Scout" article (*New Yorker*, November 8, 1952). Gruberger thought Louis Scher learned about his memory feats from Peter Lader and mentioned them to Hyman, who made the attribution to the principal subject of his profile. The "elephant memory" of Haskell Gruberger was confirmed by numerous Book Row regulars.

Gruberger believed his ability to select quality books came substantially from the courses he took at City College. The courses gave him a familiarity with authors and a store of basic knowledge that supplemented general data needed for identifying a well-made book. After City College, his interest in books and general reading steadily added to this foundation, making him a more informed and therefore better bookman.

During World War II, like many other young men of his generation, Gruberger took a long leave from his civilian occupation for service in the European war zone, while his friend Sy Silverman was on the other side of the world in the South Pacific theater of the war. Upon his return from the war, Gruberger worked for a time at the Thoms & Eron bookstore downtown on Chambers Street, near City Hall. Not long after the war he and Sy Silverman became bookselling partners by mail order in a store on West Fifty-fifth Street at the periphery of the Broadway theater district. They also opened the first incarnation of the Social Science Book Store on Twelfth Street, in the large back room of a publishing enterprise near the New School for Social Research.

The New School, long a New York City institution of intellectual distinction, was started in 1919 as an exceptionally authoritative substitute for the "academic authoritarianism" and arrogance of Ivy League bastions. The New School's Dramatic Workshop in the 1940s helped train Tennessee Williams and Marlon Brando, to drop just two famous names from a list of famous names. The lecturers and faculty included Alfred Kazin and Hannah Arendt. The New School gave the Social Science Book Store access to an impressive artistic, socially aware, and literary clientele.

The Social Science Book Store and the store on West Fifty-fifth were not walk-in bookshops. Gruberger and Silverman issued catalogues structured as much as possible to offer highly desirable books that could generate mail orders. The mail-order approach worked well for years. Gruberger considered his first retail shop for the general public was his 1967 Social Science Book Store at 85 Fourth Avenue, near Tenth Street, since his textbook store at New York University had functioned just to supply students with the texts they needed for courses. No effort was required in the textbook store to satisfy the diverse needs of many different customers. However, the ability to satisfy a wide range of book demands and tastes was a sine qua non of a successful retail business.

A Dealer Remembers Aspects and Incidents of Bookselling

A book-dealing saga that started at the age of seven gave Haskell Gruberger an exceedingly long perspective on the practices and challenges of bookselling. He remembered his customers at the Social Science Book Store falling into two categories, the "hard-core buyers" and the "floaters."

The hard-core group were the serious book buyers who came in regularly. They included book collectors and dedicated students who persistently sought books for their own sake and for their information in specific fields. They were the customers "that would make your register ring." The floaters were impulse visitors who floated down to Fourth Avenue by accident or casual curiosity after shopping at the department stores on

Thirty-fourth Street or Fifth Avenue. The floaters made occasional purchases and were welcome visitors, but they were not consistent and thus reliable sources of sales.

The partnership of Gruberger and Sy Silverman started in the 1940s and followed an on-and-off pattern; one of the off periods came in the 1950s. Gruberger for a period was associated with a bookseller and wholesaler named Bob Brown. To share expenses, they sometimes went on the road together looking for books. Gruberger noted that Brown was also a dealer in curiosa; he hired writers to produce soft-pornography fiction that he published with the titillating passages in italics to facilitate reading. Italicizing the steamy parts was like the copy of *God's Little Acre* in *Mister Roberts* in which Ensign Pulver has "underlined every erotic passage, and added exclamation points—and after a certain pornographic climax, he's inserted the words 'well written.' "

Gruberger was a surprised observer when Brown calmly accepted $250 payment from a bookseller who owed him $1,100. Brown then replenished the store's inventory on credit. In effect the bookseller got about $1,900 credit for $250. Gruberger suggested to Brown this was a dubious way to run a business. Bob Brown explained, "With the $250 I can go to the printer and get several thousand more books, sell the books, and generate cash flow. If I squeeze the man, I may get nothing. Later, as his sales pick up, he can be a good source of further orders." "That taught me a new aspect of the business," admitted Gruberger.

A quick sale he made to the notable New York book dealer and attorney Jack Bartfield alerted Gruberger to the importance of checking values and not agreeing impetuously to a sale if maximum return was the goal. Gruberger had a first edition of Albert Einstein's short essays in German that Jack Bartfield saw on his desk. Gruberger had not vetted it, though he knew it was valuable. He was not certain how valuable. Bartfield asked the price; Gruberger said $50; and Bartfield instantly answered, "You got it!" Gruberger rationalized later that he obtained the Einstein in a group of books for virtually nothing and that even if he could have gotten more for the book, he was well rewarded by the deal.

Working as a book scout, Gruberger developed an ability shared by other bookmen to judge books externally by their formats and appearances when trying to move fast in singling out those worth buying. The name of the publisher, the look of the spine, the buckram or leather material used—all these and related characteristics alerted an attentive bookman to the prospect of something interesting.

Even the physical location of a book on a shelf in a bookstore might be important. Gruberger received this insight as a young book scout in the 1930s from genial and scholarly Alfred Goldsmith. "I already knew better than to look for sleepers in another dealer's bookshop, but that's what I was doing. I was young. I found four good books with low prices, and afraid to request a dealer discount, I asked what I owed," recalled Gruberger. "He looked me over and said, 'You aren't buying these to read.' He explained that I gave myself away as I walked around the store and made selections by checking the conditions of books more than their contents. I admitted he was a good Sherlock Holmes and that I was actually trying to get by as a scout. Mr. Goldsmith invited me to join him for coffee. He closed his shop right then—exercising that friendly freedom of a bookseller—and we went to an Automat. As we sipped coffee, we talked about books and he offered me what he called good solid advice. 'When you go into a bookstore, look first at the bottom shelves and the top shelves above eye level. Those are the places routine shoppers miss most.' As I traveled across the country buying books after the war, I followed his counsel and found a lot of gems on the bottom and top shelves."

During his coast-to-coast buying trips, Gruberger noted the regional aspects affecting the prices for different authors. In the Midwest, he found that Robert Frost titles cost less than in the East; but Carl Sandburg, Frank Norris, and Theodore Dreiser books tended to cost more. These regional differences were crucially important to a bookseller acquiring books for sale in a particular territory such as Fourth Avenue, New York City.

Gruberger mentioned a personal bias in his selection of books that didn't always coincide with the wisest business choices concerning individual titles: "My first approach when I evaluated a book was to question not its worth in money but if it would grace my catalogue and add a mark of distinction. I initially wanted to know if I would be proud to sell a particular book." Using this approach, he found that his choices fortunately were often justified by the profits resulting from the sales of the books selected on the basis of their intrinsic merit.

This operating policy for acquiring books that enhanced his catalogues and gave him satisfaction when he was vindicated by their sales was paralleled for Gruberger by a conviction that he applied to collectors as well as readers: the strong feeling that all books are for reading. "My bottom line approach is, a book is meant to be read. That's the beginning point and really the only point. A book should be read," Gruberger emphasized.

He mentioned a visit he once made with a friend to the home of a collector who took special pride in his American first editions. Gruberger was impressed with a long run of Henry James firsts and admired the collector's taste and judgment until he discovered that the signatures were uncut. The books had never been read and couldn't be read until the pages were separated. He made the mistake of telling the collector with a hint of sarcasm his view that even a first edition exists for reading. Gruberger recollected, "I think I may have given the collector an impression that I believed if he didn't read a book he had no right to collect it. He kicked me out. I didn't even get dessert."

Gruberger learned from the incident the importance in certain situations of keeping his unsolicited opinions to himself. Caution, care, and sensitivity can be prudent strategies when dealing with the often touchy attitudes of collectors and readers about their book treasures if you're hoping for dessert or even just reasonable amiability.

A book-buying excursion featuring a professor at Princeton and a beloved if badly worn volume gave another illustration. Gruberger purchased over a thousand books from a French literature professor at Princeton whose library was overstocked. It happens! Loading the books, Gruberger came across a severely damaged copy of R. W. Chambers's *Beowulf* that he considered too beat-up to sell and thus not worth taking to the city. He asked the professor kindly to put it in the garbage for him. The professor exploded like a volcano erupting: "How dare you say that about a book from a library of mine!" etc. etc. etc. Cowed by the realization he had been tactless, Gruberger hurriedly took the book away as the professor raved and ranted at the outrageous affront to himself and his book. The volume really was in ghastly shape; but it *was* from the professor's library, all pages were present, and it could be read by anyone in the mood for an eighth-century Anglo-Saxon epic poem. Beware, bookmen; insult a man's book, even one he no longer needs, and you insult the man.

Not much later, back in New York at the Social Science Book Store, a professor from New York University asked for, you guessed it, a copy of

Chambers's *Beowulf.* Gruberger with some embarrassment brought forth the lamentable volume from Princeton and offered it to the professor for nothing since he was ashamed to sell it. As he held out the book with head-shaking dismay at its condition, from inside the book eleven $10 bills fell out. The professor who had been reluctant to take the book for nothing, took it. The currency that tumbled from its nest inside *Beowulf* stayed at the bookshop. Soon thereafter back came the professor to confess that while working with the tattered volume, which he valued greatly, he found three more $10 bills. The professor thought the bookseller should have them. "You can do one of two things," said Gruberger. "You can keep them or you can use them to take me and my wife to dinner." The professor chose dinner, and maybe the bookman that time without deserving it got his dessert.

Ann Gruberger, who often traveled with her husband on book-buying trips, commented during the interview, "As a book dealer's wife, traveling around the United States and also abroad to England and Europe, I've seen a lot of book dealers in many places. To me as an outsider I felt there is such a continuing romance with these people who go into the book business. To them, it is an exciting and adventurous thing. It is not so much the selling and making a profit, but the search for the book, the pursuit of the book. That's what matters most to the book dealers, I think."

FAREWELL TO BOOK ROW

Bookseller Howard Frisch remembered Haskell Gruberger as "sometimes difficult, occasionally testy, but a good book dealer." Frisch noted that Gruberger in his experience had a policy he appreciated of stating a firm price. "He never gave a discount. He told you the price and then stuck with it," said Frisch, which may suggest a reason why Gruberger refrained from asking Alfred Goldsmith for a discount on books he purchased as a scout. Remarking on his fellow bookman, in a rueful compliment seasoned with criticism, Wayne Somers said, "He was just enough of a rogue to be appealing."

In addition to the Social Science Book Store on Fourth Avenue, Haskell Gruberger operated the business known as Haskell House; and he was successful in reprinting scholarly books. He was active for many years as a mail-order bookseller in the midtown area and Greenwich Village before he established his walk-in store on Fourth Avenue in 1967. Circumstances and opportunities made his stay there relatively brief.

Gruberger actually wasn't thinking about selling his lease and taking his business outside New York. Yet his shop became part of Book Row history in 1969 after two attractive offers convinced Haskell and Ann Gruberger to leave Fourth Avenue and transfer their bookselling activities to a new place that attracted them, Hadley, Massachusetts, located in a scholarly region dense with universities and colleges, including Amherst.

The first offer, a munificent one, came from a person who wanted the space for his insurance and law business because it was conveniently close to where he lived. Thus human fates mysteriously are affected by someone's impulse to shorten his walk to work. A second offer that made giving up the Book Row lease more palatable came from Montreal's McGill University, in Quebec.

McGill wanted the stock of the Social Science Book Store for its undergraduate library and agreed to purchase all the books. Trucks arrived to transport the books to Montreal. With them were two McGill librarians, who without reducing Gruberger's payment, set aside about eighteen thousand duplicates and other books, from his stock of over seventy thousand, that they decided they didn't need for their library.

Gruberger had capital for relocation to Massachusetts and a tidy bonanza of eighteen thousand books he hadn't expected to keep. After leaving Book Row, Haskell Gruberger continued to sell books, all kinds of books, at the Old Book Store, his "Supermarket of Old and Used Books with Something for Everyone."

In the process, of course, Book Row lost another bookstore. There is some satisfaction perhaps from reflecting that students at McGill can keep warm in Canadian winters and grow wise in all seasons by reading and studying books that they probably don't know came to them from Fourth Avenue.

Leon Kramer—Leon Kramer–Books

The booksellers on Book Row predictably came with a variety of temperaments, personalities, attitudes, shapes, and sizes. Some were cranky with chips on their shoulders; others were easygoing and hospitable. Ideologically, however, most seemed to share politically a liberal to radical point of view. Jack Biblo recalled a Russian revolutionist running a bookstore nearby who gave cups of tea to those he liked and drove away those he didn't.

The label "Russian revolutionary" also suited book dealer Leon Kramer, if the adjectives "considerate," "generous," and "civilized" were attached as well, to eliminate any pejorative aspects. His cultural and ethnic background was rooted in Russian anarchism, and as a young man he was involved with the radical movements of the twentieth century that struggled to give the poor a rare share of justice and to champion the rights of oppressed workers.

"Anarchism has a broad back, like paper it endures anything," wrote Octave Mirbeau, the French playwright and novelist. Anarchism *on paper,* as well as books and publications related to other radical movements, was the long-time scholarly specialty of highly respected Leon Kramer.

Dictionary and encyclopedia definitions of anarchism generally dwell on the elimination of established order and existing governments, violently if necessary. The goal of anarchism ostensibly was the idealistic achievement of a liberated, advanced human society free from oppression, greed, and the cruelties of economic inequity. Yet, as in the case of most political ideologies, the commonly applied definition was far from accurate because it was too narrow and thus incomplete. Anarchism came to mean many things to many people. The *New York Times* (May 5, 1886) in a heavy-handed front-page blast at anarchism under the headline "Anarchy's Red Hand," after the Haymarket Riot of May 4, 1886 (blamed on anarchists but never confirmed), applied one of the public-scare meanings by identifying *all* labor meetings as "anarchistic." If the workers of the world dared unite, they quickly earned eager condemnation from the 1886 *Times.* The times and the *Times* fortunately managed to change somewhat in the following century.

To various milder radicals and liberals with no appetite whatever for bomb throwing, anarchism simply meant using peaceful means of bringing about social change. Books, pamphlets, and soapbox orations at Union Square were among the tools of persuasion to eradicate the injustices of capitalism and totalitarianism for the betterment of human lives everywhere. To bookseller Leon Kramer, by all accounts one of the kindest, least violent, and most peaceful of men, during the later decades of his life anarchism meant thousands of such books and related radical publications.

He utilized his considerable learning and expertise in the field to obtain such materials and make them available, through Leon Kramer–Books, to appreciative researchers, collectors, libraries, and institutions dependent for years on his knowledge and acquisitions to help them build distinguished collections concerning radical politics and movements.

Leon Kramer, who was also located for a period at the Bible House on Fourth Avenue, maintained his principal book business (and home) at 19 West Eighth Street. On West Eighth Street, he was situated close enough to Book Row to be considered an integral part of that community. Within the Book Row community Leon Kramer was known and admired by practically everyone. Much the same could be said about the attitude of his customers and others beyond Book Row. "Leon Kramer enjoyed a reputation with librarians and collectors as a knowledgeable and seemingly inexhaustible source of books and pamphlets on economics, socialism, anarchism, and labor movements, which he continued to sell at moderate prices. . . . He was wholly honest, intellectually and in every other way," wrote Frederick B. Adams Jr. in a posthumous tribute published by *AB* (July 16, 1962).

The 1958 *International Directory of Antiquarian Booksellers* for ABAA member Leon Kramer listed the following specialties: "Economics (History of), General Literature (Utopias), History (Russian Revolution), Political Science, Socialism." As in the case of many directories, that listing gave an incomplete representation of the scope and depth of the books and publications consistently offered by Leon Kramer–Books.

THE GENTLE RADICAL

Leon Kramer was born in Russia around 1890. About the same time a group called the Pioneers of Liberty on New York's Lower East Side established the Yiddish-language weekly *Fraye Arbeter Shtime,* which would later become highly important in Kramer's life.

The Pioneers of Liberty group was organized mainly by Jewish immigrants in 1886 to protest the harsh treatment given workers denounced and brutally attacked as anarchists after the Haymarket incident at Chicago. The Pioneers of Liberty focused on organizing and educating workers; and the first issue of their newspaper, representing over thirty Jewish workers' associations, appeared July 4, 1890. In robust and literary Yiddish, the publication would be a crusading voice in support of the labor movement and employee rights through much of the following century. It would also serve as a sort of newsprint university striving for the continuing edification of its worker-readers.

When *Fraye Arbeter Shtime* ceased publication in December 1977 it was considered the world's oldest Yiddish newspaper. The weekly was noted for its superior literary content, featuring the finest writers and poets in Yiddish, as well as for its basic journalistic functions as a source of contemporary radical and prolabor opinion. The masthead of *Fraye Arbeter Shtime* carried the words "Let the Voice of the People Be Heard!" The defiant words were taken from the dying declaration on the gallows in November 1887 of Albert Parsons, one of the four men executed by society as an act of quick revenge for the Haymarket affair, although nothing was proved against them except that they had made statements in support of anarchism.

As a youth in Russia, Leon Kramer was active in the anarchist movement that preceded the Russian Revolution. This involvement in unlawful political activities, viewed then as agitation against the government, led to his imprisonment and brief exile in Siberia. When he was free to leave Russia, the young anarchist-idealist, at the age of twenty-two, came to the United States, around 1912. Fortunately, his economic circumstances or timing kept him from making the voyage aboard the British "unsinkable" liner *Titanic,* which collided with Atlantic ice and went down that spring. Leon Kramer reached his destination and applied himself for several years to learning about his new home.

He worked at odd jobs, played chess in the parks and rented rooms, and continued his multifaceted studies of ideologies, social movements, political economy, labor, history, and international radicalism. His intense commitment to read and understand a wide range of books in the complex field he would later emphasize as a bookseller made him an exceptionally well-informed bookman. Kramer's friend Walter Goldwater, with whom he shared a love of books, chess, and radical politics, wrote in *AB* (July 16, 1962), "A number of things distinguished Leon among booksellers, but I think the main one was that he knew his field: he read the books pertinent to it, and he expanded his knowledge first, and his field second." Sol Malkin, in *AB* (July 16, 1962), observed, "He was noted throughout the international book world for his learning as a bookman and his altruism as a human."

Expanding his knowledge was a dominant concern during those first decades in America, with libraries and bookstores as his sources for the necessary books. The menial work he did to earn a living left him time for the pursuit of knowledge, which he equated with the unalienable right Americans in patriotic mode still fondly call the pursuit of happiness. His increase of knowledge about radical movements didn't decrease his belief in liberal causes and the traditional principles of anarchism to make the world a freer place for exploited people. His friend for a quarter of a century, Sol Malkin called him a philosophic anarchist, and then added, "Thinking it over . . . every dedicated bookman is probably a philosophic anarchist." Malkin meant that as a compliment, not a criticism, and so Kramer would have taken it.

Leon Kramer's voluntary roaming and drifting ceased when he joined the staff of the Yiddish newspaper *Fraye Arbeter Shtime*. Working with "kinsprits"—Christopher Morley's term for kindred spirits—Kramer was home at last, with idealistic and talented people who believed as he did in the causes of justice and equality that stirred and inspired him.

At the newspaper office, during the early 1930s he began in a serious way to collect printed materials on radical movements, economics, utopias, politics, cooperatives, and related disciplines that eventually would dominate his bookselling activities. About that time he became acquainted with Walter Goldwater, who was in the process of establishing a book business in the East Side neighborhood many were already calling Booksellers' Row. His friend Walter's new career, after living in Russia and serving radical causes, perhaps prompted Leon Kramer to consider a similar move for the unique books and pamphlets he was assembling at the offices of *Fraye Arbeter Shtime*.

Reflection became the parent of action. Kramer rented bookstore space at the Bible House and also utilized his 19 West Eighth Street residence as the location for Leon Kramer–Books. Gradually he established an outstanding reputation as a reliable source of books and related materials on radicalism worldwide. He became a leading source of advice, information, and extremely difficult to find publications for national institutions and major libraries. He guided them in their selections of the most reliable editions and supplied materials to build important collections on radicalism and associated subjects. These materials were vital to scholars and relevant to national self-interest during an era of dangerous change through World War II, the Cold War, and afterward.

Kramer was contacted frequently for information and assistance by journalists and authors in and out of the academic sector whose writings and research involved radical and anarchist topics. "His name appears over and over again in acknowledgments by authors writing on the radical movement; his help was sought by dealers, collectors, and librarians alike, and was always granted," observed Walter Goldwater. Through his timely intercession at a crucial moment, archival records of the Socialist Party of America were saved from being irretrievably discarded. With his assistance, the Socialist archives were delivered into safekeeping at the Duke University Library.

Leon Kramer communicated with libraries, institutions, and collectors by means of distinguished annual catalogues featuring radical literature and related items. The catalogues were recognized by alert recipients as more than just shopping lists; they were opportunity lists. Kramer's prices were so low that one competitor actually took the impudent liberty of listing identical items from a Kramer catalogue at prices three times higher. Frederick B. Adams Jr. pointed out that often one-third to one-half of the items listed in a new Kramer catalogue might be ordered within a fortnight. By return mail the orders rolled in as a tribute to Leon Kramer's acquisitions and his careful descriptions.

Goldwater commented on his friend's occasional brief wrath at the careless—or deceitful—mistakes he sometimes found in the catalogues of other bookstores. Errors ranged from rare to nonexistent in catalogues from Leon Kramer–Books. Anger was infrequent and short-lived for Leon Kramer. Sol Malkin remembered that only the Stalinist falsification of Russian history, in his experience, bestirred his friend to an attack of indignation. At such times he would haul out book after book to prove his points and demonstrate the abuses to which he felt truth had been subjected.

After Leon Kramer died on June 22, 1962, in New York City, Sol Malkin wrote, "In Leon, the book world has lost not just a friend and colleague but a civilized human being." The fear among Leon Kramer's friends was that his unique book business would inevitably die with its creator. However, during his long illness, his daughter Jean became increasingly active in the business. Relying on her father's catalogues, his sources, and the exceptional books he had assembled, Jean took charge and kept Leon Kramer–Books operating successfully several additional years. Walter Goldwater expressed the hope that "Leon's erudition, intelligence, and humor" would not be forgotten. That he will be long and affectionately remembered seems likely due to the praise

Bookselling partners since the 1940s and prolific authors of books about books, Madeleine Stern (left) and Leona Rostenberg exhibit at the second New York Antiquarian Book Fair in 1961. Their work for the ABAA in organizing New York events helped make book fairs a nationwide tradition.

The Fourth Avenue portico of Wanamaker's department store, the "Iron Palace," seemed a friendly port to nearby bookshops. The mammoth store was a magnet for hordes, and many shoppers paused among the books to browse and buy. (*Photograph by Louis Dienes, 1953*)

Social worker Eleanor Lowenstein switched to bookselling, married Walter Goldwater, and made her Corner Book Shop a world center for books on cooking, gastronomy, and wine. As a cook, she liked to serve canned soup in jelly jars.

The Brussel brothers, Ike and Jack, were scouts on Book Row, famous for "sleepers." Ike proclaimed himself Last of the Great Scouts. This is Jack, who ran the Atlantis Bookshop and earned a dash of notoriety by reprinting erotica classics.

Book Row's survival hinged on one vital group—the customers. This was ConEd executive, Ben Bass's friend, great collector John Thorpe. Many of his 20,000+ books came from Book Row. They returned when the Strand bought his vast library.

As a boy, Herman Graf discovered book love and then discovered Book Row where that love could be consummated for a few coins. It seems natural he'd become a publisher and produce this volume celebrating his childhood book hunting grounds.

During his years on Book Row, Shepard (Shep) Rifkin was known and loved as the wide-roaming Book Ranger. He supplemented earnings as a writer working at the Strand and Pageant. Now living in Israel, he keeps in touch with Book Row friends.

Aided by Nat Himelfarb, NYU graduate Louis Schucman long maintained his Fourth Avenue "bookstore with a scholarly bias" to find books for others. He died at 91 on December 15, 1999, exemplifying the love of reading, books, and booksellling.

Schulte's under four owners kept the name assigned by founder Theodore Schulte. Serving movie stars, a tycoon, a president, and a vast reading public, Schulte's, on Fourth Avenue since 1917, made the art of bookselling as efficient as a science.

If a customer sought a complete set of hard-to-find books, Aaron Hershbain's popular shop was a smart place to stop first. In appearance, he could have made tackles or touchdowns for the New York Giants. In fact, he was a gentle giant of books, specializing in fine sets.

The Pageant of Henry (Chip) Chafetz and Sidney Solomon was famous for prints and pamphlets as well as books in abundance. "Bookbuying is a passion, and bookselling is an adventure," wrote Chafetz in 1953. Stand aside, explorers—make way for Fourth Avenue's great adventurers.

In its early years, the Strand like its neighbors struggled to survive. Here on Ninth Street, books sold for a nickel or a dime helped founder Ben Bass soldier on and wait for better times, which *did* arrive.

Ben Bass entered the book business in 1927 on Eighth Street. He opened the Strand in 1929 at 81 Fourth Avenue using sidewalk bargains to encourage quests for "sleepers." In those start-up days, did Ben ever foresee his book-selling dynasty?

From the 1960s to the 1990s, Ben Bass's son Fred Bass proved himself an exceptional bookselling entrepreneur. He supervised the Strand's steady growth to greatness as an American legend. "I grew up in the Strand," he said.

Propelled by the city's ambition to emulate Paris's Left Bank and with the Park Commissioner's blessing, Fred Bass in the 1960s wheeled books to Central Park for a Strand bookselling bin.

Succeeding founder Ben Bass at the Strand's helm are the daughter and father team, Nancy and Fred Bass. While there's a Strand, Book Row lives! Fred and Nancy Bass keep prospects bright for the years of books ahead. (*Photograph by Marvin Mondlin, 2003*)

Here is the venerable, durable, and vital Strand—16 Miles of Books—in Summer 2003, serving the present, promising a book-filled future. The Book Row saga need never end. (*Photograph by Marvin Mondlin, 2003*)

In 1996 Steve Crowley and his Alabaster Bookshop returned antiquarian bookselling to Fourth Avenue. In October 2003, the Alabaster completed its first seven years and was well established with quality books and loyal customers for the years ahead.

he continues to receive for his dedication to his profession, for the important books he placed in safe and permanent repositories, and for his essential human goodness.

Seymour Hacker—Abbey Bookshop—Hacker Art Books

Among the thousands of bookstores located from Aden to Yugoslavia, *The World Directory of Booksellers* (1970), edited by Alexander P. Wales, included Hacker Art Books, at 54 West Fifty-seventh Street in New York City, specializing in art, architecture, bibliography, and antiquarian books. Behind the *Directory*'s succinct entry for a long distinguished Manhattan bookstore lay a bookman and Book Row saga whose beginnings could be traced to the 1920s.

Future bookman Seymour Hacker was born on the Lower East Side in 1917, the same year that Theodore Schulte moved Schulte's Book Store to Fourth Avenue and gave momentum to the establishment of Booksellers' Row. By the age of twelve, precocious book lover Seymour Hacker was a regular on Book Row, seeking books for himself and indeed already starting to practice his future trade.

The boy collected the quality magazines thrown away by residents of the apartment building in the Bronx where he lived and then sold them to receptive dealers on Book Row. During his subsequent seventy varied years as a New York book and art dealer, he would never have it better in terms of outlay versus income. The magazines cost him nothing. His personal investment was just the subway ride to Union Square and careful negotiations with the amiable dealers. Plus he had the invaluable extra dividend of roaming again among the inviting shelves of the irresistible shops.

Still a teenager, at nineteen Seymour Hacker in 1937 opened his first bookstore, the Abbey Bookshop on East Ninth Street. The Abbey was a general bookstore similar to and compatible with other small shops in the neighborhood. Around the time he reached voting age, Hacker partnered with Albert Saifer to start a book auction business located at Ninth Street and Fourth Avenue. Albert Saifer a few years later became the first treasurer of the Fourth Avenue Booksellers' Association and publisher of a nationally influential newsletter available by subscription, *The Booktrade Wants*, in which booksellers paid five cents per line to list titles they were seeking.

World War II intruded on the careers of many young bookmen, among them Seymour Hacker. He began a five-year separation from Book Row in 1941 when he joined the merchant marines. But the battle for control of the Atlantic, in which he and his fellow seamen were so dangerously involved, couldn't stop a bookman from developing opportunities to seek and sell books. You could send a Book Row regular away from Fourth Avenue aboard a transport carrying the tools of survival to England and Russia, but you couldn't stop him from haunting bookstores in all the port cities where his ships unloaded cargo. Hacker did what any bookman does in a new place— he roamed the available stores and purchased those books he could resell back home in Manhattan.

After the war, in 1946, Hacker decided he wanted to open a more specialized bookstore; and fine art books appeared a logical choice because they seemed beneficiaries of a perpetual bull market. In 1946 at 381 Bleecker Street—named after man of letters Anthony Bleecker—Hacker inaugurated the bookshop that time would make well known in both the realm of art and the world of books, Hacker Art Books.

In 1948 Hacker Art Books moved to midtown, and Book Row thus had another important alumnus in uptown and upscale Manhattan. To complement his book business, Hacker added an art gallery featuring the work of then obscure abstract expressionists. In 1950, he took a step that several other Manhattan dealers found a logical extension of bookselling. He began a publishing sideline to reprint important books as well as to introduce original works of special merit. Among the original works was a book translated by Seymour Hacker, *Paul Cézanne: Letters,* edited by John Rewald.

Hacker Art Books became a popular oasis of culture among modern artists like Willem de Kooning and Jackson Pollock. Writers and actors as well frequented the hospitable institution. One literary regular at Hacker Art Books was poet and critic Delmore Schwartz, who as an editor of *Partisan Review* rejected a story by Calder Willingham and was repaid when Willingham named a whorehouse Hotel Delmore in his first book, *End as a Man* (1947). Actor-artist Zero Mostel, a friend of Seymour Hacker, was another loyal customer. Blacklisted for his politics during the 1950s, Mostel supported his family by working as an artist with a studio on Twenty-eighth Street.

Seymour Hacker's art gallery and publishing activities were important, but they remained secondary to his first love, bookselling. He died at the age of eighty-three on December 19, 2000. His obituary by Roberta Smith in the *New York Times* (December 24, 2000) emphasized the bookman's commitment to antiquarian books. "I grew up with old books, and it sticks," Hacker declared. The *Times* obit included this description, which probably would have pleased the bookman because it was complimentary to Book Row: "A small, bright-eyed man fluent in four languages, Mr. Hacker was one of the last booksellers to learn his trade from the bookmen whose stores and stands once lined Fourth Avenue between Astor Place and Fourteenth Street."

With pride in his Book Row background, Seymour Hacker, a survivor from the great book days on Fourth Avenue, came to consider himself perhaps the "last of the dinosaurs." As did others among his Book Row contemporaries, he regretted the disappearance of smaller, individualistic bookshops, inadequately replaced by impersonal superstores where books can seem almost afterthoughts among the enveloping horde of reading accessories, videos, compact discs, sweet rolls, and cappuccinos.

This lament was ruefully and wistfully reflected in the 1998 film comedy *You've Got Mail*, in which the Tom Hanks character's superbookstore drives the Meg Ryan character's small and intimate New York bookshop out of business. "Watch it and laugh" as a reaction to the film was much less likely than "Watch it and weep" among bookmen such as Seymour Hacker and his customers with grateful memories from the decades reaching back to 1937 and the Abbey Bookshop on East Ninth.

In his later years, Hacker wondered where and if young people would still be able to develop the "mental apparatus" for bookselling. Could a hopeful answer be that young people may find the necessary will and wisdom within themselves by pondering the interesting lives and inspiring examples of that bookish band of dealers, Seymour Hacker and his Book Row colleagues?

CHAPTER FOURTEEN

BOOK ROW MEMORIES: BUYERS, BROWSERS, AND MOURNERS

*The lack of intelligence with which people use bookshops is, one supposes, no
more flagrant than the lack of intelligence with which we use all the rest of
the machinery of civilization. . . . This sharp ecstasy of discovering books for
one's self is not always widespread. There are many who, for one reason or
another, prefer to have their books found out for them. But for the complete
zealot nothing transcends the zest of pioneering for himself. . . . We visit
bookshops not so often to buy any one special book, but rather to rediscover, in
the happier and more expressive words of others, our own encumbered soul.*

—CHRISTOPHER MORLEY

THE BOOK LOVER's book lover, Christopher Morley (we never tire of
repeating that he felt about bookshops the way Will Rogers did about men
he met—liked them all), maintained in his essay "On Visiting Bookshops"
(*Safety Pins*, 1925) that visits to a bookshop are not "casual errands of reason"
but "necessary acts of devotion." That vital act of devotion was probably performed by more people, Morley among them, more often on Booksellers'
Row than can be claimed about any other neighborhood of books in this
world or any other, whether historical, existing, or future.

The booksellers of Book Row had professional reasons to lament the
passing of their way of life at the walk-in bookshops of Fourth Avenue. But
in many cases at least they had the consolation, if they wished, of selling
books by mail order or in other locations, ranging from New Jersey to New
Mexico. If rents drove them away and monster machines knocked down their
stores, they still had legitimate and satisfactory bookselling options. If maybe
not the best, there were nevertheless bona fide options.

But what about the browsers, scholars, collectors, scouts, book hunters,
teachers, writers, and book lovers who frequented Book Row, depended on
Book Row, used Book Row, found and bought books on Book Row? What
about the loyal customers who loved Book Row, who came to Fourth Avenue

day after day, year after year, for tireless wandering store to store to store? What about them? They had arguably even greater reason than the booksellers for sadness and regret. Where could they go? When their Book Row was gone, there was no other Book Row like their Book Row. Certainly not for them. It was and is to weep. We need Irving Berlin to write the lyrics.

Ah, but what a fabulous archive of book-loving world citizens it would be if it only existed, an honor roll of *all* who were there. No one, alas, managed to record the names of the book seekers who ventured to Book Row from the pioneer days of George D. Smith and Peter Stammer to the later days, when the great row had dwindled again to a struggling few.

Starting in the 1940s and continuing as long as the presence of the bookshops made it possible, both of us, Marvin Mondlin and Roy Meador, were there many times as customers, searching shop to shop, admiring books we couldn't afford (looking at beauty is its own reward), buying all the books we dared. We were there with the uncounted others, again and again. We were there reading in a corner, browsing for bargains, schmoozing with book people, and quite often buying books about books and books that were just books about everything under or beyond the sun. We had to have those books, we customers of Book Row; not to have those books was like not breathing. Our names were legion.

But no list was made of the thousands, the millions, who answered the call of the shops and made the journeys of the book faithful whenever possible. What a colossal roster it would be, though, a mammoth scroll of the celebrities, eager readers, obsessed collectors, scouts with precious tomes to sell, the famous authors and the never-heard-ofs, sharing in the mystery and miracle of books. Along with the booksellers they too should be remembered, the eager readers and book requesters and questers who were the customers of Book Row and who never ceased to miss it when it was gone.

Nathan Silver, in his excellent book about vanished city structures, *Lost New York* (1967), wrote, "The ideas of New York that are present here—though some are romantic or largely imaginary—have become part of New York experience, even to distant strangers who have only heard about them. . . . People value old things, not just for their rarity as antiques, but for their history of human use. . . . This may be a city's greatest function—its ability to present the full record of the past." Book Row as a celebrated and notable component of "lost New York" has been among the more enduring and far-reaching of the great New York ideas. Book Row lives on in the city's memories and indeed the world's memories as a vital part of the New York City past.

The loss of Book Row for countless reader-customers produced a cultural drought and intellectual dust bowl. No comparable substitute has developed, no, not even in cyberspace or those overpopulated Internet burbs. Thanks to the broadband interests and proud diversity of the booksellers there, on Book Row there wasn't just *a* book for every need, mood, or taste. Often there was a whole section of applicable books or even an entire bookstore for every taste, mood, need. The variety, independence, and heterogeneity of the dealers and their books made Book Row a haven for reading and collecting diversity where *Vive la différence* meant three cheers for nonconformity. In their place have come drearily homogenized chain stores, a global electronic whirlpool erratically accessible mainly to persistent onliners with super-human patience for slogging through vast swamps of World Wide Web distractions, and a wistfully few widely scattered individual bookshop survivors.

Book Row catered individualistically to the book demands of an international city where human diversity is an indispensable strength. Nathan Silver reminded us that while Horace Greeley advised going west, he wisely stayed put in New York. Columnist Murray Kempton, a beloved Boswell for New York, pointed out as an instance of his hometown's accommodating style that his was "the only city under the eye of God where the librettist for *Don Giovanni* could find his closest friend in the author of 'The Night Before Christmas.'" Murray Kempton didn't note what we shall, that the librettist, Lorenzo Da Ponte, was also a New York City bookseller.

Book Row issued a constant invitation to the vast wild spectrum of metropolitan possibilities. When Book Row was gone, its immensely valuable hospitality for diversity was gone as well. Reflecting on a New York without Book Row, Isaac Bashevis Singer somberly described the cultural climate that he saw developing in the United States during the 1980s: "I feel that America is waiting for a Gogol or a Sholem Aleichem, because behavior in this country has become so standardized that we are slowly losing our sense of human values. It is a result of the fact that the media are so omnipresent in this country. We are fooled by myriads of generalizations and by floods of propaganda." Book Row was a small but steady antidote to such standardization. An antidote is missed when it is gone.

Storyteller Isaac Bashevis Singer came to New York from Poland in 1935. He and his fellow refugees in the 1930s had among the bookstores of Fourth

Avenue a refuge where they could find both kindred spirits and the books needed to help master English and to find their way forward in a new land. "I began life here in furnished rooms and I ate in cafeterias. . . . My desire to learn English was very strong. I knew that if I didn't learn this language I would be lost forever," Singer recalled. He utilized the resources of the bookstores to help him learn not only the local language but also the nature of the country. He began establishing himself as a writer in Yiddish on the *Forverts* or *Jewish Daily Forward* (1897–1986). With Book Row as a prime resource, he started producing the stories that would earn and win the 1978 Nobel Prize for Literature. "Only small fish swim in schools," observed Singer, celebrating diversity and the courage of nonconformity, which were hallmarks of the Book Row reigning along Fourth Avenue when he reached America.

For decades Jimmy Breslin wrote affectionately about New York in his famous newspaper columns and included Book Row stores among his city's special amenities. One of his editors, William Brink, noted about Breslin: "He has been observed sneaking into a bookstore to buy a three-volume collection of Montaigne's essays." The stores favored by the columnist for Montaigne and others and sometimes favored with printed words of tribute were more often than not south of Fourteenth Street on Book Row.

Great authors, columnists, and everybody else within reach who wanted a book, the exact book, knew where to ask, look, search. They traveled by mail after poring over bulging catalogues from Book Row if physically going there was out of the question. It was best, of course, to go there, walk in, and carefully explore the crowded shelves oneself.

To do it right, they caught a subway and exited at Astor Place or Union Square if they lived in Brooklyn, Queens, the Bronx, or Manhattan north of Thirty-fourth Street and south of Chambers Street. They caught a plane, a train, a bus, a ship, if they lived in New Orleans, Denver, Tucson, Rio, Jerusalem, Sydney, Rome, Moscow, and said to the pilot or engineer or driver or captain, "Take me to Book Row."

They pulled on sneakers and set out afoot if they lived reasonably nearby (any mile walk in Manhattan is a pedestrian's delight) as so many readers, collectors, and writers did. Wherever they lived, whenever they could, book people headed for Book Row. There the books they wanted more likely than not, once upon a time, waited for them. Once upon a time, alas! But let not the glooms of history's what-used-to-be's prevail. Along with mourning, many of us bring pleasant memories to the wake. Heed, then, times that were, searches conducted, and books found. Listen to the memories.

REFLECTIONS FROM THE PASSING PARADE

Multitudes regret the fate of the old bookstores that served their purpose and their times and then went their way. Various customers and colleagues across the generations—patrons of the shops who constituted a passing parade of perusers and collectors—sometimes left a record of their presence or a personal recollection of Book Row's significance to them.

Starting in the 1930s, when Book Row flourished, John Nesbitt, a former janitor and seaman, inspired by his father's collection of clippings on odd but true historical events and strange tidbits from the past, began a popular series of one-reel films and a long-running radio program (initially sponsored by Cream of Milk face cream) called *The Passing Parade*. One account reported on a man who spent four years living in a cupboard. The bookstores of Book Row were hosts to a nearly century-long passing parade of book seekers and book lovers. We can get in step with the parade and share a few from the many.

AUTHORS AND EDITORS

During over three-fourths of the twentieth century the neighborhood of Book Row was home to many prominent, and of course never prominent, writers and professionals associated with publishing. They were part of the Book Row scene, some perhaps merely by walking through on the way to the subway or strolling at night past the lighted, book-filled windows. Most were regular customers in the Fourth Avenue shops. Allen Ginsberg lived at 206 East Seventh Street and was a magnet for idea-slinging, word-flinging visits by the Beats, including Jack Kerouac and William Burroughs. Dwight MacDonald lived at 117 East Tenth Street. Norman Mailer was close to Book Row and a sharp-eyed Book Row watcher when his home was at 39 First Avenue. Jack Gelber completed his play *The Connection* (1959) at 11 Pitt Street. The controversial drama about drug addicts for the Living Theater became a milestone work and catalytic influence for the Off-Broadway movement. Poet and art critic Frank O'Hara may have heard the heartbeat of Book Row and let it resonate in his urban portraits when he resided at 791 Broadway. Edward Hoagland wrote *The Peacock's Tail* (1965) while living at 521 East Fifth and 261 East Tenth Street. The bookstores were neighbors and sources for these writers. More distant authors were no less connected to the Fourth Avenue bookstores that served and honored them. They loved Book Row when it was there. They missed it when it was gone.

Renee Zuckerbrot, assistant editor, Doubleday. "Bookstores are, and have always been, important to me," wrote Renee Zuckerbrot. "When I imagine how Fourth Avenue once must have been, I can't help seeing it as a history of lost bookstores and a forgotten time. I think John Cheever called it a long-lost world, when almost everybody wore a hat."

Harry Golden, author, journalist, editor. He has been described as a man who gnawed black cigars and explored new ideas at his desk in Charlotte, North Carolina, where he edited the *Carolina Israelite*. He described himself as a fat little guy, short of breath. He never seemed short of wisdom in his books— *Only in America* (1958), *For 2¢ Plain* (1959), *Enjoy, Enjoy* (1960)—his syndicated columns, and his sixteen-page, widely quoted monthly paper. Carl Sandburg thought he exemplified Ralph Waldo Emerson's bold dictum in "Self-Reliance" (1841): "Whoso would be a man must be a nonconformist." He derived pleasure from never letting himself forget that he came from 171 Eldridge Street, on the Lower East Side, between Rivington and Delancey. It intrigued him that Rivington was named for the Revolutionary era Tory printer and publisher James Rivington, "who did not believe in America" and whose street became the entrance for "millions of immigrants from all the corners of the world, seeking political security and religious freedom." That was where Harry Golden "acquired the habit of reading books" and learned to cherish nearby Book Row. "The next time you are in New York, go down to Eighth Street and take a look at Cooper Union. It will be an inspiration to you," he wrote. "Around the corner you have the five largest secondhand bookstores in the country. In one of those stores there is a fellow by the name of Wilkes. Dream up some hundred-year-old title of a book long forgotten and out of print and he'll scrounge around the mountain of books on the floor and pull it out for you." It's too late now for the bookstores and the amazing Wilkes. But the memory is friendly.

Emma Goldman, author, editor, anarchist, feminist. During the early years of Book Row, she lived there for a decade (1903–13) at 210 East Thirteenth Street. From that address in 1906 she began publishing and distributing *Mother Earth,* a political-cultural, unconventional, anarchist journal that was often scary to the establishment of the era. The bookshops in the neighborhood where she lived served as friendly havens for discussions and intellectual warm-ups in the way European coffee shops might have served, had she stayed in Lithuania, where she was born in 1869. The bookshops were also vital providers of background materials for her contentious and forceful journal. Goldman's vocal opposition to U.S. participation in World War I took her away from Book Row to imprisonment on Ellis Island and later deportation as a "dangerous radical" to the Soviet Union in 1919. Maureen Stapleton won an Academy Award as Book Row's Emma Goldman in the 1981 feature film *Reds.*

James Atlas, essayist. In an otherwise upbeat 1980s essay, "Somewhere in New York, You Can Buy a Good Book" (*The New York Times World of New York,* 1985), James Atlas lamented that "those days are gone" when New York with Fourth Avenue had the equivalent of the Paris quays and London's Charing Cross Road bookstores. For him the city fortunately still qualified as an island of books. While reading a magazine in a Manhattan bookstore, he saw Allen Ginsberg walk in and "remembered why I'd come to New York." But the remaining book emporia were chaotically and inconveniently scattered about the city. "The bookstores that once lined both sides of the avenue have disappeared, leaving the city without a geographic center for bibliophiles," wrote Atlas. That still has an ominous sound and makes the nervous among us think of the William Butler Yeats lines "Things fall apart; the center cannot hold; / Mere anarchy is loosed upon the world," from "The Second Coming."

Howard Pyle, author, illustrator. He is best known (and most collected) for his distinctive and historically accurate illustrated children's classics such as *The Merry Adventures of Robin Hood* (1883) and *The Story of King Arthur and His Knights* (1903). As an intensely earnest book collector, he was one of the earliest and best Book Row and pre–Book Row customers. When he complained about the prices he was forced to pay for books he "had" to have, Manhattan bookseller William Evarts Benjamin tactfully responded, on October 7, 1891, "A bookseller can render far greater service to an appreciative customer by putting in his way the best books, than by giving him the benefit of lower prices and poorer material. Believe me 'the best is cheapest' in books. . . . By 'paying me for experience' I mean that as you are buying through me you are gaining experience through me. I on my part am guiding you and preventing you from making false and expensive mistakes." Early in the twentieth century, from the New York dealers, Pyle bought first editions of his favorites, Irving, Longfellow, Kingsley, Poe, Thackeray, Wordsworth. He was known to go far and pay dearly for the works of engraver Thomas Bewick, esteemed for his *General History of Quadrupeds* (1790) and *History of British Birds* (2 volumes, 1797, 1804), as well as an illustrated edition of Oliver Goldsmith's *The Deserted Village*. Pyle's library was also the beneficiary of presentation copies from literary friends such as Willa Cather, Oliver Wendell Holmes, William Dean Howells, Theodore Roosevelt. After Pyle died in 1911 in Florence, Italy, where he had gone to hone his talents as an artist, his widow, Anne Poole Pyle, in the 1930s noted that he opened a book with a "look of veneration . . . most tenderly, carefully allowing the lid to lie on his wrist with no strain to the back." Howard Pyle's library was broken up and titles from it still surface. If a Pyle volume luckily comes your way, be tender.

Thomas Wolfe, novelist. When he worked as a young English teacher at the Washington Square campus of New York University, Thomas Wolfe lived in rented rooms and small apartments several places in the vicinity of Book Row. He allowed friendly and tolerant booksellers to cash his checks and patiently listen to his limitless supply of literary opinions. He hoped New York's East Side neighborhoods and the Book Row area would provide fresh materials to complement his flood of Old Catawba (North Carolina) recollections; and he wasn't disappointed. New York sights, sounds, and people are important and sometimes dominating in three of his four autobiographical novels. In *You Can't Go Home Again* (1940), about his stand-in George Webber, Wolfe wrote, "For several years New York had been the place that he called home." In 1926–27 Wolfe lived with Aline Bernstein in a loft at 13 East

Eighth Street. From there, and later from 263 West Eleventh Street and 27 West Fifteenth Street, he often walked the Manhattan streets at night after an intense writing session on his first novel, *O Lost* (published in 1929 as *Look Homeward, Angel*). During those nocturnal strolls, some of the Book Row proprietors with stores still open might nervously anticipate his towering invasion and lusty patronage. The books he saw in the bookshops deserved the description he gave the books in the library of Mrs. Esther Jack (Aline Bernstein): The walls "were crowded with friendly volumes whose backs bore the markings of warm human hands. Obviously they had been read and read again." The same was true of the books he found on Book Row. Thomas Wolfe was a poet in prose about his city's ceaseless metamorphosis as it perpetually struggled like the phoenix to be reborn. Only the surrounding rivers were constant. "This will be an eternal and unchanging fact about that city whose only permanence is change: There will always be the great rivers flowing around it in the darkness," he wrote. Wolfe lived in the Book Row area before the eroding virus of unwanted change arrived, but his words were prophetic.

Herbert Faulkner West, author, enthusiast, collector. Among books about book collecting, those by Herbert Faulkner West were admired by Lawrence Clark Powell, and that should be good enough for the rest of us. West's *An Apology for Book Collecting* (1933) and *Modern Book Collecting for the Impecunious Amateur* (1936) are elusive, but they make cheerful reading and are well worth the seeking, taking, perusing. According to Powell, West specialized in "personal, unstandardized collecting," which probably covers over 90 percent of addicted book acquirers. West specialized, though, in the numerous works of Robert Bontine Cunninghame Grahame, about whom he wrote often and rapturously. West also took the exceptional step of praising a New York bookseller by name. In his helpful guidebook for impecunious amateurs (which may also cover a hefty percentage of collectors), West expressed affection and gratitude for his valued friend Alfred Goldsmith. He expressed his certainty that Goldsmith knew more about Walt Whitman than anyone else in America and added, "Personally I value his judgment on any writer." Booksellers tended to be thanked in person; sometimes their stores were mentioned; but those in the writing community seldom praised Book Row proprietors by name. Who can say why? Anyway, it is pleasant to have West's well-deserved paean to Alfred Goldsmith. We know Herbert West was a sage collector complacently endowed with stoicism. He wrote, "It is just as well, perhaps, when one's collection is not absolutely complete. There is still a thrill to look forward to; still a missing item to seek for. In that lies much of the joy of collecting." Quite true.

Edward Robb Ellis, author, journalist, diarist, Manhattan chronicler. When he hurt his foot in the 1950s on a newspaper assignment, he claimed his first reaction was dismay at maybe not being able to search the Fourth Avenue bookstores again. Happily Ellis walked and continued to frequent the bookshops. Mobility and access to Book Row were indispensable desiderata for the compiler of *The Ellis Diary.* Ellis had to have books, and they had to be *his* books. "I never work in libraries. Because I under-line, I can't use library books," he was quoted in William E. Farrell's "About New York" column in the *New York Times* (February 25, 1981). He even underlined and entered marginal comments in his *Encyclopaedia Britannica.* That annotated encyclopedia, of course, would be more fun to have than any monotonously unmarked edition. Ellis decided television was a disease carrier driving the world mad—a virus he intended to resist with his six-decade diary. A New York newspaperman for years, Ellis published *The Epic of New York City* (1966); *A Nation in Torment: The Great American Depression 1929–1939* (1970); *Echoes of Distant Thunder: Life in the United States 1914–1918* (1974). These massive works of microscopic history roar with the zestful curiosity of the author. They also reveal the immense resources of Book Row and Edward Robb Ellis's tireless ability "to prowl the Fourth Avenue bookstores."

Maurice Dolbier, author, critic. As a reviewer for the *New York Herald Tribune,* he received a torrent of new books from publishers each publishing season. He was a close observer of New York book people and habits. "New Yorkers do much of their reading while in motion," he wrote in "The Other Four Seasons" for a *New York Herald Tribune* anthology, *New York, New York* (1964). "Subways and buses are full of readers. . . . If the straphanger beside him drops dead, he may take his eye from the page, but only momentarily unless the deceased is known to him. 'Never ask for whom the bell tolls' is completely unnecessary advice here; we wouldn't dream of asking." Maurice

Dolbier realized and regretted that the bell in the 1960s was tolling for Book Row. "Some great secondhand bookstores are still to be found in New York . . . but on the whole this noble business has fallen upon hard times. Its heart, on Fourth Avenue, is still beating, but the beat is increasingly feeble. More and more stores of the kind that Christopher Morley immortalized in print are going out of business," he wrote. Dolbier sensed what was slowly being lost. "There were excitements and discoveries in those bargain trays outside the shops, and more inside, often including the proprietor," he noted. The new paperback stores and the chain stores were no substitute. Generations of readers would be deprived and cheated as "they grew up in a world largely without secondhand bookshops."

Imamu Amiri Baraka (LeRoi Jones), dramatist, poet, political activist. Roy Meador knew him as a proctor at the New York Law School on William Street in Lower Manhattan when he was still called LeRoi. Those of us who met him before the name change in 1968 had no doubt he was brilliantly talented and destined to be heard. Poetry was his passion and the focus of his gifts at that time. Allen Ginsberg's *Howl* (1956) influenced him as a liberating revelation that poetry could be about ordinary, real, familiar things. "It was a breakthrough for me," he wrote in *The Autobiography of LeRoi Jones* (1984, 1997). His Book Row connections included residences at 324 East Fourteenth Street and 27 Cooper Square, where he wrote *Blues People* (1963). Some of us, impressed by *Spring and So Forth* (1960), *Cuba Libre* (1961), and *Preface to a Twenty Volume Suicide Note* (1961), were surprised when substantial fame first came to him not as a poet but as a militant playwright, through his fierce trio of angry-young-black-man plays in 1964: *Dutchman, The Toilet, The Slave.* These gripping Off-Broadway hits challenged white society's perceptions of black lives and attitudes and gave momentum at the height of the civil rights movement to the development of a New York theater with a black point of view. In 1965 he founded the Black Arts Repertory Theater in Harlem. Dwelling in the Book Row neighborhood, Amiri Baraka turned to Book Row primarily for the materials he needed to write. The University Place Book Shop of Walter Goldwater and Bill French, with its African-American and African books and publications, was a particular favorite. From Bill French, whom he described as "very knowledgeable about books," Baraka obtained a complete set of *Crisis,* the magazine W. E. B. Du Bois edited for the NAACP. Bill French also delivered other out-of-print rarities pertaining to the Harlem Renaissance, an artistic and literary development that peaked in the 1920s and had a lasting impact on black art and creativity. When he started his avant-garde literary magazine *Zazen,* Baraka went on foot to place copies in the bookstores. "I think we did five hundred and in a short time they were gone. There was no money in it, of course, but we wanted to get the word out," he wrote.

VALEDICTORY

Many authors and editors, known, not so known, and unknown, valued and used Book Row. Growing up in New York when Book Row flourished, Avram Noam Chomsky relied on the Fourth Avenue shops to supply him with the scholarly and radical literature that nourished his scrappy career as author, professor, and antiwar activist. The tradition continued even in the twenty-first century as playwright John Guare, at the venerable survivor, the Strand, found a much-weathered copy of Ulysses S. Grant's *Memoirs,* which inspired the writing of *A Few Stout Individuals* (Grove Press, 2003), a drama about the writing of those memoirs, with General Grant and Mark Twain as principal players.

Frank Norris wrote, "Of all the ambitions of the Great Unpublished, the one that is strongest, the most abiding, is the ambition to get to New York." Generations later Maurice Dolbier echoed Norris: "The city acts as a magnet to ambitious young writers." In her essay "New York City: Crash Course" (*Granta* 32, spring 1990), Elizabeth Hardwick called New York "a spectacular warehouse." Now there's a succinct summation for what Book Row meant as a magnet within a magnet for members or would-be members of the writing profession.

Is it still true, we wonder, in the twenty-first century, that New York has the same powerful lure that drew Thomas Wolfe and so many others across the Hudson and along the roadways into the city? Perhaps, perhaps not. If not, here's another question with no answer: Could the passing of Booksellers' Row be among the reasons? When Gertrude Briggs was preparing to close Books 'N Things after more than half a century, a pensive customer observed, "It was bookstores like this one that initially attracted people here. . . . Now they can no longer afford to stay." Another downcast customer predicted, "And that's going to be the death of this neighborhood too."

THE BOOKSELLERS

Proprietors and employees of bookstores more often than not began their careers in books as readers, collectors, browsers, buyers. For those who grew up in the New York area, Booksellers' Row was a fascinating kingdom of books, as magical as Oz, as irresistible as Ebbets Field or Yankee Stadium. That was certainly true for Marvin Mondlin, whose connection with books began at home and grew into a love affair during the 1940s among the bookshops of Book Row. He discovered Book Row with his mother and never stopped returning. His first purchase was an organic chemistry book from a sidewalk stand on Fourth Avenue. The best browsing he found, because of fast turnover, was at the Samuel Weiser Bookstore. Yet all the shops were a browser's Elysium in which to seek and find during the 1940s and 1950s. He progressed from outside stands (seven for a quarter and up) to inside shelves (fifty cents and up). His first "big buy" was the Appleton edition of Charles Darwin. The red leather backs were dried and crumbling, but cripples or not, the volumes for him were anointed with distinction. From browsing and personal collecting, he joined in the 1950s with Victor Tamerlis to take over the space of a failed Chinese laundry and launch Amory Books at 280 West Twelfth Street. He worked as an auctioneer and appraiser, and he served for decades as an antiquarian bookman and executive at the Strand. Thus evolved a career bookseller who must live with the knowledge that "I was a teenage bibliophile" and that it happened on Book Row. Many other booksellers experienced similar relationships—let's call them love affairs—with the books of Fourth Avenue.

Maggie Donovan DuPriest. "Reading always was and always will be my main recreation. I visited New York often long before I ever thought about going into the book business on my own. I always spent hours in the shops on Fourth Avenue," wrote Maggie DuPriest. The 1977 *International Directory of Antiquarian Booksellers* had two bookshop listings for her, the Old Book Shop in Coconut Grove, Florida, and Margaret DuPriest at 720 Greenwich Street,

Manhattan, with out-of-print Americana and erudition as specialties. For this account DuPriest recalled book shopping sprees on Book Row and close friendships with Samuel Weiser, Henry Chafetz, Sidney Solomon, and others who qualified as "old-time bookmen." "You ask about famous people who visited my shop, well there were plenty, writers, artists, actors; but all my customers were important to me. Many became close friends and remain so. I never used the names of well-known customers for publicity. One of my favorite customers was a policeman who came in every week. He liked nineteenth century novels and the essays of Emerson and Thoreau, 'because they are so peaceful,' he said," DuPriest wrote. In her own stores she never really specialized because her tastes were, as she said, "very eclectic." She missed the warm and comfortable atmosphere of the small bookshops. She missed the Book Row dealers who had reverence for books, knew what was between the covers, and would share book views with customers. "I find that I miss having my shop. Even the years when it was a struggle were among the best of my life," she wrote.

Louis Wavrovics. With his brother Ernest, Louis Wavrovics was a busy book dealer in New York for many years. They were widely known as the "River Bargemen" because for a time they lived on a barge near Fourteenth Street and East River Drive. "Brother Louis is always out looking for books, you'll never get a photo of him. We're identical twins so you'll get a good idea of what he looks like from my picture," Ernest told a reporter in 1955. The 1951–52 *International Directory of Antiquarian Booksellers* had this entry: "*Wavrovics* Louis, 530 E. 14th Street. SPECIAL. *General Books.*"

Audacious, quixotic, and more often than not quite profitable deals characterized the Wavrovicses' book-buying and bookselling activities. Among their bolder, wilder, and better known ventures was the purchase of the Homer and Langley Collyer mansion. The Collyer brothers, who lived at 2078 Fifth Avenue, were eccentric recluses found dead of starvation in 1947. The Collyers carried collecting to an extreme point of obsessive hoarding. Their house was crammed with an incredible accumulation of books, magazines, journals, and tons of miscellaneous items, from several pianos to part of a Model T Ford. The Wavrovics brothers acquired the mansion with the proviso that they dispose of everything. No doubt they kept whatever books were worth the keeping. Another example of their blind optimism and sight-unseen bravado was witnessed by Marvin Mondlin at an auction. The brothers bid on and won for several hundred dollars an unopened trunk with unknown contents. That gamble too paid off opulently. The trunk was loaded with memorabilia of performer, theater manager, and concert saloon operator Tony Pastor, who was widely known as the "Father of Vaudeville." His last concert saloon, on Fourteenth Street, featured less raucous vaudeville for families.

For this account, Louis Wavrovics looked back across more than half a century since he and his brother started selling books in the 1930s and established a lasting connection with their neighbors and friends, the booksellers of Book Row. The Wavrovics Brothers specialized in histories, records and papers of New York City residents, and art objects. "I have fond memories of fellow booksellers, famous personalities, and the interesting characters that gravitate to an active bookstore in the Lower East Side area," wrote Louis Wavrovics. Thanks to the books and the book people, he declared, "I have had a very interesting life."

Wayne Somers. He knew Book Row as a student, collector, acquisitions librarian, and bibliographer in the 1960s and as a book dealer starting in 1971. Somers was the proprietor of Hammer Mountain Book Halls in the Schenectady, New York, area until 1981. He specialized in scholarly books on European history as well as French and German literature. Somers missed seeing Fourth Avenue at its peak. By the time he was searching for titles there, the real estate situation had become oppressive, and some proprietors were perhaps succumbing to the pressures. Somers remembered dealers who were unfriendly and rude with customers, including himself and his wife. He witnessed people driven from shops because they weren't buying, at least not readily enough to satisfy the bookseller.

"I recall somebody coming into one of the shops on the west side of Fourth Avenue to sell a bag of books. He was chased out before he could even show them. Perhaps the dealer knew or suspected they were stolen. . . . Portraying some of these dealers accurately could require the skills of a Rembrandt," Somers wrote. Along with his critical observations, Wayne Somers acknowledged personal kinship with the "most benighted bookseller, provided he is not actually a crook." (And who's to say for certain who is and who isn't one of those?)

In a letter paying tribute to libraries, Somers stated, "We book dealers do indeed, as Mondlin/Meador point out, perform a socially useful function in chasing down books and sifting the wheat from the chaff, but we harm our own case when we make exaggerated claims, and especially when we understate the role of libraries" (*Book Source Magazine,* May/June 2003). We'd never do that! Libraries were among Book Row's most reliable customers, for single rare volumes for academic collections and for grand-scale purchases. One beneficiary of Book Row treasures was the New York Public Library. On his arrival in the city, Leon Trotsky was told, "You absolutely must see the New York Public Library. It's open until late in the evening—think of that!" Book Row stayed open late too, as Trotsky quickly learned.

Howard Frisch. In the 1950s Howard Frisch had a bookshop at 116 Christopher Street in New York City. Later he operated by mail order through a New York post office box and maintained a walk-in antiquarian bookstore in Livingston, New York. Sharon Cherven wrote about the shop in the Daily Freeman (Kingston, New York, October 15, 1989): "One of the best things about the store is Frisch himself, who is a walking encyclopedia of literary knowledge. . . . Part of the fun is to eavesdrop, while browsing, on Frisch's conversations with serious collectors who wander in. . . . It is obvious that Frisch plays an important role in their collecting endeavors."

Frisch was another New Yorker who discovered Book Row as a boy and never quite got over his amazement. He browsed and bought on Book Row, democratically favoring several shops with his quests, first as a reader and eventually as a bookseller. "I never had a bad occurrence with any book dealer. They were always fair. So I never asked a dealer, 'Can you do any better on the price?' When you mark it, you mark it. That is the price!" he remarked. Frisch remembered that the first book he bought on Book Row, for a dollar, he sold years later for about $50.

As a dealer, he learned the inevitability of thefts. After he made a substantial purchase, in self-defense he held back the books that he expected to pay for the investment and put the rest out to take their chances. "I have stolen many books from you," someone bragged to him once at a party. "I reconciled myself," said Frisch. One customer who stood out in memory was a man who found sleepers on the outside stand. "Whenever he entered with a book I knew I made a mistake putting it outside," noted Frisch. The customer was an ex-printer who recognized items valuable for their typography and design. Whatever Frisch may have lost during those transactions, he made back later. He bought some of the ex-printer's books from his widow. Among them was a collection of Bruce Rogers's books and letters.

Everett Cunningham. At the Joyce Book Shops in Martinez, California, Everett Cunningham in the 1990s reminisced about the great book days of Book Row during an earlier time. "I was only in the trade in New York 1941–1943 and never in business on Fourth Avenue. I worked as a cataloguer and buyer for Barnes & Noble. I believe I was in about every New York store during that period." He went to the stores as a bookman, not as a "change jingler." "That's what John Campbell of the Campbell store in Philadelphia called them," Cunningham recalled, "the three-piece-suit lads who wanted to look, but not buy. They kept up the masturbatory activity of jingling the change in their pockets while they looked."

He added, "Herman Cohen, who began at Schulte's Book Store on Fourth Avenue, flatters me when he claims I know the history of the New York booksellers better than anyone." Everett Cunningham contended that like the rest of the booksellers he felt that he did nothing important. Importance is, of course, an impossible thing to measure. The fact that he remembered the Book Row of the 1940s will seem important to many.

Larry Moskowitz. As a book dealer he sought and sold modern first editions, but for himself he wanted books for reading, not rarity. Ralph B. Sipper, his friend and colleague at Joseph the Provider Books, Santa Barbara, California, wrote that while many inscribed books came their way, the only one he knew Moskowitz kept was inscribed to him by Kenneth Millar (pen name Ross Macdonald), who wrote: "To Larry Moskowitz, a man of esprit." Moskowitz as a youth loved reading and looking for books in the Fourth Avenue bookstores. He decided he wouldn't want to spend his life waiting every day in a dingy and dusty place for book seekers to show up. Interviewed for this account, he said, "I never dreamed I would become a bookseller. Yet when I found out what the rare-book business is really like, I got hooked." He began as a book scout finding books for friends in California. His first major coup was Jack Kerouac's *Book of Dreams,* the blue-cover paperback. He realized he enjoyed the hunt. "The most intriguing thing for me about the book business is not what I found yesterday but what I might find tomorrow," he said.

He bought books at the Strand, Biblo and Tannen, Pageant Book Company, and many others on Book Row. "By the time I was on the street with any regularity, most of the stores were gone or going," he observed. In 1989 Moskowitz feared that the days of the open secondhand bookshop were numbered due to rising rents and the growing difficulty of making a living. Another reason, he thought, was the physical labor demanded. "People now want to sit in a loft and provide quotes. It is easier than handling massive amounts of books," he said. "The kind of stores that were on Fourth Avenue were a tremendous resource. You could go to those stores and the books were there. They preserved them. Too few do that anymore." About the future of bookselling he remarked, "All I know is that tomorrow will be different from today. How it will be different I'm not sure. . . . Nothing is a solution."

Charles F. Heartman. Alexander Deutschberger at 117 Fourth Avenue made a young German immigrant working as a janitor on Second Avenue an offer he could have refused but didn't. Deutschberger in 1911 told Charles Heartman he would teach him the book business if he worked part-time for nothing. Heartman agreed, planning to learn all he could while gaining greater facility with English. So began one of Book Row's shortest and most productive apprenticeships. As a "student book dealer" he negotiated a purchase for pennies of German first editions. And by 1912, he was ready to start his own business, on Twenty-second Street, thus launching one of the most successful bookselling careers, coast-to-coast, in the books and for the books, with stores from Vermont to Texas. Numerous bookstore clerkships led from Fourth Avenue to success beyond Book Row. Charles Heartman, born in Braunschweig, Germany, in 1883, went further than most Book Row alumni as a specialist in Americana. He wrote, "To me it seems that only the Americana collector has reached the heights of supreme contentment." Heartman attained a reasonable altitude of contentment *selling* Americana, applying the bookselling insights that had their incubation period on Fourth Avenue.

Walter L. Caron. He succeeded Isaac Mendoza and the Mendoza sons as the owner of the renowned Isaac Mendoza Book Company on Ann Street. When he finally closed the store in February 1990, he continued for a time to use the famous name. The 1994–95 *International Directory of Antiquarian Booksellers* listed the Isaac Mendoza Book Company under Walter L. Caron, "by appointment only," at 77 West Eighty-fifth Street, not far from Columbia University, with science fiction, detective fiction, and modern firsts as specialties. Before he was associated with the store as a book dealer, Caron shopped there often as a collector. He remembered finding an underpriced set of books from the Roebling family. (John Roebling planned and began construction, and his son Washington Roebling completed construction, of the Brooklyn Bridge.) Earlier Walter Caron had roamed, browsed, and searched for sleepers among the bookshops of Fourth Avenue and beyond as a book-loving reader and collector. He cultivated and admired the amiable proprietors he met on Book Row and elsewhere. He pleased himself without hurting them when he sometimes found a valuable item priced well below its worth.

"Thoms & Eron on Chambers Street was a wonderful store. I always liked the Strand. Schulte's Book Store was another favorite. Biblo and Tannen saved things for me," he recalled for this account. Among his favorite book places was the Carol Cox Book Company after it moved from Fifty-ninth Street to a large loft near Twenty-sixth Street and Third Avenue. "I got along well with Carol Cox and his wife. He had probably the best stock in New York City because of the space. The loft was so vast if you put books down and walked ten feet you couldn't remember where you put them. I found wonderful books there. And there was where I made the worst mistake of my life," he recalled.

In the early 1950s Caron had saved for a trip to Europe when Carol Cox showed him a recently acquired collection of signed, limited, mint first editions. Cox offered them to Caron for $500. "I had the money, but with the trip and all, I thought, I can't spend five hundred dollars. I had never seen them before, and I never saw such books again," he admitted. Luckily, mistakes were few and successes many for reader–collector–book hunter Walter Caron. Decades later, he still could derive enjoyment from the thought of exceptional finds he made among low-priced discards outside the Argosy and other shops. Memories lingered too of his frequent discoveries along Book Row of hard-to-find volumes such as a book of short stories published only in England, *Turbulent Tales* by Rafael Sabatini. Thinking about the great years of Book Row and his triumphs as well as friendships there, Walter Caron noted that those experiences strengthened his perpetual love for books. He emphasized his resolve never to stop looking for and buying more books, in the tradition that began for him on Book Row.

Janice Longone. Jan Longone, founder with her husband, Dan Longone, of the internationally esteemed Wine and Food Library at Ann Arbor,

Michigan, was inspired to enter the bookselling business and specialize in cookbook and culinary materials through the example, friendship, and encouragement of Eleanor Lowenstein at her Corner Book Shop on Fourth Avenue. Jan Longone visited the Corner Book Shop regularly through the years to observe, learn, admire books, and make purchases. But Jan and Dan Longone were enthusiastic Book Row regulars long before she developed a yen to write on culinary topics and to sell cookbooks. In the 1950s, the Longones were graduate students at Cornell University in Ithaca, New York, Jan studying history, Dan working for a Ph.D. in organic chemistry. Their custom at holidays and breaks was radically different from that of most other students. They didn't head for ski resorts, Florida beaches, or other traditional student play places. "We got on a bus and headed for Manhattan," said Jan Longone. "We'd arrive about five A.M., walk around in the sleeping city, have breakfast at a place we liked, and then head for Book Row. We spent most of our breaks among the books on Fourth Avenue." Where, she wondered, can similar Jans and Dans go now, without a Book Row waiting? "Many of the proprietors were elderly, and I expected them to be gruff. But when they saw you loved books, they became friendly and helpful," she stated. Toward the end of the 1950s, after Cornell, with Dan Longone on the faculty at the University of Michigan, they continued making annual visits to check out the bookshops.

The Longones became familiar to the various dealers. One surprised Jan Longone after she walked in without advance notice following a year's absence. "I've saved something you may want," he said. She did! "The items he kept for me to consider were magnificent prints from Victor Rendu's *Ampélographie française,* published in 1857, with engravings by Eugene Grabon," said Jan Longone. The very rare and valuable book featuring the botanical display of grapes had been broken up for the plates. The Longones used some of the plates as exquisite decorations for their home and sold others. The fact that a bookman remembered her and held over a long period an item that he thought might interest her struck Jan Longone as customer service above and beyond the norm. To her it was a memorable demonstration at a personal level of New York bookselling at its finest.

Jay Platt. The number and quality of secondhand bookstores in Ann Arbor, Michigan, have fathered or mothered speculative guesses that the city is home to a reincarnation of Book Row. Those of us familiar with Fourth Avenue as well as the hometown of Walter Goldwater's and Arthur Miller's alma mater see Ann Arbor as a worthy successor but not as a resurrection of Book Row. Ann Arbor simply hasn't yet replicated Peter Stammer, Sam Dauber, the two Jacks, George and Jenny. Luckily it has had Jay Platt, who opened Ann Arbor's West Side Book Shop in 1975 after switching from a career in naval architecture and ship design. He has been called the dean of Ann Arbor booksellers because of his ABAA membership, specialties in Arctic and Antarctic exploration, and generous support for start-up booksellers.

Jay Platt told Roy Meador that in the 1970s he was on Fourth Avenue and entered one of the bookstores. His description of the bookman on duty fit Jack Biblo like a glove, so it was probably Biblo and Tannen. Platt asked for an obscure volume. "Sure," said the proprietor. He went to a shelf and casually pulled out the book requested. Jay recalled the moment as a personal epiphany: "I was impressed. Right then was when I decided I wanted to be a bookman and work in the antiquarian book business." The newborn bookseller also wanted to be someone who could step to a shelf and remove the precise book a customer wanted. In 2003, Jay Platt, another Book Row alumnus, was still doing just that.

THE READERS AND COLLECTORS

Roy Meador spent his years through high school in a small Southwestern town that had no bookstores. None. Neither new nor secondhand, can you believe it? There were a small public library, much smaller school libraries, and a magazine store where Pocket Books, Bantams, and other paperbacks began appearing in the 1940s. So there were books available to *read*—praise be—at that Oklahoma outpost. But finding hardcovers—real books—to have, to hold, and to own wasn't possible locally for the book-famished. Hitchhiking to Oklahoma City or Amarillo, where he might locate a struggling book outlet, wasn't a realistic answer. He learned, of course, about books by mail and the selective services of the Book-of-the-Month and other book clubs where paper route earnings could be invested. He signed on with several clubs and slowly formed a personal library of book club choices. Some of those books were still in use over half a century later, for example, William Rose Benét's *The Reader's Encyclopedia* (1948). But truly grasping the possibilities inherent in a genuine bookstore was not to be accomplished there at the heart of the wasteland. What else do we call a place without bookstores? In the 1950s, that small-town Roy arrived in New York City and promptly discovered Book Row, an event comparable to an amazed explorer making landfall on an uncharted isthmus between two unknown continents. At Book Row, he felt as did many others that he had left home to arrive home. If Book Row arguably wasn't exactly the Promised Land, it held the promised books silent on the shelves, waiting to be found. Here are more recollections from the Fourth Avenue passing parade.

Edwin Franko Goldman. Fourth Avenue had booksellers on the spot for every book genre from aviation to the occult to whatever. Also music. Thomas J. Gerald, formerly an orchestra leader for vaudeville and silent film palaces, in 1931 opened a bookstore on Fourth Avenue, Friendly Books and Music. He specialized in sheet music and books on musical subjects. The shop is listed at 83 Fourth Avenue in the 1936–37 *Clegg's International Directory of the World's Book Trade.* As a musician, Gerald attracted musician customers. One was band conductor and march composer Edwin Franko Goldman.

Goldman, originally from Kentucky, was an eminent musical figure in New York City from the 1890s until his death in 1956. He performed in the Metropolitan Opera orchestra, taught music at Columbia, founded the Goldman band, won fame for his summer band concerts in city parks, and bought books on Book Row. Goldman found items for his personal collection as well as materials for his numerous band instruction books at Friendly Books and Music. Thomas Gerald's store was the best place to go to find copies of books by Goldman, including *The Band Guide and Aid to Leaders* (1916) and *Band Betterment* (1934).

Aaron J. Cooke. Michigan businessman William L. Clements, through his love of books and connections with New York and London book dealers, established one of the world's greatest research libraries and repositories of rare books, the William L. Clements Library of Americana, located at the University of Michigan. Clements was inspired and tutored by the book collecting enthusiasm and knowledge of Aaron J. Cooke, a dry goods store owner in Bay City, Michigan. A Civil War veteran, Cooke from his youth was a fervent bibliophile. Above a bookcase, he displayed Erasmus's defiant admission "If I have any money, I buy books; if there is any left, I buy food and clothes for the family." In New York on buying trips for his Michigan business, Cooke spent all the time he could at auctions and in rare bookshops, carefully assembling a history collection focused on the American colonies and earlier periods. At the New York bookstores, he regularly bought more books than he wanted himself. These he took back to the Midwest and handed them on to friends at cost.

He made himself a one-man missionary for the appreciation and distribution of better books than were the usual fare then in a small Michigan town. One of his recruits for the higher religion of books was William L. Clements. At the store owner's home, he and Clements often admired and discussed Cooke's acquisitions. Cooke saw promise in his protégé and in 1903 turned the Americana collection over to Clements to continue. Cooke delivered his books to Clements with a poignant poem of his own that began, "Books I have loved so well," and ended that the books were going into the keeping of "hands that love books, fear not, no less than mine." The Aaron J. Cooke books, largely acquired from the New York bookshops, became the foundation of the library William L. Clements created.

Sonja Wohl Mirsky. Taught by an older brother from a picture book, the future Rockefeller Institute librarian began reading before she was three. Her mother believed the first thing she read was a Consolidated Edison brochure. "My parents were not free with money for ice cream and candy, but they gave us money for books," wrote Sonja Mirsky. "My older brother Rudy paid attention to my reading. When I was thirteen, he saw me reading a romance magazine. He gave me a Faulkner novel and said, 'See how good writers deal with sex.' I couldn't go to the movies until I was sixteen, but when it came to books and intellectual matters, they gave me a free hand."

She began going to Fourth Avenue in 1939 and learned gratefully that Ben Bass would let her browse as long as she pleased at the Strand. In the 1940s she became interested in mathematics and turned to Book Row for classics in the field. "When I was collecting books on ancient mathematics, Sam Weiser would hold books for me," she recalled. She also remembered Murray Dauber at Dauber & Pine as a knowledgeable and fair book dealer. Bertrand Russell's *Principia Mathematica* (1910) in three volumes she acquired at the Strand in 1948 with a gift from her uncle when she graduated from the City College of New York. She thought that Ben Bass marked the books down from $35 to $25 for her benefit. "I knew Ben Bass and cared for him very much. He was a person who, if you took the time to know him, you had a very deep friend," she wrote. The support, encouragement, and friendship Sonja Mirsky received were not forgotten. "In 1949 I began working at the Rockefeller Institute, and I bought the medical, science, and technology books we needed for the institute library whenever possible at the Strand. Ben Bass put books aside for that purpose," she noted. Sonja Mirsky began with books early in her life and continued to work with them through the decades. "I have always been surrounded by books," she wrote. She relied on Book Row from the 1930s on through the century, thanks to the remarkable ability of the Strand to stay alive and continue supplying the books she needed.

Philip Sperling. This New York and Pennsylvania business executive was noted during his business years and in retirement as a vigorous book collector active in the Grolier Club and as a research scholar and author with particular focus on the life and activities of English publisher-bookseller William Pickering (1796–1854) and his American connections. Sperling through his research, which depended in part on the acquisition of relevant materials from Book Row stores, sought to make Pickering better known and appreciated. Pickering adopted the Aldine Press trademark and produced books distinguished for their typography and for their dyed cloth instead of paper bindings. Pickering publication series included the Diamond Classics, Christian Classics, and Oxford Classics. Philip Sperling in his eighties continued to collect books, to perform tasks for the Typophiles and the American Printing History Association, and to carry out his research concerning William Pickering. As a collector and researcher, the Book Row shops were vital resources for him over many years. "Thinking about the book trade on Fourth Avenue brings back many memories, *à la recherche du temps perdu*," he wrote. "Well do I remember . . . the Bible House, Schulte's, Stammer's, and others." He reminisced about sitting on wooden benches at City Book Auction and making wonderful buys for fifty cents or less. He gave perspective, however, to the low prices by noting that the cost of lunch in those days was only about a quarter. "The Fourth Avenue bookstores from my early teens held a dear place in my life from Astor Place up to Fourteenth Street, both on the east and west sides of the avenue," stated Philip Sperling.

Joseph J. Cohen. This journalist's "forays into the book world on Fourth Avenue" began in the 1930s. His experiences in the bookshops ranged from pleasant to winning a charter membership in the large "Given a Hard Time by Peter Stammer" club. At Stammer's Bookstore he found the proprietor reading, snuggled close to a potbellied stove. Cohen may have entered just as the book engrossing Stammer reached a crucial point. The potential customer was honored with the "Stammer stare" and aggressively interrogated about his reason for the uninvited, unscheduled, and unwanted intrusion. Cohen timidly asked if there was a philosophy section. After another sharp look, the bookman in a tone beyond argument declared there was not a thing in the store that could possibly be of any interest whatever, philosophy or otherwise, to this particular invader.

Cohen remembered receiving considerably more hospitable Book Row receptions at Schulte's Book Store, Biblo and Tannen, and the Strand, when it was on Fourth Avenue. He was a reporter for the *New York Journal-American* in those days, and his beat assignment for several years was the area around Foley Square (named for Thomas F. Foley, a saloon keeper and politician), downtown near City Hall, the municipal and other government buildings, and the courthouses. "Because of my work, two secondhand bookstores I visited often were Thoms & Eron on Chambers Street and Mendoza's on Ann Street," he wrote. Cohen noted that after the closing of Thoms & Eron and with growing neglect about replenishing stock at Mendoza's, he began confining his "book-buying, book-browsing, and book-selling to the Strand which by then had opened on Broadway." "From those days to this, I have gone to the Strand," observed Cohen as he reminisced about his long association with Book Row.

Lawrence Rao. This Brooklyn-born writer became an authority on vintage radio programs as a collector of tapes and books from the 1930s–1950s golden age of the broadcast medium that perhaps more than any other challenged and rewarded the imagination. Rao mentioned that while employed in Manhattan, he derived immense pleasure from his regular "hauntings of Book

Row." He called reminiscing about the area "a joy and heartbreak" and declared, "There was no place like and no place better than Fourth Avenue to see, touch, and hold books of every sort from banged-up to beautiful." For this account he wrote, "There was so much to love about those bookshops. I especially liked being able to enter, browse, look, read, and *never* have anyone approach and ask 'may I help you?' I can't think of it as progress that the stores were replaced by high-rise apartments, antique shops, and trendy coffee places. The need for good secondhand bookshops everywhere seems to me greater than ever." In the twenty-first century, commenting that the past seldom makes a successful comeback, he observed that nothing in book-selling had developed to replace Book Row and to repeat its amenities.

Herbert T. Pratt. Acquiring old chemistry books when he was fifteen launched Herbert Pratt on a lifetime of book collecting. He acknowledged that eventually bargain-hunting became his way of life. He became a frequent visitor to Book Row, as business trips took him to New York City during the 1950s and 1960s when he worked for the DuPont Company. Except the Strand, he wrote in the *Delaware Bibliophiles Endpapers* (September 1999), "all of these stores are long gone, victims of high rents and redevelopment." Herbert Pratt returned often enough to Fourth Avenue to become well known "by sight and interest" at the various bookstores. At the book-crowded Pageant, when he walked in, someone invariably called out, "Chemistry!" "The Pageant contained thousands of books from the nineteenth century and before," Pratt recollected. He was impressed that somehow the proprietors remembered the specific location of the scientific books that could enhance his collection.

"One of my favorite stores was Dauber & Pine," he wrote. "Books were everywhere—packed on the floor and tables . . . even packed on the steps of the narrow rolling ladders that moved along the wall on a track to give access to the highest shelves." Pratt received special attention from Murray Dauber in the Dauber & Pine basement, which struck the collector as "a dimly lit cavern that burrowed under several surrounding buildings." Murray Dauber, noted Pratt, "had a spot reserved in one of the old wall cabinets where he hid away things that might interest me and would even provide a flashlight for getting around in one room in the back which had no lights at all." He was apprehensive that the back room could be a home for large, possibly literary rodents, but saw none. Concerning the vanished stores of Book Row, Herbert Pratt declared, "Neither they nor their likes will be seen again. E-mail shopping is upon us."

Stanley Nosek. Retired engineer and book collector Stan Nosek knew Book Row well as a high school student in the 1930s and again as an engineering student after World War II. He attended Stuyvesant High School, on East Fifteenth Street. The school was a short stroll from Union Square and Book Row. "I loved to walk over there and browse among the book stalls. But that was about all I could do, for the simple reason that I had no spare money," wrote Nosek. Still he enjoyed being in the presence of and examining the books even if he had to save his nickels for the subway. After wartime service in the army air force, Nosek attended the Polytechnic Institute of Brooklyn to study engineering. During that period, his Book Row sojourns were increasingly frequent, although he was still more the dedicated browser than buyer. "The book collecting bug hadn't yet bitten me. That came later. I loved books and reading but not accumulating them. I built a small bookcase, and when it was full, that was it," he remarked. Later, as with many collectors, space concerns evaporated as the urge to possess books won out. "I got the craze and started amassing books," he acknowledged. Perhaps the fertile seeds of that happy craze were initially planted in a teenage student among the bookstalls of Fourth Avenue during the 1930s.

Frederick S. Lightfoot. He attended Columbia University and became an industrial engineer. From the 1940s to the 1970s he held corporate, government, and academic positions in his field. Eventually, through the Lightfoot Collection, he was commercially active in purchasing and selling photographic, philatelic, and other paper ephemera. His Book Row connections began in the 1930s and continued until the end of his life, in 1992. Starting as a boy, Fred Lightfoot collected books, phonograph records, stamps and covers, coins, photographs, and ephemera. "Brought up in New York City during the 1930s, I had access to many dealers. Prices then were incredibly low for desirable collectibles. The standard prices for some items literally were about one-thousandth of their value today. So I could buy quite a lot then," Lightfoot wrote in 1989 for this account. He developed the weekly ritual of browsing for a few hours on Fourth Avenue every

Saturday while his younger sister received art lessons in Greenwich Village. When his sister was old enough to travel alone and he had no need to wait for her, Lightfoot spent many Saturday hours "sometimes trudging miles through bitter cold winds to cover stores from Eighth Street to the Uptown bookstores." Because of his age, young Lightfoot believed he was not taken very seriously by some of the booksellers, but this did not diminish his congenital impulse to collect books.

He remembered with gratitude those who were willing to share their knowledge with a teenager, including Jack Brussel, the Mendoza brothers, the Kraus family, and especially Alfred Goldsmith. "Frank discussions with friendly dealers were invaluable to a young person whose home and school environment shielded him from some of life's realities. There is less concern for young collectors now with Book Row no longer there," observed Lightfoot. "A teenager is generally not welcome in the specialized antiquarian places, and the small shops where they might receive some warmth and understanding are few in number. Also television has curtailed reading, and the rising prices of scholarly books reduces sales still more. These are among the reasons why fewer children are inspired to begin collecting." Through the years Fred Lightfoot closely observed the Book Row dealers and found a wide divergence of standards. "There were true gentlemen among dealers in those days, men of high integrity. At the same time, a few were more or less dishonest. Some had no compunction about offering the uninformed outrageously low prices for valuable books. One dealer in the postwar years paid only a dollar a volume for several hundred incunabula from a Brooklyn estate!" Lightfoot stated. The condition of a book depended, he noted, on whether you were buying or selling. "Various dealers overpraised condition when they sold a book, and they underrated it if you tried to sell the same book back to them," he wrote. "I still enjoy going to the Fourth Avenue area although the number of bookshops has greatly decreased, and the antiquarian books I might like to buy have either vanished or are available at prices I can't afford," concluded Fred Lightfoot. He considered it impossible to convey accurately to those who were not there the "quality of life as well as the treasures of old Fourth Avenue."

Coda to Book Row Memories

The book lovers, readers and collectors, went to Fourth Avenue and its cross streets south of Union Square when a multitude of bookshops formed America's and the world's Booksellers' Row. Many of the book seekers viewed the area as a rare and special place. When it was gone they remembered it as their sceptered isle, their other Eden, demi-Paradise, their second, book-rich home away from home, their blessed plot, their earth, their realm, their Book Row. "Where do we go now to find the books?" they wondered. Hearing no convincing or final answers, in memory they keep going back to Book Row. They keep remembering. "I don't live very much in the past," claimed Fred Lightfoot, perhaps trying to convince himself, in a letter sharing his Book Row memories. Maybe we all try not to live in the past but seldom succeed completely. "Almost everything good seems located in the past," wrote Susan Sontag in *In America* (2000). Do you know what she means? We think we do. Of course, the future too will have space and time to hold a lot of books. We'll see to that. And good memories will help.

CHAPTER FIFTEEN

THE STRAND LIVES ON
Benjamin Bass · Fred Bass · Nancy Bass

*It was thus—"Second Handbooks: Good Opening: established
business: owner leaving for Australia: must sell: 400 Pounds or
near offer." . . . The business wasn't worth Four Hundred Pounds.
You can buy a lot of second-hand books for Four Hundred Pounds
but I didn't know that then. It was just as well, perhaps. I would
have missed a lot if I hadn't set up as a bookseller. A lot? Heresy!
Sacrilege! I would have missed EVERYTHING.*
—WILLIAM YOUNG DARLING

✄ LIVING IN LONDON during the first half of 1897, Mark Twain completed
Following the Equator and put a rumor memorably to rest. Newspapers fell
prey to hearsay and got a story all wrong (not a first, or last, for newspapers).
One paper told its London reporter: "If Mark Twain very ill, five hundred
words. If dead, send one thousand." The reporter found the vigorously vertical author, who promptly informed America, with an instant candidate for
quotation books, "The reports of my death are greatly exaggerated." Similarly
let's acknowledge with refined cheers that rumors of Book Row's departure,
big sleep, final death, are also definitely somewhat exaggerated. The truth is
that Book Row is not gone, not completely, because the Strand carries on.
The Strand, praise be, still lives. And how it lives!

If bookworms held an Olympics, their Olympics committee might decide
to use the miles of books at the Strand for their marathon. They should keep
their plans quiet. If Fred Bass, who owns the Strand and runs it with his
daughter Nancy Bass, heard about such intentions for his store's 2.5 million
books, to avoid disturbing miles of browsers he'd have an antipest army on the
job before they could sound the start. After all, browsers often become buyers.

Jim Jerome, in "Book Smarts" (*People*, October 7, 2002), called the Strand
America's largest independent used bookstore and quoted Strand manager
Nancy Bass: "Our awning says '8 Miles of Books.' It's changing soon to '16

miles.' " Jerome highlighted the Strand's celebrity connections by citing famous customers and their hefty purchases as well as the store's book-renting services for major movies, such as *You've Got Mail* and *A Beautiful Mind.* Actor and bibliophile Richard Gere said, "The Strand is the most dangerous bookshop in New York. It's impossible to spend less than two hours there."

Everyone who remembers Book Row as it used to be tends to agree the Strand is a phenomenon just through the mighty feat of staying in business. The Strand adjusted as necessary through changing times and kept growing while its contemporaries from the 1920s, 1930s, 1940s, 1950s, 1960s, and 1970s one by one suffered the slings and arrows of outrageous fortune, or high rents, or aging proprietors, or too little business, and folded. Not the Strand. The Strand survived. It marched into the twenty-first century and displayed vital signs of immortality, such as expansion and renovation.

Reporting on a Strand new-book party for Simon Winchester, author of *The Professor and the Madman,* the *Knickerbocker* (June 26, 2003) alluded to the store's plans to install a personnel elevator linking four floors. The expansion project also included doubling the rare book department's space on the third floor and turning the entire second floor over to the art department. Fancy—a four-floor elevator for people, not freight, in a Book Row bookshop! The program easier to swallow was Winchester's comment that he spent a lot of time at the party signing the Strand's remainder copies of his book as well as new copies.

At the time of writing, in 2003, the Strand clearly was doing much more than simply staying in business and surviving. The Strand was thriving and prospering. At the outset of the twenty-first century (January 1, 2001), the then nearly seventy-four-year-old bookstore occupied its own building at 828 Broadway, on the corner of Twelfth Street. It then had three 10,500-square-foot floors crowded with books, including fifty thousand rare books. In 2003 all Strand numbers were expanding—added floor space of 120,000 square feet, additional rare books, art books with a floor of their own, four floors instead of three, the elevator. The store even joined the Internet and accepted orders online at www.strandbooks.com. The changes meant more of a good thing, but the Strand would stay the Strand.

In an article about the Strand for the September/October 2000 issue of *Book,* Mimi O'Connor wrote, "There is no mistaking the legendary Strand for anything but the quintessential New York bookstore. The Strand is cramped, it is disorganized, it is dusty. . . . With its high ceilings, peeling paint, ancient homemade signs featuring white stenciled letters on red construction paper ('Sell your books here,' 'These books are sorted. Do not touch') and overwhelming stacks and piles of used books, the place has the air of an institution that has been around since the dawn of time."

In addition to the vast retail space, office and administrative areas accommodated nearly two hundred Strand employees carrying out the behind-the-scenes functions of a secondhand book business that was routinely selling several million books and grossing over $20 million annually. This family-owned book monarchy—a German travel writer called it a *Boeken-jungle*—was ruled over, benignly, efficiently, and imaginatively, by Fred Bass and his daughter Nancy Bass, son and granddaughter of the founder, Benjamin Bass. If we considered the Strand as an oceangoing liner loaded with books to the Plimsoll line, Fred was the captain and Nancy Bass was the ubiquitous executive officer (on the job at Broadway and Twelfth, her title was store manager). Neither Fred nor Nancy maintained a fixed personal office space at the Strand—too confining. They needed freedom to roam widely and at will through their immense kingdom of books, which might also be condemned by FOO (Fans of Order) as a world-class farrago and monument of clutter.

The Strand has neither tried for nor won any good housekeeping awards. An air of controlled derangement and casual untidiness has deliberately and purposefully been maintained. When interviewed, Fred Bass through the years routinely paid tribute to the profitability of mild disarray, congenial messiness, and apparent disorder. He told Mimi O'Connor, "I got the store nice and neat and sales went down. That was about twenty-five or thirty years ago." "Every time I make the place too neat, business goes down," Bass was quoted by Nicholas A. Basbanes in *Biblio* (November 1998). For an article about the Strand by Michael Wels Hirschhorn in the *Wall Street Journal* (August 21, 1986), Bass stated, "I keep it a little bit sloppy. When I make it too neat, business goes down."

The message comes through loud and clear: We're dealing with well-considered bookselling ambience, attitude, process, and strategy here, not a bias against brooms or a defense of debris. In fact, appearance, as it often is, has been a blithe and messy deceiver at the Strand. The Strand from its early years was a skillfully organized bookstore offering a highly diverse collection of desirable books both popular and scholarly. Something for everyone was more than a cliché at the Strand; it was a fact of books.

The books in view at the Strand along miles of inviting and intimidating shelves were backed up by row after row of books stacked ceiling high on the tenth floor of the industrial-strength Strand building. They were stored in large boxes collectively weighing many tons and creating formidable, rectangular mountains of books separated by narrow chasmlike corridors. A tour of the Strand's tenth floor was a walk through the valley of the shadow of books. The boxes were carefully labeled for easy store identification as the books were needed for future replenishment of the downstairs retail stock. With over six thousand customers entering the Strand daily to browse and buy, there were never too many books, even though steady buying of books took place on the main floor under Fred Bass's supervision as well as off the premises through the acquisition of small to large private libraries and at auctions.

By the 1990s, the Strand had expanded to the point where superlatives regarding size were bandied about. Was the Strand the biggest secondhand book store ever, and how big was biggest? Considering the number of employees (over 130 in 1990) and the volume of books bought, shelved, and sold, the viewpoint became widespread that the Strand was indeed *numero uno* in size among secondhand bookstores. Strand employee Dick Cuffari was charged with making a realistic estimate in the 1970s after columnist George Will, a Strand customer, inquired about the size. Cuffari conducted a careful count of occupied shelves and display tables from the large basement stretching under Broadway, alias the "Strand Underground," to the third-floor rare-book sanctuary; and he factored in book counts for stored cartons. Cuffari wrote in *ABMR* (February 1990), "The final total showed us having 8.3 miles of display space . . . and we estimate that we have over two million books in the building at any one time. So when Strand claims 'eight miles of books,' be assured it's not hyperbole. I know, because I counted them all."

After Cuffari's calculation in the 1970s, the Strand certainly didn't slow down or stop growing. In the mid-1990s, the Strand gave itself more book-breathing room by adding the Strand Fulton Street Annex, with a fifteen-thousand-square-foot space, which in turn was rapidly packed with books. The nearness of the annex to the area of New York's first Booksellers' Row on Nassau Street fueled speculation that the Strand not only preserved the Book Row tradition but sponsored its rebirth downtown. So it still wasn't hyperbole in 2003 to describe the Strand as the world's largest secondhand bookstore, probably in history, with some sixteen miles of space for 2.5 million books in a state of constant turnover, and with the sky the limit.

What Fred Bass told Joseph Deitch for the *Wilson Library Bulletin* (June 1986), when he was asked what the Strand offered libraries, still applied years later, only more so. Bass replied, "Books. I've got them. More than any other book dealer and wholesaler. Two million under one roof. And of a highly varied nature. We can ship, or libraries can come in and pick for themselves. We have got the books." In the new century and new millennium, the Strand still had the books, and not only for libraries—it had books for all. The status was attained where "The constant reader's best friend" would make a more inclusive slogan than the claim that appeared on old Strand catalogues, "Your library's best friend."

Books and the Basses

The bookseller's equivalent of Horatio Alger's "rags to riches" or the politician's "log cabin to the White House" might well be "Eighth Street bookstall to the Strand." Born in Lithuania in 1901, Benjamin Bass in the United States worked in construction, first as a messenger and then as a salesman, before entering the used-book business in 1927, with a bookstall called the Pelican Book Shop on Eighth Street. In 1929 Ben Bass relocated to 81 Fourth Avenue, between Tenth and Eleventh Streets. The new site wasn't far from the geographic center of the Fourth Avenue book trade, where the bigger and better known bookstores were already defining Book Row as a New York institution. No one, of course, guessed in 1929, unless Ben Bass had a secret hunch, that the unpretentious newcomer would outlive them all.

Bass did realize that a big-billed, web-footed bird with a gular pouch for holding fish didn't really qualify as a top-notch Book Row symbol. On Fourth Avenue Ben Bass's shop retired the pelican and was reincarnated as the Strand Book Store. Some say it was named after the classy thoroughfare in London between Charing Cross Road and Fleet Street, an area known for theaters, law courts, and many addresses, with literary associations, such as the Turk's Head Coffee-House of Dr. Johnson's era. Some, though, hearing the word "Strand," don't think of a city street or a bookstore at all;

they think of Sherlock Holmes. Loyal followers of Sherlock Holmes may like to think the Bass bookshop honors the toweringly valuable issues of *Strand Magazine,* July 1891–December 1893, in which the stories that won global fame for the world's first consulting detective initially appeared.

As is often the case with a small business, the first years were difficult ones, and Ben Bass struggled to get by. He held on through the Depression and patiently gained a reputation as a reliable source of quality books in all the general categories. The store developed particular strengths in the social sciences and the humanities. Walter Goldwater in the 1930s knew Bass—whom he called Benny—as a good friend who was often short of funds but never defeated. Goldwater remembered the occasion when Ben Bass was charged by the city prosecutor with buying stolen law books. Goldwater appeared for his friend as a character witness and convinced the judge there was no plausible way honest Ben Bass could possibly know whether or not the books were stolen property. Bass was released, and on the subway heading uptown to Book Row, he said, as Goldwater remembered it, "You were just wonderful. . . . I was almost convinced myself."

In 1942 Ben Bass made the Strand Book Store a charter member of the Fourth Avenue Booksellers' Association. A little less than a decade later, during 1951, Ben Bass served for a time as the president of the association. In the 1940s, his teenage son Fred began his career at the Strand. He worked there after school. Eventually that part-time job sweeping floors, packing and shipping books, and closely watching everything going on to learn all the details of buying and selling books and running a rapidly growing bookstore evolved into a working partnership between Ben and Fred Bass.

Fred Bass attended Brooklyn College and majored in English; he later noted that he probably should have majored in business. Considering the steadily onward and upward path of the Strand under his astute direction, it strikes observers that perhaps Fred Bass should teach business administration, not study it. "I grew up in the store," Fred Bass told writer Joseph Deitch. After growing up, he stayed on to make the Strand his lifetime workplace. His apprenticeship at the store as a boy and his growing experience with books when he was there full-time allowed Fred Bass to develop into a worthy successor to Ben Bass as a knowledgeable buyer of quality books that the Strand could sell at a profit. Deitch quoted Max Harris, who wrote in the Australian magazine *Weekend,* "There are only two legendary book explorers left. One is Fred Bass, the other is in London." Fred Bass credited his ability in this crucial area to his many years spent "seeking and searching for good books—new, used, rare, or collectible."

In 1951 Marvin Mondlin began working for Ben Bass while Fred Bass was on army duty in Germany. He carried out a full range of bookstore duties as a general Man Friday. He also focused on increasing the knowledge and honing the skills that later made him a Strand vice president in charge of the rare book department and a professional appraiser and purchaser of antiquarian books. After leaving the Strand for other bookstore and publishing activities, he rejoined the staff in 1959 for what evolved into a permanent position except for a sabbatical in Europe during the 1970s. In 1986 Fred Bass remarked about his colleague that he was a principal buyer for the Strand "with great sensitivity for books and outstanding knowledge of obscurer material and its importance. And instinct for what is good."

The decade of the 1950s became a time of major upheaval for Book Row and a time for critical decisions by Ben and Fred Bass. A short distance south of the Strand, the Bible House on Fourth Avenue, which over the years had been so friendly to bookshops, was scheduled for demolition, which compelled four book businesses—Astor Place Magazine & Bookshop, Colonial Book Service, Eureka Bookshop, and Leon Kramer—to find accommodations elsewhere.

Up the street from the Bible House, the Strand and four other bookstores—Arcadia Bookshop, Friendly Book & Music Shop, Louis Schucman, Wex's Book Shop—confronted the same fate when the buildings on the east side of Fourth Avenue between Tenth and Eleventh Streets were sold. Their lease terminated, and faced with eviction, the Basses could play it safe and look for another low-rent site in a neighborhood where such sites were swiftly disappearing, or they could accept fate's dare and make a bold move upward.

Looking back, Fred Bass observed, perhaps with relief, that boldness won out. The Strand departed the aging building it had occupied for most of the twenty-seven years since 1929 and where the rent was $110 per month. It moved north to Twelfth Street and west to Broadway. The building at 828 Broadway instantly raised their monthly rent to $400, and the costs of carrying on business commensurately increased. Furthermore they weren't on familiar, reliable Fourth Avenue. Would their old customers find them?

Would new customers show up? Fred Bass admitted they had apprehensions about taking on the dual challenges of a different location containing more space to fill with respectable stock and what seemed at the time a formidable financial burden. The move was viewed by some as a dangerous act of Bass hubris and folly, doomed to flounder. How off the mark such nervous Nelly false prophets turned out to be. At 828 Broadway, the Basses had ample room to grow, innovate, experiment, and steadily build a secondhand book dynasty.

On Fourth Avenue the Strand maintained a steadily changing stock of about seventy thousand volumes, mainly in the most popular areas of the humanities, including literature, history, Americana, and fiction. At 828 Broadway, in a few years the stock doubled and kept increasing to utilize the available space. The Strand by the mid-1960s offered customers a five-hundred-thousand-book reservoir from which to choose—and nearly five times that number in the 1990s. As the volume of books increased, so did the store's areas of concentration. The Strand on Broadway gradually added major holdings in the physical and biological sciences, social sciences, the visual and performing arts. A rare book department, headed by L. Craig Anderson, a skilled antiquarian bookman and an avid collector of Mark Twain, Ezra Pound, modern art, and photography books, established the Strand as a major player in antiquarian books, limited and first editions, fine bindings, and other valuable works. This and other daring steps went well beyond the traditional practices of Book Row. The Basses seemed to realize their time had come to choose between the frustration of slow failure and the will to innovate and diversify.

Success wasn't immediate or even fast in coming, but steady and solid progress was made. In 1969, when Manuel Tarshish reported on Book Row history and status in his *Publishers Weekly* series, he wrote, "Down the street at 828 stands the store that most used-book dealers believe will be the only one left on Booksellers' Row in the years to come: Strand." The dealers, as cited by Tarshish, in 1969 were certainly not false prophets. The vindicating experience of the Strand in retrospect might be taken as a variation on Robert Frost's poem "The Road Not Taken," from *Mountain Interval* (1916). Two roads diverged for the Strand on Book Row; the Basses took the route less traveled by, which made all the difference. And what a difference.

During the 1970s the momentum of the Basses' new policies and methods propelled the Strand forward at an accelerating pace. Ben Bass, the founder, in his seventies continued to maintain his daily position overseeing operations and pricing books on the main floor at the big table near a side door to Twelfth Street. Ben Bass bought books over the counter from scouts and others with books to sell, and he swiftly entered the store's price in books brought in from outside purchases of libraries and at regularly attended book sales.

When he made over-the-counter purchases, Ben Bass reached quick decisions and typically entered prices in pencil near the gutter margins of the front endpapers. He was careful in what he bought, restricting purchases to items that he recognized as readily marketable. His buying policy, he informed Marvin Mondlin, whom he helped train as a buyer, was to pay no more than one-third of the Strand's selling price. The one-third rationale was based on a formula of replacement cost, one-third; handling and store costs, one-third; profit, one-third.

Some books in Ben Bass's rapid evaluation and pricing process inevitably received substantially lower Strand prices than their true market values might support. When recent acquisitions considered "choice" reached the new arrivals tables around Thursday afternoons, other dealers, collectors, specialists, and book scouts recognized opportunity knocking—sometimes they literally knocked one another in the fierce competition for the Strand's latest desirables. A regular crowd showed up for these unveiling events to cruise the tables for unusual books, long-sought titles, and possible sleepers, which could be construed as considerate gifts from Mr. Bass. Thus the bargain image of the Strand was allowed to flourish and ultimately benefited the store by attracting more and more customers.

After Ben Bass died, on July 28, 1978, his son was on the job and fully prepared to take over at the center table and throughout the business. As Fred Bass had previously joined his father at the Strand, Fred's daughter Nancy Bass entered the firm in the late 1980s to assist in the management and running of the business. She was well prepared for the task, with an MBA in finance and marketing from the University of Wisconsin, plus frontline experience at the Strand, where she, like her father, began learning the ropes by working at the store part-time as a teenager.

The long-range, twenty-first-century phase of the Strand might be said to have started in earnest at that point in the 1990s when Fred Bass purchased the building at 828 Broadway and achieved greater stability for the future. If the American dream traditionally has been to own your own home, the practical dream for a secondhand bookshop must be to have a place not subject to the greed of landlords or the vagaries of rising rents. The Strand after close to seven decades had a permanent home of its own.

STRAND STRATEGIES AND SOURCES

The axiom that success feeds success worked out for the Strand without a hitch in obtaining a steady supply of excellent books through the purchase of private libraries. The store's name and reputation brought the owners or sellers of many such libraries initially to the Strand. A practice that became almost a tradition developed through the years in New York and elsewhere of attorneys and banking officials charged with settling estates to contact the Strand if the properties included books. Strand representatives cooperated with estate professionals by appraising the books involved and often buying them for the Strand. Acquisitions obtained through these contacts replenished standard stock and sometimes sent antiquarian-quality volumes to the rare book department.

Persistent hustle was also part of the Strand's winning formula during the buildup years. The Basses and Marvin Mondlin made frequent buying trips outside the store as opportunities for worthwhile quantity book purchases appeared. Fred Bass and Marvin Mondlin also traveled extensively in the firm's station wagon to attend Friends of the Library sales and other large-scale book sales in outlying communities near and far. At these events, they rushed up and down aisles, filling cartons with salable volumes. Each such sale typically produced hundreds of books for the Strand. Some books were acquired at auctions, but most books came from private library purchases and from walk-in sales at the Strand. Marvin Mondlin remembered going out on frequent calls to examine thousands of books each week and to purchase heavily as the Strand's demand for books expanded with steadily increasing sales. The selling pace was stimulated with regular weekly advertisements in the *New York Times* to keep readers informed that fine books at bargain prices waited for them at the Strand. Obedient readers and collectors in ever-growing numbers showed up to browse and buy.

Book accumulators squeezed for space in city apartments were persistently reminded as well that the Strand was the place to go to sell books that had some claim to quality. The July 1988 edition of *7 Days* called the Strand "the Macy's of the old book world" and noted, "The Strand is also the best place in town to sell your unwanted books for cash on the barrelhead."

Although ostensibly a secondhand bookstore, the Strand became well known for the availability of half-price review books passed on in mint condition by reviewers and of remainders that had never been sold to individuals. Walter Caron remembered Carol Cox as the original "king of the review books." "After Carol Cox died, the Basses stepped in and began purchasing review books. From then on in that area, the Strand took off," recalled Caron.

Consumer's World (October 24, 1992), reporting on the Strand, stated, "Fred Bass, the owner, says his stock, although categorized as 'used,' contains mostly remainders, review copies and closeouts direct from publishers or retailers. The turnover in the book business is so fast these days that the Strand offers many books that are still sitting at the front of the shelf in the retail stores." The Strand's buying and pricing policy on a review copy of a desirable recent book was to pay the seller one-fourth of the dust jacket price and to sell it at one half the dust jacket price. Such bargains persuaded many readers—and even librarians—to beat a steady path to the Strand to learn what new titles had become available at half price. The temptation to enjoy a hefty discount on new books still in the bookselling mainstream came on strong. Such savings couldn't be resisted by eager readers with frugality in their genes and with the Strand only a subway stop, taxi ride, or city stroll away.

And if one lived in Cincinnati or Des Moines or Seattle, there was always the option of ordering by mail or telephone from one of the frequent no-frills but prices-that-thrill Strand catalogues. Orders by mail or telephone kept climbing as a percentage of the total sales volume until the figure rivaled the massive sales represented by the walk-in traffic on the first floor. The Strand walk-in business for years was considered a major competitor for the title of the world's largest. With the addition of the Internet to traditional book-buying methods, the Strand has gone ahead to the future while going back to the past with preservation of the old reliables: walk-in, catalogues, telephone, mail.

The readiness of the Strand to buy review copies brought the store a steady flow of books from the book-beleaguered tribe of reviewers residing in New York City and the surrounding area. With thousands of new books published each year, reviewers were deluged with volumes they had neither room nor inclination to keep permanently. So began a long-established custom among reviewers—to the Strand with review copies whenever the stacks started wobbling, produced floor sag, devoured too much room, consumed excessive oxygen, or became threatening. The Strand promised cash for the books, but even more important, space. The statue in New York Harbor obviously in recent decades misstated the prevailing reality about the United States taking in "the huddled masses"; but the Strand generally lived up to its offer to take in review copies with a reasonable likelihood of finding eventual purchasers.

In this connection, a typical Strand occurrence was reported by William Norwich in *Talk* (September 2000): "The last time I saw Liz Smith she was unloading about a thousand books outside the Strand bookstore. . . . The syndicated columnist was clearing her office of review copies, most of which she had read—or tried to read." The columnist's explanation to Norwich was: "Honey, we're just trying to make a little room. . . . Clutter is making me crazy."

In addition to the purchase of review copies, Fred Bass began purchasing large numbers of remainders to help fill the Strand shelves and to earn the store a reputation for having "new" as well as secondhand books available in quantity. Against the tendency to consider remainders insignificant books that failed to sell, Fred Bass countered that remainders just as often represented the production excess of a well-received, even popular book. He told Joseph Deitch, "No, they are not all inferior by a long shot. A publisher may have sold 300,000 copies of a work of nonfiction. It is a good book. But he has printed 320,000 copies. . . . The remainders, of course, are as good as the 300,000 he has sold. What does he do? We buy them for a different market at a lower price. We buy what the publisher has overprinted, not undersold."

The Strand's widespread network of book sources that kept fresh supplies steadily flooding into the Twelfth Street and Fulton Street buildings inevitably produced thousands of books that didn't sell. If every person somewhere has his mate, it just isn't true that for every book there is somewhere a buyer. At least not till the price goes way down. With these books, Fred Bass, in most ways the epitome of a twenty-first-century innovative bookselling entrepreneur, became a Book Row traditionalist. He refused to dump such books. Following the age-old Book Row practice of offering bargains on the sidewalk, Fred Bass filled outdoor stands with thousands of rapidly rotating books at nominal prices. "I don't make any money on them; I just don't want to throw them out," he told *Book*'s Mimi O'Connor.

In Ben Bass's day, five- and ten-cent books on street stands summoned passersby to halt and take a look. Who could afford not to find out what he might otherwise be missing? So check this stand, and the next, and maybe another after that, just in case. From an outdoor table at the Strand in the 1950s, Roy Meador acquired for ten cents the Penguin paperback edition of Apsley Cherry-Garrard's *The Worst Journey in the World,* which George Bernard Shaw helped the author write, and which richly warmed a New York reading winter for that cautious investor of a dime in a previously unknown book. The ten-cent Cherry-Garrard Penguin, incidentally, transformed that particular grateful reader into a dedicated, long-hunting, temperate-zone collector of books about Antarctica.

By 2001, considering new book costs, outdoor prices at the Strand had gone up, but not out of sight. Five paperbacks for $2 or a hardcover for $1 could still be called a good deal. Like a moat of books around the Strand on Broadway and along Twelfth Street, the stuffed shelves continued to reward book seekers with the pleasant dividends of serendipity or the book lover's art of experiencing delight from finding what you didn't know you were looking for. The Fred Bass argument in defense of remainders could be restated for outdoor discards. Many were outstanding, if surplus, books pursuing special readers in a different market.

Then too, there was possibly another sly Book Row angle to those generous outdoor bookstands. Browsers who found something irresistible had to venture inside to pay even if the asking price was more 'umble than Uriah Heep. And inside were always many more books with compelling titles on display for inspection and consideration. The effectiveness of outdoor books at producing indoor sales for secondhand bookstores may not be a study topic for a graduate thesis or a government grant, but suspicions linger that maybe book dealers weren't merely indulging in altruism with those calculatedly unkempt sidewalk bargain bins.

Enigma: If sidewalk books really didn't reap any profits and weren't designed as enticements to bring buyers indoors, why not simply deposit them outside with a bold sign, white on red, proclaiming *Free Books!* Such a gesture would give rare authenticity to that 1927 Bud De Sylva, Lew Brown, and Ray Henderson song about what the best things in life are.

The Strand historically distributed catalogues to a large mailing list as a quick, cost-effective means of informing potential customers about the availability of titles in specific categories. To get in step with the technotimes and a wired millennium, the Strand during the year 2000 was also preparing to go online at www.strandbooks.com.

Strand catalogues typically were extensive lists of books without annotated bibliographical descriptions. The general catalogues were designed simply to inform collectors, readers, and library buyers of available items. These information listings covered the different book categories maintained at the store, including the arts, biography, fiction, history, literature, religion, and travel. Catalogue recipients missed the ambience of being at the Strand and actually holding the books, but they knew what they were getting and could rely on the quality.

Catalogues from the Strand rare book room on the third floor were exceptions in that bibliographical data were supplied, including notable points and features of the books offered. Catalogue RBR-5, "Books on Books & Limited Editions Club: A Selection," from the 1980s, was representative, with 616 items listed. Numerous items came from the Strand's large stock of books from the prestigious Limited Editions Club, founded in 1929, concomitantly with the birth of the Strand on Fourth Avenue. Among the distinguished books in RBR-5 are these:

36. **BRUSSEL, I. R.** *Anglo-American First Editions.* With an introduction by Lord Esher. NY.: Sol Lewis reprint. 1981. Orig. pub. 1936. 2 vols. 8vo. Cloth, near fine, both vols. in cloth slipcase. The set: $49.50

106. DE VINNE, THEODORE L. *Manual of Printing Office Practice.* Forest Hills, N.Y.: Battery Park Book Co. reprint. 1978. Orig. pub. 1883. With an Introductory Note by Douglas C. McMurtrie. 8vo. iv + 52 pp. Ltd. ed. one of 600 copies. Cloth, near fine. $25.00

391. BRADBURY, RAY. *Martian Chronicles.* Intro. by Martin Gardner, lithographs by Joe Mugnaini. Designed by Ernst Reichl and printed by the Connecticut Printers. Bloomfield. 1974. Tall 8vo. dec. cloth, signed by author and artist. $140.00

401. CARROLL, LEWIS. *Alice's Adventures in Wonderland.* Intro. by Henry Seidel Canby. The original Tenniel illustrations re-engraved on wood by Bruno Rollitz. Designed by Frederic Warde. W. E. Rudge. Mt. Vernon. 1932. 8vo. Full red Morrocco, v.sl. rubbed. SIGNED by Mrs. Alice Hargreaves, the original Alice for whom the story was written, and Frederic Warde. In sl. worn cloth slipcase. Small neat bookplate. A beautifully preserved copy of this book, seldom offered in this condition. $700.00

An intriguing addendum to RBR-5 or any Strand catalogue would be the edition of *Candide, ou L'Optimisme* (1759) by Voltaire with a preface signed B.B., for Benjamin Bass, who occasionally indulged in literary scholarship while selling books. Those interested in the literati of Book Row might have rushed an order to the Strand to have a book with the impressions and imprint of a famous bookseller, *dans le meilleur des mondes possibles.*

THE STRAND CUSTOMERS

When year after year you apparently have more customers entering the store than any other secondhand bookshop on planet Earth, you inevitably attract every conceivable sort of person—the wise and foolish, the good and wicked, the obscure and famous, the old and young, the usual and unusual. And if you are an employee meeting customers on the main floor, you hear and must respond to every possible book-related question humans can dream up. Humans are terrific dreamer-uppers.

One writer, Joseph Deitch, visiting the Strand in 1956 for the *Wilson Library Bulletin*, heard a woman ask, "Have you anything on life after death?" She was promptly directed to the store's section on the occult, where she could find different views of the topic and also information about reincarnation, communicating with and raising the dead, foretelling the future, coping with the spirit world, and related issues if such activities were also of interest. No area of subject matter was foreign to the Strand, and no patrons, except on-the-job shoplifters, were unwelcome.

Deitch asked Fred Bass if he thought television might replace books. Ten years later the question perhaps would have been phrased differently to include computers. Bass answered in 1986, as he might in 2003 concerning television and probably other electronic gadgetry as well: "Absolute nonsense. . . . All the numbers belie the notion that TV will replace the book . . . our book buyers, those all about us here, are generally not your average TV watchers. There are people seriously interested in books—your professionals in many fields, academics and scholars, students, lovers of literature, art, and travel. People for whom books are part of their lives." The Strand after more than seven decades on Book Row was committed to helping such people keep books part of their lives. The storewide effort to honor that commitment was impressively succeeding.

The Strand has met the book needs of institutions as well as individuals on a vast scale. Through the years libraries—great and small, public, private, college, university—were among the store's regular customers. Librarians ordered from and frequently came to the Strand because they often could get considerably more for their budget money than they would through new-book outlets. Add the fact that they could also acquire important, scholarly, out-of-print books generally unavailable through other channels. The Strand deliberately cultivated library customers with substantial discounts and first choice on hard-to-find books needed by library collections.

The Strand has maintained standing arrangements with various libraries to send them quantities of books regularly selected by Strand employees based on their institutional needs. The libraries receiving books under these arrangements have had the option of returning the books they don't want to keep. The retention rates have generally been high because of the Strand's close working relationships with the libraries and knowledge of their requirements, and because the store has consistently come through with selections and prices that benefited the institutions. The store's long-standing effort to cultivate and serve public and academic libraries has made this sector a major contributor to the Strand's annual sales.

The Strand has maintained popularity among book scouts and other book dealers because of its variety and its accommodating prices. A bookseller with a customer for a particular title would find the book at the Strand and pass it on to the purchaser at a reasonable profit. The arrangement was pragmatic for all, with no losers. The Strand had its profit. So did the intermediary. And the ultimate customer had the book he coveted.

The Strand's immense stock and broad range of subjects has enabled the store to serve as a library builder as well as a library supplier. Assembling customized libraries in designated topic areas for customers, both individuals and businesses, evolved as another Strand specialty because of the widespread need. When busy moviemaker Steven Spielberg wanted a professionally compiled library of four thousand books covering the arts, history, and literature, he gave the Strand a $30,000 budget and in due course received an excellent, well-balanced library. Forming a library carefully tailored to fit each particular customer the same way a couturier would design a client's garments became a popular Strand service.

Interior decorators and others have sometimes sought books not for reading but for show. The Strand hasn't struck a haughty intellectual pose with such customers. At a price, it has provided the books. Strand books were utilized extensively to decorate sets in numerous movie and television productions. Strand volumes filled the shelves on stages for a multitude of Broadway and Off-Broadway theatrical presentations. The Strand provided books for the broadcasting areas of the *Today* show and other regular television programs striving to grant themselves the respectability of knowledge through their backdrops. The store itself became a set and provided the background scene in various films.

For instance, in the McCarthy-era thriller *The House on Carroll Street* (1988), a spirited chase occurs *inside* the Strand between the government bad guys and the liberal heroine, Emily Crane, played by Kelly McGillis. There are, of course, a few geographic and fact-bending oddities in the scene. The 1980s Strand performs as the 1950s Strand (does a nice job of acting too). Emily, telling someone to meet her, says, "Near Sheridan Square, there's a bookstore, it's quite large and it sells used books." The bookstore was never near Sheridan Square, and in the early 1950s it didn't look as it did in the film.

In one key scene, the Strand interior was on display with books in all directions. Watching, one yearned to put all the fictional tumult on pause and step inside the picture to check out the forty-eight-cent bargains prominently exhibited at tables with conspicuous Strand signs. Did the prices jibe with 1950s realities? Don't bet on it; however, most moviegoers were probably much too worried about threatened, harassed (by Mandy Patinkin), and bookish Emily Crane to care. But hey, it was just a movie, right? We shouldn't be picky. And the bookstore had a great role, which as usual it played to perfection.

Even while locating rare out-of-print books to fill gaps in an academic library's intellectual resources for students and researchers, the Strand could simultaneously deliver books by the foot or yard to decorate a wall or a room with a bookish appearance. Books chosen not for content but to foster a special mood could even be picked to harmonize with a particular color scheme at prices up to $200 a foot depending on the complexity of the challenge and the quality of the books required to achieve a desired effect.

Individual customers at the Strand included tourists who read, liked the idea of books, and dropped by for the first time because their guidebooks told them the Strand should not be missed. Joining them and ignoring them were the book-buying regulars, the ever loyal Strandites who started young and kept going back all their lives to learn "what's new." In between the first-timers and the perennials were we, the people, in our millions, who needed and wanted various books, some not so easy to track down, and who suspected from experience that the Strand was the likeliest place to find them.

The Strand's extensive roster of celebrity patrons has ranged from former CIA director William Casey, who allegedly once called the president from the rare book room, to Bette Midler—who didn't—which is some range. Spymaster Casey was a dedicated book collector who rummaged secretly in secondhand bookstores wherever he traveled; and according to the *Wall Street Journal* (August 21, 1986), he viewed the Strand as the world's best bookstore. He got around and was presumably in a position to know. Broadway actors and film stars who read—an impressive number do—have also frequented the Strand from one generation to the next to right now.

Italian author and collector Umberto Eco cherished the store's variety. He always found something different and desirable at every visit; and he called the Strand his favorite place in the United States. Some New York–based writers tended to think of the Strand as an extension of their own metropolitan homes, with acres of reference books complementing those on their domestic shelves. Fran Lebowitz, according to *New York* (April 18, 1994), whenever in New York always spent hours "plowing through the stacks of the Strand." "There's nothing like the hands-on browse through the Strand's basement" observed *New York*. The magazine quoted Lebowitz in her own defense: "I make myself believe that buying books is the same as writing books. So I have a good excuse."

Sonja Mirsky wanted no defense for the years she'd been going to the Strand and the hours she'd spent there. The future librarian discovered the Strand in 1939 and kept returning because she loved books, and the Strand tended to have the books she loved. Furthermore, she appreciated and never forgot the kindness and generosity shown her by the proprietor, Ben Bass. When she was in a position to buy books for the Rockefeller Institute library, she obtained them whenever possible at the Strand.

Reporter and writer Joseph Cohen made the Strand his exclusive secondhand bookstore because of attrition as well as preference. He liked the Strand but shared his book quests with other Book Row shops when they existed. The other shops slowly disappeared, and Cohen by necessity as well as inclination gradually confined his "browsing, buying, selling" to the survivor.

Larry Moskowitz viewed the Strand he knew and visited for decades as literally two bookstores. The early one he admired greatly. The Strand that developed later disappointed him. "The Strand was terrific in the days when you didn't know what would be available from one day to the next, and when there was a lot of good fiction at attractive prices," he recalled for this account. Moskowitz's criticism was that works of fiction previously available on the main floor were exiled to the rare book department and assigned premium prices. That step, understandably aimed at obtaining a greater return on valuable items for the Strand, reduced the appeal of the Strand's formerly impressive fiction section for Moskowitz.

"What that has done is strip the fiction downstairs of anything that is interesting . . . the fiction stock from having once been almost more impressive than anywhere else has become a bore," he stated, emphasizing that he spoke as both a bookseller and a collector. He acknowledged that his was the viewpoint of a disgruntled customer who missed the great finds and golden buys of yesteryear. He accepted that in a business sense the Strand had probably been correct to make the changes it did and to classify more volumes as higher-priced rarities. "The Strand for a long time was selling hundred-dollar books at two dollars, which allowed tremendous finds to those of us who came in. There is no reason, of course, why the Strand should sell such books for less than their value. The store deserves a greater share, and the finest books rightly should go to the rare book room."

Moskowitz's argument was one of degree. He thought the Strand policy went too far, sending nearly all fiction with any merit upstairs and rendering what was left on the main floor drab and unappealing. "I think maybe sixty percent of what is up there could be downstairs. It would make the stock more interesting; and if priced right, would sell much faster," he said. Moskowitz added, "I used to go to the Strand a lot. I don't go there nearly as much anymore, and when I do, I don't stay very long."

The availability under one roof of such a vast and varied collection of books has kept thousands of book searchers coming through the front door on Broadway year following year. And enough of them stayed long enough to find books they chose to keep. They carried those books away in sufficient quantity to keep the Strand a continuing Book Row success in finding, buying, and selling books for a phenomenally long run, and who knows, maybe ad infinitum.

THE STRAND EMPLOYEES AND ALUMNI

If the Strand emulated the universities whose libraries it helped develop and maintained an alumni association, it would comprise a fascinating collection of successful booksellers, actors, writers, entrepreneurs, scholars, perpetual students, and colorful characters.

New York City—with its large and periodically unemployed pool of talented actors, writers, musicians, artists, students, thinkers, revolutionists, and probably, truth be told, fugitives—has always been able to staff its vital service industries such as coffeehouses and bookstores with employees, part-time and full-time, possessing impressive curricula vitae and dossiers. These moonlighting workers, strongly committed to other careers, often bring to temporary jobs ample talents as well as fascinating pasts and not infrequently famous futures.

A scholarly, degree-worthy exposé with a catchy title, possibly *New York Bookstore Confidential*, probably could be done about well-known authors hired and fired at New York bookstores. Every resident of Tometown knows Tennessee Williams couldn't wrap packages or show up on time and thus had to end his brief employment at the Gotham Book Mart. If a qualified literary archaeologist receives a grant for such a study, the Strand will certainly deserve a chapter all its own, even though we turned up no proof that Richard Kimble ever worked in the Strand Underground.

The Strand's more than seventy years of bookselling and a staff that grew from Ben Bass in 1929 to nearly two hundred at the start of the next century would necessarily have a larger alumni roster than any other secondhand bookstore. The Strand's workers generally came from the city's perpetual, never diminished reservoir of talented people with determined ambitions to write, act, paint. For some, those ambitions were brilliantly fulfilled. Other students at and graduates from the unaccredited yet highly respected Strand College of Bookselling went on to distinguished careers in various phases of the book trade.

Most Strand employees came and went and were not later recognized on Broadway, movie screens, or publishers' lists. But they left warm memories behind them with their colleagues and with grateful book collectors who received their discriminating assistance in building satisfying collections. Representative perhaps among these servants of the books was William H. Floyd, who worked ten years at the Strand before his early death in 1990 at the age of thirty-six. He was a gentle bookman who considered going into the priesthood and then chose antiquarian books as a worthy alternative career. He advanced at the Strand from the review department to the position of chief researcher in the rare book room.

Steven Wise worked at the Strand for three years at the end of the 1980s. His job was to keep main floor activities functioning smoothly. He remembered the Strand as "the last bastion for bibliomaniacs," where he loved working because of the books and the camaraderie that existed among the employees. Wise had recollections of accompanying his mother on her book-browsing excursions along Book Row when he was a child.

Dennis J. Quigley was at the Strand for several years, starting in 1969 as a driver. He had been there less than a month when he had a conversation with

Ben Bass that he never forgot. He asked permission to take a week off. "Why?" the Strand owner asked. "To attend an antiwar rally in Washington, D.C." was the answer. For this account, Quigley wrote, "Ben Bass replied that the demonstration was only for the weekend. I said yes, but that I would probably wind up in jail. He laughed and said if I got thrown in jail to call him up and he would bail me out. I decided the Strand was the place for me to work."

Jan Spacek, a rare book room researcher, believed he learned more during two years in the RBR than during four years of college. He wrote that while you might not find a specific title at the Strand, "You are also not likely to leave empty-handed. The Strand repays the patient browser." Joe Rudnicki first visited Book Row with his mother in the 1950s; he later roamed the neighborhood by himself and found books that would shape his life. In 1980, after jettisoning the scary notion of accepting a "suit, power tie, and wing-tip shoes" Wall Street job, he decided on impulse, while buying a twenty-five-cent paperback at the Strand, to take a job for a few months "at this dusty old dinosaur of a bookstore." He was still there ten years later and wrote, "I love the place. That day ten years ago was perhaps the most important day of my life. What a horrible thought. And the books. Let's not forget the books. I love them."

George Wimpfheimer became a regular Strand employee in 1981. He recognized that for many the bookstore served a "halfway house" function, but he considered the venerable institution much more than that. "There are just so many good people at the Strand, and it is from these people that I have drawn my primary sustenance and learned so much," he wrote.

Ron Antonucci was a journalist and editor who gave up those activities in 1989 to work at the Strand and "return to my first love, used and rare books." He served as a researcher in the rare book room; and after he left to return to his home state, he carried back to Ohio the conviction "There is no doubt that the Strand is the finest used-book store that I've ever visited." Ron Antonucci as a grateful Strand alumnus may have been somewhat affected in his enthusiasm by bias. Yet there was ample evidence from Strand customers, employees, and alumni that the expression "finest used-book store" applied to the Strand was hyperbole free.

In its winter 2002 newsletter, the New York Metro Chapter of the Art Libraries Society of North America featured an interview with Richard Lilly, manager of the Strand's art department. Lilly noted that the Strand in the twenty-first century was continuing to thrive, with exceptional new strengths in art books. He noted the acquisition of Hacker Art Books, a Manhattan art book oasis since the 1940s. He heralded the Strand's dramatic leap to art book prominence through the formation of Hacker-Strand Art Books. John Huckans in *Book Source Monthly,* February 2002, echoed this enthusiasm: "With the Hacker purchase the Strand (after 75 years certainly a dynasty in the bookselling world) strengthens its position as one of New York's important bookish icons. There's hope."

Lilly noted the Strand's overall progress, exemplified by the improvement program, including turning the second floor over to the art department and upgrading rare books with a much larger, more attractive, air-conditioned area. About his art books specialty, Lilly speculated he might "double my staff and triple my space."

Calling himself "a classic old Fourth Avenue–type bookseller," Richard Lilly acknowledged that the Strand, including himself, had allowed the Web to come aboard the Strand in a large way, with loads of efficient electronic luggage. "Slowly we're becoming computer literate," he said. He referred to an interview of Nancy Bass by Richard Raynor in the *New York Times Magazine,* "An Actual Internet Success Story," June 9, 2002. Nancy Bass called the Strand's $250,000 Internet system "a natural progression" for the store. Bass commented, "The Internet has been a total boon." One unarguable symptom of success was the Strand's promised replacement of its red-and-white sign "Eight Miles of Books" with "Sixteen Miles of Books." Concerning the store's online experience, Lilly agreed it had become "quite clear that the Internet is one of the few successes in secondhand and out-of-print books because it draws together all kinds of disparate people all over the planet. It's also very useful for me to research prices, conditions and editions."

But along with the contemporary low hum of the Internet, we still hear the melodies of yore, books moving in and out of shelves, old cash drawers opening and closing, book people wrangling over first edition points and prices. Raynor in his *Times Magazine* report on Internet bookselling stated grandiosely that the "Internet transformed everyone on the planet into a potential used-book dealer." Those who had the books and the know-how might buy and sell books on the Net, but we'd like to hear Peter Stammer's,

Sam Dauber's, and Jack Biblo's views of them as genuine secondhand book dealers.

Book Row's Twenty-first-Century Grand Survivor

Reformer Lincoln Steffens in 1919 declared about revolutionary Russia, "I have seen the future, and it works." Perhaps it worked for a time, but certainly not as long and well as the Strand. In the twenty-first century, the Strand passed the three-quarter-century mark and obviously possessed considerable momentum for future growth. In Manhattan, the Book Row survivor was the number one target of choice when books were needed fast on any subject. After the World Trade Center tragedy of September 11, 2001, it was to the Strand that readers rushed in droves for background reading in pursuit of understanding and reassurance. Emily Eakin reported in the *New York Times*, September 18, 2001, that the Strand in a week sold twenty-seven of its forty-four copies of Eric Darton's *Divided We Stand: A Biography of New York City's World Trade Center*. Still today, when a particular book is needed, the Strand remains the place to go.

In the opening years of the twenty-first century the old bookstore has become as big a celebrity as most of the celebrities it serves; witness Jim Jerome's 2002 Strand tribute in *People*. Stars flock to the Strand, establishing their bona fides as book fanciers; and their PR releases wisely don't keep such bookish facts a secret. The report that Ben Affleck went to the Strand seeking Corman McCarthy galleys for his friend Matt Damon applied intellectual polish on the images of both actors.

About her job helping her father, Fred Bass, run the remarkable book enterprise, Nancy Bass said, "I'm able to make money doing what I love and believing in the specialness of what I'm selling." Her predecessor booksellers on Book Row, also committed to serving book lovers, might have used different words to describe their work, but most probably would have expressed the identical view of bookselling as they knew it, performed it, loved it.

CHAPTER SIXTEEN

THE LATER GENERATION
Timothy Johns · Glenn Horowitz · Steve Crowley

*Of all the inanimate objects, of all men's creations, books are the
nearest to us, for they contain our very thoughts, our ambitions,
our indignations, our illusions, our fidelity to truth, and our
persistent leaning toward error. But most of all they resemble us in
their precarious hold on life.*

—JOSEPH CONRAD

✄ THE PREVIOUS PAGES considered, revisited, and honored several generations of New York booksellers who fretted and served their hours and years
upon the stage of Fourth Avenue and nearby streets and then too often were
heard no more. But let it not be said their tales are full of sound and fury, sig-
nifying nothing. Get out of here, Macbeth! Avaunt!

Those bookmen and their bookshops signified knowledge on the march,
the dissemination of wisdom (with maybe a dash of nonsense now and then),
the spreading of words, the preservation of human insight, the sharing of
beauty. They distributed books in the big city far and wide and well beyond.
That signified plenty.

Romain Rolland declared in *Nation* (April 22, 1931), "My country is not
yesterday. My country is tomorrow." That would be a pretty sappy statement
without books. Luckily, when the Nobel-winning author entered his country
of tomorrow, he could take yesterday and the whole of the past with him,
thanks to books. That signifies.

During the 1980s, when the final curtain was gradually yet inexorably
closing on the Booksellers' Row that began in the 1890s, a lot of gloomy
things were spoken. The consensus around the surviving bookstores was
that climbing costs, aging bookmen, and the disinterest of the new generations in careers as booksellers were combining to give old Book Row its

coup de grâce. Not to moan; everything changes, and it was nice while it lasted.

Walter Goldwater morosely mentioned to the *New York Times* (May 31, 1981), "There aren't many young people entering this field. There isn't anybody to take over." But the bookselling prognosis at Goldwater's University Place Book Shop wasn't entirely bleak. When the founder died in 1985, his protégé Bill French carried on the venerable bookstore another ten years. Bill French acquired and sold a lot of books during that ten-year survival period, made readers and collectors happy, and made considerable printed information available near and far. That definitely signifies.

According to *Biblio* (November 1998), Fred Bass at the Strand thought that Book Row faded away in part because many of the booksellers there, as veterans of the Depression, held on too tightly to what they had, were reluctant to share their knowledge, and neglected to train successors. With no one prepared or inclined to take over, when a bookstore proprietor wanted to or had to retire, his shop quite often retired with him. At the Strand, however, Fred Bass was both superbly trained and fully ready to replace his father, Ben Bass.

At the Strand, with its ever-growing and rotating staff, withholding useful knowledge was clearly recognized as a shortsighted and not-good-for-business practice. The Strand through the years hired well-qualified book people when they were available. Yet many inexperienced people were also necessarily hired and taught the rudiments of bookstore operations so they could effectively apply them at the Strand. Thus the Strand functioned as an on-the-job booksellers' training academy, with buying and selling second-hand books as the entire curriculum. The rare book department at the Strand as it expanded into a major component of the business served as a basic and advanced school for scholars in antiquarian book appraisal, acquisition, pricing, cataloguing, and marketing.

Many graduates from the Strand schools in time journeyed forth into the book world to make their alma mater proud. Several former Strand employees went on to highly successful careers in other bookstores and different phases of the book trade. Onetime Strand employee Chris Coover, for example, became a vice president in the book department at the New York branch of Christie's, the auction house, whose tales of mighty sales included $82.5 million for Vincent van Gogh's *Portrait of Dr. Gachet* in 1990 and the

1994 purchase by Microsoft's Bill Gates, for $30.8 million, of a Leonardo da Vinci notebook, known as the Codex Hammer because Armand Hammer had owned it.

Bookmen who went on to brilliant antiquarian bookselling careers with traditional bookstores after their stints at the Strand included Timothy Johns and Glenn Horowitz. These gentlemen and other trained professionals with bookselling roots at the Strand were all from a later generation than the Fourth Avenue bookshop originals and eccentrics who preceded them.

Another from the later generation who had the unusual background of *not* having worked at the Strand was Steve Crowley, who committed the even more unusual act in 1996 of setting up shop to sell books at his Alabaster Bookshop on Fourth Avenue, in the same neighborhood where Book Row made history during the century before him.

These younger booksellers headed for the future and spoke to the past. What they said to reassure the past was that the earlier generations had no cause to despair about the future of books and bookselling, whether on Fourth Avenue or elsewhere. The book, mankind's only perfect invention (with the possible exception of the paper clip and the no. 2 pencil), would never disappear; no matter the amusing speculations, brouhaha, and hubbub about twenty-first-century electronic reading gadgets. The traditional book would calmly and placidly carry on as it did when "talking book" substitutes appeared. Again it would easily prevail over the clever but by comparison cumbersome book-displaying screen devices. There would still be book seekers and booksellers to maintain the book's sovereignty in the great marketplace of book lovers, readers, and collectors.

TIMOTHY JOHNS—JAMES CUMMINS, BOOKSELLER, INC.

This fact may seem incredulous and astonishing, but to become a prominent New York City bookseller you don't actually have to be born in Brooklyn, the Bronx, or Eastern Europe or be a refugee from Nazi tyranny. Timothy Johns first entered the world of people and books a long hike down the Western trail from Manhattan. He was born in Austin, Texas, on September 2, 1945, a few weeks after World War II ended and around the time the Pageant was established on Fourth Avenue by Henry Chafetz and Sidney Solomon.

Tim Johns became a skilled bookman before he reached Fourth Avenue. He studied classics and linguistics as a graduate student at the University of Texas in Austin after receiving his B.A. there in 1968. Tim Johns impressively demonstrates that distinguished bookmanship can develop in Texas, and if there, why not anywhere!

He worked as a teacher and translator, but the career of bookselling eventually became his primary commitment. During the summer of 1980, transplanted from Texas to Manhattan, he joined the staff of the Strand in the Booksellers' Row neighborhood. The Strand was already atypical as a Book Row enterprise because of its growth, staff, and scale of operations, which dwarfed what had previously been the norm along Fourth Avenue.

Tim Johns brought the Strand a depth of knowledge and range of abilities that made him a key contributor to the establishment, strengthening, and expansion of the firm's rare book department. The Strand reached beyond its original status as predominantly a secondhand book leviathan that gave only nominal recognition to rarity as a marketable asset. A concerted effort was made at the Strand to acquire more books of antiquarian quality, to screen routine acquisitions for such qualities, and to make the most of the commercial opportunities inherent in the developing rare-book trade. The Strand's rare book room sought to become a prime player in the antiquarian book field.

Tim Johns created a memorable milestone in the history of the Strand and its RBR as the compiler of the initial rare book room catalogue, RBR-1. Other catalogues followed, but RBR-1 went into the archives of the Strand as a memorable first.

Johns left the Strand in 1983 to join the well-known midtown antiquarian book business James Cummins, Bookseller, Inc., as an associate of the proprietor, James Cummins, who was an agent of the New York book collector Richard Manney and active in many celebrated rare-book deals. At a 1989 Boston Antiquarian Book Fair, on the job at his booth, Cummins remarked, as quoted by Nicholas Basbanes in *A Gentle Madness*, "The glamour of a big sale is wonderful, but this is the meat and potatoes of the business."

Cummins was once manager of the rare-book department at Brentano's when it was located at Forty-seventh Street and Fifth Avenue. That department, one of the earliest, best known, and most influential rare-book enterprises, was the 1907 brainchild, and pride and joy, of Arthur Brentano. He was the bookselling nephew of August Brentano, who founded Brentano's

Literary Emporium during the nineteenth century in the Union Square neighborhood near where Book Row evolved. John Winterich during the 1930s met Arthur Brentano, then in his eighties and still actively selling books on the floor at Brentano's. He told Winterich that one of his pleasures in the business was "getting good, solid, useful, permanent books into the hands of an appreciative buyer." That statement comes close to describing bookselling at its finest by Tim Johns and all his gone but not forgotten Book Row predecessors.

Tim Johns became a permanent associate of James Cummins, Bookseller, Inc. He was the compiler of many successful catalogues for that organization during the years that followed his affiliation with the company in 1983. The 1994–95 edition of the *International Directory of Antiquarian Booksellers* named Johns manager of the store at 699 Madison Avenue. The following specialties were listed: sporting, color plate books, private press, first editions, fine bindings, sets, English and American literature.

As a prominent bookseller from a later generation than most of the Fourth Avenue booksellers and an important contributor to the Strand success story early in his career, Tim Johns became another refutation of the bleak scenario that secondhand and antiquarian bookselling might fizzle and falter with the decline of Book Row. The older bookmen had too many successors throughout the city. Their continuing influence reached from New York to other cities and countries. The effective work of Tim Johns and others from his generation in the rare-book field should pacify the restless shades of the Book Row proprietors. True, they weren't all that easy to pacify when they were active on Fourth Avenue. Chances are they didn't become that much more amenable to pacification when they moved on. But the fact is that good, solid, useful, permanent books are still being delivered to the appreciative by knowledgeable and hardworking booksellers. That's a legacy from and connection to Book Row.

GLENN HOROWITZ—GLENN HOROWITZ BOOKS

When he worked at the Strand from the autumn of 1977 to the autumn of 1979, Glenn Horowitz was surrounded by an overwhelming number of secondhand books. Many sold for less than a dollar, with the majority available first-come, first-served "for a few dollars more" (to borrow the title of a 1966 Italian spaghetti Western starring Clint Eastwood and Lee Van Cleef). The bookselling career of this Strand alumnus dramatically proves the journey between secondhand books and antiquarian rarities can be a symbolic saga from feathers to fortunes.

In her *Newsday* column for May 13, 1990, Horowitz's wife, M. G. Lord, described her husband as a rare-book and manuscript dealer with private collections that "clutter every flat surface in our loft." She wrote about her husband's latest acquisitions at a New York auction, which she could admire on their home shelves but which, she suspected, based on past experience, wouldn't "spend many nights on our cheap motel of a bookshelf; they're bound for nobler collections." The titles and prices the columnist listed from his Sotheby's auction acquisitions were the first English-language edition of Saint Augustine's *Confessions,* $16,000; thirteen-year-old Elizabeth Barrett Browning's *The Battle of Marathon* (1819), $45,000; Mary Shelley's *Franken-stein, Or The Modern Prometheus* (1818), $70,000.

By the 1990s, a little over two decades after his learning experiences on Book Row, Glenn Horowitz was among America's leading experts on and merchants of rare books. Marvin Mondlin worked with Horowitz in the rare book room at the Strand and remembered that the young man brought considerable book knowledge with him to the job when he joined the firm. When Horowitz left the Strand to start his own business, he expressed his gratitude for the help he received and for what he had learned while there.

Horowitz became a key source of books for many notable collectors, including the New York financier Carter Burden, for whom at a Swann auction he purchased *Hike and the Aeroplane* (1912), by Sinclair Lewis writing as Tom Graham. The collector paid $19,250 for the volume. "I already had a copy of the book. It was the dust jacket I needed," Carter Burden admitted to Nicholas Basbanes.

Glenn Horowitz was a student of literature at Bennington College, in Bennington, Vermont, where he studied with Brooklyn-born novelist Bernard Malamud. After graduation, Horowitz in his early twenties headed for Book Row and his first job at the Strand. There, based on his education and knowledge, he was assigned to the rare book department.

His personal recollections of Book Row went back to the 1950s, when he had sometimes visited the bookshop of his uncle the Book Row proprietor

Haskell Gruberger. Interviewed for this account, Horowitz noted that his uncle "always appeared to me as the quintessential version of the book merchant."

Reminiscing about Book Row, he said, "By the late nineteen seventies, when I was employed at the Strand, what was left of Fourth Avenue was rather sad." He remembered the few remaining booksellers as an aging group who seemed financially on a downhill slide. "You could see these were the surviving dinosaurs who had been left behind. I didn't at the time sense that the Strand would be the culmination of the Fourth Avenue experience. The remaining shops did give a sense of what had once been a boulevard of flourishing enterprises devoted to buying and selling used books," he remarked.

At the age of twenty-three, Horowitz received an opportunity to acquire a substantial collection of twentieth-century first editions. Boldly acting on this chance took him from the Strand and into his own bookselling enterprise. "The library that became the foundation of my business was offered to me in October 1979," he recalled. A considerable amount of money was involved, but he was young enough, as he put it, not to be "petrified with anxiety" about making the leap.

"If I had known then what I know now, I would have been paralyzed with fear," he admitted when interviewed by Sheridan Sansegundo for "A Crusading Book Lover," published in the *East Hampton Star* (July 16, 1992). The article commemorated the opening at East Hampton of a Glenn Horowitz rare-book store complementing his Manhattan-based bookselling endeavors.

In Manhattan, Horowitz's operation did not include walk-in bookselling services, but his upscale shop at the Long Island resort area was designed to attract browsers and tempt buyers. He noted that his year-round store at East Hampton would strive "to appeal to people who are escaping from the pressures of the city." Book treasures filled the shelves, and comfortable armchairs invited placid perusing until the reader-buyer was at ease and reconciled to investing $1,850 for a signed copy of *Horseman, Pass By* (1961) by Larry McMurtry. (Conscientiously, that is to say *legibly,* signed McMurtrys are likely to remain a bull market thanks to the author's announced intention to stop delivering a readable signature at book signings, producing instead an effortless scrawl. In his essay "Why I Stopped Signing My Books" (*op,* July/August 2003), he mentioned two reasons: "to spare my hand" and "to avoid book buyers of the sports-card mentality." McMurtry noted he had probably signed at least thirty thousand books and added that after thinking about it, "the more wrong it seems. For the signature slowly but steadily slides attention away from the one thing that really deserves it: the book."

Glenn Horowitz specialized in nineteenth- and twentieth-century first editions. He told Sheridan Sansegundo, "In twentieth-century books, condition is essential in determining the value, and they must have the original dust jacket." East Hampton was the home of John Howard Payne, who wrote, "Home, Sweet Home." Glenn Horowitz set out to make it a home, profitable home, for a splendid group of dust-jacketed American and English firsts as well as art books and volumes that were distinguished examples of fine bookmaking.

Discussing value-adding dust jackets and their subtle distinctions, Horowitz talked about William Faulkner's *The Sound and the Fury* (1929). The jacket for the Faulkner first edition carried an advertisement for another 1929 book, *Humanity Uprooted* by Maurice Gerschon Hindus. The first-state jackets listed the Hindus volume at $3 while second-state jackets gave the price as $3.50. Horowitz explained that this trivial difference on the back of the dust jacket made the first edition with the prior jacket, carrying the lower Hindus price, worth several thousand dollars more than those with the later price, although the books they embraced were identical firsts.

Another instance of staggering dust jacket inflation concerned F. Scott Fitzgerald's *The Great Gatsby* (1925). "In good condition, without a jacket, the book is worth from $200 to $400. The same book with its original jacket will fetch $15,000 to $20,000," Horowitz declared. The Ahearns, in *Collected Books* (1998), echoed Horowitz. They listed *The Great Gatsby* with a first-state dust jacket at $25,000 and with a second-state dust jacket at $15,000. Obviously it has become extremely foolhardy and costly *not* to judge a first edition by its cover.

Speaking about his upwardly mobile bookselling career after leaving the Strand, Horowitz talked about his education as a bookman, in which trial and error played a major role. By trying and gaining insight from error, he quickly found out the importance for an antiquarian book dealer of establishing strong and lasting relationships with a steady corps of clients. As different collectors were cultivated and developed, the bookseller steadily gained awareness about what would interest each particular buyer and how best to serve his needs.

Love of books when young led Glenn Horowitz to learn all he could from them and about them. Knowledge of books in turn led him to a career of bookselling. His ardor for what he helped his clients acquire never diminished. He told Sansegundo, "Books are life and death—they contain everything we know." He called them "precious and spiritually nourishing."

"What I think motivates many people who assiduously collect books is the idea of making the world whole again," Horowitz told Philip Weiss, who wrote about their meeting in "The Book Thief, a True Tale of Bibliomania," *Harper's* (January 1994). The bookman mused that collectors are private people who create a sanctuary of books to which they can go by themselves "as often as not with a glass of whiskey in hand." Horowitz imagined book collections as organic entities in which the volumes through their titles and contents related to one another and conducted a silent, private conversation on the shelves. Weiss described the Glenn Horowitz business in Manhattan as a refuge "lined from floor to ceiling with books."

During his early years as a book dealer, Horowitz produced catalogues that focused on a broad selection of modern literature. Later, as his business and clientele expanded, he issued catalogues for substantial single-author (such as T. S. Eliot) and special-subject (such as American presidential materials) collections.

Horowitz also began doing research and investing capital to build special collections in fields that had not been sufficiently exploited. One was devoted to New York City. "If you were asked the name of somebody with a good inventory of rare books on New York City, there was nobody you could name," he said. His intention was to make his own name the correct response to such a query. "For a city that is as large, dynamic, and historically remarkable as New York, such an inventory is a must. I've been slowly building this to issue eventually what I expect will be a notable catalogue."

Another neglected area to which he gave special-collection-building efforts was abolitionist material. "It seems to me the history of slavery is one of the great issues in the history of U.S. development, and the books on the subject have been undervalued," he said. A third category was the vital period of American theater before the Civil War.

Horowitz observed that during his first decade in the business, the 1980s, the interest in rare books grew dramatically. The buying market expanded, and the value of significant rare books correspondingly increased. During the period, dealers such as Horowitz made extensive use of auctions as a source of books. "I have no objection to buying books for inventory at auction," he said. "Certain books that interest me I will buy at auction that other people may be shy about. Thus in some ways I do go slightly against the grain of the trade by taking books that interest me for resale purposes."

Concerning his overall acquisition policy, he observed, "I will buy as readily from the trade as I would buy from an auction house or private sources." An advantage of buying from the trade and at auctions over the purchase of large private libraries, he noted, was the ability to be highly selective and to eliminate handling large numbers of books that were not sufficiently valuable to justify the expense and labor required to manage them. Thus, Horowitz was cautious about purchasing a large collection simply to obtain a few worthwhile books. When he did accept a collection, his practice typically was to carry away a few books that were the "pure profit from the purchase," and to box the others for inventory. "It is rare that I find a collection that has enough books of substance to warrant the amount of money and labor required by the routine books involved," he admitted.

Concerning the rare-book trade as a whole, Horowitz lamented that a "codification of professionalism" has never been satisfactorily accomplished by those in the profession or by the Antiquarian Booksellers' Association of America. "There are so many gradations of both quality and quantity within this form of bookselling, the umbrella-trade, the rare-book trade, the used-book trade, the secondhand trade, the resale trade, they make it difficult to settle on a code of professionalism," he commented. "I think it's just a fact of life and a problem that is not going to be solved readily."

He derided the widespread complaint among some book dealers that good books are increasingly unobtainable. "Rare book dealers who say there are no good books available should have their wings clipped and sent packing into another trade. The claim that there are no good books out there anymore is demeaning to the trade and reflects negatively on those making that assumption," he insisted. Plenty of fine books were still waiting to be found by diligent seekers.

Horowitz dismissed too the familiar moans and groans about the contemporary difficulties of various rare-book enterprises related to high rents and other heavy costs of staying in business. "It's a question of management and intelligent business practice," he maintained. "Some who fill book shelves and call themselves book dealers are dreadful business people. Any business involves the responsibility of keeping financially sound. Unless you can *do* business, you are not *in* the book business." He added that if an exceptionally skilled businessman such as Fred Bass were in charge of such firms, "they would soon be making three times the profit."

Concerning the future, Horowitz thought there might be fewer streetfront bookstores, in the tradition of Book Row and Christopher Morley's *The Haunted Bookshop*, located in New York City. The reason was the formidable economic problems endemic to such businesses in various neighborhoods as those neighborhoods moved beyond marginal status. He wondered if more such bookstores might eventually locate in areas of Brooklyn, Harlem, and Manhattan's Upper West Side, where costs might for a time be less severe.

He expected, however, that rare books would continue to increase in value for several reasons. One reason was the declining numbers of the great eighteenth- and nineteenth-century books that would be available through the rare-book market as more of them settled permanently in institutions and others were lost through mishandling and deterioration. Fewer volumes meant increasing rarity and consequently greater values.

Another stimulus to rising prices, he felt, was the surge in available capital for purchasing rare books and art. New technology and international business continued steadily to make the earth wealthier, with more money everywhere accessible for intellectual and aesthetic pursuits and purchases. He feared, however, the occurrence of a major depression might sabotage the trend. "Books are probably recession-proof but not depression-proof," he noted.

He considered books ultimately safe from threats imposed by technological changes, other media, the decline of literacy, and related competitive forces that keep sneaking into a changing world. "Books will continue to be sacred objects to us," he predicted. For the hopeful accuracy of his prognostication that books will never become the artifacts of vanquished pieties, may Glenn Horowitz the book prophet in time's fullness surpass the fame of French astrologer Michel Nostradamus, who published a book of prophecies, *Centuries* (1555).

Now all would be well if similarly inspired predictions could only take William Faulkner's Nobel Prize optimism and substitute "bookstores" for "man" and "they" for "he" in the declaration "I believe that man will not merely endure: he will prevail."

So, will the bookshops ever return to Fourth Avenue the way the swallows return to Capistrano, salmon swim upstream, and American bison, when they were plentiful, made seasonal migrations? Maybe not. But on the other hand, let's not be too hasty. There have been reports that buffalo properly encouraged and protected on game preserves can make impressive comebacks. Why not bookstores?

There was the inspiring example of Steve Crowley and his calico cat, Houle, who opened their Alabaster Bookshop at 122 Fourth Avenue, near Twelfth Street, in October 1996. Crowley was the first person in two decades to take such a step in what once had been the Book Row area. This audacious return of secondhand books to the former used-book oasis startled and pleased the *New York Times* to the point of assigning Rosalie R. Radomsky for a feature article on the phenomenon. "And Then There Was One," read a caption in the February 9, 1997, *Times* story, above a street map showing where twenty-five former bookshops had once flourished and where the Alabaster now stood alone. The headline for Radomsky's report stated, "On Fourth Avenue, Going Against the Flow," and the subhead read, "When He Opened a Bookshop, Steve Crowley Became a One-Man Book Row."

Music brought Steve Crowley to New York; books kept him in the city as a dedicated bookman. He came to the city from his home in the Washington, D.C., area after graduating from Western Maryland College in 1984. He was a professional drummer during the 1980s and earned his living by taking jobs with bands. Between those gigs he filled in at the Gryphon Bookshop, a popular West Side book place at Eightieth Street and Broadway.

His part-time work in the shop and as a book scout helped pay the bills and gave him a well-rounded education in the buying and selling of quality secondhand books. One of the Gryphon owners, Henry Holman, was gratefully credited by Crowley for giving him a solid grounding in bookstore operations and the discriminating acquisition of salable stock. " 'Mentor' was certainly the word to describe Henry Holman for me and others who worked at the Gryphon," Steve Crowley said in a November 2000 interview for this account. "He was patient, considerate, and very generous with his endless store of knowledge. I began bringing back books I found and asking what he thought about them. Gradually, with Mr. Holman's guidance, I learned what was important and how to establish prices."

As he developed skills in recognizing valuable books, Crowley roamed the city and sold his finds on consignment at the Gryphon. Along with these successes and increasing acquaintance with the joys and pitfalls of book-selling through the tutelage of Henry Holman, he began to think seriously about starting a bookshop. The desire for a bookstore wasn't discouraged by his sale, for a substantial price, of an Ayn Rand first edition, *The Night of January 16th*, a play that appeared initially on a New York stage in 1935. He found the scarce volume for a dollar while scouting in the stores and on the sidewalks of New York.

Crowley decided that if he opened a bookstore, he wanted it for good busi-ness reasons to be near the Strand, which attracted endless, earnest, eager multitudes of book seekers. A small bookstore close to the Strand couldn't help but benefit symbiotically just as bookshops collectively profited in Book Row days from the steady flow of bibliophiles through the neighborhood.

He discovered the right place one day when he was bicycling on Fourth Avenue from his home on the Lower East Side. It was a space formerly occu-pied by the Abbey Bookshop, which had been run by the late George Foss. The location was around the corner from the Strand, and it had the ambi-ence of historic connection to the street's legendary bookselling past. There an independent secondhand bookstore featuring the books he would find to fill it could turn his quixotic dream into a beguiling reality. But the first and not so easy step was getting in. New York in the 1980s had become a society of careful, cautious, and suspicious screeners. "The space became available at just the right time for me, so I went for it," Crowley declared.

The ground-floor retail space was in a cooperative apartment building, and the co-op board loomed as a formidable obstacle course demanding skillful navigation. Crowley learned that he was competing against other candidates, including a beauty salon and a dress shop. He hoped Fourth Avenue's book-selling history would give his cause positive PR. He proposed to reestablish, if on a modest scale, a neighborhood tradition that had been a major New York claim to fame among book people worldwide.

An artist friend at the Gryphon prepared a painting of what the store-front would look like, displaying the name he picked. (Crowley noted that the friend, another Henry Holman bookselling protégé, later returned to England with her husband and opened a secondhand bookstore there.) He chose the name Alabaster because he liked the word for its pleasant, exotic sound; because he found a handsome pair of alabaster bookends at a flea market; and because it started with *A*. Classic phone book strategy to encourage calls wouldn't hurt. Add too that Shakespeare used the word to describe Desdemona.

The interesting and catchy name, the handsome painting of a stylish bookstore window with an appealing design, and the proprietor's realistic business plan convinced the co-op board to grant him the lease. Several weeks later, neatly furnished with the new pine shelves that Crowley had constructed and filled with his initial stock featuring literature and the arts, the Alabaster brought secondhand bookselling back to life on Fourth Avenue.

Near the end of 2000, after four successful years keeping a bookselling lamp lighted on Fourth Avenue, Steve Crowley affirmed that he was doing well and ambitious to keep selling books at the Alabaster. At the time he was still accepting drumming jobs with area bands, but drumming was now an avocation. His true calling was selling books where once Book Row had been.

Crowley noted that since he opened the Alabaster, a second new bookshop opened not far away, on Twelfth Street. The Alabaster's success in surviving four years as a start-up small business, he speculated, perhaps had been an inspiration for the Twelfth Street Books entrepreneurs to try as well. Though not exactly a Book Row revival, it might in Churchill's November 10, 1942, words be optimistically called the end of the beginning.

Crowley's store received a major boost from the *New York Times* article on February 9, 1997. Around then Andy McCarthy, with a 1997 degree in literature from New York University, became an Alabaster employee. Crowley and McCarthy entered the new millennium as the full-time staff. In 1997 the store's immediate neighbors included a vintage clothing store, a hardware store, and an Indian restaurant. At the end of 2000, the restaurant was gone and a gourmet pizza shop had taken its place.

Crowley talked about the challenges of keeping the store an interesting place for book lovers by steadily acquiring new stock. He continued to scout bookstores and sidewalk offerings throughout the New York area. The Strand often sent people who had good books the Strand didn't need over to the Alabaster. Crowley acknowledged that many of his best books came over the counter from walk-in sellers. He was especially pleased with a recently acquired set of Marc Chagall lithographs in six volumes, including twenty-four originals.

Starting in 1998, Crowley offered a service that would surely have astounded, and perhaps in some cases dismayed, the bookshop proprietors of earlier generations. He maintained an e-mail address to accommodate customers and was online with two of the major virtual bookshops populating the Internet. One of his Internet listings was a first edition of Robert C. Benchley's *Of All Things* (1921) priced at $125. A Benchley enthusiast, Crowley kept a signed Robert Benchley at home. He clearly suffered attacks of the same chronic dilemma that afflicts other book dealers: reluctance to sell books they'd rather keep.

For Internet customers, specialties listed at the Alabaster were New York, art, occult, first editions, photography. Crowley observed that in 2000 Internet purchases accounted for only about 5 percent of the Alabaster's sales, but it was an important and very welcome 5 percent. He mentioned selling another volume of Marc Chagall lithographs to a collector in Connecticut who probably would never have known about its availability without the Internet.

Such elusive items as Robert Benchley's first book, E. Annie Proulx's *Heart Song* (1988), a signed William Morris, and an original edition of Dard Hunter on papermaking could potentially reach a much greater book-buying market via the dot-com electronic trail than he could ever count on from the Fourth Avenue walk-in traffic.

Crowley's online information included an offer to "search for out-of-print, rare, used, antiquarian, and hard-to-find books." He admitted that the use of the bookstore for searches was decreasing as more customers gained access to the Internet and conducted electronic browsing on the World Wide Web for themselves. "Our finest books are displayed in a special cabinet. The problem is that walk-in customers frequently never look at them. The books we list on the Internet are brought to the attention of customers all over the world. The resulting sales make up for the decline in our search services and the business generated by successful searches," he said.

The Alabaster still, however, was first, last, and always a typical walk-in bookstore on Fourth Avenue. As in the golden age of the 1930s and 1940s, outside the neatly kept shop were four sidewalk bookstands offering discount books at $2 each. Many of the well-chosen books were attractive and appealing volumes that served the vital purpose of producing sales and also bringing customers inside. These bookstands delivered a delicate reprise of sentimental nostalgia to New Yorkers and city visitors who remembered Book Row.

Eve Claxton in *Bookstores for Book Lovers* (2000) described the Alabaster as "especially good for fiction and the arts." She wrote about the store skillfully coming through when she was struck by a sudden Proust emergency. The clerk at the Alabaster met the emergency with a 1932 set of Proust, which Claxton urgently sought for use as a birthday present. Bookstores must indeed be cherished that can rise to the occasion and meet a Proust, Rabelais, Gibbon, Irving, Twain, Edward Eggleston, Lyman Frank Baum, Ian Fleming, Zane Grey, or other literary crisis with such hurry-up efficiency.

Claxton reported that the Alabaster clerk found the desperately needed Prousts in seconds and wrapped them in plastic on a rainy day: price, $12. "The owner and his bookish employees are always happy to talk shop or trace elusive titles," she wrote. "If you listen intently you may even be able to hear the ghosts of booksellers past whispering along the avenue," she spookily hinted.

And the ghosts of booksellers past proved equal to the challenge of keeping Fourth Avenue an active if dwindled home for secondhand books. Lynn Yaeger, writing in the *New Yorker*, December 9, 2002, reported that Steve Crowley was still carrying on at the Alabaster, thriving on what Crowley described as "Strand spillover." The magazine quoted Crowley, "You know, this used to be bookstore row. People still come in all the time and say, 'Did you know there used to be fifty bookstores along here?' Now there's me." We can take that not as an epitaph for Booksellers' Row but as the unforgotten row's grateful eulogy in a new century.

In September 2003, Steve Crowley became less lonely when Michael Gallagher opened his Art & Fashion Gallery at 111 Fourth Avenue, specializing in rare books, fashion, and photography. Open-door shop bookselling then had two outlets on the Avenue. Could the future be repeating the past?

CARRYING ON

Great changes continued to take place in the technologies and locations of secondhand bookselling in the twenty-first century. The versatile and ubiquitous use of the Internet by booksellers such as Steve Crowley produced an electronically global Book Row with literally millions of books and thousands of dealers profitably involved. The scope of online book shopping and selling seemed intimidatingly complex to some who would prefer physically browsing among the actual books in an old-fashioned bookstore. As the new century rolled on, the evidence grew that the process works; the Internet moves books, lots of books.

The expertise and successes of younger bookmen such as Chris Coover, Tim Johns, and Glenn Horowitz, who trained at the Strand and moved on to other important book venues, conveyed further examples of progressive change. These highly educated bookmen with professional credentials became authorities in their work. They were indisputably the peers if not the superiors of their bookselling predecessors.

The felicitous conclusion was that secondhand, rare, and antiquarian bookselling was still being carried on effectively by outstanding practitioners, whether in traditional bookshops or in the new dot-com, world-reaching manner. And some of them, whether as students or dreamers, could in fact trace their beginnings to the shops, the shoppers, and the dedicated, eccentric, long-enduring bookselling veterans of Booksellers' Row.

CHAPTER SEVENTEEN

Book Row – Past · Present · Future

As to the rare-book game: I am very humble and shudder when I look back on my own ignorance which led me into it. I know of no game more complex. And only now have I begun to realize just how little I know about it. The actual knowledge of books— bibliography—and proper prices is insignificant when compared to the importance of knowing where they can likely be placed. And then comes the painful task of acquiring the confidence of buyers so that they'll take your copy. . . . There's many a book for which the dealer will pay 75% of resale value; because of its quick saleability; while he won't pay 35% for some overtouted slow selling plugs. . . .

It's a tough game.

—Ernest J. Wessen

In 1938 W. Somerset Maugham wrote a book to sort out his thoughts on subjects that had interested him throughout his life. He called it *The Summing Up* (1938) and stated, "To have settled one's affairs is a very good preparation to leading the rest of one's life without concern for the future. When I have finished this book I shall know where I stand." Here we have reached the summing-up stage on our journey through time to Fourth Avenue and Booksellers' Row from the end of the nineteenth century into the twenty-first. So, where *do* we stand?

"Where have we been?" and "Where do we go from here?" are basic questions that logically end a journey. Direct responses to the first question fill the preceding pages. Book Row certainly wasn't merely past history in 2003, since the Strand lived on and an active antiquarian bookstore was again functioning on Fourth Avenue. The Book Row story is an ongoing saga that encompasses more than a century as it moves forward in both reality and fiction.

The Book Row legend was alive for author John Dunning when he wrote in his World War II novel, *Two O'Clock, Eastern Wartime* (2001): "Sometimes on a Saturday he'd meet Carnahan downtown and they'd kill an afternoon prowling through the secondhand-book stores on Fourth Avenue." It seems likely that future writers telling New York stories will continue sending char-acters to Fourth Avenue, America's best-known traditional place of books.

The phenomenon of Book Row America can be said to have begun qui-etly in 1890 with the shop, called Mitchell's, of A. J. Bowden and George D. Smith at 830 Broadway and later in the 1890s, with the first go-it-alone book-store of George D. Smith at 69 Fourth Avenue. In 2003, the long record cul-minated (without ending) in the gigantic Strand at 828 Broadway (next door to the Mitchell's 1890 location!); Steve Crowley's Alabaster Bookshop at 122 Fourth Avenue; and Gallagher's at 111 Fourth Avenue; in the heart of the short stretch from Astor Place to Union Square where Book Row flourished and a lot of bookselling history was made.

Between the ambitious start-up of George D. Smith in the 1890s and the Strand, Alabaster, and Gallagher, survivors of the third millennium, came all the remarkable men and women who established the bookstores, obtained and sold the books, and gave birth to an enduring legend we permanently remember as Book Row.

Some of those dedicated, eccentric, wonderful, book-loving, knowledge-able (occasionally perhaps mad) book people populate the foregoing pages: Peter Stammer, David Kirschenbaum, Jacob Abrahams, Samuel Dauber, Nathan Pine, Alfred Goldsmith, Theodore Schulte, Will Pesky, Stanley Gilman, Samuel Weiser, Walter Goldwater, Eleanor Lowenstein, the Brussel scouts, Haskell Gruberger, and others. Among these, Haskell Gruberger alone still actively continued as a book dealer into the third millennium. But these are only some, indeed relatively few, considering the more than 110 years of bookselling on and around Fourth Avenue. The complete record of a century and all the names of all the people are unattainable. The few must represent and honor the many.

From early in the century through the 1940s we saw Book Row evolve into America's leading repository and source of old, bargain, and low-priced anti-quarian rarities for book lovers worldwide. In 1942 we took part vicariously in the formation of the Fourth Avenue Booksellers' Association, which made history as the first such association in existence.

In the 1950s we saw the Bible House, which was home and kindly mother to generations of bookstores, torn down. We saw the customer-summoning Wanamaker's department store disappear. And we saw aging sites that housed bookstores evict their bookselling tenants to rebuild as expensive co-ops, high-rent apartments, and other upscale urban uses beyond the normal means of marginal small businesses such as secondhand bookshops. (At the end of the decade, in 1959, a decision was reached at the U.S. District Court in New York City in *Grove Press Inc. v. Christenberry*. Judge Frederick van Pelt Bryan rendered the opinion that D. H. Lawrence's *Lady Chatterley's Lover* was not too shocking for the U.S. mail. The postmaster general had attacked and upheld the ban of the book as one full of "filthy words and passages" and descriptions of sexual acts. Such condemnation was, of course, a hearty sales pitch for booksellers with nerve to ignore a silly act of suppression. America in a morally mature sense was growing up, and Book Row survivors must have been amused, pleased, and a little concerned that revenue might be lost if the government would no longer help them sell a forbidden book.)

During the 1950s and 1960s as economic pressures multiplied through rent increases and as bookshop leases were lost in the name of progress (translated as the urge for greater real estate profits), the Fourth Avenue Booksellers' Association sought to alert the media and the people via publicity and public relations outreach that an internationally renowned New York City institution they would surely miss was steadily being lost.

The association accurately promoted Book Row as America's venerable counterpart of Charing Cross Road in London and the quays of the Seine in Paris. From the perspective of history, those promotional efforts in fact succeeded. To this day, the Fourth Avenue Book Row of memory is still viewed as an astonishing and colossal neighborhood of total hospitality for books, books of all subjects, shapes, sizes, values, vices, virtues. Be patient and any book ever printed and still existing outside the marble walls of treasure mausoleums eventually could be yours through Book Row. Existing no longer in reality, the Book Row of memory is still preserved as a rare American oasis of book rarities and bargains.

Cooperative advertisements sponsored by association members invited people to come to Fourth Avenue south of Union Square and "Visit the Book Center of the World." The city was asked to identify the area officially with a new street name as the Fourth Avenue Book Row. If the city heard, the city neglected to act.

Perhaps the city did see and regret what was happening to its Book Row, because the city's Department of Commerce and Public Events did offer for consideration the quixotic option of putting the threatened bookshops underground in the subway arcade between West Thirty-fourth and West Forty-second Streets. That subterranean notion struck most Fourth Avenue bookstore proprietors as a little crazy. They put up posters declaring, "The Book Row of America Will Remain As Always on Fourth Avenue." The die was cast. They would hold on while they could with rueful dignity, and Book Row would quietly fade away as the booksellers scattered and their walk-in bookshops one by one departed from Fourth Avenue.

THE LONG GOOD-BYES

At the end of Raymond Chandler's *The Long Goodbye* (1954) Philip Marlowe says, "I never saw any of them again—except the cops. No way has yet been invented to say goodbye to them." During the time that Chandler's thriller was being featured at new-book stores in the mid-1950s, the long series of good-byes to the disappearing Book Row stores began—and continued into the 1990s.

While some of the stores reopened elsewhere in New York, others moved to locations beyond the city, from Long Island to Everywhere, U.S.A. The Abbey Bookshop, owned by George Foss, was eulogized in the newspapers as the last bookstore to close its doors on Fourth Avenue. Forced to move by financial circumstances, Foss reduced his stock from over twenty-five thousand books to about five thousand and reopened at 79 East Tenth Street in much smaller quarters, at a much lower rent.

When the Abbey Bookshop left, the thoroughfare that had been so hospitable to some three dozen bookstores at one time was turned over to restaurants, dry cleaners, and apartment dwellers—but one likes to think there is still the lingering aura of several million books that had come and gone in the neighborhood over the decades. George Foss was sad to leave Fourth Avenue. His sadness was shared by book lovers from New York to the antipodes who regretted the demise of a grand tradition.

The dealers who didn't quit altogether or establish new walk-in shops at other neighborhoods generally stopped serving book buyers directly. They focused on mail-order bookselling by means of catalogues, and later in the century, by means of the Internet. In general even the bookmen who were forced away from the Fourth Avenue area continued in the profession that had been the core of their lives.

The Fourth Avenue booksellers under pressure to move on generally tended to fit the peppery insights of Ohio bookman Ernest J. Wessen, source of the famous *Midlands Notes* catalogues and the Americana specialist behind Thomas Winthrop Streeter's distinguished collection. After working most of the night on one of his catalogues, Wessen wrote another bookman, "I have no justification in writing this long screed, other than that I live in hopes that one day you'll wake up, and provide the trade with a competent rare-book dealer, so very badly needed as few are coming up." In a letter of November 4, 1941, writing to bookman Arthur Phillips, Wessen in effect lectured his whole profession: "Whether you know it or not, you're in this game for the rest of your days, and whether you arise to the level of a top-flight scout, dealer, or collector (and there's little difference between them), or sink to the level of the common dregs of those three . . . is a matter that is right up to you."

In New York a few hardy survivors kept their almost patriarchal stores alive until the 1990s. It was February 1990 before Walter Caron finally and with reluctance closed what was then the oldest book shop in New York City, the Isaac Mendoza Book Company, 1894–1990, which practiced the Book Row tradition of selling quality secondhand books a few city blocks downtown from Book Row on Ann Street.

Charles Carillo, writing in the *New York Post* (February 27, 1990), made a final tour of the nonagenarian, legendary institution and reported, "A great bookshop makes you feel as if you're at sea, and that's Mendoza's creaky wooden floors, staircases that lean this way and that, and not a level surface in sight." Walter Caron noted that a Mendoza customer had called the store one of the last oases downtown. Another customer lamented the loss of a rare place where you could spend the day if you liked in the relaxing vicinity of books. Walter Goldwater used Mendoza's as a source for stock at his own University Place Book Shop. His chosen successor, Bill French, kept the University Place Book Shop open until the end of 1995.

The poignant farewells in the 1990s of these venerable book places received appropriate sentimental attention in the New York media. The final departures of the last survivors, except for that amazing immortal maverick the Strand, both signaled and symbolized the end of an era. The end of any era always brings concerns and worries about the future.

The termination, at least for a while, of the Booksellers' Row era on Fourth Avenue was no exception. Where would secondhand- and rare-book stores find a place for themselves? Could they have faith, as Stephen Sondheim put it in a *West Side Story* lyric, that "there's a place for us"? Where would readers and collectors go to find the reasonably priced used, secondhand, rare, and antiquarian books that were as essential to them as basic tools of survival like air, food, and water?

HAIL TO THE NEW

In the autumn of 1996 when Steve Crowley returned secondhand bookselling to Fourth Avenue at number 122, the Alabaster Bookshop, with the exception of George Foss's Abbey Bookshop, was the first such bookshop launched on former Book Row's main street in two decades. Later another shop opened not far away, on Twelfth Street between University Place and Fifth Avenue, then Gallagher's in 2003. Welcomed though they were by book lovers, three bookstores in a neighborhood did not a Book Row make.

A few weeks before the birth of the Alabaster, Michael Cooper reported in the *New York Times* (August 18, 1996) about a new cluster (a short row?) of bookstores that had developed in the West Eighteenth Street area between Sixth Avenue (some say Avenue of the Americas) and Fifth Avenue. Cooper wrote, "As large bookstore chains pop up throughout the city, writers, readers, and other bibliophiles fear the demise of the independent bookseller. But in the shadow of Barnes & Noble's main store and sales annex at Fifth Avenue and Eighteenth Street, small bookstores are thriving." The small stores profited from the book traffic drawn to the area by the Barnes & Noble outlet just as Fourth Avenue stores profited from the Wanamaker's clientele.

The Eighteenth Street bookshops described by Cooper would not have been out of place or strangers on old Book Row. Books of Wonder specialized in children's books and was especially strong in L. Frank Baum books about that over-the-rainbow world of Oz, including Oz books in other languages, as the *Wonderful Wizard of Oz* (1900) centennial approached in 2000. A particular treasure at Books of Wonder was a first edition of J. R. R. Tolkien's *The Lord of the Rings* (1954–55) coupled with a holograph Tolkien letter priced at $12,500. Among used and out-of-print bookshops nearby were Academy Books, featuring scholarly and literary works, and Skyline Books and Records, which focused on literature and theater books.

After the disappearance of the Fourth Avenue Book Row, the Eighteenth Street book enclave somewhat quieted the apprehensions of book seekers that they might never again have access to fine browsing and good book buys in a single New York neighborhood. The small but thriving West Side bookshop group near a Barnes & Noble superstore gave a modicum of credibility to the theory that secondhand bookshops naturally and profitably cluster together. Thus time, that cunning maestro of change, might even in some segment of the future generate another Book Row not unlike the earlier versions to satisfy the vast and varied book needs of Manhattan dwellers and visitors. Or maybe not.

Interviewed for this account in 1989, Larry Moskowitz, speculating about the prospects for secondhand bookselling in the future, was certain only that it would go through cycles as it always had, that it would be ruled by changing times, technologies, and metropolitan circumstances. He expected tomorrow to be different from today, but different *how* was a topic for those who enjoyed the sport of guessing.

Moskowitz commented that perhaps some book dealers on Fourth Avenue thought or pretended they could go on indefinitely pretty much as they had in the past. The city changed around them; but they didn't, couldn't, or wouldn't accomplish necessary changes in harmony with the city. On the other hand, what realistic change was possible for a bookshop owner, when his rent suddenly shot out of manageable sight, except to move?

Moskowitz hazarded one prediction, that specialist bookstores would tend to increase in number in comparison with generalist bookstores. He was concerned about the challenge to books and consequently to traditional bookstores by electronic and technological innovations that were producing a few shrill predictions of the conventional book's obsolescence and disappearance. Larry Moskowitz, echoing probably every bookstore proprietor and customer who loved Book Row and the casebound products of Book Row, hoped the book would prevail—expected the book to prevail. He had no doubt there would continue to be good secondhand bookstores somewhere in New York and elsewhere to conserve books and make them available to those, whether the many or the few, who never had and never would lose the desire to read— and preferably to read a book.

As for Fourth Avenue and bookstores of the future, even with the solitary and valiant Alabaster Bookshop and Gallagher's on the job alone, who could say?

What Now, Fourth Avenue?

In the summer of 2000 the area that once had been a low-rent, patient, and understanding host for Book Row was caught up in a real estate boom and neighborhood revolution that was driving out the modest old and bringing in the luxurious, expensive new. The transformation to glitz, glamour, and staggering (for most) prices posed this question: Is there a future for anything similar to old Book Row in the sort of neighborhood that has $5,000-per-month rents on apartments in formerly rundown buildings, and condominium apartments in new towers that cost millions, just for a little living space up in the air above Manhattan? Obvious answer: probably not.

Fourteenth Street was called the crossroads of New York by an area enthusiast in a detailed real estate report by Nadine Brozan in the *New York Times* (August 13, 2000). Obviously a powerful argument can be made that at every crossroads there should be secondhand bookstores of high quality and variety such as those that used to thrive near New York's year 2000 crossroads. But no mention was made of such a special neighborhood need in a discussion that predominantly celebrated the heady promise of high-priced space, not high-quality books.

Not everyone was cheerful about the triumph of chic and the threat to diversity in what had been the city's primary region of old books. "When neighborhoods become upscale . . . diversity goes out the window," warned one resident who didn't want to lose everything the area had been in Book Row days.

One positive sign, friendly at least to the concept of secondhand bookstores, was the fact that many academic institutions remained at or close to the area, including Baruch College, Cardozo School of Law, Cooper Union, New School University, New York University, and Pratt Institute. The combined effect of these institutions produced an immense academic hub second to none. Students and books go together. Well, at one time they did. Maybe they still do.

As part of the upscale metamorphosis in progress, New York University was sponsoring the construction of large student dormitories in the area, including dormitories at and near the former site on Fourteenth Street of the famous German restaurant Luchow's, where Caruso and Paderewski dined; where Gus Kahn wrote the words for "Yes, Sir, That's My Baby"; where H. L. Mencken found solace and German beer when *American Mercury* business forced him to visit New York City from his native Baltimore.

It was at Luchow's that the Fourth Avenue Booksellers' Association held an important organizational meeting in March 1959 for considering challenges to survival and ways of meeting them. Anyway, the presence of over fifteen hundred students where Luchow's used to be should in the future provide customers for used books whenever the students can safely extricate themselves without inner traumas from their keyboards and monitors. Steve Crowley and the Alabaster as well as Gallagher's, let's optimistically hope, may still be around the corner on Fourth Avenue. But where will other bookstores with scholarly, literary, and scientific stocks be for urgent searches when footnotes and bibliographies confront students with obscure titles—online perhaps?

Virtual Bookshops and E-Reading

Concomitantly with a new century and a new millennium in 2000–2001 came an explosion of online bookshops, electronic handheld reading devices (e-books), and eager avowals by committed, card-carrying techies that traditional reading in old-fashioned books would gradually become a thing of the primitive past, since e-gadgets made e-reading so much more versatile and practical.

A typical e-gadget advertisement of the time rapturously invited book buyers and readers to reflect on the magic of having instantly at their fingertips books, journals, and magazines, with new titles promptly available simply by plugging in to a telephone line. What could be easier, simpler, faster? Those agile fingertips had virtually a whole library on tap and ready for the screening. No more untidy and time-devouring browsing through dusty, crowded shops. No more searching for titles you can't find. No more waiting for the book you want to show up. Plug in and ye shall instantly receive— assuming, of course, the title you want is e-worthy of e-you and thus appropriate for inclusion in the electronic archive of books worth preserving. What reader could ask for anything more!

Well, in fact, some, like Oliver Twist, did request more: More books, please. Real books. Those conventional readers with a bias for the familiar didn't want streamlined contraptions designed for plugging in, recharging, screen reading, and keypunching instead of page turning. They wanted more old-fashioned books, printed on paper and neatly bound in cardboard, cloth, or leather, thank you very much.

Truth be told, some readers ambitious to be in tune with the latest tech trends tried to love the new gadgets and to swear by them. Conventional readers cynically wondered just how long the fad would last before those e-readers thrust the awesome devices from their sight and picked up a real book. It's a free country, or should be, and *chacun à son goût*.

Fair or not, the idea of electronic gadgets replacing books frankly seemed to real book lovers rather like living with Guy Montag among flames, terror, and totalitarian folly inside Ray Bradbury's *Fahrenheit 451* (1953), where books threatened social order and had to be put to the torch. In a 1979 coda for his classic, Bradbury warned against monkeying recklessly with books: "It is a mad world and it will get madder if we allow the minorities, be they dwarf or giant, orangutan or dolphin, nuclear-head or water-conservationalist, pro-computerologist or Neo-Luddite, simpleton or sage, to interfere with aesthetics." Replacing books with e-substitutes also seemed to many traditionalists a case of voluntarily moving in with Winston Smith and loving Big Brother at the Ministry of Truth in George Orwell's prophetic *Nineteen Eighty-Four* (1949). "By 2050—earlier, probably—all real knowledge of Oldspeak will have disappeared. The whole literature of the past will have been destroyed. Chaucer, Shakespeare, Milton, Byron—they'll exist only in Newspeak versions, not merely changed into something different. . . . The whole climate of thought will be different. In fact there will *be* no thought," predicted Smith's friend and comrade Syme.

In March 2000, when Stephen King's novella *Riding the Bullet* was made available only in e-book format or by downloading into a computer, speculations mushroomed electronically and in print that Gutenberg's age was on the way out, that the digital era had arrived and taken command. An electronic reader at the time was marketed as the forerunner of the postprint future with grandiose predictions that e-books by 2009 would outsell regular books, that newspapers by 2018 would no longer be available on paper, and that Webster's

2020 definition of a book would emphasize a comprehensive communication format utilizing "writing on a screen."

Book collector Gordon Pfeiffer, writing in *Delaware Bibliophiles Endpapers* (September 2000), referred to these developments and wrote, "All of this has frightening implications. First of all reading from a television tube is not the same as reading from a book. They should invent another word for it such as 'eread' used 'I am going to read my eread.' Second, what will collectors collect? I've seen nothing aesthetically pleasing about software tapes or discs." Pfeiffer, wondering if books are threatened with extinction, declared as most book lovers defiantly will echo, "I sure hope not."

Among those echoers was Harold Bloom, author of *How to Read and Why*. After hearing Professor Bloom on C-SPAN's *Booknotes*, Roger Rosenblatt in a *Time* (October 16, 2000) essay wrote, "He was full of hope and sorrow for the literary life that is mistreated and unvalued today. He spoke up for Cervantes and Shakespeare. . . . He hated e-books." Another who didn't "talk digital" was Victor Navasky, publisher and editorial director of the *Nation*. As quoted in the *New Yorker* (November 13, 2000), he declared, "Everything starts with print on paper."

Granting the sovereignty of paper and printing, why not also welcome e-books and e-reading as an alternative means of conveying and receiving information, just as word processing makes a reasonable alternative to no. 2 pencils and manual typewriters? Readers have every right to peruse their books electronically if that's their druthers. Read and enjoy! Robert Bolick, a McGraw-Hill vice president, did just that, according to his op-ed piece in the *New York Times* (July 7, 2000) provocatively entitled, "Curling Up with an E-Book." He wrote about reading the e-book edition of *Extraordinary Popular Delusions and the Madness of Crowds*: "That book had pulled me into its world. It didn't matter that I was looking at a screen, that I was tapping and pushing buttons to advance the text in readable chunks; just as if I were sitting with a good print book and turning pages, nothing mattered but the magic of the book itself." Bolick discussed various e-book benefits—fifty pounds of books in a two-pound device, access to whole libraries via the Web. Maintaining that the book business "must adapt to the digital world," he concluded, "The e-book opens a world of possibilities. It is not necessarily better than printed books, nor need it supplant them. But its time is here."

Robert Bolick made a reasonable case for a reading world that accommodates both books and e-books. Yet even most readers who are comfortable with screens and push buttons would probably agree that considering the book as a desirable item to collect for permanent retention, the paper version wins every time. Charles Mackay's masterful 1841 study, *Extraordinary Popular Delusions and the Madness of Crowds,* no doubt offers a splendid e-read as it does a paper read. Yet who doubts the decision, given a choice between software that has no meaning except through an intricate device and an always ready-to-use copy of the 1841 first edition, the 1852 second edition, or even the 1932 verbatim reprint by L. C. Page & Company? The 1932 reprint carried an admiring foreword by financier Bernard M. Baruch, and a publisher's note included the following paragraph from a published interview of Baruch: "As we sat in Mr. Baruch's library, renewing an old friendship, he reached from a book-shelf a battered calf-bound volume, the perusal of which he said had saved him millions of dollars."

The book was Charles Mackay's influential work on mass psychology, communities and countries going mad, and the author's perception that people "go mad in herds, while they only recover their senses slowly, and one by one." Would Bernard Baruch have calmly handed over his paper-printed, calf-bound, digitally challenged, user-friendly companion of many readings in exchange for an e-substitute? Frankly, we doubt it. And frankly, why postulate such an exchange? Baruch could well have afforded both versions. The digital present and the paper past in the form of such fine old books can certainly unite the new and the old to serve the variegated needs of readers— may their numbers increase—in the future.

Along with a ballooning of electronic competitors utilizing devices and formats for traditional books, the online availability of books through the Internet also offered competition for bookshops. As reported by Neil Morgan in the *San Diego Union-Tribune* (June 27, 2003), during a lecture at the William Andrews Clark Memorial Library in Los Angeles, Jason Epstein, the author, editor, and founder of Anchor Books, speaking to book collectors and antiquarian booksellers, warned that the era of the printed book may end due to the transmission of books by the Internet. He noted that computer-published books could "start an era as significant as Gutenberg's." "Authors can put their books on the Internet before they finish them," Epstein stated. "They may never finish them at all." Neil Morgan looked on the bright side: Commenting on the book treasures at the Clark Library, he observed, "If books are no longer made, such collections will offer even more cultural insight."

Also, for certain, in a bleak age with only Internet-generated books, prices on traditional books will enjoy stratospheric boosts. Hang on to those old dust-jacketed, paper-filled, buckram-bound volumes!

A rapidly growing number of walk-in bookshops also utilized e-mail and made their stock available online as a proven means of supplementing in-store sales. Steve Crowley at the Alabaster Bookshop on Fourth Avenue typified the dual-service approach. The Alabaster received the bulk of its business from walk-in traffic, but the Internet gave the shop a much broader international market, and the sales thus generated were valuable contributions to the store's overall revenue. In addition to providing accessibility to his customers through e-mail, Crowley listed the Alabaster with two of the largest online bookshop consortia and found them productive.

One of these groups advertised itself as the world's largest international marketplace of used, rare, and out-of-print books, with over fifty-two hundred booksellers and 15 million books in its database. The very size of that dot-com operation as well as other so-called virtual bookshops rendered it difficult, perhaps mission impossible, for any individual bookshops, even those on the scale of the Strand, to rival such numbers. Thus readers and collectors seeking specific titles could access the Web and quite often find even obscure items quickly somewhere among the thousands of stores and millions of books listed.

Even so, there were manifest drawbacks. The customer's approach to booksellers via the Internet allowed nothing that equaled or simulated the experience of entering a real live bookstore, roaming among the shelves, and examining book after book after book in the sanguine calisthenic of reaching purchase decisions. Internet bookshops facilitated title searches, but a description on a screen didn't exactly qualify as even a remote simulation of on-site browsing among the books.

In effect, the Internet supplied a gigantic, reasonably well organized book catalogue that could sometimes benefit book buyers who knew precisely what they wanted. But for those who wanted to cruise up and down aisles, evaluate many books, thoughtfully turn the pages of tempting ones on the spot, and enjoy benign agonies of indecision, an online book journey could be only a tepid, frustrating, and disappointing trip. Lawrence and Nancy Goldstone in

Slightly Chipped make a strong case for hands-on involvement: "To attract new people, to keep the field alive, the industry needs to provide opportunities to see the books—in person—to handle the books, to speak to an educated, passionate professional. . . . With the Internet, you'll never be surprised, never find something you weren't already looking for, never see the fold-out map at the beginning of *Kidnapped.* The Internet is good for acquiring and amassing, but not for experiencing. The Internet may be more functional than going to bookshops in person; it may be more efficient; it may be more private; it may be more cost-effective; and it is certainly more convenient. It just isn't as much fun."

Yet we should not indulge in facetiously and pointlessly knocking the virtual bookshops. Instead let's rejoice that they exist and provide a reliable, alternative route to books. Just as cultural tolerance and technological reality support the argument that e-books and traditional books can exist compatibly to meet the needs of different readers, so too online, walk-in, and mail-order bookselling can be acknowledged as acceptable and compatible variations on the same theme of putting books in the hands and on the library shelves of readers and collectors.

What has to be guarded against is allowing online book marketing to force bookstores in the Book Row retail shop tradition out of business. British antiquarian bookseller Paul Minet reported in *Book Source Monthly* (November 2000) that at the 2000 Congress and Book Fair (in Edinburgh, Scotland) of the Antiquarian Booksellers' Association, many dealers stated that they had closed their retail shops and were doing business exclusively on the Internet.

Paul Minet wrote, "The nursery of the collector and the source of books for much of the trade, not to mention the clearance house for private sellers, must continue to be the retail shop." Minet recounted a friendly meeting with his bookman friend Hylton Bayntun-Coward outside a bookshop at Dulverton on the edge of Exmoor. "You can't have such personal encounters on the Internet," Minet concluded.

Clearly in the start-up years of the twenty-first century, electronic technology was having a strong and lasting impact on all aspects of human culture, including bookselling, book buying, and perhaps book reading. An incredible e-world was in the process of being discovered like new continents, explored like a terra incognita, and developed like everybody's business.

Some zealous e-world advocates blithely maintained that the Fourth Avenue bookshops and Book Row or their equivalents enjoyed a long run and dismissed them with "Have a nice history, good-bye." Now, they insisted, the modern, online bookshops humming along Dot-Com Avenue by the thousands must and would have their turn. "Stand back, paper booksellers, gangway, we're coming through, e-yi, e-yi, e-yo," blasphemed extreme e-fanatics. Bookstore sentimentalists, most with thousands of paper books on their shelves, listened politely and smiled tolerantly. There was no point arguing with zealots and wasting time that could be better spent looking for more books.

What, No Bookshops!

The wild surmise drifting in and out of twenty-first-century rhetoric, that old-fashioned books would have no lasting place in the e-world, included the inescapable conclusion that secondhand and antiquarian bookstores would also obviously have no place. The likelihood was nil that used-e-book stores would be needed to serve new generations of collectors. The idea of no bookstores brought shivers, of course, and memories of the distraught office workers in Frank Loesser's *How to Succeed in Business Without Really Trying,* with their despairing lament, "What, no coffee!" "What, no bookshops!" for many among us would strike a deeper note of horror, a sharper stab of terror.

Most of us who swarmed through Book Row in its salad days became reconciled by the 1990s to the wistful reality that it was gone. But we also decided it need not be forgotten. As Hamlet realized about his ghostly papa, we reluctantly realized about the Fourth Avenue bookshops that we were not likely in this world to look upon their like again, at least not in their former numbers and glory, with ten-cent classics on the tables outside and $2 first editions waiting for takers on shelves inside.

The science fiction hypothesis that there was perhaps somewhere nearby an alternative universe with old Book Row still intact and five-cent double-dip ice cream cones and new books with cloth covers and sewn signatures intrigued a few imaginative romantics. But where was the door and the key to that inviting cosmos? What good was it if we couldn't actually go there with an empty book bag plus a few dollars and browse the bargain bins for a healthy first edition of Mackay's 1841 classic about mass delusions and crowd madness, say, or whatever at the moment gripped our wandering readers' fancies? If we started thinking about it too much we might get teary-eyed wondering where future readers and collectors might go to find a mint first edition of *Book Row* (2004).

Many were almost as fond of the recollections as they were of the books they had accumulated through the years from the Book Row shops. If the bookshops and the cherished FOBs (Friends of Books) who ran them were gone for keeps, maybe the Fourth Avenue experience could be kept alive in memories. Indeed perhaps overindulgence while savoring nostalgia even turned some of us into book fanatics during the struggle for survival against the e-fanatics.

Perhaps slightly overdosed on nostalgia, Roy Meador in *Book Source Monthly*, "Book Row When Serendipity Was in Flower" (April 2000), stated, "When hope imagines returning to Book Row, musing can turn militant. I join the IBA (Irate Book Army), charging with weapons of prose and poetry, restoring Fourth Avenue to its bookshop majesty. . . . Unkempt yet hospitable structures are as they were, waiting amid East Side squalor for return of the books to a place that was grand to know and good to remember. Shall we dream on?"

In a paper for the Typophiles, Marvin Mondlin wrote,

> Bookselling, if one has curiosity, is a never-ending process of learning to discriminate. Most used and antiquarian booksellers, like most people, have self-imposed limitations. One dealer knows modern poetry and fiction, another art, a third history, a fourth the biological or physical sciences, yet another knows American imprints, and another still covers religion. The fields are many; and there was always a Book Row specialist who was skilled at recognizing value in an area or a group of cognate areas. Book Row also had generalists with broad and refined tastes who could see what appeared to be trivia as the important rarities they sometimes were. The generalist can see nuggets in the sand, can in a word *place* an item in terms of its cultural and commercial value.

All these varied booksellers, each proudly and authoritatively wearing different hats of expertise, were regulars in the Book Row shops.

Even if we are not likely to look upon their like again, there is this to remember: They were there in all seasons for going on ten decades, the book people and bookshops in what were very good times for bookselling, book finding, and book buying. They were there on Fourth Avenue and surrounding streets in New York City during a special century for genuine books, true books, books that did not fall apart when exposed to a second, third, or fourth reading. They were there, the booksellers and their customers, who together produced and maintained the remarkable institution that is also known and perpetually remembered as Book Row.

EPILOGUE
Book Row Forever Redux

Nonetheless, a civilization without retail booksellers is unimaginable. Like shrines and other sacred meeting places, bookstores are essential artifacts of human nature. The feel of a book taken from the shelf and held in the hand is a magical experience, linking writer to reader. . . . Tomorrow's stores will have to be what the Web cannot be: tangible, intimate, and local; communal shrines, perhaps with coffee bars offering pleasure and wisdom in the company of others who share one's interests, where the book one wants can always be found and surprises and temptations spring from every shelf.

—JASON EPSTEIN, *Book Business: Publishing Past Present and Future* (2001)

MEYER BERGER, A much-loved archaeologist of urban facts and curiosa in his *New York Times* column "About New York," in 1955 described his special beat as the "City of Endless Change." In another column that year, Berger wrote about the worsening plight of New York's antiquarian and secondhand bookselling businesses as a metropolitan change to regret. "Many now face eviction to make way for high-priced apartment houses," he wrote. The column was an advance warning of slow recession and sad days ahead for Manhattan's internationally famed secondhand book center known as Book Row, the liveliest place in America devoted to the buying and selling of antiquarian books.

Sellers and seekers of old, rare, used, secondhand, discarded, bargain, and antiquarian books could have heeded Meyer Berger's report as a social physician's rueful diagnosis and forecast of steady decline and gloomy times, though it was years too early for final epitaphs and mourning.

Book-questing individuals and institutions bent on the pursuit of elusive volumes were too busy hunting in the 1950s to worry much about the future of their cherished bookstores. If retrenchment began and fine old bookstores closed or moved elsewhere, many bookshops in the 1950s were still open and awaiting hopeful customers with shopping lists of titles, sometimes eagerly displayed, sometimes tightly protected like poker players' aces. Book Row for eager book seekers continued to be the "happy hunting ground," as Andreas Brown at New York's Gotham Book Mart labeled it. Anywhere along Book Row the very next shelf might deliver *the* book. So the view then was to let the future come in its own foul time or fair. Meanwhile let the search go on!

Journalist Edward Robb Ellis, author of *The Ellis Diary* and remembered as an American twentieth-century Pepys, in 1955 had a greater personal worry than the long-term future of New York used-book selling. He confided to his famous diary on August 2: "When my right foot was broken two months ago today as I covered a subway accident for the *World-Telegram,* here was my first reaction: 'My God! I may never be able to prowl the Fourth Avenue bookstores again.'"

Book lovers in New York City, across America, and indeed worldwide for nearly two more decades enjoyed access to Booksellers' Row, alias Book Row, that bibliopole and bibliopolist phenomenon of Fourth Avenue and environs. New York Book Row was still reasonably well, busy, with a lot of life left— the haven for lost books, refuge for readers, oasis for collectors, browser's paradise. For bookish devotees of happy endings rather than sad endings and bleak departures, Book Row was a ready refuge. Book Row then was perhaps America's number one sanctuary for happy endings, the treasure trail where the hard-to-find was often found.

Book Row then, for those of us who pursued fugitive folios, queer quartos, evasive octavos, easily outdid with reality all the make-believe of Hollywood. Somewhere in the shops of Book Row if you didn't find the book you wanted, as Christopher Morley pointed out, through serendipity you might happen on a book you wanted even more. Thus even in the endlessly changing city with soaring rents and other threatening symptoms, Book Row long continued as New York's main magnet for true book lovers of the genus and species *Homo bibliophilus.*

The stereotypes of book seekers, whether readers or collectors (some amazing individuals are actually both!), is that they come with and without bifocals, in all sizes, shapes, genders, tastes, and races. However, the stereotype of used and antiquarian booksellers typically pictures them as rather quaint, crusty, shrewd, amiably untidy, eccentric variations on Roger Mifflin in Morley's *Parnassus on Wheels* and *The Haunted Bookshop.* Actually it wouldn't be a bad old world if New York and other cities too contained blocks of bookstores run by dealers with the wit, civility, knowledge, and book-adoring panache of Roger Mifflin. But that was certainly never New York's Book Row, where booksellers ran the gamut from gentle to fierce, helpful to get-outta-here, absolutely honest to watch out!, knowing-almost-all to knowing-almost-nothing, and wide variations within these broad parameters.

Charles P. Everitt, a dealer-graduate of Book Row and author of *The Adventures of a Treasure Hunter* (1951), once cynically, maybe tongue-in-cheek, told a book scout looking for an honest dealer, "You may find me fifty percent honest, which is way above the average." The truth is, we didn't go to Book Row for lessons in virtue and verisimilitude; we went there for books acquired on our behalf by literate merchandisers who recognized the values of books as commodities. We weren't disposed to sniff indignantly if the bookseller priced to make a profit or even tried maneuvering to make a killing. Business after all is business, and we wanted the books.

Along Book Row, we found merchants with the usual human range of virtues and vices in the, for us, noble business of buying and selling books. Many, perhaps most, of the booksellers esteemed books and knew them not only as complex cultural objects expertly designed over centuries to deliver knowledge, beauty, and joy forever but also as objects of physical beauty and appeal with superb bindings and magnificent illustrations.

Alex Auswaks, in his short story "The Napoleon of Booksellers," has his protagonist declare, "Libraries are just there as book depositories. It is we who ensure books get to the people who will read and appreciate them." There's a truism repeatedly confirmed—even libraries often receive their finest books through the good offices and sharp memories of watchful book-sellers. The symbiotic process starts with the bookseller because that's his job. For decades this magical system of recycling and preserving books was diligently and expertly accomplished by the booksellers of Book Row. The Fourth Avenue book dealers exemplified the curious mingling of book sentiments linking old books, antiquarian jewels, rare and unusual books, as well as secondhand volumes for needy students and the fortunate few—simply called readers!

Most of us who visited Book Row as customers tended to view the area as an almost sacred place of books managed (at a small profit) by benign if rather seedy walking bibliographies and mobile encyclopedias who seemed reasonably ready and occasionally eager to help readers and collectors acquire all the world's knowledge in both hardcovers and paperbacks at fairly reasonable and sometimes surprisingly low prices—unless, of course, we were wealthy collectors worthy of the spectacularly priced special stuff that was either well hidden or locked in safes.

Although these East Side book emporia became celebrated as Book Row, perhaps a more apt name might have been Book Cluster. The winning title was less than accurate since a row is typically a series arranged in a reasonably straight line. Book Row showed no respect for a straight line. The stores associated with Book Row were widely scattered; and book people who began their careers on Fourth Avenue as alumni of the row took their experience, skills, and savvy not only uptown and downtown but also to other states and countries. But Book Row it was—and now in memory and history, forever remains Book Row.

Changing times and rising rents among other complex influences did bring Book Row, with a few hardy exceptions such as the Strand, to a much regretted demise before the end of the twentieth century. Yet interest in Book Row and its innumerable stories about exciting book finds, boisterous book people, and tenacious customers through the decades has never flagged. Although most shops are gone, memories linger of all those happy endings when elusive books were found and mutually satisfying transactions were completed. In bibliolore, the march of Book Row yarns goes endlessly on.

Legends grow with the years concerning the redoubtable and improbable characters who roamed, flourished, haunted, and hunted at Book Row. Book Row was in part perhaps a state of mind, a Shangri-la of first edition tales, a book land of colorful fantasies embellished in the course of years over coffee at now departed Luchow's on Fourteenth Street or any among the area's ubiquitous coffee shops tolerant of leisurely book talk over the steamy cups.

Legends, yes, but legends containing the ingredients of plain and abiding truth. Book Row was always real people engaged in a business they loved and a business they waged with considerable pleasure amid varying degrees of solvency. Even if they could have earned more as stockbrokers, airline pilots, ministers, or cattle rustlers, they invested their lives in books; and many did so in part for the satisfaction of delivering special satisfaction to their customers.

The glow of appreciation a book lover showed as he left a Book Row shop clutching a volume he had found at last after a seemingly endless and quixotic quest was seen somewhere practically every day on Book Row. It's a glow unlike any other, and the radiance could at times make even grouchy book-sellers worried about the rent feel better for delivering a bit of happiness in a cloudy world.

The Encyclopedia of New York City (Yale, 1995), edited by Kenneth T. Jackson, recognizes the validity of the place and its purpose under the simple entry "Book Row" with this description: "An area of secondhand bookstores concentrated from the late nineteenth century in seven blocks along 4th Avenue between Union Square and Astor Place."

That capsule portrait should include a restless caravan of people, book-sellers, and book buyers. They created the diverse and widely flung Book Row on and around Fourth Avenue through their shops, deals, maneuvers, bar-gaining, strategies, discoveries, purchases. They band together across an expanse of time and choreograph an endless cavalcade of book stories unfor-gettably left behind by the bookstores of Book Row.

ACKNOWLEDGMENTS

⅜ THIS PROJECT BENEFITED immensely and indispensably from the support, encouragement, guidance, and, above all, the Book Row memories of many generous individuals. Marvin Mondlin interviewed dozens of active and retired booksellers who owned or worked in bookshops on Fourth Avenue and the surrounding neighborhood from the glory days of Book Row into the twenty-first century. Marvin Mondlin and Roy Meador interviewed as well numerous book buyers and collectors who frequented Book Row through the decades and remembered it affectionately and well.

Many who were not available for personal interviews shared their memories and reflections at length through enthusiastic and detailed correspondence. The diverse experiences, stories, triumphs, failures, viewpoints, and insights of those booksellers and Book Row customers provided much of the substance, sinew, color, and content of this historical memoir about a time and place of books and the devoted people who sold and bought them.

The authors thank the following with deep appreciation for their interest in and gracious contributions to the *Book Row* endeavor. The unique recollections of those who were there and the varied expressions of support by younger book lovers eager to know about the legendary Booksellers' Row they could not experience personally facilitated and ultimately made possible this project reflecting many minds, hearts, and books.

L. CRAIG ANDERSON
RON ANTONUCCI
CHUCK ANTONY
MILTON APPLEBAUM
JACK BARTFIELD
NICHOLAS A. BASBANES
FRED BASS
NANCY BASS
TERRY BELANGER
BARBARA BERNARDINI
JACK BIBLO
TOM BISHOP

NORMAN BLAUSTEIN
BEN BLOM
MAX BRESLOW
GERTRUDE BRIGGS
HENRY VICTOR BRISTOW
BENJAMIN BROMBERG
MATTHEW BRUCCOLI
ARTHUR CARDUNER
WALTER CARON
JOSEPH CATALANO
THE REVEREND OLIVER T. CHAPIN
BEV CHENEY

Jacob Chernofsky
Diane Clark
Herman Cohen
Joseph J. Cohen
Louis Cohen
Aaron J. Cooke
Chris Coover
Steve Crowley
Dick Cuffari
Everett V. Cunningham
Howard Daitz
Nate Denenburg
Donald C. Dickinson
Louis Dienes
Wally Dobelis
Tom Dunn
Maggie DuPriest
Edward Robb Ellis
Amy Ferrante
David Fisher
Peter Thomas Fisher
Robert D. Fleck
William French
Howard Frisch
Judith Fulmer
Martin Gilbert
Linda Gochfeld, M.D.
Harry Patrick Gold
Sam Goldberg
    (of Goldberg & Hatterer)
Eugene Goldwater, M.D.
Chelsea Goodwin
Johanna Gottlieb
Thomas J. Gould
Herman Graf
Joe Grasso

Haskell Gruberger
Max Gulack
Seymour Hacker
Claiborne Hancock
Leo Hershkowitz
Richard L. Hoffman
John Holbrooke
Glenn Horowitz
John C. Huckans
Timothy Johns
William Kerr
Karen Kimball
David Kirschenbaum
Herman W. Kitchen
Philip and Carol Kitchin
Richard Kollmar
Irwin Kraft
Eugene Kramer
Bernard Kraus
Jeffrey Kraus
Louis Krup
Robert and Arline Latas
Richard Leahy
Gershon Legman
Max Leleiko
Sylvia Leleiko
Jacques Leobold
Robert Lescher and the staff
    of Lescher & Lescher, ltd.
Frederick Lightfoot
Janice Longone
Eleanor Lowenstein
Richard Lowenstein
Kim Kaufman Malin
Mary Ann Malkin
Sol M. Malkin

Maurizio Martino
L. R. Maxwell
Helen Meador
Jerry and Alice Meador
David Meyer
Wanda Miller
Paul Minet
Arthur Minters
Sonya Wohl Mirsky
Lee Mohanlall
Rina Mondlin
Maggie Morgan
Larry Moskowitz
Peter Mustardo
Barnet Newman
Tom Nicely
Gerald T. Niles, m.d.
Stanley Nosek
Irving Oaklander
The O'Leary Family
Samuel Orlinik
Jay Platt
Stephen Pober
Doug Price
Dennis J. Quigley
Lawrence Rao
Theo Rehak and the Typophiles
Ellen Reiss
Milton Reissman
Shepard Rifkin
Ray Roberts
Rita Rosenkranz
Jack Rosenzweig
Leona Rostenberg
George Rubinowitz
Joe Rudnicki

J. B. Rund
Robert Rulon-Miller
James T. Sabin
Albert Saifer
Vincent Savarino
Al Scheinbaum
Sam Scheinbaum
Clifford Scheiner, m.d.
Louis Schucman
Frank Scioscia
Steve Seskin
S. R. Shapiro
Eli Siegel
Peter Skutches
Ross Socolof
Wayne Somers
Jan Spacek
Philip Sperling
Madeleine Stern
Richard Stoddard
Jack Tannen
John Thorpe
Rachel Warren
Ernie Wavrovics
Louis Wavrovics
Robert Weinberg
Bill Weinstein
Donald Weiser
Elaine West
George P. Wimpfheimer
Steven Wise
Clarence Wolf
John Yrizarry
Michael Zinman
Irving Zucker
Renee Zuckerbrot

References

Quotations (such as have point and lack triteness) from the great old authors are an act of filial reverence on the part of the quoter.
—LOUISE IMOGEN GUINEY, *Scribner's Magazine*, JANUARY 1911.

The easiest way to make a monkey out of a man is to quote him. That remark, in itself, quoted as it stands wouldn't make much sense.
—ROBERT CHARLES BENCHLEY, *My Ten Years in a Quandary*

✂ To AVOID THE pedantic tedium of footnotes, specific books and articles utilized by the authors to provide facts and complementary information are detailed in the text at the point of use. Periodicals and newspaper issues frequently cited (e.g. *AB / Antiquarian Bookman, Biblio, Book Source Monthly,* the *New York Times, Publishers Weekly*) are not listed in the following bibliographical entries when they have already been sufficiently identified as sources. The authors are deeply appreciative to those sources and to each of the following for their information and insights that have so richly assisted in relating the story of Book Row.

Adams, Randolph G. "Librarians as Enemies of Books," *Library Quarterly,* July 1937.
Ahearn, Allen and Patricia. *Collected Books: The Guide to Values.* New York: G. P. Putnam's Sons, 1998.
Allen, George. "Old Booksellers of Philadelphia." In *Four Talks for Bibliophiles.* Philadelphia: Free Library of Philadelphia, 1958.
Anderson, Charles B.; Joseph A. Duffy; and Jocelyn D. Kahn, eds. *A Manual on Bookselling.* New York: R. R. Bowker Company, 1969.
Andrews, William Loring. *The Old Booksellers of New York and Other Papers.* New York: Dodd, Mead & Company, 1895.
Angle, Paul M. "Reference Work in the Rare-Book Room." In *The Reference Function of the Library,* edited by Pierce Butler. Boston: Gregg Press, 1972.

Atlas, James. "Somewhere in New York You Can Buy a Good Book." In *The New York Times World of New York: An Uncommon Guide to the City of Fantasies,* edited by A. M. Rosenthal and Arthur Gelb in association with Marvin Siegel. New York: Times Books, 1985.

Avrich, Paul. *Anarchist Portraits.* Princeton: Princeton University Press, 1988.

Baraka, Amiri. *The Autobiography of LeRoi Jones.* Chicago: Lawrence Hill Books, 1997.

Barzun, Jacques. *From Dawn to Decadence: 1500 to the Present.* New York: Harper-Collins, 2000.

Basbanes, Nicholas A. *A Gentle Madness.* New York: Henry Holt and Company, 1965.

———. "The Big Apple's Book Jungle," *Biblio,* November 1998.

Benchley, Robert. "Why Does Nobody Collect Me?" In *Chips off the Old Benchley.* New York: Harper & Brothers, 1949.

Bender, Thomas. *New York Intellect: A History of Intellectual Life in New York City from 1750 to the Beginnings of Our Own Time.* New York: Alfred A. Knopf, 1987.

Benedict, Stewart. *The Literary Guide to the United States.* New York: Facts on File, 1981.

Berg, A. Scott. *Max Perkins: Editor of Genius.* New York: Pocket Books, 1979.

Berger, Meyer. *Meyer Berger's New York.* New York: Random House, 1960.

Bradbury, Ray. *Fahrenheit 451* (1953), with Afterword (1979) and Coda (1982). New York: Ballantine Books, 1987.

Briggs, Harold E. *The Veterans Fight for Unity.* New York: American League of Ex-Servicemen, 1935.

———. "For Tom Briggs" and "Farewell," *Pegasus: The Poetry Quarterly of Greenwich Village,* winter 1953.

Briggs, Morris H. *Buying and Selling Rare Books.* New York: R. R. Bowker Company, 1927.

Brigham, Clarence Saunders. Introduction to *American Book Auction Catalogues, 1713–34,* compiled by George J. McKay. New York: The New York Public Library, 1937.

Brink, William, and Michael J. O'Neill. Annotations to *The World According to Breslin.* New York: Ticknor and Fields, 1984.

Britt, George, ed. *Shoe Leather and Printers' Ink.* New York: Quadrangle / The New York Times Book Co., 1974.

Brooks, Van Wyck. *From a Writer's Notebook.* New York: E. P. Dutton & Company, 1958.

Bruno, Guido. *Adventures in American Bookshops, Antique Stores and Auction Rooms.* Detroit: Douglas Book Shop, 1922.

Brussel, I. R. "Lo! The Poor Book Scout," *Antiquarian Bookman,* April 3, 1948.

———. *Anglo-American First Editions 1826–1900, East to West.* London: Constable & Co. Ltd., 1935.

———. *Anglo-American First Editions 1786–1930, West to East.* London: Constable & Co. Ltd., 1936.

Burke, Edmund. *Thoughts on the Cause of the Present Discontents.* London: J. Dodsley, 1770.

Burroughs, Edgar Rice. *Tarzan of the Apes.* Chicago: McClurg, 1914.

Burrows, Edwin G., and Mike Wallace. *Gotham: A History of New York City to 1898.* New York: Oxford University Press, 1999.

Carillo, Charles. "Last Page for City's Oldest Bookstore," *New York Post,* February 27, 1990.

Carter, John. *ABC for Book Collectors.* 5th ed. New York: Alfred A. Knopf, 1981.

Cerf, Bennett. "Trade Winds," *Saturday Review of Literature,* January 1, 1944.

Chafetz, Henry. "Book Selling on Book Row," *Want List—The Book Trade Weekly* XVIII, no. 22, January 26, 1953.

———. *The Lost Dream.* New York: Alfred A. Knopf, 1955.

———. *The Legend of Befana.* Boston: Houghton Mifflin Company, 1958.

———. *Play the Devil.* New York: C. N. Potter, 1961.

———. *Thunderbird and Other Stories.* New York: Pantheon, 1964.

Chandler, Raymond. *The Long Goodbye.* Boston: Houghton Mifflin Company, 1954.

Cherven, Sharon. "Back Roads: Hail Gems of Columbia," *Daily Freeman* (Kingston, New York), October 15, 1989.

Chesterton, G. K. Introduction to *Literary London* by Elsie M. Lang. New York: Charles Scribner's Sons, 1907.

Chew, Beverly. *Essays and Verses About Books.* New York: 1926.

Chomsky, Noam. Introduction to *Anarchism from Theory to Practice* by Daniel Guerin. New York: Monthly Review Press, 1970.

Ciardi, John. Note to *John Ciardi: A Bibliography,* compiled by William White. Detroit: Wayne State University, 1959.

Claxton, Eve. *New York's 50 Best Bookstores for Book Lovers.* New York: City & Company, 2000.

Clegg, James. *Directory of Second-Hand Booksellers and List of Public Libraries, British and Foreign.* 3rd ed. Wet Rake, Rochdale (Great Britain): James Clegg, 1891.

———. *Clegg's International Directory of Booksellers.* 4th ed. 1894.

———. *Clegg's International Directory of Booksellers.* 5th ed. 1899.

Clegg's International Directory of the World's Book Trade Booksellers, Publishers, Book Collectors, Etc. 1936–7. Vol. I, *English Speaking Countries.* New Series: No. 3. Gravesend (Great Britain): The Librarian, Lodgewood, Windmill Street, 1936.

Clinton, Alan. *Printed Ephemera.* London: Clive Bingley, 1981.

Conrad, Joseph. *Notes on Life and Letters.* Toronto: Doubleday, Page & Company, 1921.

Cuffari, Dick. "Letter: How It Was Done," *ABMR* LXVII, no. 2, February 1990.

Dannay, Frederic, and Manfred B. Lee, eds. *The Literature of Crime.* Boston: Little, Brown and Company, 1950.

Darling, William Young. *The Private Papers of a Bankrupt Bookseller.* Edinburgh: Oliver and Boyd, 1932.

——. *The Bankrupt Bookseller Speaks Again.* Edinburgh: Oliver and Boyd, 1939.

Davis, Kenneth C. *Two-Bit Culture: The Paperbacking of America.* Boston: Houghton Mifflin Company, 1984.

Deitch, Joseph. "Portrait: Fred Bass," *Wilson Library Bulletin,* June 1986.

Dickinson, Donald C. *Dictionary of American Book Collectors.* Westport, Conn.: Greenwood Press, 1986.

——. "Mr. Huntington and Mr. Smith," *Book Collector* 37, no. 3, autumn 1988.

——. "Bookdealers' Archives: A Search for Buried Treasure," *ABAA Newsletter,* spring 1997.

——. *Dictionary of American Antiquarian Book dealers.* Westport: Greenwood Press, 1998.

Diefendorf, Elizabeth, ed. *The New York Public Library's Books of the Century.* New York: Oxford University Press, 1996.

Directory of Booksellers, Newsdealers and Stationers. H. W. Wilson Company, 1910.

Dolbier, Maurice. "The Other Four Seasons." In *New York Herald Tribune Presents New York, New York.* New York: Dell Publishing Company, 1964.

Dorman, Joseph. *Arguing the World: The New York Intellectuals in Their Own Words.* New York: Free Press, 2000.

Dreiser, Theodore. *The Color of a Great City.* New York: Boni and Liveright, 1923.

Dunn, Tom. *The Pipe Smoker's Ephemiris,* spring-autumn 2000.

Dunning, John. *Booked to Die.* New York: Charles Scribner's Sons, 1992.

——. *The Bookman's Wake.* New York: Scribner, 1995.

——. *Bookscout.* Minneapolis: Dinkytown Antiquarian Books, 1998.

——. *Two O'Clock, Eastern Wartime.* New York: Scribner, 2001.

Early, Eleanor. *New York Holiday.* New York: Rinehart & Co., 1950.

Ehrlich, Eugene, and Gorton Carruth. *The Oxford Illustrated Literary Guide to the United States.* New York: Oxford University Press, 1982.

Ellis, Edward Robb. *The Epic of New York City.* New York: Old Town Books, 1990.

Emerson, Ralph Waldo. "Self-Reliance." In *Emerson: Essays and Lectures.* New York: The Library of America, 1983.

Epstein, Jason. *Book Business: Publishing Past Present and Future.* New York: W. W. Norton & Company, 2001.

Esdaile, Arundel. *The British Museum Library.* London: George Allen & Unwin, 1946.

Everitt, Charles P. *The Adventures of a Treasure Hunter.* Boston: Little, Brown and Company, 1951.

Fadiman, Anne. *Ex Libris.* New York: Farrar, Straus and Giroux, 1998.

Feinberg, Charles E. "Notes on Whitman Collections and Collectors." In *Walt Whitman: A Catalog Based upon the Collections of the Library of Congress.* Washington, D.C.: 1955.

——. Introduction to *Walt Whitman: A Selection of the Manuscripts, Books, and Association Items.* Detroit: Detroit Public Library, 1955.

——. "A Whitman Collector Destroys a Whitman Myth," *Bibliographical Society of America* 52, second quarter, 1958.

——. "Walt Whitman: Yesterday, Today, and Tomorrow," *Nassau Review* 1, no. 2, spring 1965.

——. Introduction to *Whitman at Auction 1899–1972*, compiled by Gloria A. Francis and Artem Lozynsky. Detroit: Gale Research Company, Book Tower, 1978.

Fitzgerald, F. Scott. *Dear Scott Dear Max: Fitzgerald-Perkins Correspondence*, edited by John Kuehl and Jackson Bryer. New York: Charles Scribner's Sons, 1971.

Flaubert, Gustave. *Bibliomania: A Tale*. London: The Rodale Press, 1954.

Fleck, Bob. "ABAA in 2001: Predictions and Pipe Dreams," *ABAA Newsletter,* spring 1997.

Fletcher, H. George, ed. *A Miscellany for Bibliophiles*. New York: Grastorf & Lang, 1979.

Forster, E. M. "Ronald Firbank." In *Abinger Harvest*. London: Edward Arnold, 1953.

——. "In My Library." In *Two Cheers for Democracy*. London: Penguin Books, 1965.

France, Anatole. *The Revolt of the Angels*. New York: Dodd, Mead & Company, 1914.

Frost, Robert. "The Road Not Taken." In *Mountain Interval*. New York: Henry Holt, 1916.

Gilbar, Steven. *Good Books*. New Haven: Ticknor & Fields, 1982.

Glaser, Edwin V. "The ABAA at Fifty: Notes Toward a History of the Antiquarian Booksellers' Association of America," www.abaa.org, 1999.

Gold, Harry. *The Dolphin's Path: A Bookman's Sequel to the Odyssey of Homer*. Chapel Hill: Aberdeen Book Company, 1979.

Golden, Harry. *Only in America*. Cleveland: World Publishing Company, 1958.

——. *For 2 ¢ Plain*. Cleveland: World Publishing Company, 1959.

——. *Enjoy, Enjoy!* Cleveland: World Publishing Company, 1960.

Goldsmith, Alfred, and Carolyn Wells. *A Concise Bibliography of the Works of Walt Whitman with a Supplement of Fifty Books About Whitman*. Boston: Houghton Mifflin Company, 1922.

Goldstone, Lawrence and Nancy. *Used and Rare: Travels in the Book World*. New York: St. Martin's Press, 1997.

——. *Slightly Chipped: Footnotes in Booklore*. New York: St. Martin's Press, 1999.

Goldwater, Walter. "World of Africana," *1965 AB Bookman's Yearbook*, 1965.

——. "On Collecting Incunabula," *Octavo, the Society of Bibliophiles at Brandeis University*, no. 3, fall 1972.

——. "New York City Bookshops in the 1930s and 1940s: The Recollections of Walter Goldwater," *Dictionary of Literary Biography Yearbook*, 1993.

Goodspeed, Charles E. *Yankee Bookseller*. Boston: Houghton Mifflin Company, 1937.

Greene, Graham. Introduction to *With All Faults* by David Low. Tehran: Amate Press, 1973.

Grolier 75: A Biographical Retrospective to Celebrate the Seventy-fifth Anniversary of the Grolier Club in New York. New York: The Grolier Club, 1959.

Growoll, Adolf. *The Profession of Bookselling: A Handbook of Practical Hints for the Apprentice and Bookseller.* Part I. New York: Publishers Weekly, 1893.

Guare, John. *A Few Stout Individuals.* New York: Grove Press, 2003.

Gunther, John. *Roosevelt in Retrospect.* New York: Harper & Brothers, 1950.

Haight, Anne Lyon. *Banned Books.* 2nd ed. New York: R. R. Bowker, 1955.

Hamlin, Suzanne. "What's in Store for You?" *New York Daily News,* October 21, 1979.

Handlin, Oscar. *The Uprooted.* Boston: Little, Brown and Company, 1951.

Hardwick, Elizabeth. "New York City: Crash Course," *Granta,* no. 32, spring 1990.

Heartman, Charles F. *George D. Smith Gentlemen Bookseller 1870–1920.* Privately Printed. Beauvoir Community (Mississippi): The Book Farm, 1945.

Hemingway, Ernest. *Ernest Hemingway Selected Letters 1917–1961.* Edited by Carlos Baker. New York: Charles Scribner's Sons, 1981.

Hirschorn, Michael Wels. "It May Be Bookish, But This Store Also Has a Tough Streak," *Wall Street Journal,* August 21, 1986.

Hoffman, Edwin D. "The Bookshops of New York City, 1743–1948," *New York History* XXX:1, January 1949.

Hoffman, Hester R., ed. Preface to *Bessie Graham's Bookman's Manual,* 6th ed. New York: R. R. Bowker Company, 1948.

Holliday, Robert Cortes. *Broome Street Straws.* New York: George H. Doran, 1919.

Hyman, Stanley Edgar. "Book Scout," *New Yorker,* November 8, 1952.

International Directory of Antiquarian Booksellers, 1931–32. Weimar (Germany): Straubing & Muller, 1931.

International Directory of Antiquarian Booksellers, 1951–52. Brussels: International League of Antiquarian Booksellers, 1951.

International Directory of Antiquarian Booksellers, 1958. Brussels: International League of Antiquarian Booksellers, 1958.

International Directory of Antiquarian Booksellers, 1977. Brussels: International League of Antiquarian Booksellers, 1977.

International Directory of Antiquarian Booksellers, 1986. Brussels: International League of Antiquarian Booksellers, 1986.

International Directory of Antiquarian Booksellers, 1990–91. Frankfurt (Germany): Edmund Brumme, International League of Antiquarian Booksellers, 1990.

International Directory of Antiquarian Booksellers, 1994–95. The Netherlands: International League of Antiquarian Booksellers, 1994.

Irving, Washington. "A History of New York." In *Washington Irving: History, Tales and Sketches.* New York: The Library of America, 1983.

Jacker, Corinne. *The Black Flag of Anarchy: Antistatism in the United States.* New York: Charles Scribner's Sons, 1968.

Jackson, Holbrook. *The Anatomy of Bibliomania.* New York: Charles Scribner's Sons, 1932.

Jackson, Kenneth T., ed. *The Encyclopedia of New York City.* New Haven: Yale University Press, 1995.

Jerome, Jim. "Book Smarts," *People*, October 7, 2002.

Karolides, Nicholas J.; Margaret Bald; and Dawn B. Sova. *100 Banned Books*. New York: Checkmark Books, Facts On File, 1999.

Katz, Herbert and Marjorie. *Museums USA*. Garden City: Doubleday, 1965.

Kazin, Alfred. *The Inmost Leaf.* New York: Harcourt, Brace and Company, 1955.

———. *Writing Was Everything*. Cambridge: Harvard University Press, 1995.

Kempton, Murray. *Part of Our Time: Some Monuments and Ruins of the Thirties*. New York: Simon & Schuster, 1955.

———. *Rebellions, Perversities, and Main Events*. New York: Times Books, Random House, 1994.

Kennedy, Shawn G. "For Book Lovers, Browsing by Mail," *New York Times*, October 24, 1992.

Kessner, Thomas. *The Golden Door*. New York: Oxford University Press, 1977.

Kestenbaum, Joy. "Interview: Richard Lilly, Strand Book Store," *ARLIS/New York News* 23, no. 4, winter 2002.

"The Knickerbocker," *New York Sun*, June 26, 2003.

Kraus, H. P. *A Rare Book Saga*. New York: G. P. Putnam's Sons, 1978.

Kroch, Adolph. *Bookstores Can Be Saved*. Chicago: Booksellers Catalog Service, 1952.

Kuehl, John, and Jackson Bryer, eds. *Dear Scott/Dear Max: The Fitzgerald-Perkins Correspondence*. New York: Charles Scribner's Sons, 1971.

Lambert, John. *Travels Through Canada, and the United States of North America in the Years 1806, 1807, & 1808*. 2 vols. London, 1814. Excerpts in *Mirror for Gotham: New York as Seen by Contemporaries from Dutch Days to the Present* by Bayrd Still. New York: New York University Press, 1956.

Lane, Anthony. "Take Me to Your Reader," *New Yorker*, October 16–23, 2000.

Lang, Elsie M. *Literary London*. New York: Charles Scribner's Sons, 1907.

Leab, Katherine. "Tracking Down Rare Books: The Quietest Blood Sport" in Collecting, *7 Days*, July 1988.

Leacock, Stephen. *The Methods of Mr. Sellyer*. New York: John Lane Company, 1914.

Lebowitz, Fran. "Fran Lebowitz Used Books," *New York*, April 18, 1994.

Lincoln, Waldo. "Bibliography of American Cookery Books 1742–1860." In Proceedings. Worcester (Massachusetts): American Antiquarian Society, 1930.

———. *American Cookery Books 1742–1860*. Worcester (Massachusetts): American Antiquarian Society, 1954.

Lipman, Samuel. "Walter Goldwater: A Memoir," *New Criterion*, January 1991.

Lockwood, Charles. *Manhattan Moves Uptown*. Boston: Houghton Mifflin Company, 1976.

Lopate, Phillip, ed. *Writing New York*. New York: The Library of America, 1998.

Lord, M. G. "A Pack Rat Redeemed by Choice Acquisitions," *Newsday*, May 13, 1990.

Lowenstein, Eleanor. *Bibliography of American Cookery Books 1742–1860*. Worcester (Massachusetts): American Antiquarian Society, 1972.

Lyon, I. S. *Recollections of an Old Cartman*. Newark: Daily Journal Office, 1872.

Mackay, Charles. *Extraordinary Popular Delusions and the Madness of Crowds.* Boston: L. C. Page, 1932.

MacLeish, Archibald. *A Free Man's Books: Address to the American Booksellers Association.* Mount Vernon (New York): The Peter Pauper Press, 1942.

Magee, David. *Infinite Riches.* New York: Eriksson, 1973.

Mailer, Norman. *The Naked and the Dead.* New York: Rinehart & Company, 1948.

Matthews, Jack, ed. *Rare Book Lore: Selections from the Letters of Ernest J. Wessen.* Athens (Ohio): Ohio University Press, 1992.

Maugham, W. Somerset. *The Summing Up.* Garden City: Doubleday, 1938.

Maxwell, Margaret. *Shaping a Library: William L. Clements as Collector.* Amsterdam (Netherlands): Nico Israel, 1973.

McCarthy, Mary. *The Oasis.* New York: Random House, 1949.

McMurtry, Larry. "Why I Stopped Signing My Books," *op,* July/August 2003.

Meador, Roy. *Franklin—Revolutionary Scientist.* Ann Arbor: Ann Arbor Science Publishers, 1975.

——. "New York's Most Dangerous Neighborhood," *AB,* May 29, 1978.

——. "Book Row When Serendipity Was in Flower," *Book Source Monthly,* April 2000.

Melville, Herman. *Redburn, White-Jacket, Moby Dick.* New York: The Library of America, 1983.

Minet, Paul. *Bookdealing for Profit.* London: Richard Joseph, 2000.

——. "Letter from England: The End of the Traveling Customer," *Book Source Monthly,* September 2000.

——. "Letter from England: Junketing in Edinburgh," *Book Source Monthly,* November 2000.

Mitchell, Edwin Valentine. *Morocco Bound: Adrift Among Books.* New York: Farrar & Rinehart, 1929.

Mitchell, Joseph. *McSorley's Wonderful Saloon.* New York: Duell, Sloan and Pearce, 1943.

Mondlin, Marvin. "Letter: Biggest," *ABMR* LXVII, no. 2, February 1990.

——. Typophiles paper: "72 1/2 Years Condensed to About an Hour," 1999.

——. *Appraisals: A Guide for Bookmen, Practical Methods and Essential Principles.* New York: American Sunbeam Publishers, 1997.

Montaigne, Michel. *The Essays of Montaigne,* translated by E. J. Trechmann. London: Oxford University Press, 1927.

Morgan, Neil. "Computer Age No Threat to Rare Books," *San Diego Union-Tribune,* June 27, 2003.

Morley, Christopher. *Parnassus on Wheels.* New York: Doubleday, Page & Co., 1917.

——. *The Haunted Bookshop.* New York: Doubleday, Page & Co., 1918.

——. "On Visiting Bookshops." In *Safety Pins.* London: Jonathan Cape, 1925.

——. "Bowling Green," *Saturday Review of Literature,* July 4, 1925.

Muir, Percy H. *Minding My Own Business.* London: Chatto and Windus, 1956.

Newton, A. Edward. "Budapest and I," *Atlantic,* November 1933.

——. *The Amenities of Book Collecting and Kindred Affections.* New York: The Modern Library, 1935.

Norwich, William. "Conversation: Talking Liz," *Talk,* September 2000.

Norris, Frank. *Norris: Novels and Essays.* New York: The Library of America, 1986.

O'Casey, Sean. *The Green Crow: Selected Writings.* London: Virgin Books, 1994.

O'Connor, Mimi. "New York City: The Very Heart of It," *Book,* September/October 2000.

Odell, George C. D. *Annals of the New York Stage.* New York: Columbia University Press, 1927.

O'Neill, Michael J. Foreword to *The World According to Breslin,* annotated by Michael J. O'Neill and William Brink. New York: Ticknor and Fields, 1984.

Orwell, George. *Nineteen Eighty-Four.* New York: Harcourt, Brace and Company, 1949.

Paine, Thomas. *The Age of Reason.* In *Paine: Collected Writings.* New York: The Library of America, 1995.

Payne, John R. "James F. Drake Inc., New York and Texas," *Library Chronicle of the University of Texas,* February 1972.

Peters, Jean, ed. *The Bookman's Glossary.* 5th ed. New York: R. R. Bowker, 1975.

——. *Book Collecting: A Modern Guide.* New York: R. R. Bowker, 1977.

Pfeiffer, Gordon. "E-Books: Are They Really the Future?" *Delaware Bibliophiles End-papers,* September 2000.

Phillips' Business Directory of New York City. 1902.

Powell, Lawrence Clark. *The Alchemy of Books.* Los Angeles: Ward Ritchie Press, 1954.

——. *Books in My Baggage.* Cleveland: World Publishing Company, 1960.

——. Introduction to *Infinite Riches* by David Magee. New York: Eriksson, 1973.

Pratt, Herbert T. "A Very Worthwhile Perk," *Delaware Bibliophiles Endpapers,* September 1999.

Randall, David A. *Dukedom Large Enough: Reminiscences of a Rare Book Dealer 1929–1956.* New York: Random House, 1969.

Raynor, Richard. "An Actual Internet Success Story," *New York Times Magazine,* June 9, 2002.

Rhodes, Eugene Manlove. "Pasó Por Aquí." In *Once in the Saddle.* Boston: Houghton Mifflin Company, 1927.

——. *Pasó Por Aquí.* Norman: University of Oklahoma Press, 1973.

Rolland, Romain. "Broaden, Europe, or Die! My Country Is Not Yesterday, My Country Is Tomorrow," *Nation,* April 22, 1931.

Rooney, Andy. *My War.* New York: Times Books, 1995.

Roosevelt, Franklin D. Letter to the American Booksellers Association. In *A Free Man's Books* by Archibald MacLeish. Mount Vernon (New York): The Peter Pauper Press, 1942.

Rosenbach, A. S. W. *The Unpublishable Memoirs.* New York: Mitchell Kennerley, 1917.

——. *Books and Bidders.* Boston: Little, Brown and Company, 1927.

Rosenblatt, Roger. "Essay: The Old Great Gatsby, Post-Olympics Blues," *Time*, October 16, 2000.

Rosenblum, Joseph. *American Book-Collectors and Bibliographers*. First series. Detroit: Bruccoli Clark Layman Book, Gale Research Inc., 1994.

Rosenthal, Bernard M. *The Gentle Invasion: Continental Emigre Booksellers of the Thirties and Forties and Their Impact on the Antiquarian Book Trade in the United States.* Second Sol M. Malkin Lecture in Bibliography. Book Arts Press Occasional Publication no. 4. New York: The Book Arts Press, School of Library Service, Columbia University, 1987.

Rossetti, William M., ed. *American Poems.* London: E. Moxon, Son & Co., 1872.

Rostenberg, Leona, and Madeleine Stern. *Old Books, Rare Friends.* New York: Doubleday, 1997.

Sabin, Joseph. *A Bibliography of Bibliography or a Handy Book About Books Which Relates to Books.* New York: Argonaut Press, Ltd., 1966.

Sansegundo, Sheridan. "A Crusading Book Lover," *East Hampton Star*, July 16, 1992.

Schoenherr, Ian. "Howard Pyle: Delaware Bibliophile," *Delaware Bibliophiles Endpapers*, March 2000.

Schulte, Theodore E. "The Second-Hand Book Business as an Adjunct of the Bookstore," *Publishers Weekly*, May 13, 1911.

Shay, Frank. *My Pious Friends and Drunken Companions: Songs and Ballads of Conviviality.* New York: The Macaulay Company, 1927.

Siegel, Eli. "Hymn to Fourth Avenue," *Antiquarian Bookman*, July 21, 1958. Reprinted in *The Right of Aesthetic Realism to Be Known*, December 28, 1988.

——. "Great Books; and the Kick," *The Right of Aesthetic Realism to Be Known*, December 28, 1988.

Silver, Nathan. *Lost New York.* New York: Weathervane Books, 1967.

Silverman, David W. "The Jewish Press." In *The Religious Press in America*, edited by Robert Lekachman. New York: Holt, Rinehart and Winston, 1963.

Singer, Isaac Bashevis. "Two Stories," *New Yorker*, August 21, 2000.

Singer, Isaac Bashevis, and Richard Burgin. *Conversations with Isaac Bashevis Singer.* Garden City: Doubleday, 1985.

Sipper, Ralph B. *Larry Moskowitz Man of Esprit.* Santa Barbara: Cordelia Editions, 1986.

Smith, George D., publisher. *Literary Collector* 1, no. 5, February 1901; and 2, no. 5, August 1901.

——. "American Smashes London Book Ring," *New York Sun*, July 18, 1914.

Smith's Bi-Weekly Price-Current of Books. no. 1, June 1897; no. 2, June 15, 1897; no. 3, July 15, 1897; no. 4, August 2, 1897; no. 6, October 15, 1897; no. 7, December 1897.

Sontag, Susan. *In America.* New York: Farrar, Straus and Giroux, 2000.

Sperling, Philip. "Looking for Mr. Pickering." In *A Miscellany for Bibliophiles*, edited by H. George Fletcher. New York: Grastorf & Lang, 1979.

Stephenson, Olivier. "The University Place Bookshop: A Labor of Love," *Village Voice,* June 18, 1985.

Stern, Madeleine B. *Antiquarian Bookselling in the United States: A History from the Origins to the 1940s.* Westport, Conn.: Greenwood Press, 1985.

Stern, Philip Van Doren. *The Greatest Gift.* New York: Penguin Studio, 1996.

Stevens, Wallace. *Wallace Stevens: Collected Poetry and Prose.* New York: The Library of America, 1997.

Stewart, Seumas. *Book Collecting.* New York: E. P. Dutton, 1973.

Still, Bayrd. *Mirror for Gotham: New York as Seen by Contemporaries from Dutch Days to the Present.* New York: New York University Press, 1956.

Surowiecki, James. "The Financial Page: The Most Devastating Retailer in the World," *New Yorker,* September 18, 2000.

"Talk of the Town: Review Copies," *New Yorker,* January 30, 1937.

Tannen, Jack. *How to Identify and Collect American First Editions.* New York: Arco Publishing Company, 1976.

Tanselle, G. Thomas. "The Literature of Book Collecting." In *Book Collecting: A Modern Guide,* edited by Jean Peters. New York: R. R. Bowker Company, 1977.

Targ, William, ed. *Bouillabaisse for Bibliophiles.* Metuchen, N.J.: Scarecrow Reprint Corporation, 1968.

——. Foreword to *A Miscellany for Bibliophiles,* edited by H. George Fletcher. New York: Grastorf & Lang, 1979.

Tarshish, Manuel B. "The 'Fourth Avenue' Book Trade," *Publishers Weekly,* October 20, 1969; October 27, 1969; November 3, 1969.

Tebbel, John W. *A History of Book Publishing in the United States.* Vol. II. New York: R. R. Bowker Company, 1975.

Teller, Chester James. "Of A. F. Goldsmith," *Publishers Weekly,* November 22, 1947.

Thomas, Isaiah. *The History of Printing in America.* New York: Weathervane Books, 1970.

Thompson, Francis. "In No Strange Land." In *The Concise Treasury of Great Poems,* edited by Louis Untermeyer. Garden City: Permabooks, 1953.

Tillman, Lynne. *Bookstore: The Life and Times of Jeannette Watson and Books & Co.* New York: Harcourt Brace & Company, 1999.

Valentine's Manual of Old New York. No. 7, new series. Edited by Henry Collins Brown. New York: Valentine's Manual Inc., 1923.

Wald, Alan M. *The New York Intellectuals: The Rise and Decline of the Anti-Stalinist Left from the 1930s to the 1980s.* Chapel Hill: University of North Carolina Press, 1987.

Wales, Alexander P., ed. *World Directory of Booksellers.* London: Alexander P. Wales Publishers, 1970.

Walsh, Francis, ed. *That Eager Zest: First Discoveries in the Magic World of Books.* Philadelphia: J. B. Lippincott, 1961.

Weiss, Philip. "A Book Thief, a True Tale of Bibliomania," *Harper's Magazine,* January 1994.

Weitenkampf, Frank. "Lafayette Place: An Erstwhile Literary Center." In *The Book Lover's Almanac for 1897*. New York: Duprat, 1897.

Wells, Carolyn. *Murder in the Bookshop*. Philadelphia: J. B. Lippincott, 1936.

———. *The Rest of My Life*. Philadelphia: J. B. Lippincott, 1937.

Wernick, Robert E. "The Bookseller Who Couldn't Stand to Sell His Books," *Smithsonian* 23, no. 1, April 1992.

Wessen, Ernest J. *Rare Book Lore: Selections from the Letters of Ernest J. Wessen*. edited by Jack Matthews. Athens: Ohio University Press, 1992.

West, Herbert Faulkner. *Modern Book Collecting for the Impecunious Amateur*. Boston: Little, Brown and Company, 1936.

Wharton, Edith. *Old New York*. 4 vols. New York: Appleton, 1924.

White, E. B. "Selecting School Books." In *Writings from the New Yorker 1925–1976*, edited by Rebecca M. Dale. New York: HarperCollins, 1990.

Whitman, Walt. "Mannahatta." In *Walt Whitman: Complete Poetry and Collected Prose*. New York: The Library of America, 1982.

Wilentz, Elias, ed. *The Beat Scene*. New York: Corinth Books, 1960.

Wilson, Robert A. *Modern Book Collecting*. New York: Alfred A. Knopf, 1980.

Winterich, John T. *23 Books & the Stories Behind Them*. Berkeley: Book Arts Club of the University of California, 1938.

———. "Alfred F. Goldsmith: An Appreciation," *Publishers Weekly*, November 22, 1947.

———. *Three Lantern Slides*. Urbana: University of Illinois Press, 1949.

Wolfe, Thomas. *Of Time and the River*. New York: Charles Scribner's Sons, 1935.

———. *You Can't Go Home Again*. New York: Harper & Row, 1940.

World Directory of Booksellers. Edited by Alexander P. Wales. London: Alexander P. Wales Publishers, 1970.

Zeitlin, Jake. "Who Shall Silence All the Airs and Madrigals?" In *Book Selection and Censorship in the Sixties*, edited by Eric Moon. New York: R. R. Bowker Company, 1969.

*The Island of Books: A Look Back to the Earliest Decades of Books
in New York City*

*Look for it only in books, for it is no more than a dream remembered, a
Civilization gone with the wind.*
—Ben Hecht, "Lines to Commence a Familiar Film
Not About New York"

Considering the long-ago past and eras that are gone with the wind
on wings of time will seem a waste to those who dismiss ancient history as
"weary, stale, flat, and unprofitable." Baseball manager Sparky Anderson
pointed out the futility of living in the past: "There's no future in it." A New
York book dealer, quoted by the *New York Times* (May 31, 1981), doubted the
existence of serious interest among contemporary booksellers in the vanished
shops of Fourth Avenue, which were no longer relevant to the needs and
problems of modern bookstores: "Those who remember them don't want to
be reminded, and those who don't, won't care. It's like talking about a five-
cent sandwich. No one knows what you are talking about."

Yet those who concur with Prospero's ambitious brother Antonio that
"what's past is prologue" calmly demur. Prospero in *The Tempest* expressed an
even wiser sentiment when he gave thanks for the thoughtfulness of his friend
Gonzalo, who "of his gentleness, knowing I lov'd my books . . . furnished me
from my own library with volumes that I prize above my dukedom."

The magic island to which Prospero and his daughter Miranda escaped
probably wasn't Manhattan, though there is pleasure in thinking so, considering the duke of Milan's insistence, "My library was dukedom large enough."
Good counselor Gonzalo naturally stands forth as the beau ideal of a New
York bookseller, past, present, future.

In the intriguing 1999 film *Magnolia* a frequently repeated theme—that we may be through with the past, but the past isn't through with us—seems a clear warning to the antihistory clique. Useful lessons are learned from the experiences of those who in the past traveled comparable paths and cultivated similar ground. Even if particularly worthwhile insights aren't gained, those experiences can be fascinating just for themselves. Except for a speculative minority with occult goals, don't all books pretty much focus on what's past? So read on.

In the matter of bookstores and books, New York City from its earliest days has been a city of many books, a city where the writing, publishing, selling, and reading of books take priority over many other important activities. "I'll do your brief, dispose of the garbage, fix your pipes, teach your child, chase your mugger, practice the piano, but first let me finish this chapter, thanks."

Whatever the claims (that is, pretensions) of other places, New York City has long been America's national center of book-related activities. Even with the disappearance of Book Row in the last quarter of the twentieth century, the book sovereignty of New York continued and shows no convincing signs of substantially changing any time soon.

Given these past and present facts, one has to wonder why figimag (figment of imagination) Diedrich Knickerbocker, in his *History of New York from the Beginning of the World to the End of the Dutch Dynasty* (1809, 2 volumes)— with an essential assist from spoof master Washington Irving—didn't discuss the obvious logic of assigning New Amsterdam, on the island of Manhattan, the more fitting, descriptive, and appealing name of *Booklyn*. The English also missed their golden chance to christen the city Booklyn when they took over from the Dutch in 1664 and called it New York. Booklyn still seems warmer, homier, closer to sister borough Brooklyn, and definitely more bookish than either New York City or Manhattan. Should a civic committee look into this?

It wasn't good news, at least not for fur-bearing animals, that explorer Henry Hudson took back to his East India Company employers in old Amsterdam. Although he failed his 1609 commission to locate a northeast passage to the Orient, he reported fur-trading opportunities with eager aborigines. A 1610 voyage from Amsterdam encountered the Manhattes Indians, and the game was definitely afoot for book trading to replace fur trading and for the eventual existence of Booksellers' Row on an island to be called Manhattan. Dutch Captain Adriaen Block, whose name is perpetuated by an Atlantic island near Long Island's eastern end, was first to use "Manhattes" as a name for the promising 14-mile-by-2.3 mile island with a harbor that seemed to say "Come in" to seamen.

Trade opportunities led to formation of the Dutch West India Company and establishment of a trading center on Manhattan, in the 1620s called New Netherland. Peter Minuit, director general of the province, in 1626 inaugurated the Manhattan tradition of shrewd real estate deals by negotiating the purchase of the island from the resident natives for sixty guilders' worth of cloth and trinkets. Face it, real estate and finance as well as books have always been primary New York enterprises.

Dutch settlers and later English settlers during the seventeenth century gradually made the favorably situated island known as Manhattan. "I was asking for something specific and perfect for my city, Whereupon lo! upsprang the aboriginal name. Now I see what there is in a name, a word, liquid, sane, unruly, musical, self-sufficient, I see that the word of my city is that word from of old," wrote Walt Whitman for *Leaves of Grass* in his "Mannahatta." We are free to think Whitman, an innovating poet, would have cared less about the aboriginal name if the logic of Booklyn had been thrust upon him. Historian David Dykstra thought it was important to note, "Manhattan is the centre of much of the city's activities and is often mistaken as being synonymous with New York City." Care must be taken to resist such an easy error.

It wasn't as if Knickerbocker and Irving in their rollicking 1809 tribute to the city weren't thinking about books, and very seriously, too, in Chapter I of Book IV, where they focus on "those arch Free Booters, the Book Makers, and their trusty Squires, the Book Sellers." Doubters of history's utility should question their position when they consider Knickerbocker's warning to book authors, publishers, and sellers about the crucial importance of padding:

> *If every writer were obliged to tell merely what he knew, there would soon be an end of great books. . . . A man might then carry his library in his pocket, and the whole race of book makers, book printers, book binders and book sellers might starve together; but by being entitled to tell every thing*

he thinks, and every thing he does not think—to talk about every thing he knows, or does not know—to conjecture, to doubt, to argue with himself, to laugh with and to laugh at his reader. . . . all these I say, do marvelously concur to fill the pages of books, the pockets of booksellers, and the stomachs of authors—do contribute to the amusement and edification of the reader, and redound to the glory, the encrease and the profit of the craft!

THE FIRST BOOKS PRODUCED IN NEW YORK

As Manhattan in an ever-burgeoning New York City, the Dutch island became English, and the English island became American. These transitions occurring over centuries lend credence in New York to a G. K. Chesterton wager: "The chances are a hundred to one that every man of us is living on a historic spot."

That's probably a safe bet in most cities that qualify as elderly. In Manhattan, Chesterton's odds might even be increased. "A street in London means stratum upon stratum of history, poet upon poet, battlefield upon battlefield," Chesterton wrote. The same is no less true in the City of Endless Change, as columnist Meyer Berger described New York. The pier of the Brooklyn Bridge on the Manhattan side of the East River stands over the location of America's first White House, not far from where George Washington was inaugurated as the first president. And where Booksellers' Row existed for nearly a century, during earlier centuries Dutchmen farmed, and earlier still the Lenape Indians roamed and dwelled.

English colonel Benjamin Fletcher became governor in 1692, and that soon led to the manufacture of books through the hiring of William Bradford as royal printer for the colony. London-trained William Bradford was nineteen when he emigrated to Philadelphia in 1682 and introduced "the art and mystery of printing" there in the 1680s. His print shop also became a source of books and pamphlets. One of Bradford's Pennsylvania innovations was the establishment with William Rittenhouse of America's first paper mill.

The move to New York City came in 1693. There the job of public printer was his for over half a century. Bradford established his print shop at the Sign of the Bible in lower Manhattan. Among his first jobs was a book by Nicholas Bayard and Charles Lodwick praising Colonel Fletcher for his military prowess and related exploits. "It may have been the first book ever printed in New York," observe Edwin G. Burrows and Mike Wallace in their Pulitzer Prize–winning history *Gotham* (1999). More books followed from the Bradford press. By producing the first books manufactured in the city, Bradford launched one of New York's oldest and most important continuing industries. Remove books published in New York from the world's shelves, and the space opened up would reduce many, maybe most, private and public libraries to skeletons of their former selves. In 1725, Bradford started the *New York Gazette,* the city's first regular newspaper.

Among the ifs of American history are "What if William Bradford had found a place in 1723 for a runaway from Boston with print shop training, and what if the boy had stayed put in New York?" The boy had "sold some of my books" to finance his move south. Much later as the most famous American alive, he wrote in his *Autobiography:* "Having a Trade, & supposing my self a pretty good Workman, I offer'd my Services to the Printer of the Place, old Mr. Wm. Bradford.—He could give me no Employment, having little to do, and Help enough already: But, says he, my Son at Philadelphia has lately lost his principal Hand, Aquila Rose, by Death. If you go thither I believe he may employ you."

The Philadelphia Bradford did not in fact hire Benjamin Franklin, but William Bradford helped the youth get a position at Keimer's Printing House. Observing William Bradford in action with Keimer, Franklin thought he observed a "crafty old Sophister" toying with a "Novice." Bradford, having no vacancy at New York and gaining the energetic, talented youth a place in Philadelphia, where he profited in printing and became rather active in various areas of public endeavor, clearly affected the future history of the country, the Revolution, libraries, and much more. A case can be made that New York City, by denying young Franklin a position, helped start and helped win the American Revolution over half a century later.

William Bradford's last home in New York was at Hanover Square, in the area of New York's original Printing House Square. The day he died, at ninety-two, in 1752, Bradford took a long walk through the city to which he had given its first books and newspaper. He was buried in Trinity churchyard, and the *Gazette* concluded its encomium with, "His lamp of life went out for want of oil."

After William Bradford fathered a printing and bookselling tradition in New York, many successors followed. Hugh Gaine, born in Ireland, opened a printing and bookselling business, the Bible and Crown, at Hanover Square sometime around 1750 and kept it going over forty years, producing pamphlets as well as folio, octavo, and duodecimo volumes for sale. "He began the world a poor man, but by close application to successful business through a long period of time, he acquired a large property," observed printer and book collector Isaiah Thomas in *The History of Printing in America* (1810, 2 volumes). John Holt from Virginia was another New York printer and bookseller in the eighteenth century. His property was destroyed by the British during the war, but he rebuilt and was appointed the printer to the state.

James Rivington from London made his mark as a bookseller, first in Philadelphia and then in New York. His father, Charles Rivington, was established in England as a publisher of religious books. James Rivington's New York shop was at the end of Wall Street, and he advertised as "the only London bookseller in America." Rivington enjoyed relating the story of his bookshop run-in with the Vermont warrior Ethan Allen, hero of the Revolution and author of *Reason the Only Oracle of Man* (1784). Frontiersman Allen was noted for his perpetual feuding with New Yorkers, and his visit to Rivington's boded ill. When the soldier burst in, Rivington, without letting him speak, offered him a glass of Madeira, then another, and another, and so on. "We finished two bottles of Madeira and parted as good friends," reported Rivington.

Since bookselling and printing merged well in the 1700s, Rivington added printing to produce books he could sell. One publication in two volumes was *Cooke's Voyages*. Another was Tobias Smollett's *History of England*, which allegedly brought in ten thousand pounds, then the largest amount earned by a single work. A royalist during the Revolution, Rivington rode out the war. He continued to sell books in New York with the coming of peace and benefited from the port city's tolerance for dissent. He left his name behind on one of the city's streets.

The New York habit of tolerance didn't cope with the fury that hit the city in 1765 due to the infamous Stamp Act. Demonstrators attacked the home of a major who aimed to cram the stamps down disobedient throats, and destroyed with household furnishings "a Libiry of Books."

Robert Hodge learned printing at his native Edinburgh and during the 1770s began printing and selling books in New York with a shop on Maiden

Lane. Fleeing the city in 1776, he abandoned unbound books in sheets to the British troops. At war's end, he resumed bookselling and printing and, according to Isaiah Thomas, was sufficiently diligent and frugal for several years to sell his stock and retire in those pre-Florida times to a Brooklyn estate.

Garret Noel, credited with introducing New York's first circulating library in 1763, ran a bookstore and publishing business next door to the Merchant's Coffee House. It was in the Long Room of the Merchants' Coffee House that Leonard Bleecker and John Pintard in 1791 began holding weekly stock auctions. When the auctions weren't in progress, brokers and stock dealers talked business around a tree on Wall Street—the start of something destined to be very New York and very big. In February 1792, an exchange office to serve stock dealers opened at 22 Wall Street. Thus the stock market genie left the bottle while Garret Noel and his partner Ebenezer Hazard sold books nearby.

BOOKSELLING AND PUBLISHING IN THE NINETEENTH CENTURY

The Long Room of the Merchants' Coffee House stepped up in class from mere stock marketing when it became the site in June 1802 of a major book event, one of the first literary fairs in the United States. Booksellers from across the nation assembled at the Coffee House for five days, during which time nearly half a million books sold. New York was beginning to assert its importance as a bookselling metropolis. On Evacuation Day (November 25, 1783), when the last dejected British troops left the city, New York had five active bookstores. Nineteen years later at the time of the book fair, there were thirty booksellers, and many more appeared as the city expanded northward. Soon after the literary fair in 1802, city booksellers banded together cooperatively as the New York Association of Booksellers.

A leader among the booksellers at the turn of the nineteenth century was Hocquet Caritat, who ran a popular bookstore on Broadway. During 1801, the first year of the new century, in a city hall reading room he sponsored a literary assembly where writers and readers talked about books. Caritat was less successful than Benjamin Franklin at Philadelphia with a similar effort; but he had the chutzpah for a then scandalously bold step to expand participation—in 1803 he asked women to attend the sessions as well as men. Caritat also started a circulating library to stimulate learning and advance the liberal principles of the French Revolution among American workmen.

Caritat's business partner was auctioneer John Fellows, who proved his commitment to radical ideals as a friend and champion of controversial Thomas Paine ("My country is the world and my religion is to do good"). Fellows was the original American publisher for Paine's critical assessment of the Bible, *The Age of Reason* (1794) ("When I see throughout the greatest part of this book, scarcely any thing but a history of the grossest vices, and a collection of the most paltry and contemptible tales, I cannot dishonour my Creator by calling it by his name").

Travelers in the city noticed the air of optimism and the burgeoning markets of a city on the move. Some commented about the booksellers. John Lambert visited New York in 1807 and 1808 on behalf of Canadian business and wrote a widely read account that appeared in three editions, *Travels Through Canada, and the United States of North America, in the Years 1806, 1807 & 1808*. Lambert described New York as "the first city in the United States for wealth, commerce, and population. . . . The booksellers and printers of New York are numerous, and in general men of property." Lambert noted the progress made since the 1780s, with land values soaring from $50 to $1,500. He saluted the city's public library for its "rare and valuable books" and the availability of public reading rooms and circulating libraries supported by the booksellers. A spectacle he considered worth mentioning, along with wheeling and dealing, at the Tontine coffee house was the presence of people reading. Say, maybe the past *is* prologue.

The city's commercial center of gravity moved northward in leaps and spasms, almost in the manner of electrons obeying Bohr's quantum theory. First came Lower Manhattan, where the earliest communities accommodated settlers and their few imported books. As towns evolved into a city, Nassau Street and a few other bookselling areas developed their trade with books from overseas but also with a growing number of volumes "printed in the United States of America." It was no coincidence that Nassau Street bookselling took place in close proximity to the nineteenth-century locations of leading New York publications.

Nassau intersected with Park Row, which geographically helped frame Printing House Square. Park Row became a site of reminiscent sentiment to New York newspaper reporters and editors the same as Book Row did to book lovers and those in the book trade. Martin Green of the *New York Journal* and the *Evening World* arrived at Printing House Square in 1897 and in *Shoeleather and Printers' Ink* (1974) recalled: "The intangible odor of printers' ink, beer, whiskey, and delivery horses was overpowering and pleasant. The cries of newsboys were as music to my ears." Green lamented that with New York newspapers reduced in number and scattered about the city, young people venturing to the city for newspaper jobs could no longer experience the lush atmosphere of Park Row. "In no section is there such an authentic newspaper atmosphere as made Park Row what it was in its heyday," he observed.

Madeleine B. Stern, in *Antiquarian Bookselling in the United States: A History from the Origins to the 1940s* (1985), focused on New York City in chapter 3 and paid tribute to the booksellers and their customers. The back room "Den" of Charles Wiley's New Street Bookstore was a literary rendezvous. There James Fenimore Cooper hosted "Cooper's Lunch," which became the Bread and Cheese Club, where the city's leading authors and artists could meet, form friendships, and discuss their common challenges as artists in a mercantile society.

In the 1820s book publishing became a leading and lucrative Manhattan enterprise. Indeed the city emerged at an accelerating pace as the national center of book publishing, thanks to the popularity of William Cullen Bryant, James Fenimore Cooper, Washington Irving, and other authors identified with the city and its bookmakers and booksellers. Credit for the triumph of New York publishing was due as well to the 363-mile (580-kilometer) Erie Canal, which, after eight years under construction, was officially opened for traffic along its full length on October 25, 1825. As part of the celebratory ceremonies for the occasion kegs of Lake Erie water were carried aboard the *Seneca Chief* and added to the Atlantic at New York. The Atlantic didn't need Erie water, but western markets quickly demonstrated a need and welcome for New York books. The canal linked the port of New York with Lake Erie at Buffalo, and gave booksellers access to large and expanding markets in the Midwest territories and farther still via the Mississippi and Ohio Rivers. Countless boxes of books were barged across New York to Lake Erie and transported from there to waiting readers. Thus books from Manhattan moved in large quantities to Michigan, Ohio, Indiana, Illinois, and points west. It was a case of manifest destiny for the American continent applied to the book business.

As a prime transportation artery, the canal was a critical factor before the development of railroads in the ascendancy of New York as a mercantile power. And it was a bonanza for New York book sales as crates of books headed west with other merchandise aboard the barges. Those who look for symbolic and symbiotic connections may find one in the fact that the year the canal opened, a Massachusetts storekeeper named Daniel Appleton moved to New York and opened a store to sell groceries and books. As so often in New York, selling books led to producing them. In the 1830s Appleton moved into publishing, and D. Appleton & Co. began its long history with a three-inch-square 1831 book entitled *Crumbs from the Master's Table*. Appleton's sons carried on after his death in 1849. Appleton highlights in the century's second half were the first American edition of *Alice in Wonderland* and the sale of about 35 million copies of *Webster's Blue Back Speller* between 1855 and 1890.

Charles Wiley operated a bookstore in New York as early as 1807 and was among the booksellers who benefited from the publishing boom. His success owed not a little to the fact that thirty-one-year old Cooper entered his establishment in 1821 with the manuscript of *The Spy* (1821). Cooper started writing when a bad novel infuriated him, and he told his wife he could do better. Her challenge to prove it made him try. What he initially wrote, a novel entitled *Precaution* (1820), was a flop—"hopelessly bad," declared William Lyon Phelps later. But Cooper was no quitter. He kept writing and became America's first author with an international audience. In a famous put-down, Mark Twain reviewed a single Cooper passage and claimed it broke a record by scoring 114 literary offenses out of a possible 115. Whatever the quality of Cooper's prose, it greatly profited himself and his publisher. He moved to the city to work near his publisher and began writing the many books we know about but haven't necessarily read.

Before the Bread and Cheese Club there had been the Lads of Kilkenny, to which Washington Irving belonged, and after it came the 1829 Sketch Club in a continuing series of literary and social fraternities. The club-forming impulse among the literati (have New York's water, coffee, and liquor supplies been checked for a viral explanation?) was exemplified in the twentieth century by the celebrated Algonquin Round Table, where wit became an obsession on West Forty-fourth Street. The twenty-first century no doubt will continue New York's tradition of wit.

Without evolving into organized conclaves, various groups of the "writing, thinking, and talking set" developed the custom of meeting at the city's bookstores. The Bartlett and Welford shop at the Astor House, which included rare books in its line, became such an intellectual assembly area. The Astor House, another John Jacob Astor creation, opened in 1836 and began life as the Park Hotel just west of City Hall Park on Broadway. With 309 rooms, and bathroom facilities on *every* floor, it was a grand granite edifice for the 1830s. The bookstore lured bibliophiles. In an age when some politicians weren't afraid to be bookish, former New York Mayor Philip Hone wrote in his diary on June 3, 1840: "Old Books: *I purchased this morning at Bartlett & Welford's bookstore a fine old Oxford copy of Shakespeare in six volumes quarto, printed 1744.*" The diarist-mayor who presided over the opening of the Erie Canal made several other purchases that spring morning before escaping the bookshop.

A contender for the title "most colorful and versatile character" among Manhattan booksellers in the first half of the century was a Jewish-born former professor and Catholic priest, seditious poet, opera librettist, translator, lover (as a priest in Venice he caroused with Casanova), and London rare-book dealer. As a librettist his credits included—are you ready?—*Le Nozze di Figaro, Don Giovanni,* and *Così Fan Tutte* with a musician named Mozart. He was born in 1749 in a ghetto near Venice and named Emanuele Conegliano. After his widowed father married a Catholic, the teenager became a seminarian. Later he changed his name to Lorenzo Da Ponte, derived from "Abbate Da Ponte," meaning someone who has studied to be a priest. To avoid arrest for debt, he immigrated from London to New York. There in a bookstore he cultivated a new friend, teacher and poet Clement Clarke Moore, the author of "Account of a Visit from St. Nicholas" (1825). Moore got Da Ponte work as a tutor and encouraged him to open a bookstore, which proved popular among Columbia College students when Columbia was located downtown. Through Moore he also obtained a professorship in Italian at Columbia, and thus may well have been the school's first Jewish-born, former-Catholic-priest, bookstore-operating professor. Eventually he sold his outstanding library of Italian books to Columbia. Da Ponte also found time in his eighties before his death in 1838 to establish the city's first theater for opera, the Italian Opera House. Look on Lorenzo Da Ponte and discard the stereotype notion that booksellers are necessarily cautious, sensitive, reclusive.

Among nineteenth-century Manhattan booksellers was George Philip Philes. Born at Ithaca, New York, in 1828, he opened his New York bookstore in 1854. Philes was noted for his extraordinary knowledge of old books and his skill as a bibliographer and linguist. He compiled the *Catalogue of the Library of Andrew J. Odell* (1878–79, 2 volumes) and was an assistant to the bibliographer and historian Henry Harrisse in preparing the *Bibliotheca Americana Vetustissima*. From 1861 to 1863 he published the *Philobiblon*, remembered as a source of bibliophilic information and anecdote.

Another lower-Manhattan bookseller was peripatetic William Gowans, who was born in Scotland and whose stores moved from Chatham to Liberty to Fulton to Centre and eventually settled on Nassau Street booksellers' row. William Loring Andrews in *The Old Booksellers of New York* (1895) indicates that Gowans began selling old books in New York during 1830. He was twenty-nine when he opened his own shop on Chatham Street in 1832. By the 1860s, Gowans was known as the "Antiquarian of Nassau Street." By adding to his stock through auctions and the purchase of entire libraries, Gowans was a forerunner of such latter-day New York bookmen as George D. Smith. His establishment was famously crowded with teetering eight- to ten-feet-high stalagmites of books. Customers used sperm-oil lamps in the unlighted basement to conduct searches. Imagine using such a lamp to seek a first edition of *Moby-Dick or The Whale* (1851) amid floor-to-ceiling books. Among those who braved the stacks at Gowans's through the decades were literary luminaries and collectors. His customers included John James Audubon, Henry Ward Beecher, William Cullen Bryant, Washington Irving, and Henry Longfellow. Whether luminary or collector, each customer abided by Gowans's fixed prices in front, which he called "unalterable as the laws of the Medes and Persians." What each book had cost him was noted in code at the bottom of page 25.

By operating a walk-in shop, issuing regular catalogues, publishing reprints, and preparing bibliographical notes, Gowans could be viewed as America's first complete bookman, contended Roger E. Stoddard in the fourth Sol M. Malkin Lecture in Bibliography, in 1990. At one time Gowans lodged in the same house as Edgar Allan Poe. Poe and the antiquarian often talked; and Gowans wrote that he never saw the poet-storyteller intoxicated but rather that Poe was always "courteous, gentlemanly and intelligent." Knowing Poe's reputation, dare we wonder about Gowans's relationship with a stimulating liquid product of his native Scotland? In 1870 when he retired, Gowans owned a stock of some three hundred thousand books and "pamphlets innumerable." He died that year, which raises doubt about the wisdom of retirement for bookmen.

If some bookmen were nomads in Manhattan, others roamed greater distances in their cravings to disseminate books. One was John Hamilton Still, another Scot, who arrived in California from New York during Gold Rush days in 1849 aboard the *Griffen* and is credited with starting the first bookstore in San Francisco. Instead of digging for nuggets, he chose to sell nuggets of literature. Still had several different shops, including one named the New York Cheap Bookstore. Along with his San Francisco operations, Still maintained a location on Nassau Street called California Booksellers and News Agents.

Back in Manhattan, a Nassau Street bookselling neighbor of Gowans was Joseph Sabin, who became well known as an American bibliographer and bibliophile. Sabin began on Canal Street in the 1850s to market "antique miscellaneous fine books." He moved to Nassau Street after buying out fellow dealer Michael Noonan's new and secondhand stock in 1864. Born in England in 1821, he served as a fourteen-year-old apprentice to an Oxford bookseller. Sabin was well known in the nineteenth century as a bookman of many roles. In 1861 he joined with H. A. Jennings to start a book auction business. His sales from 1864 to 1874 were said to exceed a million dollars.

Among Sabin's own books was the ambitiously titled *A Bibliography of Bibliography or a Handy Book About Books Which Relate to Books* (1877), for which he found a pithy epigraph: " 'To aim at learning without bookes is with Danaides, to draw water in a sieve.'—R. Williams, 1630." In the preface, Sabin identified librarians as a group for which the book was done, thanked a librarian who helped him, and added, "When librarians in general can approach his standard of library intelligence, there will cease to be that plentiful lack of knowledge by which some of them are now distinguished." Compliments were complicated in 1877.

Sabin stands out for his cataloguing of great collections, editorship of the *American Bibliopolist,* and compilation of *Bibliotheca Americana: A Dictionary of Books Relating to America from Its Discovery to the Present Time* (1868–84, 14 volumes). That project led to the suggestion his epitaph should be "killed by a dictionary." Through his store passed Shakespeare first folios, Jonsons, Spensers, Miltons, and countless comparable antiquarian volumes. The high quality of Sabin's collections helped justify labeling Nassau Street the Rialto of old books.

An observer of the New York book scene was I. S. Lyon, who wrote in *Recollections of an Old Cartman* (1872), "I have rarely met with a bookseller who knew anything about the character of the books that passed through his hands. . . . The exceptions to this rule are generally to be found among the dealers in old second-hand books. . . . There is always some satisfaction in *seeing* and *handling* a rare and valuable book, and hearing its secret history descanted upon, even if you are not able to become the owner of it."

Some of the many names that appear on the New York City roster of early book merchants are James Eastburn, Samuel Loudon, Thomas and James Swords, Charles Smith, Charles Woodward, T. H. Morrell, Calvan Blanchard, Samuel Rayner, Charles B. Norton, John Doyle, M'Elrath and Bangs, "Old Hollingsworth," and "Old Cronin." They sold books; let their names be remembered. Another was John Bradburn, whose specialties interestingly were medicine and theology. Still another was Charles S. Francis from Boston, who opened a bookstore on Broadway in 1826. Among his customers were Aaron Burr (U.S. vice president), DeWitt Clinton (mayor, governor, senator), and James Audubon (artist). Francis printed the American edition of Audubon's *Birds of America*. Publishing firsts for Francis include Shakespeare's works in America and *Mother Goose Melodies*. All served the cause of books; let their names be remembered.

WHY FOURTH AVENUE?

The leap to Fourth Avenue and low-priced books ironically involved one of America's richest men and his revenue from the Lafayette Street homes—with Astors, Delanos, and Vanderbilts among the residents—that for a time were a synonym for Manhattan swankiness. The tycoon was John Jacob Astor, who invested his immense gains from the fur trade and Oriental tea in New York real estate and watched his fortune swell. In 1804 he paid $45,000 for what became Lafayette Place, and two decades later began selling Lafayette building lots at $45,000 each. It's not whom you know, but what you hold—and when—that counts most. Astor made Lafayette Place pay big in the first half of the century; in the second half, as New

York commerce headed north, the area declined to tenements, factories, and warehouses.

When John Jacob Astor died in 1848, his will designated $400,000 for the endowment and foundation of a public library. The Astor Library that resulted opened at Sixth Street and Lafayette in 1854 and is remembered as the first free public reference library in the United States and a vital element in the evolution of today's New York Public Library. At that time shops for secondhand books in the city were scattered from Nassau Street to the Bowery. The library, according to Burrows and Wallace in *Gotham*, was a catalyst for the gradual development of Fourth Avenue into New York's primary center for antiquarian books.

A year following the appearance of the Astor Library, an unconnected event (unless there is an intangible connection at work throughout the world of books—which wouldn't surprise us) was the formation by New York book publishers of the New York Publishers Association, to encourage cooperation and facilitate reaching nationwide outlets for books. The publishers had recognized what booksellers realized earlier: the practical merit of professional cooperation within areas of common interest. An inaugural banquet for six hundred was held at the Crystal Palace. "This self-congratulatory conclave of authors and editors marked publishing's arrival as a full-fledged metropolitan industry," Burrows and Wallace observe in *Gotham*.

Change and mobility were dynamically alive in New York during the 1800s, but many citizens as always were anxious about the portents of change. Would city life turn out better, or bitter? It was an era, wrote Edith Wharton, "when people shuddered at the perils of living north of Union Square." Perhaps that was a subtle factor too when the Fourteenth Street border of Union Square became the northern boundary of Book Row. Following the Civil War, the Fourteenth Street–Union Square area increasingly gained cachet as an effective place to conduct commerce. Major department stores moved in, such as Rowland Macy's store at Fourteenth Street and Sixth Avenue. These stores especially attracted women shoppers to what became known as Ladies' Mile.

During later decades, the area north of Eighth Street gradually evolved as a fashionable shopping area. Near Grace Church were two large sellers, publishers, and importers of books, Gustav Stechert at 810 Broadway and B. Westermann & Co. at 812 Broadway. In the vicinity of Union Square were the Literary Gallery of William Evarts Benjamin at 22 East Sixteenth Street and Charles Scribner and Sons, future publishers of Hemingway, Fitzgerald, and Wolfe, on Fifth Avenue between Twenty-first and Twenty-second Streets. The nation's leading haven of fine music, Steinway Hall, was erected in 1866 at 109–111 East Fourteenth Street. Thomas Bender, in *New York Intellect: A History of Intellectual Life in New York City from 1750 to the Beginnings of Our Own Time* (1987), describes the Union Square vicinity early in the 1890s: "The Square and its precincts, more than any other place in the city in the Gilded Age, represented to the city and to others the cultural complexity and role of the nation's metropolis. . . . The Metropolitan Museum of Art's first home was on Fourteenth Street [128 West], the New York Historical Society was just to the east on Second Avenue, while the Astor Library, the New York Society Library, and New York University were just to the south."

The full flowering of Fourth Avenue's Book Row was still in the future, but the last quarter of the nineteenth century brought to the neighborhood one of the two sine qua non requirements for bookselling: first, good books; second, customers who want them. Theaters and restaurants as well as bookstores flocked to the Union Square neighborhood and flourished there until the next Manhattan migration northward. When that migration began, the fertile seeds of Book Row were in place.

Significant book-related activities in the area prior to the reality of Book Row should be noted. Madeleine B. Stern and Leona Rostenberg, in "American Bookselling: Historical Perspectives," in the 1976 *AB*, recognized the unique accomplishment of Francis G. Leon, a Polish nobleman and scholar. After the Polish revolution of 1863, Francis Leon joined his brother Adam in New York. By 1878 Adam Leon was the proprietor of a cigar store at Washington Square East; and Francis Leon began selling books from the same address. Early in 1884, Francis Leon opened a cellar bookstore at 3 West Twenty-third Street. Before the move, Leon began issuing catalogues offering details in seven languages about new and rare books and bookbinding services when needed.

From his new location, Leon in 1885 issued his *Catalogue of First Editions of American Authors*, featuring literary giants of the age. Writing about American books in the preface, Leon stated, "Blurred in type and printed on indifferent paper, as some of them are, these first examples of the writings of our great authors are today, in many cases, worth their weight in gold." The catalogue is recognized as the first about American firsts, a bibliographic milestone in American bookselling, and a strong motivator for collecting first editions. An unbound edition of the catalogue cost $1; a deluxe edition bound in half morocco was $2. The catalogue listed *Huckleberry Finn* at $2.75; *The Scarlet Letter* at $12.50; and *Leaves of Grass* at $15. These are representative entries among over fifteen hundred items.

Stern and Rostenberg commented on the impact of the catalogue: "A Polish refugee had turned the minds of collectors from Caxton and Shakespeare, Hugo and Montaigne, to Franklin and Irving, Poe and Longfellow. He had, in effect, supplied a gap in American book collecting." When it was possible, Leon returned to his Polish estates. In 1891, after the sale and auction of his stock, he was no longer a New York bookseller. Yet his cultivation of collectors and the strategic whetting of their appetites for first editions continued functioning as permanent literary fertilizer for the start-up shops soon to appear on Book Row.

A Sicilian immigrant with entrepreneurial ideas had a newspaper stand in front of the New York Hotel for years. In 1860, he boldly invested his savings in the bulk purchase of a London newspaper which covered a sporting event, the Heenan-Sayer fight. He then parlayed his remarkable earnings from this coup in a large newsstand at Union Square selling foreign and domestic papers. His name was Agosto Brentano, and he utilized his name boldly when he launched Brentano's Literary Emporium in the centennial year, 1876, to sell books as well as other publications. From that beginning came a bookstore chain that took the name Brentano wherever books were sold. His initial store, continuing a New York tradition, became a place of rendezvous as well as books. According to Edwin D. Hoffman in "The Bookshops of New York City, 1743–1948" (*New York History* XXX:1, January 1949), the emporium served such customers as former president Ulysses S. Grant and had a "musty corner" where lingerers such as Henry Ward Beecher, Edwin Booth, and Artemus Ward could smoke, joke, and exchange stories.

Dodd, Mead & Company was another eminent publisher that began with particular emphasis on bookselling. Moses W. Dodd became a New York bookseller and publisher in 1839. His sons Frank and Robert Dodd joined the company in 1859 and 1873 respectively. Hitherto Dodd, Mead had sold only new books. Robert Dodd's job was to develop a new department for rare books and manuscripts. He put together a staff that included William

Evarts Benjamin, James F. Drake, and George H. Richmond, all of whom would establish successful book businesses. Another member of the star staff was Luther S. Livingston. When Dodd, Mead in 1895 put out the first volume of *American Book Prices Current*, Livingston was identified as the chief compiler. One obscure Dodd, Mead employee was a teenage stock boy whose name became permanently linked with Fourth Avenue and bookselling, George D. Smith.

As part of the city's northward flow, Dodd, Mead moved to the corner of Broadway and Eighth Street in 1880. The retail store was open from 7:30 A.M. until six P.M., and was closed only on Sundays. An exception to those hours occurred during the blizzard of 1888, which began Monday, March 12, and ended Tuesday with the city at a standstill. The store like much else in New York was stymied by the storm and its paralyzing aftermath. One employee recalled walking to work down Broadway from midtown through an eerily quiet city to reach the store, where he sold only one book all day, a Philadelphia guidebook.

Dodd, Mead moved to other locations in subsequent years, with a general uptown progression. In 1910 the company dropped its bookselling operations to concentrate on publishing. Robert Dodd joined with the Dodd, Mead cataloguer Luther S. Livingston to establish Dodd & Livingston Rare Books, an influential institution serving distinguished collectors. After the partnership dissolved in 1914, Robert Dodd sold antiquarian books from a Book Row shop at Fourth Avenue and Thirteenth Street until his 1917 retirement. Dodd helped many collectors build superb private libraries. One collector allegedly asked another, "Well, what's in the rest of your library?" Answer: "Dodd only knows." Dodd is remembered as one of the dominant individuals during the development of antiquarian bookselling in America and along Book Row.

THE STAGE IS SET, THE PLAYERS APPEAR

Just before Book Row received its cue to enter came the turn of the distinctive Lafayette group to form a New York book oasis. Frank Weitenkampf, who eventually became chief of the New York Public Library's Art and Print Divisions, began his long library career in 1881 as a teenager working at the Astor Library. In an article, "Lafayette Place: An Erstwhile

Literary Center," for *The Book-Lover's Almanac for 1897*, Weitenkampf recalled that in Lafayette Place and its environs, the presses of Theodore Low De Vinne and J. J. Little were churning out publications and books. The De Vinne Press building at 399 Lafayette housed the manifold activities of Theodore De Vinne, noted as a leading U.S. printer in the nineteenth century. He was also an authority on the history of printing and typography and the author of important works related to these subjects, including *The Invention of Printing* (1876) and *The Practice of Typography* (1900–1904), a series of manuals.

Theodore De Vinne was born Christmas Day 1828, and his career was a fine gift to bibliophiles. He learned printing as a boy at Fishkill, New York, and in 1849 began working for Manhattan printer Francis Hart. He became Hart's foreman in 1850, and in 1859 a member of the firm. Printing books was De Vinne's specialty, and he directed production of many important works including the *Century Dictionary* and *The Book of Common Prayer*. Among the business's serial publications were *St. Nicholas*, *Century Magazine*, and *Scribner's Monthly*.

In 1883 the firm's name changed to Theodore L. De Vinne and Company, which became a printing plant of international distinction. De Vinne was a founding member of the Grolier Club, formed in 1884 to encourage serious book collecting as well as "literary study and the arts of the book." In the club's early years, De Vinne edited or wrote many of the Grolier publications and his firm printed them.

Other publishers were also busy in the area. And with book manufacturing in full swing at Lafayette Place, it was natural that numerous binderies were drawn to the neighborhood. Weitenkampf named several publications associated at different times with Lafayette Place: the *Critic*, *Current Literature*, the *Magazine of American History*, the *Review of Reviews*.

Yet the tides of New York business were never still for long. Other commercial trends "crowded out this once drowsy spot and its peculiar literary flavor," Weitenkampf observed. He mentioned how Lafayette and Astor Place were affected as business "passed northward, leaving them high and dry." He recalled the "chain of factors concerned in the production and sale of literary ware which ultimately might find its way to the old auction rooms of Bangs (over Scribner's) or be offered on the counters of dealers in second-hand books on Fourth Avenue."

Fourth Avenue! The designated successor to Nassau Street's Book Row and to Lafayette Place. Had its moment in time finally begun to appear in the century's final years? It had!

Yet the new Booksellers' Row would have to be deliberately unlike its predecessors in the changing city. A different kind of New York City was taking shape, with a restlessly diverse population. The new Book Row must serve during a nervous, pulsing, anything-goes era. Soon the more leisurely—let's say it, the more refined—bookselling milieu of the eighteenth and nineteenth centuries would be gone. Then the genteel classes with little need for penny-pinching were those that read or pretended to read. To thrive, indeed to survive, the new Book Row must be wide open, more democratic, less fancy, less elite, less discriminating. Book Row would welcome the great collectors (they could afford the high-priced rarities!); but it would be egalitarian from the start, and anybody who sought books to own and read would be welcome.

The secondhand book merchants on Fourth Avenue would serve not just knowledgeable, wealthy collectors, but also a vast throng of general book buyers. When customers appeared for books to read (at bargain prices), they must be satisfied so they would come back again. And again. Antiquarian bookselling on Book Row had to be wide enough—and wise enough—to serve *all* who read or collected books and to help them get and keep the book habit.

Fourth Avenue's Book Row could never have developed as it did if the shops that sprang up had functioned under the patrician notion of "the best books for the best people." As always, book knowledge was a primary stock in trade of these operations, but quantity sales were a crucial key to pay the rent. Special knowledge might bring in exceptional and exciting items to lure financially robust collectors; but volume would bring in readers, including those with a mere dime or quarter to invest on Shakespeare or, why not, Agatha Christie and Zane Grey, the former New York City dentist who translated the American West into best sellers.

The timing of Book Row's gradual appearance, starting in the fin de siècle period, had clear-cut historical reasons behind it. Book Row came when it did because Book Row was required by the people's need in the crowded city for information, education, answers, escape, hope, entertainment. Only inexpensive books offered easy access to mental riches, respite from woes, reprieve from drudgery, sometimes even solutions to life's nagging problems. The northward movement of publishing and other commerce and a population of millions, coupled with the necessity of books for learning, support, dignity, pleasure—all these and more dictated the existence of Book Row.

A seemingly never-ending line of vessels entered the port during those years. These ships from Europe and other continents landed scared, hopeful immigrants—the uprooted, as Oscar Handlin called them—by the tens of thousands, soon by the hundreds of thousands. Many of the new volunteer Americans packed into rented rooms on Manhattan's Lower East Side— within easy walking distance of Book Row. Most who passed through "the golden door" came to the New World with little more than themselves. They wanted help to know what they had to know. Some found Book Row. All needed books (although all didn't *know* they needed books). Books were tools to pick ghetto locks and escape to better lives. Those who knew found books at the libraries and on Book Row, the city's best answer to the need for books of one's own.

So Book Row happened. During the 1890s, issues of James Clegg's *Directory of Secondhand Booksellers* showed a steady increase in the listings of secondhand booksellers on Fourth Avenue and adjacent streets. The *Clegg's International Directory of Booksellers for 1899*, fifth edition, in its New York section describes the city having a population of 2 million; and it lists several pages of new and secondhand shops to supply those millions with books. Some of the 1899 secondhand shops have addresses on or about Fourth Avenue.

Thus, in 1899, Book Row was no longer an idea like a Messiah whose time was foretold. Book Row was taking shape. Over a fifth of a millennium after William Bradford printed and sold books on the island to serve a tiny population, Book Row would put books, every kind of book, within easy and ready reach of millions.

At the cusp of the twentieth century, Fourth Avenue was poised to serve as an American secondhand book center on a par with the London antiquarian businesses "pitched betwixt Heaven and Charing Cross," as Francis Thompson put it; an equal of the famous booksellers along the quays of the Seine in Paris; the peer of the ancient secondhand book stalls in the Liulichang section of imperial Peking. Early in that new century, Book Row began to shape its destiny as an international oasis of biblioplenty to book lovers everywhere.

✂ MARVIN MONDLIN was born in Brooklyn; served in the wartime Merchant Marine; educated at Cornell, CCNY, and Brooklyn College; and was a student of Aesthetic Realism with Eli Siegel. In the antiquarian book trade since 1951, he has served as an appraiser, book auctioneer, proprietor of book businesses in New York and Belgium, and estate book buyer for the Strand since 1974. His writings include *Appraisals: A Guide for Bookmen.* A notable photographer, he knew and photographed the people and places of Book Row for over half a century. His affiliations include the Antiquarian Booksellers Association of America, the Appraisers Association of America, and The Typophiles. He lives with his wife Rina Mondlin in Manhattan near Book Row.

✂ ROY MEADOR was born in Oklahoma, served in the U. S. Navy, and was educated at the University of Southern California and Columbia. He lived in Manhattan as a technical and promotional writer, migrating west when a city apartment accommodated no more Book Row irresistibles. His articles on authors, books, sports, chess, history have appeared widely. He is a regular contributor to *Book Source Magazine.* He has written brochures and grant proposals for university, corporate, state, and federal clients. His books include *Franklin—Revolutionary Scientist, Future Energy Alternatives, Guidelines for Preparing Proposals,* and others on energy and the challenges of technology. He lives in Ann Arbor with his wife Helen Meador surrounded by 1,000s of books—and growing—many of them from Book Row.

Aberdeen Book Company — 1
America's Bookshop — 4
Anchor Bookshop — 2
Arcadia Bookshop — 20
Astor Place Magazine And Bookshop — 7
Atlantis Bookshop — 8
Biblo and Tannen — 9
Books 'N Things — 25
Colonial Book Service — 10
Corner Bookshop — 11
Eureka Bookshop — 12
4th Avenue Bookstore — 13
Friendly Music Shop — 23
Gilman's Bookstore — 14
Green Bookstore — 19
A. Hershbain — 16
Leon Kramer — 17
Pageant Bookshop — 18
Raven Bookshop — 5
Louis Schucman — 3
Schulte's Bookstore — 21
Stammer's Bookstore — 22
Strand Bookstore — 6
(Vanity Fair) — 15
Samuel Weiser Bookstore — 24

Within a radius of a mile of the 4th Ave. Booksellers---

Stechert-Hafner, Barnes & Noble, Dauber & Pine, University Place Bookshop, Seven Bookhunters, Verry-Fisher, Gabriel Engel, A. Buschke, Louis Wavrovics, Abrahams Magazine Service, Joseph Kling, American Book Auction, William Salloch, O'Malley's Book Store, Scientific Library Service, Old Hickory Bookshop, S.R. Shapiro, Martin's Bookshop, Henry George Fiedler, F. Thomas Heller, Walter J. Johnson, American Scholar, Ben Bloomfield, Wex's.

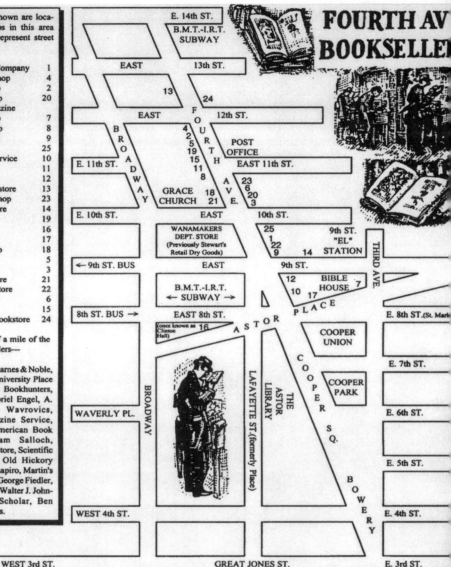

FOURTH AV
BOOKSELLER

FOURTH AVENUE BOOKSELLERS & A FEW LANDMARKS OF NOTE East of Broadway (a few still remainin
MAP c. 1950 Orig. drawn by Mahlon Blaine with a few historical modifications [not drawn to scale].